THE SOVIET MILITARY AND THE COMMUNIST PARTY

The Soviet Military and the Communist Party

BY ROMAN KOLKOWICZ

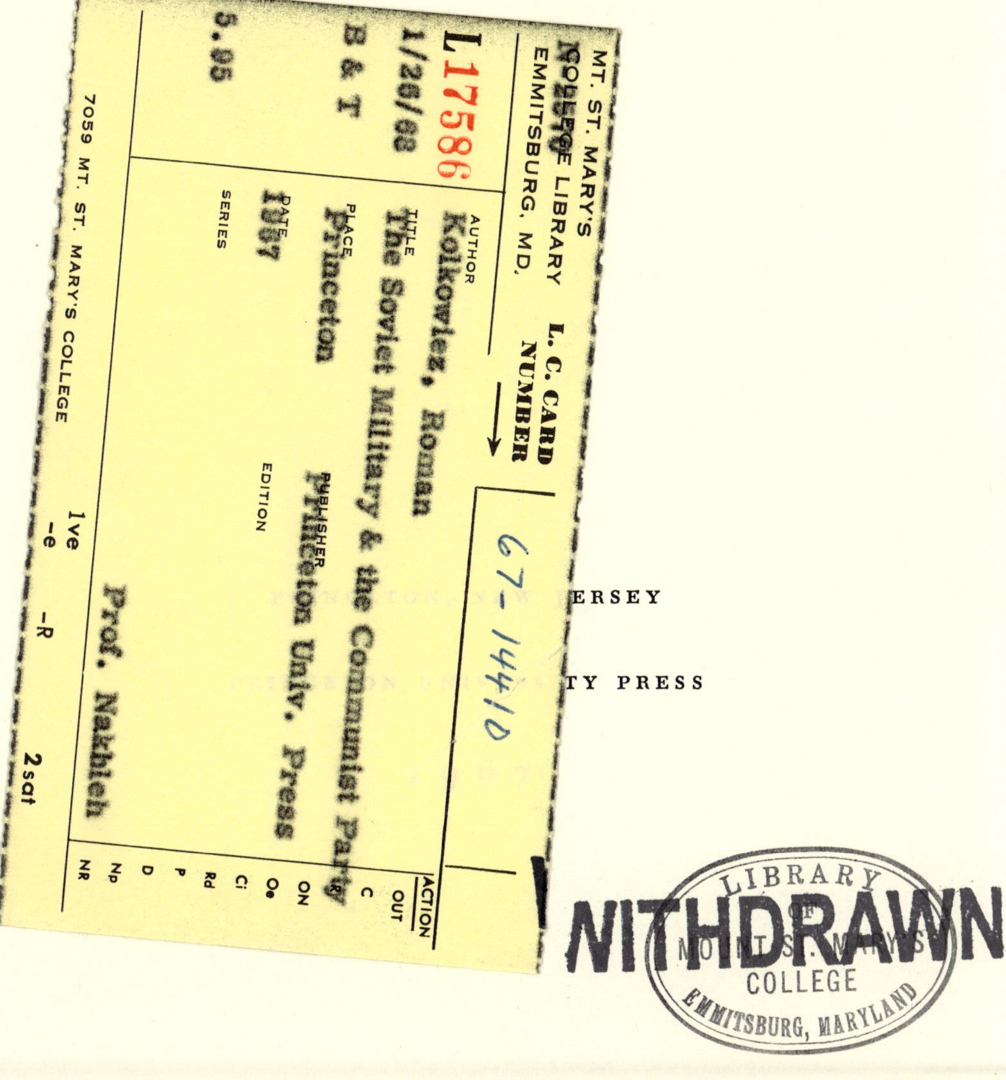

ERSEY

TY PRESS

Published 1967 by Princeton University Press

L. C. Card: 67-14410

Printed in the United States of America
by Princeton University Press

TO MY FATHER AND MOTHER

Preface

The Soviet Military and the Communist Party is a study of institutions in conflict. In a broad analytical treatment of the complex relationship of the two dominant institutions in the Soviet Union, it seeks to assess the military's influence in Party and government, and by extension the military's role in the economy and in society in general. To this end, the author examines the areas where the interests of the Communist Party and the military establishment coincide and those where they conflict; the manner in which the two protagonists press their respective claims, defend their interests, and play on one another; the historical perspective of that interplay; and recent changes in the internal and external affairs of the Soviet Union which have substantially altered the traditional pattern of the relationship. With its main focus on the period since Stalin's death, the study analyzes the mounting influence of the Soviet officer corps on the formulation of military policy and doctrine and on the Party's internal affairs. It concludes with the author's estimate of future developments in the unstable relationship between the two powerful institutions whose interaction so profoundly affects Soviet politics.

The book was completed while the author was still a staff member of The RAND Corporation, since when he has joined the staff of the Institute for Defense Analyses. An earlier and less fully developed version was submitted to the University of Chicago as a doctoral dissertation.

The study was prepared as a contribution to The RAND Corporation's continuing program of research undertaken for United States Air Force Project RAND.

Acknowledgments

Although the views expressed in this book are solely my responsibility, they were substantially influenced by the suggestions and criticism of many of my colleagues at The RAND Corporation. For a better understanding of the complex problems to which I have addressed myself I am especially indebted to B. Brodie, H. S. Dinerstein, A. L. Horelick, T. W. Wolfe, and R. L. Garthoff. A. L. George, J. M. Goldsen, I. C. C. Graham, and J. C. Hogan gave invariably helpful counsel.

I also owe a debt of gratitude to Professors Jeremy Azrael, Herman Finer, and Morton A. Kaplan of the University of Chicago.

Sibylle Crane vastly improved the draft by editing it with skill and intelligence. Lilita Dzirkals provided useful research and bibliographical assistance. And special recognition goes to Eugenia Arensburger, who proofread the manuscript, and to Rosalie Fonoroff and Roselle Foy, who typed the several drafts of this study with unstinting care.

To my wife, Helene, whose understanding and unselfish support were a source of strength during the long months of research and writing, I affectionately acknowledge here my immense debt.

R. K.

Washington, D.C.
September 1966

Contents

THE SOVIET MILITARY
AND THE COMMUNIST PARTY

In a Communist society no one will even think about a standing army. Why would one need it?

F. ENGELS, 1845

A standing army is an army that is divorced from the people. . . .

V. I. LENIN, 1903

Our principle is to have the Party control the gun and never allow the gun to control the Party. . . .

MAO TSE-TUNG, 1938

V. I. Lenin frequently stressed that every class, and that includes the proletariat, consolidates its power solely by means of a regular army.

From a CPSU publication, 1959

History knows of many armies; in none, however, was the role so significant for the fate of mankind, the aim so noble, and the accomplishment so brilliant as in the army born of the Great October.

Krasnaia zvezda
February 24, 1965

I · Introduction

The essential characteristics of authoritarian political systems are internal coercion and external militancy, and to achieve these postures the ruling elites must maintain powerful security organs and large military establishments. A vital difference, however, between the internal instruments of coercion and the military institutions in authoritarian states is that the former usually are organically part of the ruling Party's apparatus and intensely loyal to the dictator, while the latter, though not necessarily disloyal, seek to dissociate themselves from the Party apparatus and its controls, to cultivate their own professional and institutional values, and to remain aloof from politics and the larger society. Communist Party leaders have found this propensity of the military a source of grave concern. Indeed, their inability to make the military a fully integrated part of the Party-dominated system illustrates a vital defect in the structure of one-party autocratic systems.

The Communist Party of the Soviet Union claims hegemony within the state, and, on the basis of their common ideological commitment, demands primary loyalty from all, individuals as well as institutions. Any institution, therefore, that seeks to close itself off from the regime's scrutiny and interference, and whose members look on their profession as a guild, represents a threat to the Party. If, moreover, its members not only resent the Party's domination but are the instruments of the country's defense, and thus are both indispensable and potentially dangerous, the Party is forced constantly to take elaborate measures to contain such an institution without undermining its strength. It is the purpose of this book to investigate the relationship between the Communist Party and the military establishment in the Soviet Union, a relationship which includes areas of common interest and interdependence as well as sharp clashes of ideas and objectives, and which, because of its complexity and inherent conflict, strongly affects the politics of the Soviet Union.

This is not to say that the problems attending the relations between military establishments and their political authorities are peculiar to authoritarian and dictatorial regimes; they exist in other political systems, and their severity is increasing. Indeed, one of the most striking political developments of our time has been the growing importance of the "military factor" in international and national affairs. If we adapt Clausewitz's famous definition of war to the realities of the last fifteen years, we might say that "the threat of war" has become "a continuation of politics by other means."

Introduction

The preoccupation with the danger of thermonuclear war, which today affects all political activity of the major world powers, is of course due to the very nature of modern military weapons: their total destructiveness, which could spell the end of all human life within a brief space of time, and their technical complexity, which surpasses the understanding of laymen and political decision-makers. One consequence of the growing sophistication of the art and the means of warfare has been a change in the role and the complexion of the professional military. In the past, large military establishments tended to be closed guilds whose professional training varied little from generation to generation and whose chief claim to professionalism rested on a nominal military education and such well-established virtues as ability to command and obey and adherence to a code of honor. The modern military establishment presents a radically different picture. Today's officer may be a technician, a manager of large projects that involve collaboration with businessmen and industrialists, a coordinator of complex industrial-logistic activities, a statistician, or even a decision-maker with direct influence on the nation's economy and manpower. The military establishment, as a result of its impact on the national economy, has come to exercise great influence both on a country's political processes and on the private lives of its citizens.

How does this change from the military's traditional role affect its relations with the civilian political leadership? Has the enlarged scope of its function and influence altered the balance between the "specialists in violence," as Harold D. Lasswell calls the military professionals, and the civilian authorities? Most Western students of political-military affairs seem to agree that it has. The growing volume of writings on the nature of civil-military relations and on the role of the military in society reveals concern about the increasing role of the defense establishments in the various nations and the possible effect of this change on the traditional political equilibrium. A recent study views this development as follows:

> Arms are no longer the sole concern of the warriors: the whole state is involved, and not merely in the diversion of limited resources to military needs. The demarcation line between the "civil" and "military" in assessing the elements of national policy has become blurred.[1]

[1] Walter Millis, Harvey Mansfield, and Harold Stein, *Arms and the State*, The Twentieth Century Fund, New York, 1958, p. 5.

Lasswell, in a reassessment of his hypothesis of the garrison-state, finds that "the arena of world politics is moving toward the domination of specialists on violence."[2] Morris Janowitz says: "The military have accumulated considerable power, and that power protrudes into the political fabric of contemporary society." Although he qualifies this statement by speaking of the "restraint and unease" with which the military exercise their influence on political matters, he concludes that "it is outmoded to think in terms of maintaining traditional forms of political controls" over them in view of the growing professionalization and intellectualism among the military professionals and of the "recent striking technological developments in the military. . . ."[3]

The British political scientist S. E. Finer sees the "military as an independent political force which constitutes a distinct and peculiar political phenomenon." Their frequent involvement in politics, he says, is not "a mere set of ephemeral, exceptional and isolated adventures. On the contrary, it does emphatically suggest that we are in the presence of a peculiar political phenomenon: one that is abiding, deep-seated and distinctive."[4] Samuel P. Huntington describes the changing relationship between civilian and military authority as only one aspect of "the new roles of the military elites in world politics resulting from the balance of terror, technological advancement . . . the process of modernization and the increased importance of general and regional collective security arrangements."[5]

Finally, it is relevant to recall here former President Eisenhower's warning, on his departure from office, about the growing threat of the "military-industrial complex" to the democratic principles of government.[6] It was an implicit reference to the growing complexity and scope of the defense establishment, to the intensive professionalization and specialization of the military professionals, and to the rising influence of the military factor in nonmilitary spheres.

Much of the recent literature on civil-military relations deals with Western societies today, with former colonial areas, and with the

[2] "The Garrison-State Hypothesis Today," *Changing Patterns of Military Politics*, ed. Samuel P. Huntington, The Free Press of Glencoe, Inc., New York, 1962, p. 51.

[3] *The Professional Soldier*, The Free Press of Glencoe, Ill., 1960, p. viii.

[4] *The Man on Horseback: The Role of the Military in Politics*, Frederick A. Praeger, Inc., New York, 1962, p. 4.

[5] "The New Military Politics," *Changing Patterns of Military Politics*, p. 13. See also Gene M. Lyons, "The New Civil-Military Relations," *American Political Science Review*, No. 55, March 1961, pp. 53-63.

[6] *The Nation*, No. 14, October 28, 1961, p. 276.

former dictatorships of Germany, Japan, and Italy. Thus far, comparatively little has been written on the relations between civilian and military authorities in the countries of the Soviet bloc. Indeed, not many years ago, most of the Western writers on Soviet affairs seemed to share Churchill's image of the Soviet Union as a riddle, a mystery, and an enigma. Frequently, their accounts of life and politics in the USSR transmitted their vision of a rule of terror over an undifferentiated populace, and of a small group of men whose Byzantine intrigues and struggles for power absolutely determined the fate of the state, its institutions, and the individual citizens. Such accounts reduced all political activity to a single stage at the apex of the Party hierarchy.

In defense of this simplistic presentation of a complex society we must remember how relatively little information on the Soviet Union was available to the West for many years, so that researchers had to make the most of official communications and the occasional statements of Party leaders, and had to try to derive both meaning and facts from the often laborious scrutiny of this output for any inconsistencies and irregularities. This task was the more difficult because of the distorted, idealized view of the Soviet scene—an idyllic picture of a classless, tranquil, and wisely guided society—that was propagated by the Party-controlled media.

Though the cumulative efforts of a generation of Western students of the USSR gradually permitted a much broader understanding of political relationships, institutional structures, and socio-economic processes, traditional views about the static character of the Soviet Union persisted; Soviet society was presumed by many to be permanently "frozen" in an ideologically and politically determined mold and firmly ruled by the Party, the changes in the top leadership notwithstanding.

In reality, as we know, underneath the inhibiting burden of Stalin's long rule, the Soviet Union was changing. It was becoming a complex industrial society, divided into a number of new functional and social groupings and developing a vast bureaucracy, and it included several institutions with strong loyalties and parochial interests, each striving for a greater measure of autonomy. For a time, the Party apparatus, centrally controlled from the top, successfully straddled and synthesized these differences among institutions and social groups, aided in this effort by the terror machine. With the death of Stalin, however, and the gradual loosening of political controls that followed it, social and political life in the Soviet Union became less monolithic, and the divergent institutional claims, which theretofore had been suppressed, became perceptible pressures upon the Party.

The growing body of available information on the Soviet Union, the trend toward moderation in the country's political and social life, and the pressures for emancipation among the European satellites caused many Western students of communist affairs to abandon the static view of the Soviet Union, and to base their emphasis on the expectation of change. Thus, much recent research is focused on social and political change, and is devoted to an analysis of Soviet phenomena which starts with the premise that Soviet society is in transition.

The present study belongs to this category. It investigates the pressures and demands that are brought to bear upon the Party leadership by one institution striving for greater autonomy. We shall approach this inquiry into the relations between Party and military, the two most powerful bureaucracies, by defining and analyzing the areas where their interests converge and those where they conflict. In doing so, we must try to free ourselves of all popular preconceptions about the Soviet military, which run the gamut from "The Red Army is an offensive juggernaut with overwhelming influence on Party policy" to "The Soviet officer corps has no voice in policy, and its members are unquestioningly and deeply loyal to the Party."

The Soviet military establishment as it is here presented is neither a body of faceless, totally submissive soldiers nor a militant praetorian guard; rather, it is shown as an institution with certain interests, values, and objectives that it has in common with military establishments in other societies. However, while these institutional similarities are stressed, careful consideration is given to the effects that its peculiar social and political environment has upon the Soviet military. Indeed, the conflicts that arise for that establishment from the hostility of its environment are at the center of this study, which tries to answer the question: How does an institution with a well-defined system of values and distinct interests and objectives retain its identity and the necessary degree of autonomy in the face of constant intrusion and manipulation by the ruling elite?

Another major task has been to discern how the ruling elite of the Party satisfies the demands of the several institutions for resources and status when to meet such demands fully would mean overburdening the country's economy and jeopardizing political objectives or even threatening the entire internal political balance. The case of the military is here used as an example of the serious, and at times critical, political strains that are created when such demands are subordinated to other social priorities or are denied altogether.

Finally, this book seeks to illuminate the complex and somewhat precarious relationship between the Party and the military establishment which arises from the fact that, notwithstanding its distrust of the officer corps and its fears of "Bonapartism," the Party must grant the military the degree of professional and institutional freedom that a military establishment needs if it is to remain a formidable factor in its country's foreign policy. The Party's attitude and policy toward the military, therefore, are the result of a delicate balance between two conflicting motivations: the desire for hegemony within the state, and the need to maintain a strong military-political posture before the rest of the world.

Part One

The Nature of Institutional Conflicts

II · The Dynamics of Party-Military Relations

A · *THE CONFLICT*

Among the many difficulties that attend an investigation of the role of the Soviet military, the primary one is that of recognizing and defining the military's separate institutional identity: its interests, policies, objectives, and values. The Communist Party denies the military such a distinct identity.[1] Through all available media it seeks constantly to reinforce an image of the military as a fully integrated part of the totalitarian system. And a large network of political controls within the military organization is designed to keep the latter fully responsive to Party guidance, initiative, indoctrination, and other forms of manipulation. This effort, however, has not always succeeded in suppressing the many strains and disagreements that exist between the two institutions. At various points in Soviet history, as will be shown, these disagreements have brought about critical tensions in their relations. Indeed, as this study sets out to demonstrate, the relationship between the Communist Party and the Soviet military is essentially conflict-prone and thus presents a perennial threat to the political stability of the Soviet state.

The history of Party-military[2] relations presents a study in conflicts created by a certain incompatibility between the sole holder of power in the state and one of the main instruments of that power. The Party's pervasive endeavor to hold on to its monopoly of power is related to its expectation of challenge from organized groups within society. This wariness, moreover, is closely tied to the constant unease that afflicts the political authorities in totalitarian states because of the absence of provisions for the orderly transfer of power when changes in leadership become necessary, and the consequent opportunity for rival groups to assert themselves. In this context the military appears to the Party as a potential challenger, who must be

[1] Friedrich and Brzezinski maintain that totalitarian parties exert vast efforts "to prevent the armed forces from developing a distinct identity of their own" and that this results in a situation where the military lives "in an atmosphere of an armed camp surrounded by enemies." They also find that, among various totalitarian systems under investigation, "the Soviet handling of the army . . . comes closest to the model image of the complete integration of the military into the totalitarian movement." Carl J. Friedrich and Z. K. Brzezinski, *Totalitarian Dictatorship and Autocracy*, Frederick A. Praeger, Inc., New York, 1956, p. 281.

[2] The term "Party" is used throughout to include the elite and the professionals in the Party apparatus. The term "military" denotes those members of the armed forces who are not political officers, and whose interests and objectives reflect primarily the institutional interests of the military establishment.

controlled and manipulated at all times to prevent any power-seeking elements from threatening the Party's monopoly. Among the various groups in the society that cause the Party anxiety and prompt it to maintain controls within them, the military represents a special case, because of the instruments of violence which it commands. In dealing with it, the Party must balance the usefulness of any coercive measures against the possibility of demoralizing and weakening the country's military forces. It must reconcile its obvious need for an effective military organization, which demands broad professional autonomy, with the constant concern that such an organization could some day reject Party controls and make its own political claims. Whether or not the historical evidence substantiates the Party's fear of Bonapartism in the Soviet military, the very existence of the fear, and the extensive safeguards against the eventuality of Bonapartism, endow the military with a vital role in Soviet politics. And though it might be argued that the demands and interests of the military thus far have been largely professional and institutional in nature, even such narrow demands assume political significance in the Soviet context: The Party's inability or unwillingness to modify its autonomous position raises the modest efforts of other groups toward professional autonomy or institutional privacy to the level of a contest and makes them appear as a challenge to the Party's hegemony.

In dealing with their military establishment, the Communist Party leaders thus frequently seem to obstruct their own ends in an irrational manner. On the one hand, they pursue an ambitious foreign policy, predicated to a large extent on the continued viability of a powerful military capability, and invest a substantial share of their GNP, and large numbers of scarce scientific and technical personnel, in the development and maintenance of this military juggernaut. On the other hand, the Party antagonizes the military leadership and burdens a modern war machine with the archaic impediment of a political control system.

Throughout the past four and a half decades, relations between the Party and the military in the Soviet Union have been marked by instability, tension, and conflict. This has been so despite the fact that about 80 per cent of all armed forces personnel are Communists or Komsomols; that the officer corps is one of the most preferentially treated groups in society; and that the military has a sizable number of representatives in the high Party councils. The Party's extensive effort to control, manipulate, and indoctrinate the military has not always prevented the crystallization of a "military" point of view and the expression of opposition or self-interested demands. Nor, apparently, has friction between the two institutions been mitigated by the awareness that they are both parts of the Establishment, whose interests are not served by internecine conflicts and tensions. The reasons must be sought in the unique political context of the Soviet Union. In this context, even the relatively limited professional-institutional interests and objectives of the military take on disproportionate importance, mostly because of the Party's exaggerated distrust of all institutions and its unconditional insistence on a power monopoly that permits it not only to make decisions for the whole system, but also to conduct their implementation and to control its execution. Along with this political *sine qua non* the Party jealously guards its powers to define the public and private goals of the citizens, to initiate or interdict public discussion on certain issues, and to cultivate an image of its own infallibility.

The Party's total involvement with all facets of behavior and activity, both social and national, causes its leaders to view any criticism or opposition as a possible danger, a potential precedent that could upset the rigid internal *status quo.* If the recalcitrants or opponents are few and expendable, the Party leaders face only a minor problem in silencing them. They can remove them from positions of power or influence, intimidate them, and even, as was the practice in the past, kill them. However, when unwillingness to submit to the Party's rule comes from large professional groups whose services are vital to the well-being or even the survival of the regime, then the Party has the much greater problem of suppressing their self-assertiveness while continuing to employ their professional skills. It has attempted to do this in the past by seeking to have loyal Party zealots in the professions. In the case of the military, however, the search for such a synthesis led to various collectivist schemes whose central objective was to prevent military elitism, but whose major effect has been to lower discipline, morale, and military effectiveness.

What can be said about the political role of the Soviet military establishment, an up-to-date military machine that has been forced to wear a horse collar of ideological and political controls? The very words "political role" harbor ambiguities. Since a large number of activities of citizens or institutions may be viewed as political—from saluting the flag, to the acts of voting and paying taxes, up to a direct military takeover of government—we must first agree on a definition of what constitutes a significant "political act" and a "political role."

In the United States, an American general's testimony to a Congressional Committee, if it contradicts the President's official policy, may in most cases be viewed as a political act of only very limited importance, not as an institutional challenge of the civil authorities by the military establishment. (General MacArthur's opposition to President Truman was something of an exception because of its broader and more immediate consequences.) In authoritarian societies, such as the Soviet Union or the former Nazi Germany, challenges from the military establishments are of a different magnitude. These establishments are in the anomalous position of being a central factor in the survival of the regime and in its ambitious expansionistic policies—receiving large portions of the country's economic output (frequently at great expense to the rest of society) as well as possessing vast means of coercion—and being at the same time denied, not only any role in the political sphere, but also the freedom to practice the military profession without political impediments. This anomaly derives from the absence of regularized procedures for the transfer of political power and from the Party's insistence on its hegemony, two factors that lead to an unstable equilibrium between the power of the Party and that of the major institutions (the "pillars") within the state. In such a delicately balanced system of power relationships, any major challenge to the balancer, the Party, is a threat to the equilibrium, to the *status quo*. Thus, acts by military representatives that would be considered of little consequence in Western democracies take on political significance in authoritarian societies, because they could, in sufficient numbers or under certain conditions, change that vital internal balance.

In trying to define the political role of the military, we shall apply several criteria by which to measure the significance of the military's manifestations of self-assertiveness and of opposition to Party views, policies, or interests. These criteria are not in the nature of an ideal model, nor are they purely theoretical. Rather, they are derived from the prevailing political norms and institutional power arrangements in the Soviet Union, and take into account the Party's dominant position in the state, its intolerance of any form of expressed opposition, and its constant fear of military insubordination and the military's intrusion into Party politics. In exploring the whole range of interaction between Party and military, we shall have to examine their individual historic roles in the Soviet state; their complementary and divergent objectives; the methods and means by which they seek to influence and manipulate each other; and the "systemic parameters," or broad powerful contraints, which limit their freedom of arbitrary action in this interplay.

In the following, our main interest will be directed at the Party's relation with the military between 1953 and 1963. The earlier period, on which a number of studies are already available,[3] will be touched on only to the extent necessary to an understanding of the problems. The chief reasons for concentrating on the post-Stalin period are the availability of many Soviet public sources, and, most important, the significant change that took place in Party-military relations during that time. It was a period when the military publicly questioned some of the Party's major military policies and the wisdom of certain of its statements and measures, and at times openly opposed the ruling Party elite. More than ever, the relations between Party and military became a dialogue between two powerful institutional bureaucracies, some of whose vital interests had come into conflict.

This dialogue will be viewed here, first, as an open debate, during the ten years after Stalin's death, between the Party and some military circles on a range of substantive issues. Secondly, we shall look at it as a political conflict, of longer duration, between two major institutions which continue to make claims on each other. Its political quality derives largely from the Party's image of its own authority in the state, which permits the military at best a subordinate political function, and from the military's opposition to this distribution of roles. While the Party has retained the initiative throughout most of the dialogue, there have been times when the military was able to assert its views and gain some concessions.

B · THE INTERACTION BETWEEN PARTY AND MILITARY

1. The Role of the CPSU in the Soviet State

The factor that helps to shape life in the Soviet Union more than any other is the Communist Party's dominant position within the state. The Party has sought to ensure the preservation of its dictatorial powers, which might be described as its fundamental imperative and primary objective, by numerous doctrinal formulas, policy declarations, institutional arrangements, massive indoctrination, and coercion.

[3] The two most comprehensive and authoritative studies of Party-military relations in the Soviet Union have dealt only with the 1917-1941 period: D. Fedotoff-White, *The Growth of the Red Army*, Princeton University Press, Princeton, N.J., 1944; John Erickson, *The Soviet High Command, 1918-1941*, St. Martin's Press, Inc., New York, 1962.

In 1918 Lenin said: "Dictatorship is power based directly upon force and unrestricted by any laws. The revolutionary dictatorship of the proletariat is power won and maintained by violence . . . power that is unrestricted by any laws. . . ."[4] In 1920 he reiterated this definition.[5] That same year, he also stated that the "will of a class may sometimes be carried out by a dictator, who at times may do more alone and who is frequently more necessary."[6] Stalin, in 1926, saw "the highest expression of the leading role of the Party in the Soviet Union . . . in the fact that not a single important political or organizational question is decided by any Soviet or mass organization without guiding directions from the Party."[7] On another occasion, Stalin emphasized that the Party "does not share, and must not share guidance of the state with any other party."[8] Khrushchev continued to uphold this traditional viewpoint: "The reactionary forces," he said, "assert that the dictatorship of the proletariat is a cruel power. This is true. . . ."[9]

The institutional arrangements by which the Party seeks to retain its autonomy are formidable, and they are enforced without scruples. Vyshinskii has described the "dictatorial mechanism" with disarming frankness:

> Stalin demonstrated the "mechanism" of the dictatorship of the proletariat; the transmission belts, the "levers," the "directing force," the sum total of which constitutes the system of the dictatorship of the proletariat, of which Lenin spoke. Here we see the Party (the main guiding force in the system of the dictatorship of the proletariat), . . . the trade unions (a school of Communism . . .), the Soviets (. . . a direct expression of the dictatorship of the proletariat), the cooperatives (facilitating contact between the vanguard and the masses of the peasantry), . . . the Komsomol (which helps the Party, provides reserves for all other mass organizations . . .).[10]

[4] "Proletarian Revolution and Renegade Kautsky," *Selected Works*, International Publishers, New York, 1943, Vol. 7, p. 123.

[5] "State and Proletarian Dictatorship," *ibid.*, p. 254.

[6] "Speech to the 9th Congress of RKP(b)," March 31, 1920, *ibid.*, Vol. 8, p. 222.

[7] "On Problems of Leninism," *Problems of Leninism*, Foreign Languages Publishing House, Moscow, 1940, p. 135.

[8] "The Reply to Comrade Yan-sky," *Bol'shevik*, No. 7-8, 1927, as cited in *Soviet World Outlook*, U.S. Department of State, July 1959, p. 57.

[9] Speech at the Csepel Iron Works (Hungary), Budapest radio broadcast, April 9, 1958.

[10] "Teachings of Lenin and Stalin on the Proletarian Revolution and the State," *Soviet News*, London, 1948, pp. 66-67.

Vyshinskii omitted the terror machine from this list. But, without it, his description clearly indicates the Party elite's i of the Party's role in the state and of its relationship with the lace, that vast, amorphous entity which the Party must consi manipulate by means of "levers" and "mechanisms" in an effc keep it malleable and committed, and to prevent it from que: ing the direction by the Party.

The manifestation of any form of opposition, disagreement, even passive noninvolvement by any group or individual in rel to Party policies, objectives, views, or personalities is anathema t Party elite. In these forceful words of Karl Radek, "Even a shadow of opposing oneself to the Party signifies the political d of a fighter for socialism, his going over into the camp of the posts of the counterrevolution."[11]

The leaders' constant wariness of potential opponents and c lengers, and the readiness, if necessary, to take radical meas against any dissidents, apply to members of the Party as well a outsiders. They are reflected in Khrushchev's remark that " Communist Party guards the unity of its ranks like the apple of eye";[12] in a directive by Lenin to the effect that "The Commu Parties . . . must periodically purge the membership of the P organizations"; and in Khrushchev's warning that "The Commu must act like a surgeon who takes a sharp knife and operates on m body to cut out malignant growths and thus make possible the furt development and strengthening of the organism."[13]

The history of the Soviet Union is indeed filled with the ghosts victims of the Party's wrath—individuals, professional groups, tire classes, and ethnic communities—whom the Party leadersh regarded either as obstacles to its exercise of absolute power or as o right enemies, actual or potential. One of the reasons for the Part ruthlessness, its institutionalized distrust of all citizens, and its p petual fear of potential opponents lies in the communist ideology self, according to which all historical processes are based on conflict- class conflict, economic conflict, political conflict, and so forth—an struggle and violence between opposing forces thus become the a cepted norms in political and social life.

11 "Speech to the XVIIth Congress of VKP(b)," *Stenographic Report of th XVIIth Party Congress*, Partizdat, Moscow, 1934, p. 628.

12 Speech to the Seventh Congress of the Bulgarian Communist Party, Bulgaria radio broadcast, June 4, 1958.

13 *Pravda*, January 14, 1957.

Another reason for the Party's pervasive distrust may lie in the circumstances of its origins, under the watchful eyes of the czarist secret police. The need to maintain constant vigilance against spies and provocateurs prompted the Party in those days to develop an elaborate system of protective measures, from limiting the size of Party cells to periodic purges, which became part of its normal *modus operandi* when it came into power.

However, the most convincing reason for the Party's institutionalized suspicion of any citizen or group of citizens that could pose a threat to its absolute power must be sought in the lack of established procedures for the transfer of powers both within the Party and within the state. In the absence of such formal provisions, authority in the Party goes to the strongest or the most cunning faction, in a process which is characterized by Byzantine maneuvers and countermaneuvers.[14] Once in power, the leader and his faction exert constant efforts to remain there, making use of the vast machinery of police, Party, and government to prevent the coalescence of any organized opposition and to destroy any challengers.

Aside from the desire to maintain its authoritarian position in the state and the ruling faction's dictatorial position within its own ranks, the Party has other reasons for practicing distrust and coercion. Among them are the need to mobilize the citizens for the fulfillment of Party goals, the importance of maintaining internal stability by the threat or the actuality of coercion, and the wish to pursue radical political, social, and economic policies without opposition from the citizens.

To be sure, since the death of Stalin, the Party has abandoned some of its former methods of dealing with the citizenry. It no longer shoots the avowed opponents of its ruling elite, but consigns them to political obscurity. However, although methods may have changed, the essential objective remains the same; it is to forestall or suppress any opposition to the Party on sensitive issues and on questions or policies of major importance.

2. *Changes in the Role of the Military*

Ever since the Revolution, the Communist Party has relied on a professional standing army for the defense of the socialist state.[15]

[14] The secrecy of these palace politics, its effect on Soviet and international developments, and the Western desire to be informed on the process and future impact of this factional turbulence within the Communist Party are reflected in the emergence of a field of study sometimes referred to as Kremlinology or Sovietology.

[15] See Chapter III.

During the 1920's, when the ebbing revolutionary zeal of Communists in the rest of Europe and the rise of fascist movements combined to isolate the Soviet Union and confirm its fear of a "capitalist encirclement," Stalin's desire for a modern military establishment led to a series of far-reaching changes in the socio-economic structure in the Soviet Union. Through a policy of collectivization and industrialization, large sums of investment capital were to be extracted from the agricultural sector and invested in a large-scale heavy industry that would furnish the basis for a military organization well-enough equipped for defensive and political purposes.

Though Trotsky is correctly described as the creator of the Red Army, it was Stalin, during his long rule of the Soviet state, who shaped its characteristics, defined its internal role, and set the limits to its freedom of action. After the establishment of the Soviet state in the aftermath of the Revolution, Trotsky had been willing to sacrifice some of the Red Army's professionalism and military viability for the sake of ideological continuity and legitimacy. Stalin, who was less concerned with ideology than with pragmatic problems of statecraft, saw the necessity of maintaining a professional military establishment[16] and, having prevailed over Trotsky in the intra-Party struggle, proceeded to mold the Red Army to fit his needs. His advocacy of a standing army did not bespeak the militarist or martinet in him. If anything, Stalin was even more distrustful of professional military establishments than Trotsky, as evidenced by his introduction of strong political controls from the very beginning, by his denial of full authority (*edinonachalie*) to the commanders, and by his strengthening the security organs' authority in the military establishment. The military did win concessions and privileges from Stalin, but these were intended to keep the army loyal to the regime and to make it proficient; they were outweighed by negative measures and practices which resulted in severe curtailment of professional freedom, authority, and institutional self-esteem. Although the military emerged from the early intra-Party struggles with several gains, it found itself the captive of the Party elite, living in an "atmosphere of an

[16] At the VIIIth Party Congress, which dealt a crushing blow to utopian and revolutionary schemes for an armed proletariat and may be regarded as a triumph for Soviet military professionalism, Stalin said unequivocally: "Either we will create a real worker-peasant, strongly disciplined regular army and defend the Republic, or we will not do it and our cause will be lost." Cited in *KPSS i stroitel'-stvo Vooruzhennykh Sil SSSR, 1918-iiun' 1941* (The CPSU and the Development of the Armed Forces of the USSR, 1918-June 1941), Voenizdat, Moscow, 1959, p. 121.

armed camp surrounded by enemies."[17] Its official role in the Soviet state, as it evolved in the early years, was unquestioningly to execute the policies and directives of the Communist Party elite; to protect the state and the regime and to put down challengers to the Party's hegemony within and without; to accept and tolerate the presence of Party functionaries in its midst even at the expense of interference with military efficiency and authority; and to be a citizen army, permeated with egalitarian virtues while performing in a disciplined, effective manner.

The major test of the Red Army came during World War II, when it dramatically proved its crucial role by successfully defending the state against German aggression despite the handicaps under which it suffered as a result of the 1937 purges and Stalin's handling of mobilization and other organizational problems on the eve of the hostilities. Since the war, Soviet foreign policy has become a grand strategic design with many commitments in various areas of the globe, a policy based on the viability of the Soviet army as well as on the political exploitation of this military capability. As long as the Party leaders adhere to the present dynamic, expansionistic foreign policy—and there is little reason to believe that the policy will change in the foreseeable future—the military will continue to have a vital role in the Party's scheme.

As a result of these postwar developments, the position of the military, once strictly subordinate to that of the Party and closely integrated with the Party's interests in the state, has become progressively less subordinate and more self-assertive. Since the death of Stalin, in particular, the role of the military, and its relations with the Party, have undergone a discernible change. Among the many factors which have contributed to this change, the most important have been the modification of the terror machine, the effects of de-Stalinization, the more moderate political and social climate in the Soviet Union, and the growing complexity of warfare.

3. *The Conflicting Interests and Objectives of Party and Military*

Although the Party distrusts most institutions and individuals, its apprehensions are unique in the case of the military because of the latter's structure, function, spiritual values, and, above all, certain inherent characteristics. First of these is the vast physical power, the weapons, equipment, men, and logistic means, at the military's dis-

[17] Friedrich and Brzezinski, *Totalitarian Dictatorship*, p. 281.

posal. Second is the fact that the military mechanism, with its closely integrated organization, responds to a few commands and can therefore, in theory, be rapidly mobilized for action over large areas of the country. Third, the military tends to be a closed group, and as such breeds elitist values; sharing the experiences, the schooling, and the jargon common to their career, its members are cliquish, with a strong sense of solidarity. Finally, its officers are trained to command, to demand obedience, and to respond to a chain of command.

Indeed, many of the Soviet military's characteristics are those of all large professional establishments, regardless of their political-social environment: (a) high professionalization and demands for professional autonomy; (b) a professional ethos, including strict codes of honor and discipline; and (c) an organizational structure whose levels of authority are easily discernible and stable.

These institutional propensities of the military clash with the Party's ideal image of an open institution, one easy to penetrate and manipulate. However, the Party is unwilling and even unable to alter these characteristics, because to do so would require radical measures that might endanger military viability. Yet it is also unwilling to accept their unchecked existence. This dilemma creates difficult choices for the Party, which accents this contradictory situation by denying the military any actual autonomy while firmly demanding from it the kind of results that could be achieved best if such professional autonomy were granted. It is almost as if the Party leaders hoped to be able to create not only a "new man" but also a "new institution," which they expect to be *sui generis* in terms of organization, structure, and values, and yet to resemble other orthodox military establishments in performance.

The contradictoriness and incompatibility of certain basic characteristics of the military and the features that the Party would have it exhibit become readily apparent if one juxtaposes them as follows:

"Natural" Military Traits	*Traits Desired by the Party*
Elitism	Egalitarianism
Professional autonomy	Subordination to ideology
Nationalism	Proletarian internationalism
Detachment from society	Involvement with society
Heroic symbolism	Anonymity

That the military traits in the left column are indeed "natural" can be seen in the fact that they have tended to emerge whenever the Soviet military has been in a position which permitted it some freedom from the coercive controls of the Party: in the early 1930's, during World War II, and in the brief period of Zhukov's tenure in the Ministry of Defense.

The incompatibility between the Party's ideal model of a thoroughly politicized instrument of the socialist state (which must also be militarily effective and disciplined) on the one hand, and the military's "natural" tendencies toward orthodoxy on the other, creates friction and tension between the two institutions, the range of whose conflicts will be described below.

a. Conflicts of Ideology and Organization. A perennial source of tensions is the Party's antimilitary ideology, which clashes with the military's own institutional beliefs. As we look at the relations between Party and military, we see two institutions, with distinct ideologies and conflicting institutional interests, in a state of uneasy coexistence, both striving for exclusiveness, elitism, and detachment from the rest of the society; both subscribing to similar formalized codes of beliefs and behavior; both cultivating an almost messianic self-image. How can these exclusive ideologies accommodate themselves to each other in view of the Party's claim to hegemony?

(1) Communist ideologues often find it awkward to define their attitude to standing professional armies. Originally, such armies were seen as the exploiting instruments of the ruling classes, which, by definition, had no place in a classless communist society. The despised power of the state was personified in "barracks and bivouac, saber and musket, mustache and uniform."[18] Says Reinhard Höhn, a prominent German student of Marxist views of the military: "According to the Communist Manifesto, the Army becomes unnecessary in the classless society. It [the classless society] knows no socialist soldiers and no socialist officer."[19] However, the need to translate the doctrine into reality, and the sobering facts of political power, convinced Marx, and even more so Engels, that the only way for the revolution to succeed would be "through modern means of war and modern military art against modern means of war and modern military art."[20] Professor Höhn states that, after the experience of the disastrous Paris Commune uprising, Marx and Engels viewed "the idea of abolishing standing armies and introducing the general arming of the people (*allgemeine Volksbewaffnung*) which

[18] Karl Marx and Friedrich Engels, *Ausgewählte Schriften*, Vol. 1, p. 241, cited in Reinhard Höhn, *Sozialismus und Heer*, Verlag Dr. Max Gehlen, Bad Homburg, 2nd ed., 1961, Vol. 1, p. 34.

[19] Höhn, p. 35.

[20] *Ibid.*, p. 52.

had so excited the minds of that time, as a bourgeois utopia."[21] Höhn maintains that, gradually, Marx and Engels arrived at the realization that the army was no longer outside the realm of consideration, as it had been in the Communist Manifesto; they came to view it as a power factor, which must be included in the revolutionary world strategy.[22]

In the communist *Weltanschauung*, wars play a vital role in the realization of communist goals. "War," says Marx, ". . . puts a nation to the test . . . [it] imposes the death sentence on all social institutions which have lost their vitality."[23] Engels maintains that the only "right wars" of large dimensions are those that serve the purpose of the revolution. Lenin reiterates approvingly Clausewitz's dictum that "War is simply a continuation of politics by other (i.e., violent) means," adding that "this has always been the standpoint of Marx and Engels, who regarded every war as the continuation of the politics of the given interested powers. . . ."[24] In 1917 Lenin was even more emphatic when he wrote that "Socialists cannot, without ceasing to be Socialists, be opposed to all war."[25]

Yet, while warfare as such was thus accepted as a key factor in victory, the communist leaders' views of professional armies were never as explicitly direct, nor were they unequivocal. In 1903 Lenin wrote: "A standing army is an army that is divorced from the people and trained to shoot down the people. . . . A standing army is not in the least necessary to protect the country from an attack of the enemy; a people's militia is sufficient."[26] Two years later, he changed his mind: ". . . great historical questions can be solved only by violence, and the organization of violence in the modern struggle is a military organization."[27] Like Marx and Engels before him, Lenin may have observed the futility of spontaneous mass uprisings against standing professional armies (in his case it would have been the czarist army in the uprising of 1905) and taken the position that the communist movement needed a professional military organization to reach its objectives. However, Party leaders had to maintain the doctrinal fiction of the eventual withering away of the state, of which the military is an essential factor, and of the superfluity of the pro-

[21] *Ibid.*, p. 70. [22] *Ibid.*, pp. 70-71. [23] *Ibid.*, p. 69.

[24] "Collapse of the Second International," *Selected Works*, Lawrence & Wishart, Ltd., London, 1936, Vol. 5, pp. 179-180.

[25] "Military Program of Proletarian Revolution," *Collected Works*, International Publishers, New York, 1942, Vol. 19, p. 362.

[26] "To the Rural Poor," *Selected Works*, Vol. 2, p. 281.

[27] "Revolutionary Army and Revolutionary Government," *ibid.*, Vol. 3, p. 313.

fessional army in the classless communist society. They therefore devised various formulas by which to justify the maintenance of a professional army. Under Lenin and Stalin it was the threat of "capitalistic encirclement"; under Khrushchev the rationale went as follows:

> We are devoting great attention to our army only because we are forced to do so. Since the capitalist countries cannot think of existing without armies we must also have an army. . . .[28]

Such avowed misgivings about the maintenance of professional armies seem to have been largely rhetorical statements for the sake of ideological continuity and legitimacy. The Party leaders' apprehension about the role of the professional army in a communist state, on the other hand, is genuine. It stems from uncertainty about their ability to exercise constant, effective control over the "experts in violence," with their well-integrated organization, whose institutional objectives frequently diverge from those of the Party. The latter, to state the conflict in its simplest terms, is a group of "experts in violence" of a much broader scope, who cannot tolerate any significant opposition to their hegemony within the state.

(2) Some Western students of military affairs have compared the ideology of the military to that of the Church. Other scholars have drawn the parallel between Church and Party, among them Zbigniew Brzezinski, who states that "both movements see themselves as the exclusive standard-bearers of an absolutely correct and normatively all-embracing vision of reality."[29] It follows, then, that there are certain similarities also between the Party and the military. Indeed, to the extent that the Party may be described as a dedicated, exclusive elite, which deals with and serves society but stands apart, and which owes its cohesion to the institutional values upheld by a dogma, these characteristics can be transferred almost without qualification to the officer corps of most military establishments. Studies which stress similarities between military and Church doctrine deal chiefly with Western or noncommunist military establishments, but their theses are applicable also to the Soviet military, with its very similar structure, internal procedures, and idealized self-image.

The theme which is common to most of these views is that the pro-

[28] Interview with Iverach McDonald of the London *Times*, January 31, 1958, reported in *Pravda*, February 16, 1958.

[29] "From the Other Shore," *Encounter*, No. 3, 1963, p. 78. For a striking example of the Party functionaries' moralistic-theistic view of the Party, see Appendix F.

fession of the officer is strongly motivated by selfless devotion to spiritual and patriotic values, making it more of a "calling" than a job. Walter Millis observes that "Military service stands by itself. It has some of the qualities of priesthood, of a professional civil service . . . of an academic order."[30] The British General Sir John Winthrop Hackett sees the military calling as "one of the fundamental pursuits" and compares the profession of an officer to those of "the priest, the healer, the lawgiver."[31] Morris Janowitz refers to this similarity of priesthood and officer profession in the United States on several occasions. He cites, among others, a naval captain: "The naval profession is much like the ministry. You dedicate life to a purpose."[32] And, in Germany, von Seeckt has remarked on the tradition of the officer: "The form changes but the spirit remains as of old. It is the spirit of selfless devotion to duty."[33]

Communist Party experts on military affairs, well aware of this idealized image and self-image of military professionals, deny that it exists in the Soviet army. One of them, in a major work on militarism, has accused militarists of employing "the doctrines of the ruling church and various religious movements."[34] (He is obviously referring to Western militarists, since, according to Party dogma, there can be no militarism in a classless society or in a society whose classes are in a "nonantagonistic relationship.") The author, V. I. Skopin, strongly attacks this "ideology of militarism," which he accuses of embodying an "idealistic philosophy." Methodically he uncovers and condemns these "idealistic" views which strive "to show the 'beauty' and 'wisdom' [of military life] and the 'benefits derived from war for the welfare of mankind.'"

[30] Walter Millis, "Puzzle of the 'Military Mind,'" *The New York Times Magazine*, November 18, 1962, p. 155.

[31] "The Profession of Arms, Part II: Today and Tomorrow," *Military Review*, Vol. 43, No. 11, November 1963, p. 57.

[32] *The Professional Soldier*, p. 115.

[33] Cited in Samuel P. Huntington, *The Soldier and the State*, Harvard University Press, Cambridge, 1957, p. 51.

[34] V. I. Skopin, *Militarizm: istoricheskie ocherki* (Militarism: Historical Essays), ed. Major General Professor N. V. Pukhovskii, 2nd ed., Voenizdat, Moscow, 1957, p. 35. Skopin lists the following, among others, as typical examples of militaristic "idealistic philosophy": "Eternal peace is possible only in the cemetery" (Leibnitz); "War is a celebration of the one who is best" (Hegel); "I counsel you war, not toil" (Nietzsche); "War—that's a purifying fire! It heals the spirit of the nation" (Mussolini). Facetiously, one might add to Skopin's list of "decadent" Western views of militarism such statements as "War . . . puts a nation to the test . . . [it] imposes the death sentence on all social institutions which have lost their vitality" (Marx); "Socialists cannot, without ceasing to be Socialists, be opposed to all war" (Lenin); and Stalin's calling war a "kind of test of the Soviet system."

However, while Communist Party ideologues express themselves in these contemptuous terms, Soviet military leaders and publicists, concerned about the deteriorating morale of their officers, speak proudly of the beauty of the military profession. Major General Makeev, who is the influential editor-in-chief of the Defense Ministry's central organ, *Krasnaia zvezda,* recently asserted that "the concept of military honor has existed since time immemorial: it is as ancient as armies. . . . Even in the old Russian army there existed good traditions—bravery, selfless dedication and military expertise were revered." He also made an interesting distinction between the officer and the soldier:

> There is a saying: the soldier is at war even in peacetime. But the soldier serves his prescribed time and departs into the reserves. The officer—he is also a soldier, but he is at war for a lifetime. . . . How many inconveniences, deprivations and trials! But the officer withstands all, overcomes all, he does not lose courage. He holds high his honor, the honor of the officer and citizen.[35]

A conflict of ideologies is inevitable in view of the Party's attempt to neutralize, equalize, and "depersonalize" all institutions and groups and claim exclusive features only for itself, and, at the same time, of the inherent tendency of all professional-institutional groupings to develop characteristics and personalities of their own.

b. Substantive Disagreements. Since the very beginnings of the Soviet state and the Red Army, the Party has maintained in the military establishment a multiple control network whose purpose it is to secure information, to indoctrinate and manipulate the military, to supervise and control the professional and private activities of officers and men, and, finally, to coerce the recalcitrant or anti-Party elements.

The military has seldom opposed or even questioned the principle of having some measure of political indoctrination or supervision. It does, however, resent and oppose any excessive pressure from the control machinery that substantially interferes with the performance of professional duties.

Disagreements have centered also around issues of strategy. Before World War II, the Soviets had no distinct, indigenous strategic doctrine, although there was some cross-fertilization from the German army in the pre-Hitler era. During the war, Stalin launched

[35] *Izvestiia,* February 12, 1963.

several new strategic concepts. These were subsequently formalized in a "scientific military doctrine," whose basic features were a set of "permanent factors," or immutable laws of warfare, and several "temporary factors," which were changeable with conditions.

Stalin's death and the ensuing struggles for power within the Party freed the military from a long silence. One by one, the Stalinist formulas were exposed to discussion, their failings and merits were analyzed publicly, and most of them were rejected. The introduction of thermonuclear strategic missiles and other advanced weapons and equipment led to a drastic change in Soviet strategy. But not all parts of the military welcomed this change. While the rejection of the obsolete Stalinist formulas had met with general approval, some aspects of the new Soviet strategic doctrine encountered strong opposition from the theater forces, which were most severely affected by the change, and some of whose spokesmen questioned its wisdom. The result was a continuous debate between the Party and the "traditionalists" (the theater forces) as well as between the "traditionalists" and the "radicals" (the military supporters of the new, Khrushchevian strategic doctrine).

Another source of tensions has been the Party leadership's divide-and-rule policy, by which it accords preferential treatment to favored factions within the military, and excludes other, politically unaligned officers from the highest Party councils and military positions.

While Stalin tended to reserve the highest military positions for "political generals," Khrushchev entrusted these vital positions to professional officers who had shown courage and ability during the war. These officers, who owe much of their career and thrust to prominence to Khrushchev (they are here called the Stalingrad Group, because the origins of their special relationship with Khrushchev go back to the battle of Stalingrad in 1942-1943), constitute the present Soviet High Command. They represent a strong beachhead of the Party in the military, because many of them, although capable professionals, tend to give primary weight to political considerations.

In the various substantive disagreements between the Party and the military, the Stalingrad Group, until recently, faithfully followed the lead of Khrushchev. In the doctrinal-strategic debate, many of its members advocate greater reliance on strategic missile-nuclear forces and a reduced role for the theater forces; on the role of the political control organs, they tend to support the Party line.

One of the debates in which the Stalingrad Group has largely championed the Party view, sometimes in strikingly unmilitary fashion, has been that on the "historical issues." This arose after Stalin's death, with pressures exerted by the military on the Party for a formal reassessment of the history of World War II that would accord the role of the military proper recognition as a main factor in the victory over the German invaders. The earlier official version had absolved Stalin and the Party from any responsibility for events in the initial period of the war, when the Red Army suffered disastrous defeats, by placing the blame on the military, either openly or obliquely. At the same time, it had given Stalin and the Party the lion's share of the credit for the ultimate victory, with no more than laudatory mention for the military. It has been the contention of the military, since Stalin's death, that the Party must take on at least part of the blame for the mistakes and share some of the credit for the achievements of the war years.

4. The Party's Methods of Controlling the Military

The measures by which the Party deals with the military range from the positive (the granting of socio-economic privileges, political cooptation, and acquiescence in military demands), through the "prophylactic" (indoctrination and supervision), to the negative (intimidation and coercion). The objective of all these measures is to maintain high levels of effectiveness, discipline, and morale in the military and at the same time to prevent or eradicate any elitist, "Bonapartist," anti-Party sentiments or movements in its ranks.

a. Positive Measures. The Party grants the professional officer impressive privileges and allowances, which in the past placed the officer almost automatically among the socio-economic elite. This has been somewhat less true in recent years, not so much through deliberate action on the part of the government as because of the rising standard of living in the larger society and the greater availability of goods and services. But the higher officer and his family still continue to enjoy a privileged existence."[36]

[36] See *L'goty, pensii i posobiia voennosluzhashchim i ikh sem'iam: spravochnik* (Privileges, Pensions and Allowances for Military Personnel and Their Families: A Handbook), Voenizdat, Moscow, 1958, 260 pp.; A. I. Kotlar and B. V. Kozhevnikov, *Voprosy pensionnogo obespecheniia voennosluzhashchikh i ikh semei* (Problems of Pension Provisions for Military Personnel and Their Families), Voenizdat, Moscow, 1956; *Posobiia, pensii i l'goty voennosluzhashchim i ikh sem'iam* (Allowances, Pensions and Privileges for Military Personnel and Their Families), Voenizdat, Moscow, 1943; *Krasnaia zvezda*, May 9, 1956; M. Martens, "Providing for the Soviet Officer," *Bulletin of the Institute for the Study of the USSR*, No. 2, February 1956, pp. 26-32.

The extent of the officer's attachment to his rather agreeable way of life, and his very strong reluctance to give it up, are evident from the bitterness with which officers have reacted to the periodic reductions of the armed forces.[37] An officer who is forcibly retired, or transferred to the reserves, before his normal tour of duty is over and before he is entitled to a full pension, faces a bleak future in an unfriendly social environment. The Party *apparatchiks* are well aware of this situation, which gives them a powerful hold over the individual officer and which they manipulate to their own advantage.

The Party also coopts a certain number of prominent military leaders into the highest Party councils, such as the Central Committee and the Central Auditing Commission, thereby bringing them close to the decision-making centers where, theoretically, they may present the military's point of view and look out for the military's interests. In practice, however, most of those chosen for such representation are ideologically close to the Party's point of view and tend to give priority to political considerations over the purely institutional military interests.[38]

b. "Prophylactic" Measures. The Party elite tends to view the citizenry with suspicion and distrust. By and large, it subscribes to the view that the individual in Soviet society must be made to feel that he has no alternative but to fulfill the role assigned to him, and must be placed under strict controls that limit his freedom to make unorthodox judgments. With respect to the military, this idea is being put into practice in a variety of ways: through an elaborate system of indoctrination, supervision, and manipulation, and through the deliberate creation of unease and distrust, by having different ranks mix with one another at Party meetings and encouraging the low-ranking officers publicly to criticize their superiors.[39]

These measures are designed to keep the officer committed and loyal, to give him a set of objectives and values similar to those of the Party, and to imbue him with a negative view of the external world and an idealized image of Soviet reality, making him thereby into the "new Soviet man."[40]

c. Negative Measures. Although "prophylaxis" is the preferred method for keeping the military loyal as well as strong, the Party also resorts at times to the harsher measures of intimidation, black-

[37] See Chapter V, pp. 153-154.
[38] See Chapter VI, *passim*, and Chapter VII, p. 242.
[39] See Chapters III and IV, *passim*. [40] See Chapter IV, pp. 93-94.

mail, and coercion, and Soviet officers well recall the notorious purges (*chistki*) of the Stalinist era. In the post-Stalin period, with its more moderate methods, the Party has used a most effective means of ridding itself of undesirables in the military: the periodic massive reductions of the armed forces and the dismissal of individual officers. Furthermore, it maintains provocateurs and informers within the military units, who report the private and professional activities of their personnel to the political organs, providing the latter with dossiers that can be used for blackmail. The political control organs also play a major role during the yearly attestations of the officers, and their approval is indispensable to the officers' careers.

5. *The Resources of the Military*

Given the Party's initiative and controlling power in the relationship with the military, what, we must now ask, are the military's resources and methods for questioning, neutralizing, challenging, or opposing the Party's dominance?

a. Professional Expertise. The age of atomic and nuclear warfare has transformed most large military establishments from tradition-ridden organizations, whose leadership was predicated chiefly on its ability to lead men in combat and maintain discipline, into vast bureaucracies based on complex equipment and weapons. The new elite in these establishments consists to an ever greater extent of technocrats in uniform; their officers must understand technology, economics, and logistics, and must be able to manage large projects which overlap with the civilian economy.

In the Soviet Union, this new situation is acknowledged by prominent military and Party leaders. Marshal Zakharov, Chief of the General Staff, has warned that, whereas "in past wars gaps in the military and technical knowledge of a commander were sometimes made up by his native intuition, . . . it is very risky to rely on intuition in nuclear warfare, under conditions of rapid and highly mobile military operations."[41] Zakharov's temporary successor, Marshal Biriuzov, in a similar vein, believed that to the "officer-specialists belongs the future of our armed forces."[42]

With officer training increasingly complex, time-consuming, expensive, and exacting, any wholesale purges or massive replacements would seriously weaken the Soviet military, which even now

[41] *Krasnaia zvezda*, October 12, 1962.

[42] Cited in *Voennyi inzhener—aktivnyi vospitatel'* (The Military Engineer—An Active Educator), Voenizdat, Moscow, 1962, p. 5.

suffers from a shortage of technically trained officers. The knowledge of their indispensability has caused officers in the technical and elite services[43] to assert themselves more freely and often *vis-à-vis* the Party *apparatchiks*. The Party's attempts to place political officers in commanding positions and commanders in Party positions, so as to prevent situations where professional officers insist on greater independence and immunity, have not been very successful. By and large, therefore, the Party recognizes the importance of the military professional and interferes in his functions with greater circumspection than in the past.

b. Institutional Resilience. The Soviet officer corps retains many of the characteristics of guild-like institutions in all societies, despite the Party's constant efforts to eradicate them. Officers "cover up" for one another, further each other's careers, protect and favor their former comrades, and in other ways cultivate a sense of solidarity, in alliance against hostile surroundings. This cohesiveness and camaraderie is summed up in a sentence from the military's central organ, *Krasnaia zvezda*: "In a society where each man is a brother to his fellow-man, even an unknown soldier is best friend to each of us."[44] The corporateness of the officer corps is strengthened by tradition, by pride in the craft, and by a patriotic sense of serving the fatherland.

These qualities have given the military establishment the resilience that has enabled it to raise effective obstacles to the Party's almost obsessive endeavor to break down the military's natural independence. They are the mark of the military's institutional identity and strength. Though Stalin gained temporary mastery in this struggle by brutally cutting down the dissidents in the officer corps, his heirs in the Kremlin are no longer able, and are probably unwilling, to risk such a showdown.

c. Political Alliances. The inherent instability of power arrangements in the Soviet state has forced contenders for power to seek alliances with the major social groupings (the governmental bureaucracy, the Party professionals, the military, the terror machine, among others), either to protect a monopoly of power or to ensure against the possibility of a showdown in a future crisis. During periods of firm leadership and internal stability, the Party unequivocally dominates the state and is able to keep those institutions sufficiently divided and rigidly controlled. However, when the Party's hold is

[43] See Chapter VIII, *passim*, for a detailed analysis of this situation.
[44] October 13, 1962.

weakened—by internecine power struggles, succession crises, or external military threats—the groups that have formerly been kept submissive and politically impotent tend to gain in stature and influence.

The military establishment, being a well-integrated organization with a cohesive structure and powerful weapons and logistic facilities, is in an excellent position to exploit those occasions of division and other weaknesses in the Party and to fill the partial void of authority that they create. Stalin used to anticipate any danger of the military's political assertion in such situations, whether real or imaginary, by striking out at the military with preemptive measures designed to induce a state of near-shock. His successors do not exercise or enjoy the same freedom of action. Like Stalin, however, they have tried to bind the military to themselves through political alliances and personal ties intended to keep the military elite committed to the regime; to ensure cooperation and responsiveness in the High Command; and to divide the military leadership by favoring some segments and excluding others from such a preferential relationship with the Party rulers.

This last attempt, however, does not always succeed as intended. There have been times when military leaders in political alliance with the Party elite have found opportunity to exploit the military's implicit political weight and indispensability in the event of a crisis to their personal benefit as well as to the advantage of the military in general.

6. *Constraints on the Relationship of Party and Military*

The interaction of these two large institutional bureaucracies in the Soviet state—the conflicts and occasional clashes that result from the Party's constant attempt to impose its dominance on the military and from the military's resistance to the Party's stranglehold—suggests an uneasy balance between the objectives of external policy and concerns of internal political power. If the two institutions have nevertheless coexisted, on the whole, in a workable manner, we may assume that there are certain implicit "rules of the game," which set limits to the arbitrariness of both protagonists and prevent their interaction from becoming totally destructive.

a. "The Rules of the Game." The historical pattern of Party-military relations shows periods of relative tranquillity followed by gathering tensions, which culminate in crisis (sometimes averted through some radical preemptive action by the Party). This crisis or near-crisis has always, in the past, ended in victory for the Party, and been followed by another period of relative tranquillity. One of the most interesting aspects of this "cyclical" pattern is the fact that, in almost every case, the deterioration of relations followed upon a period when the Party was exceptionally dependent on the support of the military because of either international or domestic developments. Its temporary need of the military caused the Party to relax some of its controls and to grant officers unusual concessions and greater professional autonomy. This usually led to greater self-assertiveness on the part of the military, which in turn worried the Party as foreshadowing an emancipation from its political controls that could prove a threat to its dominant position in the state. Stalin, at such moments, was willing to sacrifice military effectiveness to political considerations and take strong action to subdue the military; his successors have sought more moderate and conciliatory means of maintaining their dominance over the armed forces.

Apart from these fluctuations in degree and method, the pattern of the relationship might be summed up as follows: When the Party is strong and untroubled, the military's voice and institutional role in the state are minor; when the Party is threatened from within or without, the military rises above its subordinate role and enters the public political stage. And since the totalitarian Soviet state, with its expansionistic foreign policy and its lack of provision for the orderly transfer of power, is likely to face frequent crisis situations, the military will on those occasions find itself in a favorable, perhaps even a central, position on the political stage.

b. The Effects of Political Changes in the Soviet Union and the Communist Bloc. In the past, the Party was able to manipulate the military with relative impunity, because the price for an embittered and hostile officer corps, though high, was not unbearable. Since the death of Stalin, various conditions, the results of social changes in the Soviet Union and countries of the communist bloc, have set limits to such freedom of manipulation.

Stalin's rule of terror kept the military, along with other professional and social groups, in a state of insecurity and political impotence. Moreover, his near-deification during his lifetime also prevented the emergence into lasting prominence of any other persons or groups, no matter how great their achievement in the service of Party or state. After Stalin's death, the situation changed considerably: The terror machine was largely discredited and moved to the background of political life; the Party was weakened by the internal power struggles of several of its factions; and far-reaching schisms within the Soviet bloc further complicated the CPSU's drive for control of the communist movement. These and other developments freed the military from the oppressive terror of the Stalin period, enhanced its role as a vital institution in the event of intra-Party power struggles, and stressed its importance to the Party's power position both within and outside the bloc. The result was a significant change also in the relationship between Party and military: Whereas formerly the Party had determined the nature of their relations by being able to muzzle the military where their views, objectives, and demands diverged, the military now assumed a new role and became an active partner in the Party's formulation of military policy.

c. The Impact of Technology on the Art of War. The weapons, equipment, and dynamics of modern warfare are radically different from those of the past. Decisive victories, or at least the destruction of the opponent, can be achieved in a matter of hours, even minutes. The impact on the military establishment of this technological change, with its implications for future warfare, has in turn affected the relations between Party and military. It has repeatedly forced the Party to subordinate ideological-political considerations to purely military ends, and has set further limits to its arbitrary handling of the military. Although the Party has not given up its intensive efforts to keep the military controlled and indoctrinated, it has had to shift tactics, to become more amenable to the military's proposals and demands, and more circumspect in its dealings with the armed forces. In addition, the growing influx of new technocrats into the military has aggravated the problem of internal control, since these young specialists tend to resent and oppose the Party's political involvement and activity on the grounds that it drastically interferes with their vital duties. Although the Party is disturbed by demands for professional autonomy, it is inclined to give in to them whenever they come from the elite forces, which form the backbone of the Soviet defense establishment.[45]

[45] Thus, General Epishev, the head of the Main Political Administration of the Soviet Army and Navy (MPA), has complained about the fact that certain missile forces have for years refused to forward reports on various Party-prescribed political activities within their units (*Kommunist Vooruzhennykh Sil*, No. 15, August 1962, p. 39). On the other hand, Colonel General Tolubko, First Deputy Commander of the Strategic Missile Forces, has issued a sharp request that officers under his command be left free of duties not directly connected with their professional functions (*Krasnaia zvezda*, January 8, 1963).

In short, the growing complexity and proliferation of military equipment and weapons, and the greater need for military professionals able to attend to them, have set new boundaries to the Party's rule over the military, for they have heightened its dependence on the experts, forcing it to treat them with circumspection.

III · The Historical Perspective

The preceding chapter has acquainted the reader with the multitude of problems inherent in, and responsible for, the conflict-ridden relationship between the Communist Party elite and the Soviet military establishment. We have suggested that the dynamics of that relationship are set in motion by two contradictory interests of the Party: its need for a strong and effective military to support an expansionist foreign policy, and its intolerance of even a modicum of professional autonomy in any major institution lest it lead to political influence. We have shown the "rules of the game," under which the Party maintains as strict a system of political and ideological control over the military as its own strength and the needs of the moment permit, but is willing to accord the officer corps status, privilege, and a voice in policy at times when the military is in a relatively powerful position and less inclined to tolerate such pressure. We must now go on to ask how Party and military, the two major institutions in the Soviet state, came to assume their respective roles in this game.

The history of the Soviet Union shows sporadic open crises between Party and military that suggest the instability in their relationship and the possibility of an essential incompatibility. As we shall try to demonstrate, these occasional dramatic eruptions are part of a recurrent cycle, in which Party and military pass from a state of relative tranquillity through rising tensions to open crisis and, upon solution of the crisis, back to tranquillity. Moreover, the cyclical recurrence of these consecutive stages is inevitable because of a basic conflict in the roles of the two establishments and the objective circumstances surrounding their relationship. In the past, every cycle has meant the temporary deterioration, if not the actual rupture, of relations, the result of the Party's anxiety at the military's growing self-assertiveness and of its fear of an ultimate challenge to its political hegemony. In almost every instance, the Party has been willing to sacrifice some degree of military efficiency for the sake of suppressing this assumed threat to its autonomy, an indication that, in the final assessment of alternatives, political considerations outweigh concern about the efficacy of the defense establishment.

A · *THE FORMATIVE PERIOD: 1917-1924*

The events of this period are a key to our understanding of the whole history of Party-military relations, because it was during these few years that the Red Army developed its structure, organization, and domestic role.

The early years were marked by debates and disagreements within the Party as to the future form and role of the military. This turbulence was due to the simple fact that the Bolsheviks had no clear concept of what their military arm should be. As Soviet interpreters themselves now see it, "Lenin and the Communist Party did not yet have [in 1917] a thoroughly formulated view of the methods and forms of the military organization of the proletarian state and of the principles of its military structure."[1]

The one thing, however, of which the early Bolshevik leaders were quite sure was the need to demoralize the old Russian army, so that it would be useless to the Provisional Government in the fight against the revolutionaries. They therefore concentrated their major effort within the army on undermining the will to fight by promoting disobedience, spreading pacifist ideas, and otherwise stirring up the soldiers' imagination with simple, appealing slogans. Lenin's and Trotsky's political and psychological adroitness in so exploiting the mood and needs of the masses of peasants in the army accelerated the corrosion of morale that was already under way. Mass desertions, fraternization with the enemy, and disobedience plagued the old Russian army, and the damage was only intensified by the futile disciplinary efforts of Kerensky, and by Kornilov's brutal executions among disobedient units. In the fall of 1917 the Russian army had ceased to exist as a viable military organization.[2] To guard against the possibility of a revival, the Bolsheviks passed the decree on gradual demobilization, on November 23, 1917, as one of their first acts after coming to power.[3] It was followed by decrees on the introduction of the elective command principle and equalization of ranks.[4] The

[1] *KPSS i stroitel'stvo Vooruzhennykh Sil SSSR, 1918-iiun' 1941* (The CPSU and the Development of the Armed Forces of the USSR, 1918-June 1941), Voenizdat, Moscow, 1959, p. 11.

[2] Kh. I. Muratov, *Revoliutsionnoe dvizhenie v russkoi armii v 1917 g.* (The Revolutionary Movement in the Russian Army in 1917), Voenizdat, Moscow, 1958, cites a report of the Chief of Staff of the 12th Army, General Posokhov, who said: ". . . the Army just doesn't exist."

[3] *KPSS o Vooruzhennykh Silakh Sovetskogo Soiuza: sbornik dokumentov, 1917-1958* (The CPSU on the Armed Forces of the Soviet Union: A Collection of Documents, 1917-1958), Gospolitizdat, Moscow, 1958, pp. 20-27. This collection of documents contains some of the basic writings, decrees, and policy declarations of the CPSU regarding the Red Army. Some of the documents had never been published before their appearance in this volume, in 1958. See also *KPSS i stroitel'stvo Vooruzhennykh Sil*, p. 45.

[4] *KPSS i stroitel'stvo Vooruzhennykh Sil*, p. 14.

combined effect of these measures was to reduce the army in numbers and remove aristocratic and bourgeois officers from positions of authority.

Having thus destroyed the old army, the Bolsheviks had to replace it with another military force if they were to be able to resist the onslaught of the counterrevolutionary forces. The existing Red Guards, although they had been adequate to dealing with the garrisons of Petersburg and Moscow during the October Revolution, were "incapable of opposing the enemy armies" because of "insufficient numbers . . . and the absence of proper centralization [of authority]."[5] Lenin proposed the creation of a "Socialist Army," which was to consist of factory workers who had been approved for membership, but the suggestion was abandoned shortly after it had been made. Instead, at the Third All-Russian Congress, in January 1918, the Bolshevik elite accepted the idea of a professional, class-based army.[6] And on January 28, Lenin signed the decree that brought into existence the Workers and Peasants Red Army (RKKA).

The new Red Army was at first far from the formidable military machine it was to become, for the Marxists' traditional distrust of standing professional armies, as well as the near-anarchic condition of the country, caused its founders to proceed cautiously. The plan was to decentralize the army, using the principle of voluntary recruitment and elected commanders. However, the divisive forces within the military—parochial interests, lack of centralized authority, multiple Party committees and Party cells, and friction between officers and enlisted men—nullified all efforts to make the army into an effective fighting force. Consequently, in the "breathing space" (*peredyshka*) afforded the Party by the Brest Litovsk peace treaty with Germany, Trotsky, with Lenin's approval, undertook to remove the destructive elements from the Red Army and to transform it into an efficient professional force. In so doing, Trotsky alienated many of his colleagues in the Party, including Stalin, Voroshilov, and Frunze, and eventually brought about his own defeat. But out of the conflicting views and ensuing debates on the proper form and role of the military that figured prominently in the Party's activities between 1918 and 1924, there emerged the Red Army as we know it today.

The many views and proposals advanced in the discussions over form and function fell essentially into two main categories. The

[5] *Ibid.*, p. 11. [6] *Ibid.*, p. 47.

crucial question that divided them was whether the Red Army was to be a truly "revolutionary" army based on ideological tenets, or whether it should be a professional army unaffected by ideology. Advocates of the former favored (1) a minimum of centralized control and maximum reliance on local Party control for military units (that is to say, a territorial militia as opposed to standing professional cadres); (2) the abolition of rigid discipline, ranks, and traditional military virtues, and their replacement by a system in which commanders were elected and orders might be questioned; (3) voluntary recruitment as opposed to compulsory service; (4) local, rather than central, control of Party organizations and political organs in military units; and (5) revolutionary military doctrine in place of orthodox strategy. By contrast, the proponents of a professional army of standing cadres advocated hierarchic organization, strict discipline, and centralized control in a military institution that would operate according to traditional strategic concepts.

The Red Army as it emerged from the dispute of the early years was a compromise between these two extremes. Well on the way to becoming an organization of professional cadres, it still retained several characteristics of the revolutionary army. Most of these seemed designed to preserve the revolutionary appearance, although in all vital aspects the army was professional and centralized. Eventually, even those few vestiges of the Red Army's revolutionary origins were abandoned, and the professional military establishment of today differs from its counterparts in other large industrial societies only in one major feature: It is the military arm of a single political party, to which it owes indisputable allegiance and by which it is rigidly controlled.

The main protagonists in the early debates on the Party's military policies and on the form and the role of the Red Army were Trotsky and his followers on the one hand, and, on the other, the opponents of Trotsky's ideas who centered around Stalin.

Trotsky had proposed two stages of development for the military organism he was seeking to build. In the first, under the pressure of counterrevolutionary threats within and without the Soviet Union, the Party was to disregard ideological formulas and create a military force capable of fending off the enemies. In the second stage, after victory and internal stabilization, the Party would be free to create, at a more leisurely pace, a truly revolutionary army guided by ideological imperatives.

For the first stage, Trotsky urged rigid centralization of the military, the inclusion of officers from the old army (*voenspets*), strict discipline in the units, the abandoning of the election of commanders, compulsory military service, and orthodox strategy. In the second stage, he proposed transforming the Red Army into a territorial militia, by decentralizing authority, minimizing the role of political commissars, and doing away with class-oriented recruitment as well as with the controlling power of the military over the secret police and political organs within the army.

Trotsky's recommendations for the first stage of the Red Army's development were based primarily on the urgency of the military situation and the acute need to preserve and expand the newly won Soviet power. His rationale for the second stage was similarly pragmatic: Since the overriding problems, once the regime had consolidated its power and repulsed the external and internal enemies, were economic, Trotsky argued the economic advantages of a part-time arrangement, by which proletarians and "near-proletarians" could continue to work in factories and villages while spending part of their time in military training—an arrangement, he pointed out, that would also accord more nearly with the model of the socialist system.

Though Trotsky's proposals had the support of Lenin, they generated widespread dissatisfaction and opposition both among the military and in the Party. This opposition consisted of divergent groups, the most prominent among them being the circle that gathered around Stalin. The latter, though a fervent advocate of a centralized standing army, saw his position threatened by Trotsky's growing power and found it expedient, therefore, to attack him on the grounds that he would destroy the revolutionary army by including officers from the old army and adopting orthodox strategy. Other factions in opposition to Trotsky were those who interpreted the communist ideology very literally and opposed any measures tending toward militarization, the centralization of military authority, and orthodox strategy. Trotsky's intellectual and personal arrogance did not help his cause; on the contrary, it contributed to uniting his various critics in a single, concerted opposition. A further source of dissension in the Party was the personal animosity between Trotsky and Stalin.

The first major salvo in the intra-Party struggle over the future of the Red Army took place at the Eighth Party Congress, which met from March 18 to March 23, 1919. It succeeded in defining some of the fundamental characteristics of the Red Army as well as the temporary features designed to enable the country to deal with the then acute counterrevolutionary threat, both internal and external. The decisions of the Eighth Congress with respect to the Red Army may be summed up as follows:

(1) The Red Army was to have "a definite class character."[7]
(2) It was to include "Military Specialists."[8]
(3) The elective principle was to be abolished.[9]
(4) The army should be highly centralized.[10]
(5) For the duration of the civil war, the army would be a "standing" and "regular" one; thereafter, it would take on a militia form.[11]
(6) The role of military commissars was to be enhanced.[12] Specifically, (a) they were to guide the activities of the Party organizations in the units; (b) they were to control the "attestation" of the commanding personnel;[13] and (c) the system of military commissars was to be centralized under a member of the Central Committee, who would perform that function as a member of the *Revvoensovet Respubliki* (Revolutionary Military Council of the Republic).[14]
(7) The *Osobye Otdely* (Special Sections, secret police) in large units were to be under the control of the commissars, and their general activity was to be centrally supervised by *Osobye Otdely* of the Republic.[15]

The Eighth Party Congress thus strongly affirmed the Party's intention to create a professional military force and laid down some of its basic features. Yet the controversy within the Party and the military did not abate. Until 1925, at the next five Party congresses and on other major occasions, the Party continued to suffer from the heated dispute over the definition of the Red Army. It was during this turbulent period that the eventual outline of the structure, internal organization, and political role of the military was developed. The utopian proposals of the Left Communists, the Bukharinites, the "Military Opposition," and others fell by the wayside, and today's Red Army reflects essentially a synthesis of the ideas of the two main protagonists in the conflict.[16]

The basic agreement between Trotsky and Stalin that made it possible to arrive at a synthesis of their divergent viewpoints was on

[7] *KPSS o Vooruzhennykh Silakh*, p. 49.
[8] *Ibid.*, p. 50. [9] *Ibid.* [10] *Ibid.*, p. 53. [11] *Ibid.*, pp. 55 and 54.
[12] *Ibid.*, p. 57. [13] *Ibid.*, p. 62. [14] *Ibid.*, p. 63. [15] *Ibid.*
[16] For details of the "Military Opposition," see Chapter IV, p. 81, fn. 4.

the immediate need for a disciplined and centralized professional army. But Trotsky envisaged a gradual changeover to an ultimately more "revolutionary," ideologically oriented army, whereas Stalin and his supporters rejected that aim in favor of a permanent standing army. Trotsky, even though he introduced the political commissars into the Red Army (thereby adopting the practice of the Provisional Government), thought of them as playing only a limited role in the long run, while he favored increasingly wider functions for the intra-military and local Party organizations. Stalin, on the other hand, viewed the central political organs not only as playing a vital role during the formative period but as permanent instruments by which the Party leader could keep the military under close control. As pointed out earlier, Trotsky, the almost singlehanded creator of the Red Army as a disciplined and centralized military organism, nevertheless viewed this professional body as only a temporary expedient against the counterrevolutionary enemies, which in due course would be transformed into the kind of territorial militia he believed to be appropriate for the socialist state. Stalin, on the other hand, who wanted a perpetual standing army, was to plan the country's entire economy around the needs of such an army after he came to power.

It might be said that the Red Army in its ultimate form owes its existence to three main factors: Trotsky's capacity for pragmatic improvisation under stress; Stalin's vast personal power designs, combined with his practical understanding of statecraft; and the conditions that prevailed at the army's birth—the political and military threats to the new Bolshevik government—which persuaded Trotsky and other Party leaders to shelve their ideological preference for a people's army in favor of the more effective organism.

The problems and issues did not, however, crystallize immediately after the October Revolution. In the early period of 1917-1918, the antimilitary bias of prerevolutionary days continued to prevail in the Party's deliberations and activities. Preferences, therefore, lay initially with the Red Guards, with the short-lived Socialist Army of volunteers, and with other utopian schemes. Only in the face of growing counterrevolutionary stirrings did the Party leadership reverse itself and begin to build a more orthodox military force based on conscription and including czarist officers,[17] at the sacrifice

[17] Lenin underlined the importance of military specialists to the defense of the Revolution by stating that ". . . only officers—colonels and generals from the czarist armies—know military science." Cited in Major General V. F. Loboda's *Komandnye kadry i zakonodatel'stvo o kadrakh v razvitii Vooruzhennykh Sil SSSR* (The Com-

of cherished ideological and organizational tenets and despite the violent opposition of various factions in the Party.

During the early 1920's, however, the mounting economic difficulties, which eventually led to the New Economic Policy (NEP), made the promilitary cause highly unpopular.[18] With the disappearance of acute external threats came a growing reluctance to maintain large professional military formations, which ideologically and economically were anathema to many in the Party. This mood was reflected in Trotsky's proposals for decentralization of military authority, a more loosely organized and locally controlled military organization, and the narrowing of the role of political commissars accompanied by enlarged authority for local Party organizations.[19]

The years of the civil war, however, also produced a type of communist military man who, having once tasted power and status, was not easily reconciled to the Party's antimilitary measures of the NEP period that followed. These military professionals therefore sought to serve their own interests by aligning themselves with the anti-Trotsky elements in Party and military. At the same time, even as Trotsky was publicly expounding and implementing his policies,

---

manding Cadres and Legislation on Cadres in the Development of the Armed Forces of the USSR), Voenizdat, Moscow, 1960, p. 32.

The widespread opposition to the inclusion of military specialists from the old army is reflected in the memoirs of S. I. Aralov. According to Aralov, there was a special meeting convened in the Kremlin on March 24-26, 1918, which was attended by Lenin and forty or fifty military personalities. In the course of it, the problem was heatedly debated, and "the majority of the participants expressed opposition to the inclusion of the military specialists." Only thanks to Lenin's passionate arguments in favor of inclusion was the program eventually adopted. *KPSS i stroitel'stvo Vooruzhennykh Sil*, pp. 67-69.

[18] Fedotoff-White summarized the prevailing mood in the Soviet Union as follows: "The years of Civil War, added to those of the World War, spread weariness and dislike for military life, not only among the peasant rank and file soldiers, but also among some of the communist element in the military and political hierarchy of the army. The army was deprived of the privileged position it held during the war years. . . ." D. Fedotoff-White, *The Growth of the Red Army*, Princeton University Press, Princeton, N.J., 1944, p. 183.

The antimilitary sentiments were reflected by Trotsky, who in January 1921 said: ". . . our enormous military machine has put everybody's back up. . . . Everyone is dreaming of reducing it to a minimum." L. Trotsky, *Kak vooruzhalas' revoliutsiia* (How the Revolution Armed), Vol. 3, Book 1, Moscow, 1924, p. 8.

[19] The concern of the promilitary faction about the antimilitary sentiment and apathy among the population and the Party is reflected in these statements by Frunze in 1922: "The Party and the working class . . . have turned themselves spiritually to peace" and "lazily and drowsily move the wheels of the military machine." M. V. Frunze, *Izbrannye proizvedeniia* (Selected Works), Partizdat, Moscow, 1934, pp. 49 and 78, respectively.

the faction around Stalin was consolidating its power and placing its own men in vital positions in the military and in the Party. The years 1920-1925 thus became a period of struggle between proponents of military retrenchment and the advocates of a strong and centralized Red Army.

The Ninth Party Congress (March 29-April 5, 1920) approved the transformation of the Red Army into a militia of the territorial type,[20] but the sudden flare-up of hostilities on the Polish front made this proposal somewhat premature. Once the differences with Poland were settled, however, the Party enforced a compromise plan, under which it retained a cadre army of 560,000 men, while the rest of the army gradually was replaced by the territorial-militia structure.

The measures proposed and enacted under Trotsky's authority, though they reflected the needs, conditions, and capabilities of the Soviet Union during the NEP period, alienated those military officers who, in the words of Fedotoff-White, ". . . realized that in the militia, organized along the original lines suggested by Trotsky, there would be no room for their professional careers."[21] While Trotsky was becoming ever more embroiled in the Party's internal struggles, the proponents of a professional standing army, with M. V. Frunze (at the time Commander-in-Chief of the southern front) as their main organizer, quietly pursued their objectives.

Even in the early 1920's, despite the many obstacles created by the deteriorating economic and social conditions, this "promilitary" movement managed to consolidate its position. Its gradual gains were to be seen in (a) the nucleus of a cadre army that was retained; (b) the rescinding of regulations under which military units were to participate in nonmilitary work in the civilian economy;[22] (c) the centralization of military authority; (d) the enhanced role of the political control organs;[23] (e) the introduction of some ranks and insignias;[24]

[20] *KPSS o Vooruzhennykh Silakh*, p. 161.

[21] *Ibid.*, p. 193. The strong promilitary viewpoint at the time was reflected by Frunze, who stated that, if a choice were given him between a regular army numbering from 1.5 to 2 million men and the kind of army that combined cadres with features of the territorial militia, in his opinion the first would have all the advantages from the military standpoint. Fedotoff-White, *The Growth of the Red Army*, pp. 193-194.

[22] *KPSS o Vooruzhennykh Silakh*, p. 193.

[23] The Tenth Party Congress decided "to retain the political apparatus of the Red Army . . . to improve and strengthen its organization; to strengthen its ties with local Party organization, while at the same time retaining full independence of the apparatus." *Ibid.*, p. 192.

[24] Loboda, *Komandnye kadry*, p. 51.

(f) the gradual professionalization of officer careers;[25] (g) significant measures for the professional education of Red Army officers;[26] (h) the prohibition of local Party control over intramilitary affairs;[27] and (i) the replacement of some of Trotsky's men in the military and political control hierarchy with pro-Stalin, promilitary personnel. The most significant of these achievements, in the long run, were the preservation of a centrally guided political control system, the abolition of local controls over the military, and the replacement of pro-Trotsky with pro-Stalin commanders.

The preservation and subsequent strengthening of the political control system involved bitter debates and struggles both within the Party and in the military. Opposition to the political commissar system, which had gathered momentum in individual military units,[28] first burst into the open in the forum of the Tenth Party Congress, in 1921, where the Military Opposition proposed the curtailment and even the liquidation of the system.[29] However, the suggestion was overruled, and the congress went on record as determined to strengthen the political control organs.[30] Agitation against the commissar system nevertheless grew in 1922; it culminated, in 1923, in the appearance of the notorious Circular 200.[31]

[25] *KPSS o Vooruzhennykh Silakh*, p. 192.

[26] Fedotoff-White, *The Growth of the Red Army*, pp. 199-229.

[27] "Local Party organizations may not change decisions and instructions of the PUR and of the political departments concerning Party-political activities in the units of the Red Army and Navy." A Central Committee Instruction of June 27, 1921, cited in *KPSS o Vooruzhennykh Silakh*, p. 212. (For an explanation of "PUR," see fn. 35 below.)

[28] *KPSS i stroitel'stvo Vooruzhennykh Sil*, pp. 221-224. In 1920, I. T. Smilga, erstwhile head of the MPA, spoke of "signs of decay of the institution of military commissars." Fedotoff-White, p. 230.

[29] Fedotoff-White, p. 230.

[30] *KPSS o Vooruzhennykh Silakh*, p. 192. On October 31, 1921, the Central Committee published lengthy instructions on the relations between the political organs and the Party cells in the military. In Point 4, it stated: "General direction of activity of the regimental *biuro* of cells of RKP, concerning political work in the military units, belongs to the representative sections to which they are subordinated." See "Instruktsiia TsK RKP(b) organizatsiiam iacheek RKP(b) Krasnoi Armii i Flota v tylu i na fronte" (Instruction of the RKP[b] Central Committee to the RKP[b] Cell Organizations of the Red Army and Fleet in the Rear and at the Front), cited in *KPSS o Vooruzhennykh Silakh*, p. 216.

[31] The affair of Circular 200 is indicative of the wide schism in the military and the political organs on the issue of the commissar system. Circular 200 was published and distributed without the Central Committee's knowledge. It was allegedly written by the head of the PUR himself (Antonov-Ovseenko), who was a Trotsky appointee. The circular enabled the dissident members of the military and the political organs to advocate at many meetings an elective system of political organs, restriction of their activities, and transferring of their activities to the Party cells.

A reflection of the anti-commissar feeling in the military was the publication, by the Central Committee, of instructions entitled *O komissarakh i politrabotnikakh v Krasnoi Armii* (About Commissars and Political Workers in the Red Army) in 1922. The main points of these instructions were that those political workers who could not get along with commanders should be replaced; that others should be sent back to school for better education; and that special attention should be given to political workers from low social classes, who were apt to cause friction within the units.[32]

By early 1923, the situation between the pro- and the anti-commissar factions had reached a stalemate, which the Twelfth Party Congress, in April of that year, was unable to break. In the wake of the congress, however, the military received new instructions, parts of which greatly extended the powers of the commissars.[33]

Throughout the period of this controversy, Trotsky had continued to alienate sectors of the Party and the military.[34] After Lenin's death, Stalin, with the support of the Zinoviev-Kamenev faction, the Red commanders, and the majority of the political commissars, set out to oust Trotsky from the *Revvoensovet Respubliki.* As preliminary steps to that end, Antonov-Ovseenko was removed from the PUR[35] and replaced with Bubnov, and the political structure within the

---

The circular was condemned by the Thirteenth Party Congress and annulled by the PUR. Another circular, No. 32, dated February 3, 1924, and issued by the new head of PUR, Bubnov, put an end to the opposition's hopes for decentralization of the political control machinery.

[32] *KPSS o Vooruzhennykh Silakh*, pp. 230-233.

[33] *Ibid.*, p. 272. Among the ten points in the instructions that related to the position of the commissars, one read, "The military commissar is a fully authoritative representative of the Party, being responsible to it for the political activities of the given unit" (Point 52); and another, "The Regimental collective and cell do not intervene in the decisions of the military commissar" (Point 53).

[34] An additional source of conflict between Trotsky and the military was created by heated debates on the appropriate military strategy and doctrine for the Red Army. While Trotsky proposed strategic concepts similar to the traditional, orthodox ones (in which he was supported by Svechin and other military specialists), such new Red commanders as Voroshilov, Frunze, and Tukhachevskii advocated several variants of the revolutionary doctrine: Voroshilov was for stress on guerrilla tactics and maneuvers; Frunze was for a unitary military doctrine based on offense and rapid maneuver; and Tukhachevskii proposed that the Red Army should become the military arm of the Communist International.

[35] The PUR was originally called *Politicheskoe Upravlenie Raboche-Krest'ianskoi Krasnoi Armii,* or PURKKA (Political Administration of the Workers and Peasants Red Army). It later became *Glavnoe Politicheskoe Upravlenie Sovetskoi Armii i Voenno-Morskogo Flota* (The Main Political Administration of the Soviet Army and Navy, or MPA). For a description of the MPA, see pp. 83 and 123-124 below.

military was strengthened by the appointment of several Stalinists to key positions in the military.

On January 14, 1924, the plenum of the Party's Central Committee created a special commission to investigate the state of readiness and the capabilities of the armed forces. Its members included Stalin, Andreev, Frunze, Gusev, Shvernik, and Ordzhonikidze. The commission reported its findings to the February plenum of the Central Committee, which subsequently announced its concern about the Red Army's viability. The entire maneuver was almost certainly part of a plan for ousting Trotsky from the position of People's Commissar for War.[36]

On March 11, 1924, Frunze's appointment as Deputy Chairman of the *Revvoensovet* and Deputy Commissar for Military and Naval Affairs marked the beginning of his succession of Trotsky as head of the country's armed forces.[37] On January 26, 1925, he actually assumed Trotsky's post, which the latter relinquished without a fight. Even had he chosen to fight, he probably could no longer have mustered any effective support. The *Revvoensovet Respubliki* was reorganized, and among its new members were the Stalinists Voroshilov, Ordzhonikidze, Bubnov, and Kamenev.

Although the 1917-1925 cycle ended in the rehabilitation of the military professionals, it was a Pyrrhic victory. The officers gained acceptance as a permanent institution and were assured of high economic and social status, but, in return, they had to accept the Party's ubiquitous control system and the *apparatchiks'* overriding authority in military matters, and resign themselves to being loyal vassals of the Party leader. Stalin's insistence, from the very beginning, on strong political controls and limited authority for the military suggests that, notwithstanding his practical championship of a strong army, his innate distrust of the professional military was as great as Trotsky's.

B · MODERNIZATION AND PROFESSIONALIZATION OF THE RED ARMY: 1925-1937

The Red Army as it emerged from the turbulent period of the early 1920's combined traits of the professional army with charac-

[36] In a recent Soviet history of this period, the authors state that "the first measure of the RKP(b) Central Committee that was intended to improve the Red Army was the ouster of Trotsky and his associates from leading military organs." *KPSS i stroitel'stvo Vooruzhennykh Sil*, p. 227.

[37] *Ibid.*

teristics that had been grafted onto it by Stalin owing to his anti-militarist bias. The former were introduced during the time of the "Military Reforms"[38] under the leadership of Frunze; the latter were at least partly the vestiges of the revolutionary period.

The chief concessions that the Red Army won from the Party in the transitional period of the Military Reforms were (a) the retention of a nucleus of professional military cadres in an army of 560,000 and in the territorial divisions;[39] (b) partial authority to command (limited *edinonachalie*);[40] (c) an extensive military-educational program for modernizing the officer corps;[41] and (d) more stable relations between the commanders and the Party-political control organs.

These gains were balanced by the following shortcomings, the concessions of the military to the Party's influence: (a) division of authority in the units between military commissars and commanders; (b) lack of career stability for the officers;[42] and (c) the dualism that resulted from combining territorial militia and professional cadres in a single structure. Despite the constraints on the military, however, the Red Army remained a viable organization, which in the span of a dozen years was to grow into a modern military establishment not unlike others in Western Europe.

1. A Time of Transition, 1925-1928

In 1925, Frunze died while undergoing surgery, and the responsibility for the military amalgam inherited from Trotsky fell to Voro-

[38] For an analysis of this important stage in the development of the Red Army, see Fedotoff-White, *The Growth of the Red Army*, pp. 199-276, and, especially, I. B. Berkhin, *Voennaia reforma v SSSR, 1924-1925 gg.* (Military Reform in the USSR, 1924-1925), Voenizdat, Moscow, 1958.

[39] See Fedotoff-White, p. 201, for statistics on the composition of the cadres.

[40] In 1926, the then head of the MPA, A. S. Bubnov, stated that among commanders of companies only 7 per cent were *edinonachal'niks.* He pointed out that, unless the commanders became involved in Party affairs and thereby earned the trust of the Party leadership, "they will be *edinonachal'niks* in name only, while their assistants for political affairs will in reality carry out the functions of a Party-political leader." Bubnov, *O Krasnoi Armii* (On the Red Army), Voenizdat, Moscow, 1958, pp. 152-153. See also the Central Committee Statement, "On *Edinonachalie* in the Red Army," of March 6, 1925, which affirmed that only those commanders who were members of the Party in good standing would be given full *edinonachalie. KPSS o Vooruzhennykh Silakh*, pp. 280-281.

[41] See Fedotoff-White, *The Growth of the Red Army*, *passim*, and John Erickson, *The Soviet High Command, 1918-1941*, St. Martin's Press, New York, 1962, for details on the growth of the military educational institutions in the Red Army.

[42] The legal provisions which formally guaranteed the military position of the commander were established in 1935. See p. 54 below.

shilov. In the short time that he was in office, Frunze had left his mark on the Red Army. The task of shaping that amorphous body into a viable organism was not easy. One of the obstacles was the presence of such opposite and conflicting forces and interest groups as officers from the imperial army; former NCOs of the old army who had risen under the communist rule to some of the highest positions in the military; former Red Guards; and the graduates of the short-term command courses, known as "Red Commanders." Another difficulty lay in the prominence of the military commissars, who jealously guarded their prerogatives. Finally, the cultural and social disparities among commanders created antagonism and inhibited any spirit of camaraderie.

Although the Party made some efforts to raise the economic and social status of the commanders and, through the network of short courses, to improve the level of professional and technical skill, it did not do so with any sense of urgency. The Red Army continued to suffer from lack of modern equipment and weapons; the careers of its officers remained uncertain in the absence of legal guarantees; the military commissars usurped much of the commanders' authority, to the latter's great resentment;[43] and the "pacifistic" and antimilitary spirit that had prevailed in Soviet society and in the Party during the NEP period continued to make itself felt throughout the country.

During this period of transition, Stalin developed the technique he was to use in all his dealings with the military. His method may be described as a "balancing act," in which every concession to the military's professional and institutional interests (broader commanding authority, professional rank and status, economic and social privileges, etc.) was accompanied by a tightening of political and police controls. Only during periods when Stalin had acute need of the military's expertise and good will did he forgo the "balancing" of concessions by stricter controls. However, these ephemeral moments of relaxation were usually followed by periods of renewed restraint, if not outright coercion, of the military.

Between 1925 and 1928, the above-mentioned gains of the commanders were diminished in a number of ways. The influence of the Party collectives in the units was severely reduced, while that of

[43] Ill-feeling between commanding and political personnel became so widespread that the Central Committee issued this sharp warning: ". . . the Central Committee finds it necessary to announce that during the past year friction occurred between the commanding and political personnel. The Central Committee views such occurrences as absolutely intolerable in the Red Army and destructive to its combat abilities." See *KPSS o Vooruzhennykh Silakh*, pp. 306-307.

the commissars was strongly upgraded.[44] Moreover, such seeming privileges as the commanders' right of *edinonachalie* were rendered almost ineffectual by the qualifications attached to them. And the distinction drawn between commanders who were Party members and those who were not resulted in the latter's becoming "yes-men . . . unable, psychologically, to exercise command."[45] After 1928, however, this situation underwent a radical change, as Stalin became increasingly worried by the specter of "capitalist encirclement," and began his drive for the country's industrialization, designed, among other aims, to give the military the technical basis for extensive modernization.

2. *Prominence of the Red Army in Stalin's Social Planning, 1928-1936*

The inauguration of the first Five Year Plan was one of the three important dates of the postrevolutionary period.[46] Its impact on the army can hardly be overestimated, for it meant the beginning of a large-scale military industry, including such automotive products as airplane engines and various types of motor vehicles.

Plans for industrialization had been extensively discussed as early as 1925, at the Fourteenth Party Congress, which issued a policy guide to the Central Committee "to undertake all necessary measures to strengthen the defense capabilities of the country and the might of the Red Army and the Red Fleet, the naval fleet as well as the air fleet."[47] But in the two years following, Stalin's plans for massive industrialization met strong opposition within the Party, as the issue was debated in a series of Central Committee meetings.[48]

In 1927, after the Party's propaganda machine had built up the threat of an imperialist conspiracy against the Soviet Union,[49] Stalin

[44] See "O rabote voennykh iacheek" (On the Activities of the Military [Party] Cells), a Central Committee decree of December 10, 1928, in *KPSS o Vooruzhennykh Silakh*, pp. 308-311.

[45] See Fedotoff-White, *The Growth of the Red Army*, p. 209.

[46] W. H. Chamberlain, *Russia's Iron Age*, Little, Brown & Co., Boston, 1934, p. 41; and Fedotoff-White, p. 277.

[47] See *KPSS i stroitel'stvo Vooruzhennykh Sil*, p. 252.

[48] At the April 1926 plenum of the Central Committee; at the Fourth Congress of the Soviets in April 1927; at the Fifteenth Party Conference in October-November 1926.

[49] Several incidents were greatly blown up by the Soviet press. (a) On May 12, 1927, in the so-called Arkos affair, the British government seized the files of the Anglo-Soviet Trade Corporation, accused the Soviet government of espionage and anti-British activities, and announced its intention to sever diplomatic and trade relations with the Soviet Union. (b) At about the same time, the Soviets announced that they had discovered a large network of anti-Soviet agents in Latvia,

succeeded in having his initial proposals accepted at the August plenum of the unified Central Committee and Central Control Commission, which declared that "the danger of a counterrevolutionary war against the USSR is the most urgent problem of our time."[50] Several months later, the Fifteenth Party Congress convened in Moscow, and approved "the directives for establishment of the first Five Year Plan."[51]

The decisions of the Fifteenth Party Congress were seen as being "of overwhelming importance to the further growth of the economic and military might of the USSR and to the strengthening of the Red Army."[52] The congress emphasized that in executing the Five Year Plan "maximum attention must be given to a most rapid development of those aspects of the national economy in general, and industry in particular, which will carry the main burden in ensuring the military and economic viability of the country in times of war." Furthermore, it stressed the need to collectivize agriculture. And it formally ousted Zinoviev and Trotsky from the Party.[53]

Once committed to the intensive development of the economic aspects of the military establishment, Stalin initiated a number of measures intended to enhance the profession of the officer, his authority and prestige.

(a) In September 1929, the head of the MPA, A. Bubnov, was appointed People's Commissar for Education, a move designed to provide the growing officer corps with better-trained and better-educated commanders and specialists.[54] Presumably, the choice of Bubnov was dictated by the desire not only to have curricula oriented toward military needs, but also to ensure that this education had a strong ideological basis. Stalin viewed the military as a school of communism, in which large numbers of youth from diverse ethnic,

---

Lithuania, and Poland who were planning to undertake massive sabotage and antirevolutionary measures against the Soviet Union. (c) On June 7, 1927, the Soviet Ambassador to Poland, P. L. Voikov, was killed by the alleged British agent Koverda. (d) Several bombs were tossed into a Party club in Leningrad, allegedly by anti-Soviet agents, injuring thirty people. These agents also were said to have organized the murder of the GPU head for Belorussia, and to be planning to explode the Kremlin and the Bolshoi Theatre. On June 1, *Pravda*'s nearly hysterical reaction to these various acts in a sense gave away the scheme behind this sudden propaganda campaign, for it stressed the Central Committee's plea that citizens give their attention to the Red Army and to the defense needs of the country. See *KPSS i stroitel'stvo*, pp. 264-266.

[50] *Ibid.*, p. 268. [51] *Ibid.*, p. 269. [52] *Ibid.* [53] *Ibid.*, p. 271.

[54] Fedotoff-White, *The Growth of the Red Army*, p. 297.

economic, and geographic backgrounds could be indoctrinated and assimilated.

(b) In 1927, a massive paramilitary youth organization, the OSOAVIAKHIM movement, was created from several voluntary groups that had dealt mainly with propaganda and agitation.[55] While its predecessors had merely stressed "defense-consciousness," the OSOAVIAKHIM concentrated on actual military training.

(c) In 1928, the Revolutionary Military Council of the USSR issued a statement which became the dividing line in the development of the Soviet officer corps.[56] Its avowed purpose was to guarantee the stability of service positions of commanding personnel. Under its many provisions, commanders were entitled to a personal rank that they retained even when they retired from the service; age limits for active service were raised, to the benefit of officers' careers;[57] each service category was given a specified rate of pay; and the commanding personnel were placed in a special category which formally divided them from the political supervisory personnel (as well as from administrative and medical officers), a change that further emphasized the growing role of the commanders.

Stalin continued, however, to offset these professional and socio-economic concessions to the military professionals by various political controls. The Field Regulations of 1929, in Paragraph 18, clearly defined the role of the political commissar, who, along with the commander, was to bear full responsibility for the military and political efficacy of the units.[58]

Despite the substantial role of the commissars, however, the changes in favor of the commanding personnel aroused opposition

[55] OSOAVIAKHIM (the Society for Promotion of Aviation and Chemical Defense) was founded in 1927 from the four voluntary organizations that had existed since the early 1920's: OSO, ODVF, Aviakhim, and VNO. It grew very rapidly, to 2,950,000 in 1927, 5,100,000 (1929), 11,000,000 (1931), and an estimated 20,000,000 in 1932. As early as 1927, OSOAVIAKHIM established thousands of Rifle Circles, Pilot Groups, etc. In 1948, it was replaced with three new organizations (DOSARM, DOSAV, and DOSFLOT), and in September 1951 these were united once more, into the present DOSAAF (Voluntary Society for Assistance to the Army, Air Force, and Navy). See Erich F. Pruck, *Der rote Soldat*, Günter Olzog Verlag, Munich, 1961, pp. 200-201; J. M. Mackintosh, "The Red Army, 1920-1936," *The Red Army*, ed. B. H. Liddell-Hart, Harcourt, Brace and Company, New York, 1956, pp. 56-57; Erickson, *The Soviet High Command*, pp. 307-308.

[56] For details of the 1928 Statute, see Loboda, *Komandnye kadry*, pp. 50-57.

[57] *Ibid.*

[58] See the Central Committee's resolution of February 25, 1929, "O kommandnom i politicheskom sostave RKKA" (On the Commanding and Political Composition of the Red Army), in *KPSS o Vooruzhennykh Silakh*, pp. 312-315, which laid down the details of the commissars' role in the Red Army.

from the political organs, which feared that an unchecked development of this kind could result in the ascendance of the commanders over the commissars. Most outspoken in this antimilitary opposition was a group at the Tolmachev Military-Political Academy in Belorussia, which denounced those Central Committee decrees and announcements that upgraded the authority of the commander, and insisted on the right of Communist Party members in the units to criticize not only the commander's personal and political acts but also his military judgment (a license that would have rendered futile all efforts to place the Red Army on a professional basis and would have meant a return to the anarchy of the revolutionary period). The "Tolmachev heresy," which had found many adherents in the political organs in the military, was put down in December of 1928.[59]

In the summer of 1930, the Sixteenth Party Congress "entered the Party annals as the congress . . . [which] undertook the liquidation of the *kulaks* as a class."[60] It also decided that the primary task of the moment was "the intensive development of the branches of industry which increase the defense capabilities of the Soviet Union."[61] The Seventeenth Party Conference (January 30-February 4, 1932) and the Seventeenth Party Congress (January 26-February 10, 1934) addressed their deliberations to the difficult task of collectivization and continued industrialization. At a great cost in human suffering and deprivation, the growing industrial basis of the Soviet economy began to provide the Red Army with large quantities of new weapons, equipment, and logistic facilities.

The victory of the Nazi party in Germany, the increasingly anti-Soviet attitudes of the successive governments in Poland, and the rather ambiguous policies of the French and British caused the

[59] For details of the Tolmachev heresy and the so-called intramilitary opposition, see Iu. P. Petrov, "Nekotorye voprosy partiino-politicheskoi raboty v Vooruzhennykh Silakh v predvoennye gody" (Some Problems of Party-Political Work in the Armed Forces in the Prewar Years), *Voprosy istorii KPSS*, No. 11, November 1963, pp. 57-72; and *KPSS i stroitel'stvo*, pp. 285-286. The leaders of the intramilitary opposition were Ia. L. Berman, M. M. Landa, and M. S. Dietgarev. For other Soviet treatments of the Tolmachev heresy, see Colonel Iu. P. Petrov, "Deiatel'nost' Kommunisticheskoi partii po provedeniiu edinonachaliia v Vooruzhennykh Silakh, 1925-1931 gody" (The Activity of the Communist Party in Introducing *Edinonachalie* in the Armed Forces, 1925-1931), *Voenno-istoricheskii zhurnal*, No. 5, May 1963, pp. 3-11; and A. Binevich and Z. Serebrianskii, "Slavnyi syn Kommunisticheskoi partii" (An Illustrious Son of the Communist Party), *Voenno-istoricheskii zhurnal*, No. 3, March 1963, pp. 35-48.

[60] *KPSS i stroitel'stvo*, p. 309.

[61] *Ibid.*, p. 310.

Soviet Union discernible anxiety. With revolutionary hopes for Europe virtually gone, and in the face of the rising fascist threat and the spreading war in the Far East, the Soviets, in a series of measures, undertook to create the kind of modern military organization that could protect the achievements of the October Revolution.

(1) Between 1934 and 1935, the standing army was increased from 562,000 to 1,300,000 men.[62] (2) On March 15, 1934, a new Commissariat of Defense replaced the separate commissariats of the Army and Navy. Voroshilov became head of the Commissariat of Defense, with Gamarnik, then head of the MPA, as his First Deputy and Tukhachevskii as another Deputy.[63] (3) The Revolutionary Military Council, the vehicle of the collegiate command principle, was abolished and replaced with the Military Council, which was to play a largely consultative role, and the collegiate principle was abandoned throughout the military.[64] (4) In 1935, the Staff of the Red Army was transformed into the General Staff, under General Egorov, with a "substantial increase of its role."[65]

Along with these measures aimed at a more centralized and effective military command, the Party made a number of concessions calculated to enhance the personal and professional prestige of the officers. In September 1935, the commanding personnel were given new personal ranks, which ranged from lieutenant to Marshal of the Soviet Union.[66] Another major gain for the officers was the provision that rank could be rescinded only through a court order, not, as in the past, by an administrative ruling.[67] In addition, substantial improvements in the socio-economic conditions of commanders made the latter into a privileged elite; "the lean and cold days of the NEP were definitely over."[68] Having gained in professional freedom and stature, career security, and socio-economic status, the Soviet officer corps also experienced preferential treatment when it escaped relatively unscathed from the purges of 1934, which severely affected the

[62] For details on the growth and composition of the cadres during the period, see Michel Garder, *Histoire de l'Armée Soviétique*, Plon, Paris, 1959, pp. 94-110; and Erickson, *The Soviet High Command*, pp. 325-404 and Appendix 1.

[63] *KPSS i stroitel'stvo*, p. 344.

[64] Fedotoff-White, *The Growth of the Red Army*, p. 358.

[65] *KPSS i stroitel'stvo*, p. 344.

[66] However, the rank of General and the designation "officer" were not introduced until May 8, 1940. For details on the ranks of 1935, see Loboda, *Komandnye kadry*, pp. 62-66.

[67] *Ibid.*, p. 66.

[68] Fedotoff-White, p. 379. The author also cites statistics which show that Red Army commanders gained substantial pay increases—an average of 286 per cent—between 1934 and 1939.

civilian Party organizations.[69] Furthermore, under Paragraph 50 of the 1935 Statute, commanders could no longer be arrested by civil organs without special authorization by the Commissar of Defense, which set them apart from the rest of the population. However, it was not long before the inexorable laws of the totalitarian system caught up with this trend.

3. The Purges of 1937

In August 1936, leading Party members Zinoviev and Kamenev, together with several of their supporters, were tried as members of the "Trotskyite-Zinovievite Center." They were executed on August 25, five days after the beginning of the trial.[70] That this was to be only the beginning of a wave of terror was hinted at during the trial in denunciations of such famous Party leaders as Bukharin, Tomskii, Rykov, Radek, and Sokol'nikov. Another ominous fact was that two of the accused, Mrachkovskii and Smirnov, both well-known military leaders, had been questioned at length not only by the prosecutor, Vyshinskii, but by Stalin himself, who sought confessions from them.

The second major trial, against the "anti-Soviet Trotskyite Center," opened in Moscow on January 21, 1937. The accused this time included Radek and Piatakov, both ranking members of the Party. On its second day, prosecutor Vyshinskii, in his interrogation of Radek, dwelt on details that connected Tukhachevskii with Putna and the Trotskyites.[71] Although Radek defended Tukhachevskii's innocence, the military had been put on notice.

In April, the press began to carry articles that were highly critical of members of the High Command, and Tukhachevskii's plans to attend the coronation of King George VI in London were canceled. On May 11, the commissar system was reintroduced into the military,

[69] Erickson (p. 374) compares the percentage of purged Party members in the military (4.3 per cent) with those purged in the civilian organizations (17 per cent).

[70] Zinoviev and Kamenev had joined the Party in 1901 and risen to high positions in it by the mid-1920's. Under Stalin, they were excluded from the Party in 1927, reinstated in 1928, excluded again in 1932, reinstated once more in 1933, and excluded finally in 1934, preliminary to their trial in 1936. For details of the trial, see Werner Scharndorff, *Moskaus permanente Säuberung*, Günter Olzog Verlag, Munich, 1964, pp. 170-183.

[71] General V. K. Putna, the then military attaché in London, was accused of being "a most active participant in the terrorist activities of the Trotskyists" and a link between the high military leaders accused of treason and the Trotskyists. Scharndorff, p. 182.

bringing back the dual-control system. On June 9, Tukhachevskii and two close collaborators, Iakir and Uborevich, were relieved of their commands. On June 11, *Pravda* announced that the military leaders Tukhachevskii, Uborevich, Iakir, Eideman, Kork, Primakov, Putna, and Feldman were under arrest and the charges against them had been investigated; the following day it reported that the eight men had been executed for having violated the military oath and for treason. This was the beginning of Stalin's purge of the military, which was to devastate the officer corps of the Red Army.[72]

The events of 1925-1937 thus illustrate the cyclical pattern of Party-military relations. Having dealt with much of the internal Party opposition, Stalin embarked on the industrialization, collectivization, and militarization of Soviet society. His commitment to these new policies led directly to the Red Army's gain in authority, professional freedom, and socio-economic standing and to the circumspection with which Stalin now treated the officer corps, for he was determined that nothing should be allowed to interfere with the efficiency of military processes. The new professional elite escaped the two "cold purges" of 1929 and 1934 with only minor damage; it acquired, and for a time was able to hold on to, the special rights and privileges, economic advantages, and symbols of power of authority that have been discussed above.

However, in time the steamroller of the purges overtook the military, leaving it politically and professionally emasculated. The fact

[72] See Erickson (pp. 404-509) for a detailed history of events connected with the purge of the military. Leonard Schapiro lists the following as possible causes of Stalin's drastic measures: (a) Opposition from some military leaders to certain aspects of the collectivization. He observes that, on this issue, commanders and political officers were unanimous. (b) The military's growing self-assertiveness and stature, which, though far from approximating "rebellion or disloyalty," may have begun to look to Stalin like a "threat to his position." (c) Substantial military support for Bukharin. Allegedly, all the senior officers on the Central Committee supported the majority against Stalin during the Central Committee meeting in the autumn of 1936, with the exception of Voroshilov and Budennyi. Tukhachevskii, Gamarnik, and Bliukher, who had voted for Bukharin and against Stalin and Ezhov, were later eliminated. (d) The military's frequent opposition to political controls. Schapiro stresses, however, that "the military purge must be viewed as part of the process that was taking place in the country as a whole." He adds: "Seen in this light, the temptation to look for rational explanations ought perhaps to be resisted. For, when once terror had been let loose on so vast a scale among the Party, intellectual and professional *élite* generally, the logic of common caution may well have made it seem imperative to Stalin that the Army should not be allowed to remain the only part of society immune from his assault." Leonard Schapiro, "The Great Purge," *The Red Army*, ed. B. H. Liddell-Hart, Harcourt, Brace and Company, New York, 1956, pp. 65-72. See also L. Schapiro, *The Communist Party of the Soviet Union*, Random House, New York, 1960, pp. 399-434.

that Stalin was willing to destroy his High Command and thousands of middle-level commanders at the very moment of a rising danger of war in Europe bears out the earlier assertion that, in the last analysis, the Party rulers placed the retention of political hegemony in the state ahead of other objectives.

C · *THE PURGES AND THEIR AFTERMATH: 1937-1941*

Soviet writers now acknowledge the disastrous effect on the Red Army of the purges that began in 1934 with "the villainous killing of S. M. Kirov . . . and grew sharply in the fall of 1936":[73]

> The repressions caused great losses in the armed forces. They took place under conditions of growing danger of foreign aggression against the Soviet Union and were directed against the most skilled sectors of the commanding personnel in the army and navy, who possessed extensive theoretical abilities and rich experience in Soviet military construction. Their destructive consequences became manifest in the preparation of the Soviet country to repulse aggression and were one of the causes of the heavy losses suffered by Soviet forces in the initial period of the Great Patriotic War.[74]

The momentum of the purging of ranking members of the military establishment carried over into the middle and lower levels of the officer corps and left the military community in a state of shock. Stalin, having urged the prosecutors "to massacre the military cadres,"[75] then undertook once more to tighten the political-police controls within the military and to abrogate the commanders' authority.

When Gamarnik, the head of the MPA, committed suicide, Stalin in December 1937 appointed Mekhlis, the former editor of *Pravda*, to succeed him.[76] Mekhlis' regime in the MPA was marked by the

[73] See Iu. P. Petrov, *Partiinoe stroitel'stvo v Sovetskoi Armii i Flote, 1918-1961* (Party Development in the Soviet Army and Navy, 1918-1961), Voenizdat, Moscow, 1964, p. 229. Petrov's book is a comprehensive review of the Party's measures to politicize and control the Red Army. (The intensification of the purges in the fall of 1936 coincided with Stalin's appointment of Yezhov as head of the NKVD, the instrument of the purges. The period of greatest excesses, therefore, is sometimes known as *Yezhovshchina*, the era of Yezhov.)

[74] *Ibid.*, pp. 302-303. [75] *Ibid.*, p. 300.

[76] It is noteworthy that in some of the major crises between the Party and the military, the dictator's main instrument for politicizing and controlling the military failed to remain completely loyal to him. In the tension of the early 1920's, the then head of the MPA, Antonov-Ovseenko, sided with the military against the political organs. In 1937, Gamarnik was also accused of sympathizing with the

oppression not only of the commanders but of the entire officer corps.

1. Stalin's Methods for the Suppression of Military Authority

Stalin's deep distrust of the military manifested itself in the course of 1937 and 1938 in various attempts to reduce the commanders' authority, to reinstitute severe control and supervision, to create an aura of fear and suspicion in the military, and to settle old scores both in the officer corps and in the political control organs.

In May 1937, Stalin ordered the creation of Military Councils, which were to be the supreme bodies in military districts and larger commands. Initially, membership of the Councils was to consist of the district commander, the head of the Political Administration, and the "regular political worker freed from his other duties"[77] (a euphemism for a member of the secret police). In July, the membership was enlarged by the inclusion of Party secretaries of *oblast'* (regional) and *krai* (district) committees.[78] At the middle levels—that is to say, in corps, division, brigade, and regiment—Stalin injected military commissars; at the lower levels, *politruks* (political guides).[79] In March 1938, he introduced collective leadership at the very top of the military hierarchy by creating the Supreme Military Council.[80] All these measures added to the demoralization of the commanders, who were no longer free to make decisions, or to issue even a single order, without the express approval of the control organs.

In August 1937, Stalin urged a conference of political workers "to eradicate the enemies of the people."[81] The following January, at the plenum of the Central Committee, he demanded "the bolshevization of the whole Red Army," and again stressed the need to cleanse the military of the enemies of the people, adding that one

---

military, and the MPA apparatus he had created suffered extensive purges. More recently, in the early 1960's, when relations between Party and military were again deteriorating, Khrushchev apparently found the regime of Marshal Golikov in the MPA too lax and lacking in *partiinost'* (Party consciousness), and replaced him with the Party *apparatchik* Epishev, who had once been Deputy Minister of State Security.

[77] Petrov, p. 305. See also *ibid.*, pp. 453 and 462, for details on the reintroduction of "regular cadre members from the political organs" into the Military Councils after they had been removed during the war, and on Zhukov's attempts to rid the military of these functionaries after he became Minister of Defense in 1955.

[78] *Ibid.*, p. 306. [79] *Ibid.*, p. 303.

[80] *Ibid.*, p. 306. The Supreme Military Soviet had been abolished in 1934.

[81] *Ibid.*, p. 300.

must not forget "the quiet ones, people who are politically spineless."[82]

In this intensified effort to subjugate the military, the Komsomol was to play an unprecedentedly active role, as Stalin and Mekhlis undoubtedly distrusted the political organs that bore the imprint of Gamarnik.[83] Zealous young Communists were recruited for the Komsomol in large numbers, and the Central Committee Decree of March 1938 called the Komsomol "the helper of the Party organizations in the army" and its activities "an inseparable part of all Party-political work in the military."[84]

The effects of the events of 1937 and 1938 on the Red Army were soon apparent. The purges virtually annihilated the skilled military professionals at the higher and middle levels; they destroyed nearly half of all lower-ranking command personnel; and they prompted an influx of mediocre and poorly skilled young officers to replace those purged. Since this massive blow to the ranks of professionally trained officers took place just as the Red Army was beginning to receive large amounts of new equipment and weapons, which needed skilled personnel, the ascendance of inexperienced young men from the reserves, the Komsomol, and the political organs was particularly detrimental to the efficiency of the armed forces, adding greatly to the general disorganizaton and decline of morale. The low state of

[82] *Ibid.*, p. 301.

[83] Petrov, "Nekotorye voprosy," *Voprosy istorii KPSS*, November 1963, p. 66.

[84] At the November 1962 plenum of the Central Committee, S. P. Pavlov, General Secretary of the Komsomol (VLKSM), vividly described the Komsomol's real activities during the purges: "In 1935, on the orders of Stalin, the Komsomol's activities became reorganized. What was the nature of these changes? Personally taking over the leadership of the Komsomol, Stalin made several observations on the nature of the Komsomol's work. As is known, the Komsomol at the time was involved in concrete economic tasks. Now, after Stalin's personal direction, the Komsomol was to cease participation in economic construction and become a special 'highly skilled educational apparatus. . . .' It became obvious—and this was clear as black and white—that the very first task of the Komsomol's total educational work was the urgent need to look for and recognize the enemy, who must be put away by force, through the methods of economic pressure, organizational-political isolation and methods of physical destruction." Petrov, *Partiinoe stroitel'stvo*, pp. 320-321. See also Fedotoff-White, *The Growth of the Red Army*, p. 409.

Petrov cites statistics on the massive recruitment of Komsomol members in the military, following the new statute on the Komsomol issued by the Central Committee in March 1938: 359,000 new Komsomol members were recruited in the Red Army in 1938, bringing the total to 798,500; 346,000 were recruited in 1939; 257,000 in 1940; and by mid-1941 there were 1,726,000 Komsomols in the Red Army. The main supporter and moving power behind this massive inclusion of the Komsomol in Party activities was Zhdanov.

morale and discipline in the Red Army was clearly reflected in Voroshilov's report to Stalin in 1938:

> The foundations of discipline and comradeship are crumbling. No one dares to trust his fellow, either superior or subordinate. I hear the same is true in the navy. Both forces are demoralized.[85]

Estimates vary as to the precise figures, but most writers on the subject agree that the damage to the Red Army caused by the purges was catastrophic. John Erickson, in his authoritative study, cites the following statistics on military personnel killed in the purges: 3 (out of 5) marshals; all 11 Deputy Commissars of Defense; 75 (out of 80) members of the Military Soviet; all military district commanders who held that position in June 1937; 13 (out of 15) army commanders; 57 (out of 85) corps commanders; 110 (out of 195) divisional commanders; 220 (out of 406) brigade commanders; and somewhere between 15,000 and 30,000 (out of an estimated 75,000 to 80,000) officers at regimental level and below.[86] To replenish these losses, according to the Soviet historian Petrov, Stalin recalled to active service "tens of thousands of commanders from the reserves, mainly those from the middle levels."[87] Moreover, because of the shortage of cadres, "many commanders were appointed who did not have a chance to improve their skills at various posts before being appointed to high positions."[88] The extent of the turnover in officer personnel is evident in Petrov's estimate that, already in 1937, the "new" men in command positions[89] totaled 60 per cent in the infantry, 45 per cent in the motorized forces, and 25 per cent in aviation.

In 1938, after the January plenum of the Central Committee, Stalin began to apply the brakes to the momentum of the purges by ordering, among other things, a massive drive to recruit military personnel for the Party. This move was most likely dictated by the fact that many of the Party members in the military had been purged, and the number of those who remained was low. It is also true, however, that, in times of stress, the Party leadership has almost invariably resorted to massive recruitment.

The recruitment drive yielded rapid results. To the total of 147,500 Party members (including about 30,000 candidates) in the military

[85] Walter Duranty, *The Kremlin and the People*, Reynal & Hitchcock, New York, 1941, p. 127.

[86] *The Soviet High Command*, pp. 504-506.

[87] Petrov, "Nekotorye voprosy," p. 61. [88] *Ibid.*

[89] Petrov, *Partiinoe stroitel'stvo*, p. 304.

in 1937, only 1,330 of whom were junior officers and men,[90] 101,000 new members were added in 1938. In 1939, their number rose to 350,000; by the middle of 1941, to 560,800.[91]

At the same time, there was an effort to build up the political control organs, which had also suffered in the purges. By 1940, the number of political officers (about 70,000) was three times that of 1937, but many of them were of low caliber, with little political or formal education and limited military training. Some 16,000 of these political workers were members of the Komsomol who served mostly as assistants to the *politruks*.[92]

The Red Army of 1938-1939 was involved in military operations against the Japanese in the Far East. It was shortly to occupy Poland in alliance with Germany, and to fight Finland in a strange David-and-Goliath war. These occasions only served to make more apparent the debilitating effects that the purges had had on the military. In a blatant reversal of policy, therefore, Stalin set about conciliating the Red Army and becoming its benefactor.

2. *The Campaigns in Poland and Finland*

On September 15, 1939, Soviet troops began to concentrate on the Polish border, and in the early morning of September 17, mechanized Soviet cavalry swept into Poland. The Soviet occupation of Polish territories, the fruit of the Nazi-Soviet Pact, was accomplished with only minor skirmishes. Soviet troops advanced easily, covering about 60 miles during the first day alone.[93] Even under such auspicious circumstances, however, the Red Army "showed deficiencies in the organization and direction of the forces."[94]

Though Poland was occupied with relative ease, the Soviet attempt to annex Finnish territories revealed to a stunned world some of the inherent weaknesses of the Soviet army as well as the bravery

[90] *Ibid.*, pp. 304 and 312.

[91] Petrov, "Nekotorye voprosy," p. 65. After the outbreak of war, Stalin began another massive recruitment drive into the Party among the military, with the following results: By the end of 1941, there were 1.3 million Party members and candidates in the military (42 per cent of total Party membership); by the end of 1942, over 2 million members and candidates (54 per cent of Party membership); and by the end of 1945, 3.5 million members and candidates (60 per cent of Party membership). See I. F. Pobezhimov, *Pravovoe regulirovanie stroitel'stva Sovetskoi Armii i Flota* (Legal Regulation of the Development of the Soviet Army and Navy), Gosiurizdat, Moscow, 1960, p. 90.

[92] Petrov, *Partiinoe stroitel'stvo*, p. 309.

[93] Colonel G. I. Antonov, "The March into Poland," *The Red Army*, pp. 73-78.

[94] Petrov, *Partiinoe stroitel'stvo*, p. 333.

of individual soldiers. The Russo-Finnish war, which began in November 1939 and ended in 1940, was the first major test of the Red Army, and it did not show the Russian giant up favorably. With an investment of about 1.5 million troops and vast quantities of weapons and equipment, it took the Soviets over three months to subdue the little Finnish army, which never exceeded 200,000 poorly armed soldiers. In the process, according to their official and undoubtedly conservative estimates, the Soviets suffered 200,000 casualties, including 68,000 dead.[95]

After the armistice with the Finns and a reassessment of the campaign, Stalin abandoned his "antimilitary" policy toward the Red Army. Instead, through a series of reforms, he now set out to create a highly professional, elitist officer corps, entrusted with broad authority and freed from much of the earlier intrusion of political doctrine and propaganda.

3. *Reconciling the Military*

Stalin's reforms followed upon extensive debates in the Main Military Soviet on the lessons of the Finnish war.[96] On May 8, 1940, Marshal Timoshenko replaced Voroshilov as People's Commissar for Defense, and this move was followed, in quick succession, by a series of measures designed to sharpen the professional qualities and raise the discipline of the Red Army, and to enhance the prestige, authority, and social status of its commanders.

(1) On May 8, the Presidium of the Supreme Soviet approved the introduction of the titles "general" and "admiral" into the Soviet Armed Forces.[97] As a result, out of more than a thousand officers who were promoted to senior commands in June, 479 received the rank of Major General.[98]

(2) On May 16, Order No. 160 laid down new training principles

[95] Lieutenant General Kurt Dittmar, "The Red Army in the Finnish War," *The Red Army*, p. 85.

[96] Erickson, p. 553. The Supreme Military Council (Glavnyi Voennyi Sovet RKKA) was established by the Central Committee on March 13, 1938. Among its eleven members were Stalin, Mekhlis, and Budennyi. Its chief function was to establish policy guidelines for the Red Army. *Ibid.*, p. 478.

[97] See Loboda, *Komandnye kadry*, pp. 71-72, for details on the introduction of the new military titles.

[98] Among the various officers who received promotion were: Zhukov, Meretskov, and Tiulenev (to General of the Army); Anapasenko and Gorodovikov (to Colonel General); Konev, Sokolovskii, Golikov, Chuikov, Eremenko, Batov, Vatutin, and Kirponos (to Lieutenant General); and Rokossovskii, Vasilevskii, Biriuzov, Tolbukhin, and Leliushenko (to Major General).

for the Red Army, stressing the simulation of combat conditions, high levels of combat readiness, and the priority of military training over political indoctrination.[99]

(3) On August 12, the institution of military commissars was abolished, and *edinonachalie* was reintroduced, though only at the tactical level.[100]

(4) On October 12, a new Disciplinary Code replaced the old code of 1925. Its provisions were remarkable in a socialist state: the commander's orders had to be carried out unquestioningly; there were severe punishments for insubordination; and an obligatory salute symbolized the new, harsh discipline.[101]

(5) The standard of living and general conditions of the military were substantially improved.[102]

(6) The authority and functions of the political organs were confined mainly to activities related to education and indoctrination.[103]

As a consequence of these changes, the military became a privileged institution, and the officer corps enjoyed both professional freedom and social and economic privileges, with little interference from the Party-political organs. The new elite of younger commanders that emerged from the purges trained the renascent Red Army and attempted to undo the damages of the purges by creating a powerful Soviet juggernaut. Yet, as we shall see, the fruits of these efforts were of little avail against the initial onslaught of the Nazi armies, in 1941, when the political miscalculations of the dictator, combined

[99] See Erickson, *The Soviet High Command*, p. 554.

[100] Petrov, *Partiinoe stroitel'stvo*, p. 326. Collective responsibility (*kollegial'nost'*) was retained, however, in the Military Councils of districts, fronts, armies, fleets, and flotillas, as well as in the Supreme Military Soviet.

[101] Petrov, whose views are those of a Party *apparatchik*, describes the then growing militaristic trends in the Red Army as follows: "The mass repressions [the purges], which had strongly undermined the authority and prestige of the commanding and political personnel, had a negative effect on military discipline. This became clear especially during the Soviet-Finnish conflict. However, instead of painstaking work to strengthen discipline on the basis of [political indoctrination and education] . . . they began to introduce compulsive measures. Some leading workers in the National Commissariat of Defense and in a number of districts attempted to idealize the relations between the soldiers and commanders which existed in the old army." *Ibid.*, p. 336.

[102] See Loboda, *Komandnye kadry*, pp. 72-75.

[103] During July and August, the political departments and sections in the military were transformed into departments and sections for political propaganda. Petrov views these changes as having "narrowed their [the political organs'] role as Party organs in the armed forces, and limited their activities, in reality, to only one aspect of Party-political work—propaganda and agitation." Petrov, *Partiinoe stroitel'stvo*, p. 335.

with the effects of massive reorganization in the military, resulted in the near-collapse of the Red Army.

The events of 1937-1941 further illustrate the cyclical nature of the relations between Party and military. Threats, real or imagined, from the military had caused Stalin to take a hard line with them, which was softened, after the crisis of the purges, by conciliatory measures that included even the cooptation of a large number of generals into the Central Committee.[104] With growing external threats and the rising need for a strong army, Stalin, as we have seen, completely reversed his former position and freed the military from oppressive constraints, granting them unprecedented privileges and prerogatives. The cycle was completed, however, after the first weeks of the Nazi attack, when Stalin reintroduced military commissars, and in various ways clamped down on the authority, prestige, and professional freedom of the officer corps.

D · THE MILITARY'S ULTIMATE TEST: 1941-1945

On June 22, 1941, the German armies attacked the Soviet Union and pushed eastward over the collapsing Soviet defenses. The thrust of the German offensive seemingly caught the Soviet High Command by surprise and caused near-panic in Moscow. In the following weeks, the Germans captured large numbers of Soviet soldiers and enormous quantities of weapons and equipment, while relentlessly pursuing the retreating, badly disorganized Red Army.[105] The Soviet Union and the Communist Party leadership were faced with the gravest crisis of their history.

Among the first measures by which Stalin sought to deal with the rapidly deteriorating situation were: (a) the creation of the State Committee for Defense (*Gosudarstvennyi Komitet Oborony*, or GKO), in which was vested complete power over all governmental and

[104] See Chapter X, pp. 330-331.

[105] The German Chief of the General Staff, General von Halder, recorded in his diary on June 22 that "tactical surprise of the enemy has apparently been achieved along the entire line. . . . The enemy was surprised by the German attack." On June 23 he noted: "I very much doubt that the enemy High Command really has a unified and organized control of the situation." And on July 8 he observed that "The enemy is no longer in a position to organize a continuous front, even behind strong terrain features." (General Franz von Halder, "Diary: Campaign in Russia" [unpublished manuscript], cited in R. L. Garthoff, *Soviet Military Doctrine*, The Free Press, Glencoe, Ill., 1953, p. 426.) According to Halder, the Soviets suffered over three million casualties, including the loss of over two million prisoners, in the first four months of the war. (*Ibid.*, p. 428.)

military organs in the Soviet Union;[106] (b) concentration of all military authority in the newly created Supreme Headquarters Staff (*Stavka Verkhovnogo Glavnokomandovaniia*, or *Stavka*);[107] and (c) the reintroduction of the military commissars.[108] In addition, Stalin dispatched to the front a number of ranking Party members, whose tasks were to supervise different sectors of the front lines, to coordinate the military, industrial, and civilian activities within these sectors, and to restore morale and discipline among military and civilians.[109]

With these measures, Stalin implicitly placed the onus for the initial disasters on the military. His subsequent policy, in which he deprived the commanders of most of their authority to undertake independent action, except with respect to minor tactical measures, and returned to very strict political controls at all levels of the armed forces, was further proof of his distrust of the military even under conditions of severe crisis. Actually, the major responsibility for the country's inadequate preparedness in the face of the German attack belonged to Stalin himself.[110] In the spring of 1941,

106 *Kommunisticheskaia partiia v period Velikoi Otechestvennoi voiny, iiun' 1941-1945 god* (The Communist Party During the Great Patriotic War, June 1941-1945); Gospolitizdat, Moscow, 1961, p. 88. A collection of rules, regulations, decrees, etc., issued by the Party and government during World War II.

107 The *Stavka* was established on July 10, 1941, and was headed by Stalin. See *Boevoi put' Sovetskikh Vooruzhennykh Sil* (The Battle Path of the Soviet Armed Forces), Voenizdat, Moscow, 1960, p. 264.

108 The eleven-point Directive on the introduction of military commissars was issued on July 16, 1941. The authority of the commissars was to be impressive indeed. Paragraph 2 of the Directive stated that "The military commissar is the direct representative of the Party and government in the Red Army, and carries alongside with the commander full responsibility for the carrying out by the unit of military tasks, for its firmness in combat. . . ." Paragraph 5 stipulated that "The military commissar must report, at the right time, to the Supreme Command and government about commanders and political workers who are unworthy of the name of commanders and political workers. . . ." Paragraph 8 said: "The military commissar must . . . conduct merciless struggles against cowards, panic-mongers and deserters, with a firm hand establishing revolutionary order and military discipline. Coordinating his activities with the organs of the third department [Security Organs] of the National Commissariat of Defense, the military commissar must thoroughly eradicate any kind of treason." See *KPSS o Vooruzhennykh Silakh*, pp. 358-361.

109 Among the ranking Party members sent to the front were Khrushchev, Zhdanov, Suslov, Brezhnev, Ponomarenko, and Epishev. See Petrov, *Partiinoe stroitel'stvo*, pp. 348-354.

110 While blaming Stalin for having miscalculated German intentions, Party historians continue to find others upon whom to place a major share of the burden. Zhukov and Timoshenko are frequently singled out as having contributed to the

Churchill, among others, had sent him confidential information about German troop movements in the direction of the Soviet borders, but the Soviets persistently denied such "rumors," accusing the Western imperialists of perfidious attempts to harm Soviet-German relations.[111] Just one week before the German attack, the official news agency TASS condemned as pernicious the speculations of foreign, especially English, newspapers about an impending war between the Soviet Union and Germany. "According to Soviet circles," said TASS, "rumors about German intentions to break the pact and undertake an attack on the USSR are without any grounds. . . ."[112] Even when German bombers were attacking cities in western Russia, Stalin is reported to have told Zhukov that this was only an act of provocation by individual German generals.[113] General Boldin reports in his memoirs that, when he asked Marshal Timoshenko for instructions during the first few hours of the German attack, Timoshenko told him to await further orders before doing anything, emphasizing that "Comrade Stalin does not permit us to open artillery fire on the Germans."[114]

As the German armies spilled into Russia, organization, discipline, and morale among the Soviet forces neared collapse.[115] In less than three weeks, the Red Army retreated 600 kilometers, and its losses in men and equipment were staggering.[116] Throughout the summer and fall of 1941, the Germans continued to advance, until the arrival of the severe winter weather stopped them before Moscow. In the spring of 1942, however, they launched a new massive offensive to-

---

initial disasters, but it is Beria who comes in for the most critical description: "Beria actually opened the aerial space of the USSR, having forbidden the border troops and the units of the Red Army to undertake any operations against the trespassers of the aerial borders of the USSR." *Partiia v bor'be za uprochenie i razvitie sotsialisticheskogo obshchestva. Usilenie oborony strany* (The Party in the Struggle for the Strengthening and Development of the Socialist Society. The Strengthening of the Country's Defense), Moskovskii rabochii, Moscow, 1962, p. 25.

[111] *Ibid.*, pp. 23-26. [112] *Ibid.*, p. 74.

[113] General of the Army I. V. Tiulenev, *Cherez tri voiny* (Through Three Wars), Voenizdat, Moscow, 1960, p. 141.

[114] Colonel General I. V. Boldin, *Stranitsy zhizni* (Pages from Life), Voenizdat, Moscow, 1961, p. 85.

[115] See Boldin, pp. 92-100, for details on demoralization and confusion in the Red Army during those initial days of the war.

[116] *Ideologicheskaia rabota KPSS na fronte (1941-1945)* (Ideological Work of the CPSU at the Front [1941-1945]), Voenizdat, Moscow, 1960, p. 19. See also Matthew P. Gallagher, *The Soviet History of World War II: Myths, Memoirs, and Realities*, Frederick A. Praeger, Inc., New York, 1963, pp. 4-15.

ward the southeast, sweeping around the Soviet defenses at Kharkov and on the southern flank, and pressing on toward the strategically vital area of Stalingrad. The defense of that city now was presented by Stalin as the crucial task of the Red Army, and the outcome of the battle for Stalingrad as decisive for the whole war effort.[117]

To make the defense of Stalingrad possible, Stalin transferred there most of the available reserves, dispatched his best and most trusted generals from the *Stavka*, and placed Khrushchev in charge of the over-all political effort as a member of the Military Council.[118] Furthermore, to raise the morale and motivation of the military, he ordered a number of changes affecting military authority and political controls, and designed to appeal to the patriotism of the defenders.

Thus, in June 1942, A. S. Shcherbakov became head of the MPA, replacing Mekhlis, whose regime in the political control organs had been deeply resented by the military professionals.[119] Next, Stalin ordered a thorough cleansing of the MPA's functionaries in the military, presumably with the aim of ousting those who were tainted by the Mekhlis regime and the purges.[120] On October 9, 1942, during the most critical battles in southern Russia, Stalin once more abolished the military commissars and established full *edinonachalie* for the commanders.[121] This measure "raised the authority of commanders and made possible the strengthening of discipline and order in the armed forces."[122]

Stalin also showered the military with new status symbols, ranks, medals, and other accolades: (a) He introduced the term "officer," which in the past had been condemned by the Party as incompatible with a socialist army.[123] (b) Red Army ranks were strictly separated, and, except for the special rank of Marshal of the Soviet Union, all military personnel were divided into four categories: privates, sergeants, officers, and generals.[124] (c) The additional "Marshal" and

[117] See Chapter VII, pp. 227-228, for details. See also Marshal V. I. Chuikov, *Nachalo puti* (Beginning of the Road), Voenizdat, Moscow, 1959, p. 194. According to Chuikov, the political organs instructed the soldiers that "Only one cause will be accepted as a correct reason for leaving one's position—death."

[118] See Chapter VII, pp. 227-230.

[119] *Ideologicheskaia rabota KPSS*, p. 88.

[120] See Lieutenant General A. Pigurnov, in *Voenno-istoricheskii zhurnal*, No. 4, April 1961, pp. 47-56, for details on the opposition of political commissars to the pending abolition of their functions. See also *Ideologicheskaia rabota KPSS*, p. 88.

[121] *KPSS o Vooruzhennykh Silakh*, pp. 370-372.

[122] *Ideologicheskaia rabota KPSS*, p. 115.

[123] Loboda, *Komandnye kadry*, p. 85. [124] *Ibid.*

"Chief Marshal" of a military arm were introduced, to be equivalent in rank to a General of the Army.[125] (d) Military units that had manifested special excellence were classified as Guards Units.[126] (e) Military epaulettes were added to uniforms, pointing up differences in rank.[127] (f) Ranking military personnel and their families received special socio-economic privileges and rights, and all families of military personnel were given financial and educational prerogatives and other assistance.[128]

The successful battle of Stalingrad was the watershed in the Russo-German war. The Red Army gained the initiative, which with brief interruptions it maintained until the end of the war. Having encircled and captured large German armies at Stalingrad, the Soviets pressed forward in 1943, rolling west with impressive momentum. Though the Germans mounted a powerful counteroffensive in the summer, the Soviets held on and eventually broke that thrust. In a series of massive offensives along a broad front, the Soviet forces broke into East European territories in 1944, crushing the retreating Germans in their path.

As the threat to the survival of the Soviet state subsided, Stalin began little by little to reassert the Party's influence in the Red Army, while continuing to placate the military. His relaxation of controls had clearly been only a temporary tactical expedient, but it had enabled the military to ascend to a highly privileged position, and had created a large elite of military officers who, for the first time, were enjoying the glory and prestige of victors, and the freedom to make many (albeit only tactical) decisions without having to consult their political "advisors." Moreover, these officers had had the more intangible but exhilarating experience of camaraderie under fire, and the novel privilege of crossing the borders of the Soviet Union and observing some of the realities of capitalist society.

In 1943-1944, Stalin began to reestablish Party-political controls in the military. Without disturbing the semblance of full *edinonachalie* in the units, he ordered the structure of the Party organization to be changed in such a way as to strengthen controls at the lowest

[125] *Sbornik zakonov SSSR i ukazov Prezidiuma Verkhovnogo Soveta SSSR, 1938-1961 gg.* (Collection of USSR Laws and USSR Supreme Soviet Presidium Decrees, 1938-1961), "Izvestiia Sovetov deputatov trud. SSSR," Moscow, 1961, p. 394.

[126] *Ibid.*, p. 396.

[127] Loboda, *Komandnye kadry*, p. 85.

[128] *Ibid.*, pp. 84-86 and 113-150. See also *Osnovy sovetskogo voennogo zakonodatel'stva* (The Foundations of Soviet Military Legislation), Voenizdat, Moscow, 1961.

levels of the military hierarchy. In May 1943, the Central Committee issued an instruction which introduced primary Party organizations at battalion level, and Party organizations at the company level.[129] This move, which facilitated closer political supervision and more intensive indoctrination of the military, was no doubt prompted partly by the impending entrance of the Soviet forces into non-Soviet territories.

At a special meeting on July 15, 1944, the MPA emphasized the importance of strengthening ideological work in the military. Shcherbakov, looking already beyond the end of the war, spoke of a continuing threat of capitalist encirclement and of the need to sharpen the controls necessary to withstand future attempts at capitalist subversion.[130] The need for heightened political activity within the military was emphasized at the meeting:

> The Party realized that, during the past three years of the Great Patriotic War, many changes had taken place in the personnel of the armed forces. Large numbers of citizens had been drafted into the armed forces who earlier lived in territories occupied by the Germans. These citizens had spent a substantial amount of time under the pernicious influence of fascist ideology and had become separated from the life of the Soviet nation. It was necessary to strengthen the political education of young soldiers in the spirit of the ideas of Soviet patriotism and hatred of the enemy.[131]

The Party's concern about the possible impact that an encounter with the social and economic realities of Central Europe might have on the Soviet military is reflected in this account, which appeared in a later MPA publication:

> During combat beyond the borders of our country, ideological work in the Red Army became substantially strengthened. It took on specific characteristics and qualities in connection with the existence of Soviet soldiers on foreign territory. There, Soviet soldiers saw around themselves the decadent social system which was based on private property and exploitation. They eagerly looked at everything, they learned and compared. All of this demanded improvement of the patriotic education of Red Army soldiers, sergeants and commanders, and daily explanations of the diversion-

[129] *KPSS o Vooruzhennykh Silakh*, pp. 377-378.
[130] *Ideologicheskaia rabota KPSS*, p. 178.
[131] *Ibid.*

> ary ideological activities of the enemy, and a sensible explanation of the superiority of the Soviet socialist system.[132]

How strongly Soviet military personnel reacted to the non-Soviet style of life is apparent from this comment:

> When our unit entered East Prussia, many of the soldiers were wondering about the large quantities of well-fed cows . . . the multitude of household objects and agricultural machinery in the farmsheds. It was necessary to give a correct explanation about all of this to help the Soviet soldiers understand what they had seen in Germany.[133]

The political "educators" thus were in the difficult position of depending on old ideological formulas to explain matters that were real and could not easily be conjured away by dogma:

> The educators reacted quickly to all impressions of the Red Army soldiers and attempted appropriately and convincingly to explain to their comrades-in-arms all the questions which came up. . . . Once a sub-unit was passing through a village [when] the soldier Shishkin said: "Take a look, friends. All these houses are covered with iron [tin] roofs, not as in our village. They sure live well here, damn it." [Whereupon] the agitator immediately answered: "Sure they have lots of iron for their roofs, but for tractors, nothing."[134]

In 1944-1945, the Party-political organs were again exercising control in the military units,[135] and the officer corps was beginning once more to feel the heavy hand of the dictator. Shcherbakov had died, and in May 1945 a protégé of Zhdanov, Colonel General I. V. Shikin, took over the MPA. His regime was marked by a sharp curtailment of the commanders' authority and the ascendance of the political organs.

By 1946, the Red Army had been greatly reduced in numbers through demobilization; its wartime hero, Marshal Zhukov, had been relegated to the obscurity of a command in a remote military district, and the Party organs were busy minimizing the military's contribution to victory and giving all the credit to Stalin and the Party.[136] Having saved the country from collapse, the military was being deprived of the historical claim to its share in the victory, and forced once again to submit to rigid political and police controls.

[132] *Ibid.*, p. 231. [133] *Ibid.*, p. 236. [134] *Ibid.*, p. 234.
[135] *Ibid.*, p. 254. [136] See Chapter VII, pp. 239-240.

E · TOWARD THE END OF AN ERA: 1945-1953

The Soviet Union emerged from the war as the most powerful state in Europe, having turned back the German aggressors, withstood the threat of internal collapse, and extended Soviet political power into Central Europe. But the price for this achievement had been staggering: The country's industry and agriculture had suffered greatly; its western territories were in ruins; and the most productive sector of the population had been seriously reduced in numbers. A weary people was faced with the task of repairing these ravages of war, while the government had to consolidate its political gains and rebuild the economy.

The Party approached this challenge by tightening its hold over society and over the military, and creating an image of Stalin as the invincible and infallible leader and the savior of the nation. In building up this myth, the Party necessarily obscured the role of the Red Army and its contribution to the war.[137] And the remaining years of Stalin's rule were years of tribulation for the victorious officers and men of the Soviet military.

In this postwar period, as before, we thus observe the familiar cycle in the relations of Party and military: (a) the Party's tightened controls over the military, once the threat of foreign aggression has passed, including actual demotion of some military leaders and the general subordination of the officer corps; (b) a period of increasingly repressive measures, as the dictator set about cleansing the whole social system of any obstacles, challengers, and potential opponents; (c) with the growth of certain external[138] and internal[139] problems, a slight easing of the pressures on the officers and a few steps aimed at reconciling them; and, finally, (d) after Stalin's death,

[137] For an authoritative treatment of Soviet trends in historical writings on World War II and related issues, see Gallagher, *World War II*. See also Chapters VI and VII below.

[138] The U.S. commitment to the idea of "containment," which was manifested in repeated statements, rising military allocations, and the formation of regional anti-Soviet defense pacts, as well as the rapid economic recovery of Western Europe with American economic assistance, must have caused rising concern in the Party.

[139] Despite some successes in the postwar reconstruction of Soviet industry, the agricultural sector continued to lag and to be a major weakness in Soviet economy. Thus, the growing tensions among potential successors to Stalin were frequently articulated in terms of who would be best able to "clean up the agricultural mess." See Robert Conquest, *Power and Policy in the USSR*, St. Martin's Press, New York, 1961, pp. 112-128; Schapiro, *The Communist Party of the Soviet Union*, pp. 505-527. Furthermore, the secession of Yugoslavia from the bloc set in motion a number of disturbing events, including the purge of the Zhdanovites and plans for a purge of Beria and the security organs.

and in the course of the severe struggle among his heirs, the military's rise from obscurity to the position of a prominent institution wooed by all the warring factions in the Party.

1. The Apotheosis of Stalin

Soon after the end of hostilities, the Party's propaganda apparatus began to create the official version of the events just past, assigning credits, creating heroes, and delimiting the sphere of issues, events, and personalities that could properly be dealt with in the Soviet press.[140] On February 9, 1946, in a speech to a gathering of "electors" in Moscow, Stalin pointed the direction for the historical treatment of the war and indicated the subordinate role to be assigned to the military. Victory had been won mostly through the efforts of the Party and its organizational and ideological genius, he said, and "it would be a [great] mistake to say that we won only because of the gallantry of our troops."[141]

Soviet historians and military writers, well attuned to the signals of the dictator, quickly began to write a history of the war in which Stalin emerged as the savior of his country and the Party as a whole received the credit for victory. Stalin himself continued to reinforce this interpretation. In 1947, he wrote his famous reply to Colonel Razin, in which he questioned the military abilities of Lenin while presenting himself as the mastermind that brought about victory in the last war.[142]

The military's fall from grace was clearly evident as early as February 1946, during the events celebrating Armed Forces Day, and again later, at the first anniversary of Victory Day. Marshal Zhukov's name was significantly omitted from the articles, reports, and descriptions that appeared in *Pravda* in connection with these affairs, and there were few other military names or references in the Party press. Zhukov next was demoted from his prominent position as Commander-in-Chief of the Ground Forces and relegated to the command of a military district.[143] In addition to these public signs of the military's deflated role in the postwar society, some equally convincing, though less well-known, changes in the military itself left no doubt as to Stalin's intentions.

[140] See Chapter VI.

[141] Cited in Gallagher, *World War II*, p. 40.

[142] See *ibid.*, pp. 51-57.

[143] Zhukov's post went to his old adversary, Marshal I. Konev, while he himself was given command of the Odessa Military District.

2. The Rise of Zhdanov

Early in 1945, Zhdanov returned from the front to Moscow, where presumably he embarked on a struggle with Malenkov for primacy in the Party under Stalin. His rise to great power was immediately felt, both in the Party and in the military. After March 1946, Zhdanov's name ranked third, after Stalin and Malenkov, in the listings of Party dignitaries.[144]

Zhdanov's ascendance made itself felt in various spheres of Soviet life. A strong champion of "ideological discipline" and a believer in the imminent economic collapse of capitalism and the possibilities of a revolutionary offensive by the Cominform, Zhdanov instituted a strict Party regime in the arts, literature, and social sciences, and urged the subordination of all professional and personal objectives and loyalties to the interests and ideology of the Party.

Zhdanov's influence on the military was transmitted through the new head of the MPA, General I. V. Shikin, who had served under Zhdanov in the Leningrad Military District and during the war years. Shikin's appointment to the MPA signaled the end of the military's relative independence and ushered in another era of strong control and massive indoctrination by the Party.

In March 1946, the separate ministries of the Army and Navy were abolished, and the military establishment was centralized with the creation of the Ministry of the Armed Forces.[145] Shikin, as the head of a centralized MPA, now initiated a number of measures intended to raise the authority and scope of activity of the political control organs. Thus, he created three Political Administrations, immediately subordinate to his own, in the Army, Air Force, and Navy, respectively, and gave them wide authority.[146] Early in 1947, the Central Committee approved a decree on the political organs in the armed forces which "expressed high appreciation of the activities of the political organs during . . . the war," and emphasized that "under peaceful conditions, when the education and training of personnel became the primary task, the significance and role of the political organs has grown even further."[147]

These and subsequent measures of the Party and the MPA revealed the outline of Stalin's postwar policy toward the military: The Red

[144] For details on the rise and fall of Zhdanov, see Conquest, *Power and Policy*, pp. 79-111, and Schapiro, *The Communist Party of the Soviet Union*, pp. 507-511.

[145] Pobezhimov, *Pravovoe regulirovanie stroitel'stva*, p. 108.

[146] Petrov, *Partiinoe stroitel'stvo*, p. 445.

[147] *Ibid.*

Army was to be a closed institution of military professionals.[148] Military authority was to be minimal at the lower and middle levels, and less limited at the higher levels, where, presumably, it would be vested in politically trustworthy generals. The political control organs were to reassume extensive authority, replacing the quasi-elective, more nearly democratic Party organizations within individual units.[149] The commanders were to be a "kept" elite, who would enjoy many economic and social privileges in return for their tolerance of ubiquitous political controls. And Party recruitment among military personnel was to be limited almost exclusively to officer personnel.[150]

In carrying out this policy, Shikin and others took a number of measures designed to enhance the position of the political organs and to reduce the influence of the Party organizations. In May 1947, the old Lenin Military-Political Academy was reopened, to become the center at which promising political and military personnel were trained for ranking positions in the MPA apparatus.[151] In August 1947, the Central Committee created a special commission to study the problem of improving the impact of political indoctrination and supervision at the lower levels of the military community. The commission recommended strengthening the Party organizations' role in the military mostly through their more active inclusion in the organizational and operational affairs of the units, but its recommendations were not followed until 1950-1951, presumably because of opposition from the MPA, which feared interference with the authority of the political organs.[152]

[148] According to Petrov (p. 450), "Stalin single-mindedly and subjectively viewed the armed forces as a closed organization. He frequently stressed the predominance in the military of coercive elements as being its characteristic aspect. This attitude concealed the basic qualities of the armed forces of a socialist country."

[149] *Ibid.*, p. 451.

[150] Petrov (p. 443) cites the following statistics on Party recruitment: (a) In 1940, the Party recruited eighteen times as many privates as in 1948. (b) In 1948, privates and sergeants made up only 3 per cent of all military Party members. (In 1957, after Zhukov's ouster, and during Khrushchev's massive reform program in the military, which was aimed at destroying the elitist tendencies of the officer corps, the Party again actively recruited sergeants and privates for the Party organizations.) (c) In 1947, 50 per cent of all primary Party organizations contained fewer than fifteen members and candidates; 15 per cent contained fewer than five people; and most of the company-level organizations "fell apart."

[151] *Ibid.*, p. 447.

[152] *Ibid.*, p. 452. For descriptions of, and the distinction between, the Party organizations and the political organs, see Chapter IV, pp. 87-88.

The influence of Zhdanov and Shikin resulted in the political emasculation of the military. Deprived, by the apotheosis of Stalin, of even its claim to having played a major and heroic part in saving the country from succumbing to the Nazi armies, the military ceased to have any voice in the affairs of Party and state, and its leaders were relegated to the peripheries of the Soviet empire,[153] while political functionaries once again controlled the thought and the activities of rank and file as well as officer corps.

3. The Fall of Zhdanov

While Stalin's position remained undisputed, his lieutenants were jostling for power and prominence, the more fiercely so in view of the dictator's advancing age and poor health. Zhdanov's star, which had shone brightly in 1946 and 1947, began to dim after the defection of Yugoslavia from Moscow's fold, since Zhdanov was closely associated with that fiasco.[154] He died in August 1948, and his former rivals, Malenkov and Khrushchev, thereupon assumed greater powers. Many of Zhdanov's associates in the Party, both in government and among the military, were purged in the so-called Leningrad Affair of 1949-1950,[155] the first of the series of purges on a much broader scale that were to take place in subsequent years.

With Malenkov, Khrushchev, Beria, and their respective followers filling the vacuum created by Zhdanov's death, the struggle for power and position became ever more intense, as the contenders, in vying for the domination of Party and state, carried out plots and counterplots in the shadow of the aging autocrat. First, Zhdanov's associates were purged in the Leningrad Affair. Between 1951 and 1953, the purges and intrigues in Georgia and Mingrelia were aimed at the followers of Beria, who were briefly reinstated after Stalin's death, only to be definitively purged after Beria's fall.[156] The Slansky trial of November 1952 revealed the increasingly anti-

[153] See Chapter VII, pp. 239-243.

[154] See Conquest, pp. 91-94, for a description of and speculations on Zhdanov's involvement with the Yugoslav affair.

[155] The purge of the Zhdanovites was extensive. It included the economist, planner, and minister N. A. Voznesenskii; the secretary of the Central Committee A. A. Kuznetsov; all five secretaries of the Leningrad City Committee, which was Zhdanov's home base (Popkov, Kapustin, Nikolaev, Sintsov, and Levin); all five secretaries of the Leningrad Provincial Committee; various members of the Party and city organs in Leningrad; and, finally, General Shikin, head of the MPA, himself. Of those purged, only Shikin remained alive, and was eventually rehabilitated. See Conquest, pp. 96-97.

[156] *Ibid.*, pp. 129-153 and 195-226.

Semitic overtones of the Party purges that were growing in intensity in the Soviet Union and elsewhere in the bloc. Among them, the Doctors' Plot, staged just before Stalin's death, was undoubtedly meant to be the point of departure for a wholesale purge in the Soviet Union.[157]

Toward the end of his life, Stalin apparently was preparing a purge among his Party associates and in the security organs which was to include Beria. He seems to have intended to spare the military, however, and indeed made several conciliatory gestures toward the military hierarchy that could only have been designed to mollify them and ensure their neutrality in the impending crisis.

In March 1949, Marshal Vasilevskii replaced the "political general," Bulganin, as Minister of Defense. In May 1949, General Shikin was relieved of his position as head of the MPA, a victim of the anti-Zhdanov purges, and was replaced with Colonel General F. F. Kuznetsov. In February 1950, the Defense Ministry was again divided into separate ministries of Army and Navy, and the MPA also was divided into two corresponding suborgans, with a resultant loss in authority and influence. General Kuznetsov remained as head of the political organs in the army, and Admiral Zakharov became head of the political organs in the navy. In 1950 and 1951, Zhukov made several public appearances, the first since he had become commander of the Odessa Military District. At the Nineteenth Party Congress, in October 1952, an unusually large number of ranking military professionals were given membership in the Central Committee.[158] And, finally, the Doctors' Plot was being staged in a manner suggesting that it was meant to enhance the military's role in the state.[159]

[157] This hypothesis seems to be shared by most Western writers on the Soviet Union: cf. Conquest, pp. 154-191; Schapiro, pp. 542-546; George Paloczi-Horvath, *Khrushchev: The Making of a Dictator*, Little, Brown and Company, Boston, 1960, pp. 125-129; Myron Rush, *The Rise of Khrushchev*, Public Affairs Press, Washington, 1958, p. 17; Konrad Kellen, *Khrushchev: A Political Portrait*, Frederick A. Praeger, Inc., New York, 1961, p. 89.

[158] Vasilevskii, Sokolovskii, Konev, and Admiral N. G. Kuznetsov were appointed as full members, while twenty-six other marshals, generals, and admirals (including Zhukov) were appointed as candidate members. See Chapter VII, p. 242, for details.

[159] Though conclusive evidence to that effect is not available, writers on Soviet affairs point to an official announcement by the Party, according to which the alleged plotters intended to "undermine the health of leading Soviet personnel, to put them out of action and to weaken the defense of the country. They sought to put out of action Marshal A. M. Vasilevskii, Marshal L. A. Govorov, Marshal I. S. Konev, General of the Army S. M. Shtemenko, Admiral G. I. Levchenko, and others. . . ." *Pravda*, January 13, 1953.

At the same time, however, Stalin was balancing these promilitary gestures with measures that seemed designed to tighten political controls in the armed forces. In July 1950, "the Central Committee passed a new, important decision intended to strengthen the Party's leadership in the army and navy."[160]

> Military Councils of Force Groups, districts, fleets, armies, and flotillas are transformed from advisory organs to the commanders, into responsible collective organs authorized to direct all aspects of life and activities of the troops. At the same time, the position of a Military Council member from the cadres of political workers is restored.[161]

That same year, Stalin also abolished the political organizations at battalion level and moved them up to the regiment, while introducing the *zampolits* at company level.[162] This change was most likely dictated by the fact that there were not enough Party members at the battalion level to maintain a full-fledged organization.[163] Furthermore, by moving the primary Party organization to the regiment and establishing *zampolits* in the company, Stalin was actually streamlining political controls throughout the chain of command while ostensibly relieving the battalions of the burden of Party functionaries.

In Stalin's lifetime, the military remained a thoroughly controlled elite, with a semblance of professional autonomy, which, in response to pressures, was allowed to play a limited role in Party politics. However, by keeping the military a closed institution, a condition that favors the development of elitist propensities and practices, Stalin was laying the groundwork for its future emergence as a cohesive institutional organism that would claim a more prominent role in Soviet life.

160 Petrov, *Partiinoe stroitel'stvo*, p. 453.

161 *Ibid.* The reference to the "member from the cadres of political workers" as being promoted to membership of the Military Councils refers in actuality to a member of the security organs. In time of crisis the Party has in the past transformed the Military Council into a collective body of broad responsibility and full authority in the district, and placd a security organ member on it for tighter supervision. Zhukov, after assuming the Ministry of Defense, tried to liquidate the "position of membership on the Military Councils from the cadres of political workers." *Ibid.*, p. 462.

162 For details of the role and functions of the *zampolit* (*zamestitel' po politicheskoi chasti*), see Chapter IV, p. 87, and Appendix E.

163 Petrov, p. 443.

4. The Death of Stalin

The events following the death of Stalin—the rise of Malenkov, Beria's plotting and subsequent fall, Khrushchev's eventual displacement of Malenkov as the dominant leader in the Party, and his assumption of full powers after 1957—all of these have been extensively analyzed in the West and need no further treatment here.[164] We shall therefore emphasize only those events that illuminate the military's rise from obscurity into political prominence and strengthen our hypothesis about the cyclical nature of Party-military relations.

The death of Stalin removed the linchpin which had held together all the elements of power in the Soviet state. In the ensuing struggle among his lieutenants, the Party was greatly weakened as its leaders plotted against each other, seeking support from other institutions and power centers, which thus gained in influence. Foremost among those that benefited by the Party's relative weakness was the military. While the details of the succession struggles are still uncertain, it is quite clear that the military played some major role in the fall of Beria and in the subsequent ouster of Malenkov and the anti-Party group. The known facts are: (a) Within a week after Stalin's death, the Ministry of War and the Ministry of the Navy were combined under Bulganin, and Zhukov joined Vasilevskii and Kuznetsov by becoming First Deputy Minister.[165] (b) The same Central Committee plenum which approved Beria's ouster coopted Zhukov for Beria's seat.[166] (c) Within the next few months, a number

[164] Conquest, pp. 195-227; Schapiro, pp. 547-553; Paloczi-Horvath, pp. 130-145; Kellen, pp. 88-116.

[165] Raymond L. Garthoff, "The Marshals and the Party: Soviet Civil-Military Relations in the Postwar Period," *Total War and Cold War: Problems in Civilian Control of the Military*, ed. Harry Coles, Ohio State University Press, Columbus, 1962, p. 249.

[166] *Ibid.* Conquest's speculations on the role of the military in the ouster of Beria seem very convincing, and are further strengthened by the fact that two military men, Konev and Moskalenko, known to be associates of Khrushchev, were named as members of the tribunal which "tried" Beria. See Conquest, Appendix VI, p. 444. It may be of interest to compare the time of Beria's death by firing squad, generally accepted as having taken place between June 26 and July 10, with the meeting of the Party *aktiv* of the Ministry of Defense which was reported in the July 16 issue of *Pravda*. The meeting, which was attended by Bulganin, Zhukov, Sokolovskii, Budennyi, and Govorov among others representing the collective military establishment, vowed that the military "will in the future remain the loyal and reliable support of the Central Committee of the Party." This unusual public avowal of the military's support to the collective Party leadership at the time of Beria's death may have been indicative of the military's *a priori* or *ex post facto* support of Khrushchev and Malenkov. Furthermore, the military's long-standing hatred of Beria may have been another strong factor in his ouster and

of generals and admirals received striking promotions, and several military leaders who had been in disgrace were rehabilitated.[167] (d) The MPA was taken over by General Zheltov, during whose regime the hold of the political organs over the military was relatively weak.

Gradually at first, military men began to speak out publicly, as representatives of a professional group, criticizing the dead dictator's military thought as sterile, calling for a correct historical appraisal of the military's role in World War II, and demanding greater freedom to practice their profession without interference from ignominious controls.[168]

In the 1945-1953 period, as in earlier years, the military's position *vis-à-vis* the Party improved whenever the Party suffered internal dissension or faced external dangers. Yet, although at various times the military might have been in a position to press its claims vigorously and lastingly, it failed to take full advantage of those moments and thus eventually succumbed again to the Party's grip.

---

death. Marshal Voronov reports in his memoirs that, during the war, Beria tried to obtain 50,000 guns for his NKVD troops while the military desperately needed every gun available to fight the Germans. When Stalin told him that he had decided to give him only 10,000, the rest to be sent to the front, Beria, on leaving Stalin's office, raced after the generals who had also been present and had persuaded Stalin not to give him the guns, and shouted: "You just wait, we will cut your guts out!" Chief Marshal of Artillery N. N. Voronov, *Na sluzhbe voennoi* (In the Military Service), Voenizdat, Moscow, 1963, p. 195. Tiulenev, in *Cherez tri voiny*, pp. 196-197, cites details of Beria's destructive behavior in the Caucasus during the German offensive.

[167] Garthoff, in *Total War and Cold War*, p. 249.

[168] See Chapters V, VI, and VII.

IV · The Party's Control System in the Military

Most military establishments resemble one another in organization, structure, and routine. They are predictable organisms, because they operate according to a rigid formula of explicit procedures that make for stable relationships among the various levels of the hierarchy. An essential aspect of military life is the fact that the power to initiate or terminate a function or action derives unequivocally from well-established and easily identifiable sources. Authority in the military flows naturally and unmistakably from the top to the bottom. The stable, well-regulated procedures of the military would be severely shaken if any source of authority outside the regular chain of command were to issue commands in an *ad hoc* manner; if several sources of authority coexisted in a loosely defined fashion; or if military procedures were subjected to the constant scrutiny of committees composed of ranks and civilians from outside the units so reviewed.

In the Soviet Union, however, most units, institutes, staffs, and other groups in the military establishment have precisely such multiple sources of authority. As a result, the typical Soviet military unit is a microcosm of the tensions and conflicts that have beset the Red Army as a whole since its very creation. These internal tensions have not succeeded in crippling the Soviet military, but they frequently cause inertia and low morale, and their cumulative effect at times is such as to pose a challenge to the Party.

The Soviet Party leaders are very well aware of the disruptive effects of having multiple sources of authority within individual military units. However, since the military's political reliability is to them a matter of even greater concern than its technical and administrative viability, they accept this risk as the price they must pay for ensuring full control over their military establishment. Any tendency toward arbitrariness in dealing with the military is tempered, to be sure, by considerations of efficiency as well as of morale, and the Party's complex system of controls, therefore, is so designed as to strike a balance between the permissiveness needed to maintain morale, discipline, efficiency, and readiness at desirable levels, and the degree of coercion that will prevent the military from becoming too self-assertive.

The Party's Control System

A · HISTORICAL BACKGROUND OF THE POLITICAL CONTROL SYSTEM

Ironically, the Bolsheviks did not invent the system of military commissars but adopted it from practices instituted by the Provisional Government of Kerensky in the old Russian army.[1] When first introduced in the Red Army, the commissar system met with much opposition, and it was permanently adopted only after violent debate among the Party leaders. Though there were small numbers of military commissars already toward the end of 1917, their chief function then was to bolster the morale and loyalty of the troops. Political activities among the majority of units were being controlled by local civilian Party organizations. However, when Trotsky subsequently decided to use large numbers of officers from the old army as military specialists in the Red Army, it became imperative to have their activities supervised by Communists, and this led to the introduction of military commissars on a large scale, and to the controversy that broke out over this move.[2]

Opposition came from different quarters: (a) from the more prominent military specialists who feared "dual authority in the military";[3] (b) from the local Party organizations, which were reluctant to give up their authority in the units to the centrally controlled commissars; (c) from the Left Communists and the Military Opposition, who opposed all centralized control of Party-political activities;[4] (d) from among some of the commissars themselves; and

[1] For an excellent summary of these problems, see Littleton B. Atkinson, *Dual Command in the Red Army*, Air University Documentary Research Study, Maxwell Air Force Base, Alabama, 1950, pp. 1-13.

[2] *KPSS i stroitel'stvo Vooruzhennykh Sil SSSR, 1918-iiun' 1941* (The CPSU and the Development of the Armed Forces of the USSR, 1918-June 1941), Voenizdat, Moscow, 1959, p. 77.

[3] *Ibid.*

[4] A recent Soviet work describes the Left Communists as "military romantics" who consider the revolutionary Red Army "an absurdity," maintaining that a "revolutionary war should be conducted not with an army but by the whole nation" and that "the new Red Army is nothing more than the recreation of the old army." *Ibid.*, p. 44.

The Military Opposition consisted of spokesmen of several Party factions which, during the vital proceedings at the Eighth Party Congress (March 1919), attempted to oppose the creation of a centralized standing army. Since these factions included the Left Communists, the *Partizanshchina* (guerrilla-war advocates who rejected discipline and military rules), and the proponents of local Party control over military units, it is not surprising that they favored voluntary enlistment, the election of commanders, the retention of guerrilla units, and guerrilla methods. By the same token, they opposed centralized control of the military, strict discipline, general mobilization, and a prominent role for military commissars. *Ibid.*, p. 121.

(e) even from Trotsky, who regarded the commissars as superfluous once the civil war and the Polish war were over.

The main support for the military commissar system came from (a) the majority of the commissars; (b) the "Red Commanders" (most of them noncommissioned officers from the old army who now occupied major positions and commands); and (c) the clique around Stalin, including Voroshilov, Budennyi, and Frunze. Stalin and those of his associates who had themselves served as commissars in the Red Army during the civil war understood the vital role of the commissar in maintaining political control within the military.

The political control structure in the Red Army was born in the spring of 1918, when military commissars were attached to individual units.[5] Their function was defined, and their position formalized, in April 1918, through a decree which established the military commissar as "the direct political organ of Soviet power in the army." On April 8, 1918, the Central Committee of the Party asked the Defense Commissariat to centralize the various activities of the commissars by creating the All-Russian Bureau of Military Commissars.

The next important move to centralize Party-political activities in the military took place on December 5, 1918, when the Revolutionary Military Council of the Republic (*Revvoensovet Respubliki*) in its Order No. 337 created political organs at all Fronts (army groups), armies, and divisional levels, thereby rescinding the power of the local civilian and intramilitary Party organizations to direct political activities in the Red Army.[6]

See also documents on the Eighth Party Congress in *KPSS o Vooruzhennykh Silakh Sovetskogo Soiuza: sbornik dokumentov, 1917-1958* (The CPSU on the Armed Forces of the Soviet Union: A Collection of Documents, 1917-1958), Gospolitizdat, Moscow, 1958, pp. 49-64.

[5] See P. A. Golub, "Kogda zhe byl uchrezhden institut voennykh komissarov Krasnoi Armii?" (When Was the Red Army Institute of Military Commissars Founded?), *Voprosy istorii KPSS*, No. 4, April 1962, pp. 155-160, for the most recent treatment of that problem.

[6] *Partiino-politicheskaia rabota v Sovetskoi Armii i Voenno-Morskom Flote* (Party-political Activities in the Soviet Army and Navy), Voenizdat, Moscow, 1960, p. 10. This move was most likely an attempt to deal with the anarchic growth of Party cells and committees in units which did not desire centralized direction and at times actively opposed centralization of authority and control. This sudden growth of local Party organizations in the units represented a major obstacle to the creation of the disciplined, viable army needed to fight counterrevolutionary attacks. In October 1918, there were 1,300 Party cells in the military, comprising 35,000 Party members; in February 1919, 1,500 cells, with 122,000 members; and in the autumn of 1919, 6,919 cells, with 300,000 Party members. Cited in I. F. Pobezhimov, *Pravovoe regulirovanie stroitel'stva Sovetskoi Armii i Flota* (Legal

The Eighth Party Congress (March 1919) did much to enhance the role of the political organs and promote the centralization of their functions. It abolished the All-Russian Bureau of Military Commissars, which did not wield enough authority. In its place, the Congress created the Political Department at the *Revvoensovet* of the Republic, which in turn was changed, in May 1919, into the Main Political Administration of the Red Army (MPA), headed by a member of the Central Committee. Toward the end of 1919, Party commissions were created at the regimental and divisional levels as appellative bodies that were to investigate grievances and pass on disciplinary problems.[7] In December of that year, the Central Committee also formalized the role of the Party organization in the military by decreeing that the basic organization was to be the company cell, and the next level, the regimental cell.[8]

The main impetus behind the introduction of political commissars and the vesting of central control in the MPA had been the presence in the Red Army of large numbers of officers from the old army (whose services were indispensable not only during the civil war but for some time thereafter, as there were virtually no trained officers among the Communists) and the need, therefore, to supervise the activities of men who felt no ideological bond with the new regime. After the cessation of hostilities, however, and once large numbers of trained Communists had begun to take over commands in the military, the continued maintenance of those strict controls became a matter of controversy in the Party. As the Red Army was transformed into a territorial militia with a small nucleus of cadre troops, and as the class principle continued to govern the selection of personnel for the army and militia, the *raison d'être* of the commissars became questionable. Trotsky and several others did indeed minimize the need for the continued maintenance of the system of centralized political organs, but Stalin and his associates not only favored its retention but undertook to strengthen the authority and influence of the commissars. With Trotsky's removal from the *Revvoensovet* in 1925, Stalin's view inevitably prevailed, and the political control

---

Regulation of the Development of the Soviet Army and Navy), Gosiurizdat, Moscow, 1960, p. 37.

By an order of the *Revvoensovet Respubliki* of October 14, 1919, the central Party organs also established the function and position of the *politruk* (political guide) at the company level, who assumed direction of Party-political work in the lower units and displaced the authority of the Party cell. *Ibid.*, p. 36.

[7] *KPSS i stroitel'stvo Vooruzhennykh Sil*, p. 135.

[8] *Ibid.*, p. 157.

organs became the cornerstone upon which he created the Red Army. Although he adjusted their role to the prevailing conditions and exigencies, he always fell back on them in times of impending or actual crisis in the military.

B · THE STRUCTURE OF THE CONTROL SYSTEM

Administratively, the political control system is divided into three main plateaus, which correspond to the major subdivisions of the military establishment:

(1) the Main Political Administration (MPA), which parallels the Ministry of Defense;

(2) the Political Departments, which parallel the Military District, Force Group, or Fleet; and

(3) the Political Sections, which are parallel to the *soedinenie* (of approximately divisional level).

Each of these military divisions has its own administrative organization, with its stated size and function: The ministerial level deals with policy and broad administration; the district level has operational as well as administrative responsibilities; and the *soedinenie* is largely operational.

From the lowest squad up to the Ministry of Defense, the military is permeated with an array of Party-political control organs, each of which is administratively subordinated to the next higher level. The central decision-making body in this complex of control instruments is the Main Political Administration of the Soviet Army and Navy (MPA).

1. The Main Political Administration

The MPA operates as an independent body within the Ministry of Defense. Organizationally, it is a section of the Central Committee, to which it is directly responsible.[9] Its internal structure is as follows:

[9] In an official instruction to the political organs, the role of the MPA is described as follows: "The Communist Party is the organizer and leader of the Soviet Army and Navy. In this lies the main source of [the military's] strength. The Communist Party exercises its leadership of the Armed Forces through the Military Councils, commanders, political organs, and Party organizations. At the head of the political organs stands the Main Political Administration . . . which operates as a section of the CC CPSU." (*Partiino-politicheskaia rabota*, p. 46.) The link between the MPA and the Ministry of Defense was substantially weakened in the period after Stalin's death when Zhukov was in charge of the Ministry. Since Zhukov's ouster, it has once more become close.

(a) head of the MPA
(b) deputy heads
(c) the administration for Party-organizational and political-organs affairs in the Ground Forces
(d) the administration for propaganda and agitation
(e) the administration for cadres
(f) the administration for management of political organs in the various arms
(g) various administrative sections
(h) the Party commission at the MPA[10]

The authority of the MPA, though always extensive, fluctuates with the political climate in the state and with the personality of its head. Indeed, the rank and prestige of the head, and his political standing, often are an indication of the current status of the MPA. In the 1953-1957 period, immediately after Stalin's death, when the military was reasserting itself and Zhukov was Minister of Defense, the relatively limited power of the MPA was symbolized by the fact that its then head, Zheltov, did not rise above the rank of colonel general and was not coopted into the Central Committee. Significantly, Golikov, who took over the MPA after Zhukov's ouster, became a member of the Central Committee and was given the highest rank, that of a Marshal of the Soviet Union.

Within the central apparatus of the Ministry of Defense, the MPA maintains Political Departments (recently transformed into Party Committees). Their main function is to conduct political education, and to observe and transmit information on personnel, including top military leaders.[11]

Through the levels of the political control machinery subordinate to it, the MPA directs all Party-political activities in the military, and

[10] The difference in wording between (c) and (f) indicates that, whereas the MPA directly controls the activities of political organs in the Ground Forces, it has less immediate access to political control activities in the other services. The reason may be that such specialized and highly technical services as the Strategic Missile Forces, the Air Force, and the Submarine Fleet successfully hold out against too close scrutiny and excessive indoctrination by the MPA. With respect to (h), it might be explained that Party commissions attached to the various military organizations usually serve as appellative bodies which review complaints, disputes, and other conflicts among Party members of the organization. The MPA commission, in recent years, has also become involved in the affairs of the central apparatus of the Ministry of Defense.

[11] See *Kommunist Vooruzhennykh Sil*, No. 15, August 1962, pp. 38-41, where Epishev describes the events of the Party *aktiv* meeting in the Ground Forces headquarters.

it "regularly reports to the Central Committee about the political morale of the military personnel, the military readiness of units, and the political activities in the armed forces."[12]

2. The Political Departments

The Military District, the Force Group, and the Fleet represent the second plateau of the military hierarchy, the Military District being the main territorial-administrative unit of the Soviet army. Zhukov, during his tenure in the Ministry of Defense, attempted to stress the commander's authority over that of the Party-political organs. After his departure, however, the Party reinstated the Military Council as the main authoritative body within the district.[13] Normally, the Military Council consists of the district commander, the head of the district's Political Department, and the ranking civilian Party functionary in the district; occasionally, there will also be a representative of the police and security organs and the deputy commander of the district.[14]

The Political Department controls the Political Sections, the Party, and the Komsomol organizations at the divisional level, and the *zampolits* at the regimental level. It is responsible for Party-political work among the units, as well as for their military training and discipline, their political morale, and their military readiness.[15]

3. The Political Sections

The main operational center of the political control system is at the level of the *soedinenie*, or larger unit.[16] The Political Section of the *soedinenie* plans, directs, and controls the activities of all subordinate levels. Its head, who serves also as the *zampolit* (political

[12] *Na strazhe rodiny stroiashchei kommunizm* (Guarding the Fatherland Which Is Building Communism), Voenizdat, Moscow, 1962, p. 273. This is a large "educational text for political studies" issued by the MPA.

[13] See Malinovskii, in *Resheniia oktiabr'skogo Plenuma TsK KPSS v deistvii* (Decisions of the CPSU Central Committee October Plenum in Action), ed. Colonel S. M. Borzunov, Voenizdat, Moscow, 1959, p. 8.

[14] For details, see Chapter V, pp. 124-126.

[15] *Na strazhe rodiny*, p. 274.

[16] In Soviet nomenclature, the standard organizational elements are as follows:

Soedinenie (formation): rifle and cavalry divisions, tank and mechanized brigades.

Chast' (unit): the basic organization of a single arm or service. It is the smallest organization with balanced staff and services. It varies in size from brigade to battalion, but is most frequently of regimental size.

Podrazdelenie (element): This applies to lesser secondary components of *soedinenie*, and varies in size between battalion and company.

deputy to the commander) of the *soedinenie*, is the most powerful member of the Party commission attached to the *soedinenie*, with the added prerogatives of the military officer acting within the authority afforded by his rank. The Political Section of the *soedinenie* supervises and actively manages the three lower levels of the military-political hierarchy—regiment, battalion, and company.

(a) At the *chast'* (regimental) level, the political organs are headed by the regimental *zampolit*, whose full-time staff consists of the secretary of the Party *biuro*, the regimental propagandist, the head of the regimental club, and the secretary of the Komsomol organization, and who, in addition, has the part-time services of agitators, lecturers, and other functionaries.[17]

(b) The structure of the political organs at battalion level is roughly similar to that of the regiment.

(c) At the level of the company, it is usual to have a *partorg* (Party organizer) instead of a *zampolit*. The importance of the political organs in the company has fluctuated in the past: During periods of military assertiveness, the Party would confine most of its activity to areas upward in the hierarchy and not interfere with the smaller units. Whenever it was in a position to reestablish strong controls in the military, the battalion and company levels tended to become the loci of greatest activity, since they afforded the political officers intimate contact with the troops.

C · THE INSTRUMENTS OF CONTROL

Four separate sources of authority are distinguishable in most military units: the political organs; the military chain of command; the local Party organs; and the *prokuratura* and secret police. It is not unlikely that the Party favors a certain degree of mutual distrust among them, for their competitiveness not only prevents collusion but permits the Party to play off one against the other and, in effect, to control the controllers.

1. The Political Organs

This control system, as we have seen, parallels the military organization, from the lowest levels up to the Ministry of Defense, and the political organs coexist with the military authority without being responsible to it. Their main function is to direct the Party and

[17] For details on organizational structure and distribution of functions, see Appendix E.

Komsomol organizations within the units, and to use them to indoctrinate, inform, and coerce members of these units in line with the Party's objectives.

The Party organizations are of several kinds, depending on their location within the military hierarchy: The *Party Committee* is usually to be found at the higher levels (Ministry of Defense, Military Institutes, Military District, and division). It is nominally an elective body with substantial powers of decision concerning Party affairs as well as the military and political activities of the parent organization. The *Primary Party Organization* (PPO) is the basic operational unit of the Communist Party in the military. It used to be located at the regimental level, but recently was moved down to the battalion.[18] The *Party Organization* operates as a separate section of the Primary Party Organization at the level just below that of the PPO. Lowest in the hierarchy is the *Party Group*, which consists of a small number of Party members or candidates at the company, platoon, or squad level. The *Party Commission* may also be considered part of this organizational structure of the Party in the military, but it is not part of the descending hierarchy, and is not concerned with operational problems. Rather, it serves as an appellate or revisory body at divisional and higher levels.[19]

The structure of the Komsomol organization is roughly similar to that of the Party organizations. Together with the political organs, the Party and Komsomol organizations form essentially a single organizational unit, since the political officers in reality control all three.

2. *The Military Chain of Command*

Although the officers are the main object of the controls maintained by the Party, the latter in turn uses them as one of its means of con-

[18] Beginning in the summer of 1960, Party Committees were being introduced at the regimental level, while the PPO was moved downward to battalion and company.

[19] In the past ten years, the status and functions of the Party Commission have been fluctuating according to the political climate. Originally established as a form of Party review board at the division and higher levels, it is now essentially a tool used by the head of the Political Department at the military district level. It reviews intra-Party complaints and reported offenses, applications for Party membership, and the personal files and other problems of Party members; and it adjudicates Party organizations and political organs. See *Nekotorye voprosy partiino-organizatsionnoi raboty v Sovetskoi Armii i Flote* (Some Problems of Party-Organizational Work in the Soviet Army and Navy), Voenizdat, Moscow, 1959, pp. 84-87.

trolling the military establishment by seeking to promote politically loyal personnel and by involving officers actively in Party affairs. However, this attempt of the Party has not been very successful, for the commanding personnel tends to feel primarily attached to its professional responsibility and to view Party-political demands as a nuisance that must be tolerated.

3. *Local Party Organs*

As a check on the state of political activity within units, civilian Party functionaries may take part in the life of the units. Established during the civil war, this practice was abandoned for a while, as local Party functionaries were thought to interfere too much in military activities. In times of intramilitary turbulence, however, the Party leadership has repeatedly fallen back on the local Party organs, which became ubiquitous in the wake of Zhukov's ouster. Their functionaries frequently participate in the meetings and other activities of the political organs and Party organizations within the units. Professionally uncommitted, they serve the Party as an external control link to the military.[20]

4. Prokuratura *and Secret Police*

The functions of these institutions in the military units are preventive and coercive, the *prokuratura*'s concern being criminal and economic offenses, and that of the secret police being political misconduct and offenses against the Party. In these two elements the Party leadership has not only another external, militarily uncommitted source of information but also an instrument of compulsion.[21]

[20] This intrusion of local Party organs into the activities of the units had been largely curtailed during Zhukov's tenure in the Ministry of Defense. After his ouster, it was vigorously reinstated by Khrushchev with the aid of the political organs. The intensified collaboration between the military and local Party and social organizations has been referred to in many official pronouncements and writings. Of significance is this statement, found in a political educational handbook for officers: "A close relationship of the military with Party, Soviet, and Komsomol organizations, with collectives of factories, *sovkhozes*, and *kolkhozes*, helps soldiers and officers better to understand general national interests, and it prevents the development of caste systems. . . ." *V pomoshch' ofitseram izuchaiushchim marksist-sko-leninskuiu teoriiu* (An Aid to Officers Studying Marxist-Leninist Theory), Voenizdat, Moscow, 1959, p. 125. See also R. Kolkowicz, *The Use of Soviet Military Labor in the Civilian Economy: A Study of Military "Shefstvo,"* The RAND Corporation, RM-3360-PR, November 1962.

[21] We shall not discuss here the scope and details of the functions performed by the *prokuratura* and security organs in the military, but shall merely list them among the various other controlling instruments.

D · *METHODS OF CONTROL*

Notwithstanding the extensive, and often confusing, Soviet literature on the variety of functions performed by political organs, Party organizations, Komsomols, and others, only the political organs possess real authority to direct, maintain, and control the political, and to a large extent the military, activities within the units, and the subsidiary organizations serve them mainly as tools and levers for indoctrination and control, without sharing their power. To grasp the essential conflict between commanding personnel and Party organs, therefore, we must take a close look at the role of the political organs in the military as reflected in some of the instructions, and definitions of objectives and functions, issued to them by the Party.

General objectives:

> The political organs strive, in their work, to strengthen the military might of the Soviet Army and Navy, by *guarding daily the uninterrupted influence of the Party* on all activities and affairs of the Armed Forces. . . .[22]

> They must always approach problems in such a manner that the interests of the Party and government, the *interests of communism, are given priority.*[23]

> The Party's demand that *all aspects of military life be systematically penetrated* obligates the political organs to analyze systematically the state of military training . . . to discover at the right time deficiencies in the education of personnel . . . and to define concrete measures [for the removal of such deficiencies].[24]

> The Communist Party is the organizer and leader of the Soviet Army and Navy. In this lies the main source of [the Army's and Navy's] strength. The Communist Party exercises its leadership of the Armed Forces through the military councils, commanders, political organs, and Party organizations. At the head of the political organs stands the Main Political Administration . . . which operates as a section of the CC CPSU.[25]

[22] *Partiino-politicheskaia rabota*, p. 47. This and eight of the following nine quotations are excerpts from the same official handbook, intended for "commanders and Party-political workers" to assist them "in the organization of Party-political work among the personnel of the Soviet Army and Navy." Some of the instructions have also been published in other handbooks, pamphlets, and the like. (Italics in all quotations have been added.)

[23] P. 49. [24] P. 57. [25] P. 46.

The political organs must *extend their influence into all facets of the activities and the existence of the forces,* to become involved with everything upon which may depend the military readiness, political education, discipline, and state of political morale of the personnel. Consequently, political organs deal with the most varied problems of military life, training, and education of personnel.[26]

[The political organs must] *react to even the smallest deviations from Marxism-Leninism, to any opposition to the policies* and directions of the Party, and must analyze and deal with all problems in such a manner that the interests of the Party and government are given first place.[27]

SOME SPECIFIC DUTIES:

The *zampolit* is responsible for the work of the Party organizations. Together with the Party *biuro* he organizes Party work in the regiment and in the units. [He] concerns himself with the improvement of living conditions [of the personnel, and] reports to the regimental commander and head of the Political Department of *soedinenie* on the political morale of the personnel and on the political measures undertaken.[28]

The *zampolit* supervises the selection of study groups, and sees to it that political studies are carried on strictly according to the study plans and strictly in accordance with the schedules, to *ensure that soldiers, sailors, and sergeants do not leave their studies for administrative and other duties.*[29]

CONTROLLING FUNCTIONS:

Serious attention must be given to the *recording of discussions* [during Party meetings when *kritika/samokritika* is performed]. Here it is necessary to note the gist of every comment, and to put down precisely the basic thought expressed by the Communist as well as his suggestions. It is incorrect to take down only the names of the participants in the discussions without indicating the contents of their statements.[30]

[26] P. 49. [27] *Ibid.* [28] P. 68. [29] P. 70.

[30] *Nekotorye voprosy partiino-organizatsionnoi raboty v Sovetskikh Vooruzhennykh Silakh* (Some Problems of Party-Organizational Work in the Soviet Armed Forces), Voenizdat, Moscow, 1963, p. 61. For a discussion of the technique of *kritika/samokritika*, see pp. 94-96 below.

> An important factor in the organizational work of the political organs, and inseparably related to checks and controls, is Party information. A well-established informational system enables the political organs always to be on top of things and to *react at the right time to deficiencies in the activities of the officer personnel* and in the Party and Komsomol organizations. Party information must correctly define the state of political morale among personnel and the levels of military discipline.[31]

These few excerpts from the large body of directives that the Party issues to the political organs indicate the broad scope of the political control organs' role in the military. Their essential functions may be summed up as (a) to observe activities in the units and to pass the information to higher levels of the apparatus; (b) to "politicize" military personnel through intensive indoctrination and political education; (c) to regulate the advancement of officers so that only those who are desirable from the Party's point of view are promoted to positions of authority; (d) to supervise and control military as well as political activities within the unit; and (e) to prompt desired action or conduct through intimidation, threats of dismissal, public humiliation, or outright coercion.

[31] *Partiino-politicheskaia rabota*, p. 51. Among the many pamphlets, symposia, document collections, and articles which deal with the role of the Party-political organs in the military, some of the most significant and useful publications are: *K novomu pod"emu partiino-politicheskoi raboty v Sovetskoi Armii i Flote* (Toward a New Intensification of Party-Political Work in the Soviet Army and Navy), ed. Major General Z. S. Osipov, Voenizdat, Moscow, 1960. (This collection of articles by the top Soviet military leaders reflects the strong loyalty of the Stalingrad Group to Khrushchev's military policies, with specific emphasis on political controls.) *Partiinaia organizatsiia chasti, korablia* (The Party Organization of *Chast'* and Ship), Voenizdat, Moscow, 1960. (A collection of articles by the top functionaries of the political organs, including one by Malinovskii on the growing role of the Party within the military.) *Resheniia oktiabr'skogo Plenuma TsK KPSS v deistvii* (Decisions of the CPSU Central Committee October Plenum in Action), Voenizdat, Moscow, 1959. (A collection of articles by top leaders in the military and the political organs, stressing the changes in political indoctrination and controls after Zhukov's ouster.) *V pomoshch' ofitseram izuchaiushchim marksistsko-leninskuiu teoriiu* (An Aid to Officers Studying Marxist-Leninist Theory), Voenizdat, Moscow, 1959. (A collection of articles and some official statements by top leaders in the military and the political organs which stress the Party's supreme role in the military.) *Marksistsko-leninskaia ucheba ofitserov* (The Marxist-Leninist Training of Officers), Voenizdat, Moscow, 1957. (This collection of articles by a number of generals was published during the Zhukov era in the military. A comparison between the articles in this book and more recent publications on the same subject shows the Zhukov influence: in the 1957 volume, great stress was placed on the fact that political education should be an integral part of military life, i.e., that ideology should serve the military rather than vice versa.) For a longer list of pamphlets and other publications pertinent to this subject, see the Bibliography at the end of this volume.

The objectives behind these functions are to promote a sense of loyalty and self-sacrifice among military personnel; to uncover undesirable trends and have the means to deal with them; to guide activities into desired directions; and to keep the military establishment open to constant Party scrutiny.

1. Indoctrination

The political organs' most pervasive function is that of indoctrination, through which the Party tries to mold the new Soviet man and imbue him with a *Weltanschauung* favorable to the Party's interests and policies. Thus, the political organs are instructed

> . . . to explain thoroughly the advantages of the Soviet society and state system over the capitalistic system; to indicate the successes in building communism in our country . . . and to inculcate in soldiers a love for their motherland and an indestructible faith in the ultimate victory of communism in the whole world.[32]

A large portion of the daily activities of the Soviet officer and soldier is taken up by repetition of the little understood Marxist-Leninist litany, and the military press does everything possible to add to political indoctrination. Periodicals and dailies repeat sterile formulas *ad infinitum*, and countless handbooks and textbooks add to this verbiage. Though the military consumer of this constant diet of political rhetoric may be numbed into a state of stupor, the Party leadership believes in the method as a way of realizing Makarenko's ideas on communist education,[33] a belief that is reinforced by its reliance on Pavlov's theory of human behavior.

[32] *Partiino-politicheskaia rabota*, p. 53. Mikhail Kalinin, one of the main ideologues of the military, has defined the process of molding the new Soviet man as "instilling a definite world outlook, a system of morality and rules of human intercourse, fashioning specific traits of character, will, habits, and tastes." Cited in Louis Nemzer, "Civil-Military Relations in the USSR," unpublished manuscript, p. 147.

[33] In Makarenko's system of communist education, the individual must be made to feel that he has no alternative to fulfilling the role assigned to him; he must be placed under rigorous controls which sharply limit his capacity to make unapproved judgments. Consequently, Makarenko advocates imposing the strictest possible controls over activities, human relationships, and expressed attitudes. See Nemzer, p. 172. See also Colonel G. D. Lukov, Candidate of Pedagogical Sciences, *Vospitanie voli u sovetskikh voinov* (Training the Will of Soviet Soldiers), Voenizdat, Moscow, 1961; Lieutenant Colonel M. I. D'iachenko, Candidate of Pedagogical Sciences, *Individual'nyi podkhod v vospitanii voinov* (The Individual Approach in the Training of Soldiers), Voenizdat, Moscow, 1962; Colonel M. P. Korobeinikov, Candidate of Pedagogical Sciences, *Serzhantu o psikhologii* (To the Sergeant Regarding Psychology), Voenizdat, Moscow, 1962; *Kommunisticheskaia moral' i*

Many Party functionaries recognize the sterility of the jargon used in indoctrination and demand radical improvement of methods, but the routine approach thus far has prevailed. Despite its anaesthetizing effects, it would be a mistake to minimize the usefulness of this kind of indoctrination. The information available to the Soviet citizen is at best sketchy and distorted, and this is especially true of the closed community of the military. In the absence of other evidence and better knowledge, the bland diet of ideological, political, and social information becomes the only basis for dealing with the distant and the abstract.[34] Only with respect to domestic problems can the soldier use his own experience in a proper evaluation of the facts and the ideas that are fed him by the propagandists.

In the final analysis, indoctrination succeeds in a number of ways: It describes to the soldier the face of his enemy, making it credible through constant repetition and by denying him other sources of reference; it reminds him constantly of his duty; and it generates in him a willingness to fight and suffer for the goals established and rationalized by the Party.[35]

2. Kritika/samokritika

The custom of "criticism and self-criticism" has been raised to the level of an ethical imperative of communism. Essentially, it is a

---

voinskii dolg (Communist Morality and the Soldier's Duty), Voenizdat, Moscow, 1960; Colonel P. Kashirin, Candidate of Philosophical Sciences, *Rol' moral'nogo faktora v sovremennykh voinakh* (The Role of the Moral Factor in Modern Wars), Voenizdat, Moscow, 1953.

[34] In 1957, in an interview with *New York Times* correspondent James Reston, Khrushchev cynically answered Reston's question concerning the Soviet readers' lack of access to the foreign press: "Our people feel no need to read American newspapers. . . . Soviet people want to know the truth . . . which helps them to understand world events more clearly. As for your [American] papers, they print a lot of untruth and misinformation. Why should we force that on our readers?" *Pravda*, October 11, 1957.

[35] The vital importance to the Party of controlled information and indoctrination is reflected in the following statements of Party leaders: ". . . the press is our main ideological weapon. . . . Just as an army cannot fight without weapons, so the Party cannot successfully carry out its ideological work without such a sharp and militant weapon as the press." (N. S. Khrushchev, "Za tesnuiu sviaz' literatury i iskusstva s zhizn'iu naroda" [For a Close Tie of Literature and Art with the Life of the People], *Kommunist*, No. 12, 1957, p. 23.) "The periodical and non-periodical press . . . must be entirely subordinated to the Central Committee of the Party." (Lenin, "Conditions of Affiliation to the Communist International," *Selected Works*, International Publishers, New York, 1943, Vol. 1, p. 204.) "The role of a paper is not confined solely to the spreading of ideas, to political education. . . . A paper is not merely a collective propagandist and collective agitator. It is also a collective organizer." (Lenin, "Where To Begin," *Selected Works*, Lawrence & Wishart, Ltd., London, 1936, Vol. 2, p. 21.)

method by which Party members confess their sins against the Party and demand that their comrades do the same. This ritual is usually performed at Party meetings, where rank, position, and seniority are relatively unimportant, and all participants, especially among the younger Party members, are encouraged to criticize publicly any action of those present which does not meet the standards or interests of the Party.

Introduced in the early Bolshevik days, the *kritika/samokritika* method has been an extremely useful instrument and channel of information, which thrives on personal jealousies and animosities within the units. The Party never ceases to exhort its members, high and low, to avail themselves of this device at Party meetings, and insists that the proceedings of such meetings be recorded in detail. Inevitably, higher military commanders resent this intrusion by lower-ranking members of their commands into their professional and private activities, yet the Party, acknowledging this resentment and citing examples of it, constantly urges its members not to let it intimidate them and deter them from criticizing their peers and superiors.[36] In support of this effort, the military press reports the cases of officers who have threatened or even punished subordinates after being criticized by them at Party meetings in their units, and who, in turn, have been punished, demoted, or dismissed.[37]

The *kritika/samokritika* method is a self-policing device built into the military units. From the Party's point of view, it operates best

[36] During the period of tensions between the commanding personnel and the political organs, in the late 1920's and early 1930's, Stalin continually exhorted the military to use *kritika/samokritika*. (*KPSS o Vooruzhennykh Silakh Sovetskogo Soiuza: sbornik dokumentov, 1917-1958* [The CPSU on the Armed Forces of the Soviet Union: A Collection of Documents, 1917-1958], Gosizdat politicheskoi literatury, Moscow, 1958, pp. 309-311.) By contrast, Zhukov was accused, after his ouster, of having fostered negative attitudes toward *kritika/samokritika*. (Marshal Golikov, speech at the Twenty-second Party Congress, in *XXII s"ezd Kommunisticheskoi partii Sovetskogo Soiuza: stenograficheskii otchet* [The Twenty-second Congress of the CPSU: Stenographic Record], Gospolitizdat, Moscow, 1962, Vol. 3, p. 67.) Marshal Malinovskii reaffirmed the need to use the *kritika/samokritika* weapon rigorously to cleanse the military, pointing out that Stalin, though he had committed various offenses, had taught the military that one useful lesson. (*Resheniia oktiabr'skogo Plenuma*, pp. 17-18; *Partiinaia organizatsiia chasti, korablia*, pp. 5-6.) See also Marshal Grechko, *K novomu pod"emu*, p. 27. In the aftermath of the Cuban missile debacle, which seems to have generated much tension between Party and military, the military press also carried many articles urging more intensive use of *kritika/samokritika*.

[37] See Appendix F for the account of a case in which a general who had been subjected to public criticism by members of his own unit attempted to punish the critics, and was in turn punished by the Party organs for trying to do so.

when it is most needed, that is to say, during periods of stress, when personal tensions are greatest and when activities that could be considered "anti-Party" cause resentment or jealousy among unit members who do not participate in them.

3. *Generating Synthetic Enthusiasm*

Another major function of the Party-political organs in the military is to create and maintain an atmosphere of constant activity, productive enthusiasm, competition, and self-sacrificing endeavor. From the military point of view, this frenetic, goal-setting activity is destructive, for it produces large amounts of official documents, regulations, reports, red tape, and statistics which not only burden the commanding personnel inordinately but also result in frequent meaningless inspection visits from higher staffs and political organs. However, this system has the merit of providing the top-level military and political administrations with a statistical picture (though not necessarily a realistic one) of activities in the lower units, and it also offers one of the few incentives for extra activities to individual soldiers and to units as a whole.[38]

4. *Artificial Tension and Insecurity*

One of the Party's fears, connected with its apprehensions about military elitism, caste tendencies, and Bonapartism, is the shielding of the officers' life and activities from Party scrutiny. To prevent such "closure," the Party demands that most intramilitary affairs be conducted by collective action, which presumably serves to inhibit elitist trends. On the assumption that elitism thrives on exclusion, most activities in military units are conducted on the principle of inclusion, and implementing the "collective will" (a crosscut of the unit's membership from all ranks) becomes the normal *modus ope-*

[38] *Krasnaia zvezda* of November 14, 1962, carried an article sharply attacking the so-called "dead souls" problem, i.e., the fact that in many units, though they carry on their rolls full complements of officers and men, a large number of the personnel spend much of their time on activities which have little to do with the program of the unit. These activities involve "extra" duties (presumably political education and indoctrination), but also plain paper-shuffling and red tape: "Instead of useful work aimed at giving practical assistance to the commanders of the units . . . staff officers keep themselves busy by collecting various reports, keeping battalion and company commanders away from their duties." The author of the article, a Colonel Taratorin, sarcastically described the poor state of affairs of one unit he had visited. During an eight-month period, the unit had to respond to 1,598 documents, reports, etc., sent down from headquarters, and these 1,598 original documents grew to 6,363 when all enclosures and attachments were added.

randi in matters of ethics, honor, criticism, goal-setting, and discipline.

One of the Party's objectives in its control of the military is to keep officers and men in a permanent state of flux. Thus, for example, it adds to the insecurity of the officer by keeping him guessing about his personnel "profile." Since the political organs' assessment of his conduct is of vital importance at promotion time, the officer becomes liable to manipulation by the Political Section of his unit, to being played off against other officers, and to being used as an informer and in other clandestine functions.

Similarly exploited is the fear that many officers have of being demobilized, or transferred to the reserves, prior to the end of their normal tour of duty, with the implied risk of not being eligible for optimum pension or retirement benefits, and the bleak prospect of a greatly reduced economic and social status "on the outside."[39]

The political organs and Party and Komsomol functionaries also see to it that officers and men are kept constantly busy during duty hours and frequently in their free time as well. Thus, they take an active part in planning a large variety of educational, social, and cultural activities in which the military personnel is encouraged to participate. This is an effective way of keeping the military under surveillance at all times, and of channeling their activities into directions that are desirable to the Party and leave room for very little individual initiative.

In short, the network of controls that the Party maintains within the military so as to prevent its becoming a traditional elitist body invades every aspect of the professional and private life of officer and soldier. Inevitably, however, a system that keeps the military in a condition of insecurity and suspicion has its corrosive effects, which the Party leadership attempts to counteract with hypocritical assertions of the military commander's supreme authority in his unit on most matters. Moreover, the control network itself can become a danger to the regime, and the Party, in recognition of this threat, creates enough tension and rivalry among the various control links to make sure that the controller also is controlled, and that there will be no coalescence of special interests and no collusion between con-

[39] After the announcement of the reduction of the Soviet army which was to release 250,000 officers beginning in January 1960, there appeared numerous articles dealing with the lot of the retired, demobilized, or transferred officers. Most of these were purely propagandistic, but some were strikingly candid. See *Literaturnaia gazeta*, May 24, 1960; *Pravda*, January 20, 1960, and January 19, 1961; Loboda, *Komandnye kadry*, p. 103.

trolled and controller. Party leaders no doubt remember those critical periods of conflict between Party and military when the political control network failed to act in the best interests of the Party. Thus, in the 1920's, the heads of the MPA, Smilga and Antonov-Ovseenko, supported Trotsky in his antimilitaristic activities, proposing at one time the curbing of the political organs' authority and function. During the 1937 purges of the military, the head of MPA, Gamarnik, committed suicide, since presumably he had supported the military in its struggle with Stalin. Between 1953 and 1957, Zheltov, who then was head of MPA, took a rather ambivalent stand in the various Party-military conflicts of that period. And his successor, Marshal Golikov, administered the organization in a manner that may have been too moderate for Khrushchev, who in 1962 replaced him with the much more vigorous and pro-Party Epishev.

Part Two

Institutional Dialogues: The Conflicts of Interests, Objectives, and Values

Having introduced the reader to the historical, organizational, and ideological factors that enter into the relations between Party and military in the Soviet Union, we can now go on to examine the range of issues and events that have shaped these relations in the past decade.

Despite their many common objectives, the Party and the military disagree on such crucial issues as (a) the extent of the officers' professional freedom, (b) the military's historical role in the Soviet state, and (c) the degree of the military's institutional autonomy. These sources of conflict are due, on the one hand, to the Party's drive to integrate the military establishment into the monolithic socialist society led by the communist elite, and, on the other hand, to the military's strong resistance to any pressures aimed at interference with its institutional prerogatives, its sense of professional identity, and its primary loyalties. The professional officers, therefore, oppose the Party's insistence on ubiquitous controls within the armed forces, which they regard as an encroachment on their professional freedom; they strongly resent the Party's past efforts to reduce their contribution to victory over foreign aggressors to but one of many equivalent contributions by a large number of social institutions; and they resist the various ways in which the Party seeks to undermine the military's institutional autonomy. Denying that it breeds "elitism," as the Party *apparat* alleges, they argue that such autonomy is essential to a high level of performance. The political leaders, for their part, in an effort to forestall the development of a closed, autonomous military community, have tried to create special elite groups within the higher levels of the officer corps whose careers are closely bound to their own and whom they look to as their "beachhead" in the High Command.

In ordering his research materials and findings, the author has chosen to present the recurrent conflicts between the main protagonists—the Party and the military—not by historical period but in the context of the main issues and through discussions of the protagonists' differing value systems and objectives. Although each of the next three chapters deals with a particular conflict between the Party and the military and with the dialogue of the two institutions on that issue, the narrative approach used within the chapter will enable the reader to recognize, in the history of the most recent decade, the continuation of cyclical tensions and conflicts that were described at length in Chapter III. The events of the next three

chapters lend themselves to the following breakdown by two major cycles:

1953 to 1958	Early 1953:	A mounting crisis, interrupted by Stalin's death
	1953-1955:	A period of transition, with a relatively weak Party strongly dependent on the military
	1955-1957:	Gathering tensions between Party and military, with the Party still internally divided
	1957-1958:	Resolution of conflict; Zhukov ousted
1958 to 1964	1958-1960:	Relative tranquillity in Party-military relations
	1960-1961:	Gathering tensions between Khrushchev and some military circles
	1961-1962:	Worsening of Party-military relations, culminating in a contained crisis as a result of the Cuban fiasco in October 1962
	1963-1964:	Resolution of conflict through avoidance of open break between Khrushchev and the military and by the establishment of a *modus vivendi*, followed by the ouster of Khrushchev

V · The Dialogue on Professional Autonomy: Military Independence vs. Political Integration

A · *THE GENERAL PROBLEM*

A remarkable feature of the communist state is the ruthless subordination of the interests and objectives of all social institutions to those of the Communist Party. Ironically, therefore, in a system that has so many characteristics of the authoritarian garrison state, the instruments of violence play a relatively minor role, for they must submit to the bureaucratic elite in the Party hierarchy, whose avowed aim is the integration of all social institutions into a homogeneous, monolithic whole. However, the military's institutional interests, objectives, and values, and the range of external factors and circumstances supporting them, tend to favor its resistance to the total subordination desired by the Party elite. In the following, we shall examine more closely this essential incompatibility between the Party's ideal model of the fully integrated military establishment, and the military's continuous efforts to free itself from the subordinate role that this demands and from the oppressive controls and intrusions of the Party. Although the relations between Party and military are analyzed here from the point of view of their antagonisms, the two protagonists do, of course, have a large number of mutually complementary objectives and common interests. Yet, despite these strong ties, the relationship between the two most powerful institutions in the Soviet state is often strained and at times hostile, and it occasionally borders on the critical.[1]

The present chapter examines the tensions and conflicts that have afflicted the relations between the military and the Party (viewed here as distinct institutional entities) during the post-Stalin period, particularly those conflicts arising from the military's efforts to assert its claim to professional autonomy and the Party's constant attempts to deprive the military of the full exercise of that prerogative. The two main issues under analysis are (1) the Party's efforts to impose very rigid political controls at all levels of the military hierarchy and the military's strong resistance to such pressures, and (2) the Party's usurpation of the function of military planner and strategic innovator and the military's opposition to measures which it regards as in-

[1] See Chapter III, where these historical incompatibilities are systematically analyzed through the thesis of a cyclic recurrence of conflicts between the two institutions.

jurious not only to its own institutional interests but also to the defensive capabilities of the country.

The conflicts described in this chapter are central to our understanding of the relation between Party and military, since they go back to deeply rooted sources of mistrust and antagonism. In seeking to politicize and control the officer corps, the Party is revealing its fears of the elitism that it believes will develop among a group of professionals who possess vast means of violence. It knows, moreover, that an officer corps allowed to become a closed institution could grow into a dangerous rival for power in the state. In an effort to break down the protective walls that the military seeks to erect, the Party divides and subdivides authority horizontally, vertically, and diagonally, hoping thereby to prevent the coalescence of power and authority at focal points; and it gathers the commanders together in collective bodies in which they are open to scrutiny and criticism. While controls and political indoctrination serve to prevent disloyalty in the military and to eliminate conditions that lead to elitism, the Party has still other concerns. Since the death of Stalin, and with the growing complexity of warfare, the military has sought to obtain a larger role in high-level planning and the formulation of strategic doctrine and military policy. The Party leadership, on the other hand, trying to prevent the military from gaining greater professional autonomy, has made major military decisions and launched innovations against overwhelming military opposition. While the military leaders' overt concern is about the possible harm to the defensive capabilities of the nation that may come of military policies created by civilians, their implicit fears center on the damage to the military's institutional interests that is inherent in the usurpation of their prerogatives by civilian amateurs. The Party elite and its spokesmen, on the other hand, regard military policy and the evolution of a strategic doctrine as the exclusive domain of the political decision-makers.[2]

The military's objection to excessive political controls and its opposition to the Party's invasion of the strategic-doctrinal domain are aspects of the central struggle for influence between the two institutions. At stake in this larger conflict are the military's professional autonomy and the Party's political hegemony. Although, objectively speaking, these are not mutually exclusive ends, the Party apparently

[2] For recent evidence of these antagonisms, see R. Kolkowicz, *Soviet Strategic Debates: An Important Recent Addendum*, The RAND Corporation, P-2936, July 1964.

sees them as such; as in zero-sum games, where any advantage of one adversary is at the expense of the other adversary, so the Party elite regards any increment in the military's prerogatives and authority as its own loss and therefore as a challenge.

B · THE MALENKOV INTERREGNUM: ISSUES UNDER DISPUTE

After the death of Stalin, the complex political power system, formerly held together by the dictator as if by a linchpin, became factionalized. Several men with diverse sources of political power entered into a tense, unstable coalition, a leadership which, from the the start, promised to be short-lived.

The spokesmen of four politically powerful institutions—the security organs, the Party, the governmental and managerial bureaucracy, and the military—maneuvered for position in the ensuing power struggles in the Party. The security organs suffered a debilitating blow with the fall of Beria.[3] Of the remaining three institutions, only the Party *apparat* and the bureaucracy, with Khrushchev and Malenkov as their respective spokesmen, publicly expressed political aspirations and claims to a political role.[4] As Khrushchev and Malenkov became locked in a tense competition for control of the Party, the military establishment suddenly found itself in a position of great advantage, as its vote and support could be decisive in this factional struggle. Thus, after long suppression under Stalin, the Soviet marshals and generals emerged into the political arena. Raised in the shadow of Stalin's dictatorship, they had been trained to stay out of the frequent cabals in the Party hierarchy. Now a strong institution that enjoyed certain prerogatives as well as public acclaim, the military was being wooed by the contending factions and stood to gain much from their struggles for domination of the Party. Given the contenders' delicately balanced relationship with one another, it seemed unlikely that they would voluntarily incur the animosity of the officer corps by publicly advocating policies

[3] For descriptions of the fall of Beria, see Robert Conquest, *Power and Policy in the USSR*, St. Martin's Press, New York, 1961, pp. 218-227, 440-447.

[4] For select historical renditions of and opinions on the events of that period, see Lazar Pistrak, *The Grand Tactician: Khrushchev's Rise to Power*, Frederick A. Praeger, Inc., New York, 1961; Leonard Schapiro, *The Communist Party of the Soviet Union*, Random House, New York, 1960, pp. 528-590; Myron Rush, *The Rise of Khrushchev*, Public Affairs Press, Washington, D. C., 1958; George Paloczi-Horvath, *Khrushchev: The Making of a Dictator*, Little, Brown and Company, Boston, 1960; and Conquest, *Power and Policy*.

that ran counter to the military's interests. Yet that is precisely what happened: Malenkov, by subordinating the military's institutional demands to other social and political priorities, succeeded in angering the officers, who thereupon threw their support to the faction headed by Khrushchev and precipitated Malenkov's political demise.

The policies and other issues that caused conflicts between the military and Malenkov on one hand, and between Malenkov and Khrushchev on the other, are central to our understanding of the military establishment's institutional interests and the nature of the recurrent dissension between the civilian decision-makers in the Party and the professional officers. Essentially, such conflicts are engendered by the dilemma of the political leaders who, in the allocation of resources and social functions, must balance the demands of various institutions in such a way that external, internal, and ideological interests are reconciled amicably, or, if that proves impossible, must see to it that the slighted sector is mollified, and if need be coerced, to the point of acquiescence. While the Party leaders are in a good position to balance institutional demands from the various social sectors during periods of internal harmony, they cannot do so in times of intra-Party power struggles, when factions within the Party are seeking support from without. It is during such periods of political strife and intrigue, when the rigid authoritarian control structure has been disrupted by the sudden death or ouster of the dictator or some other internal crisis, that institutions and factions outside the Party ascend to political prominence, ephemeral though it may turn out to be, and by the weight of their support influence the outcome of the struggle for power.

In the most general terms, the institutional interests and objectives of the military establishment are determined by the nature of its function, which is to defend the country against aggression by the organized and rational use of means of violence. This social function naturally enjoys first priority whenever international tensions are high, when war threatens, and during an actual war. At times of international relaxation or détente, during periods of political and diplomatic passivity, or when socio-economic needs are paramount, the role of the military becomes secondary in importance. The officers of the Soviet Union are no doubt as patriotic as those of other national armies, and presumably they also welcome increased consumer production and social welfare. At the same time, their more urgent and immediate objectives center on the institutional interests of the military and, within that broad concern, on the individual officer's personal and professional interests. Consequently, the military must continually impress upon the political decision-makers the urgency of maintaining a large and efficient military establishment; of assigning the military a prominent, or at least a positive, social role; and of subordinating other social and economic objectives, and the allocations necessary to their achievement, to the paramount demands of national defense.

The institutional aims of the Soviet military as they emerged in the conflict with Malenkov were as follows:

(1) Maintenance of a high level of investment in heavy industry, since this sector of the economy is the foundation of the defense industry.

(2) Maintenance of a certain level of international political tension (by depicting the opponent as dangerous, aggressive, and unpredictable), sufficient to provide the rationale for large military budgets and allocations.

(3) Continuously high levels of the military budgets and expenditures necessary to an effective military establishment, as significant reductions of military budgets would destroy or cripple existing military programs and weaken established institutional empires.

The above may be described as generic institutional interests of large military establishments in all industrialized societies. There are, however, a number of other institutional objectives that derive from the particular socio-political context of the Soviet Union, and are likely to be found only in similar totalitarian societies. Their manifestation is part of the military's struggle against a political environment that seeks to deprive it of some of its "natural" attributes. In this sense, then, the following aims, peculiar to the Soviet military establishment in its opposition to the Party's pervasive attempts to control it politically and to usurp some central military functions, are but an extension of the traditional interests of all military institutions:

(1) The degree of professional authority and institutional independence that will enable military leaders to formulate strategic doctrine, conduct military planning at the highest level, and execute established military policy.

(2) Retention of commanding authority at all levels of the military hierarchy, instead of a system under which the political con-

trol organs bestow and withdraw such authority and thus wield a powerful instrument for keeping the commanders malleable and preventing elitism.

(3) Cultivation of a positive, even noble, image of the military as the defender of state and people; as the main contributor to past victories over external enemies; and as the bulwark of the Party in its pursuit of foreign policy.

Most of these military objectives were frustrated by Stalin, who suppressed such institutional and professional aspirations partly by the employment of the terror machine and partly by placing himself at the center of all things and admitting no loyalties other than to himself. After his death, however, many of the interests and proclivities that had previously been denied began to assert themselves. The military, held in check throughout the decades of Stalinist rule, flexed its muscles and tested the limits of its institutional freedom. In view of the division within Party ranks, the time seemed opportune for such a test. In the twenty-two months between March 1953 and January 1955, the military opposed those Party leaders who advocated policies that not only ran counter to the hopes of the military kindled by Stalin's death but, if carried out, would have deeply undermined those traditional institutional interests that even Stalin felt compelled to respect. By throwing their support to the faction in the Party that publicly supported their interests, the military revealed, for the first time in decades, that it could be a crucial factor in the Soviet state in times of internal division and collective rule.

1. Heavy vs. Consumer Industry

After the removal of Beria from the ranks of would-be successors to Stalin, the collective leadership that combined the various factions in the Party in an uneasy coalition began to define a number of policies designed to undo the Stalinist heritage and move the Soviet Union in new directions. Of cardinal importance in this effort was the plan for a radical change in Soviet economic planning and allocations, based on a new assessment of the international political situation and of domestic economic and social needs and priorities. In August 1953 Premier Malenkov addressed the Supreme Soviet in a speech whose central and potentially most controversial proposal concerned this shift in the investment and allocation policy:

> . . . our main task—ensuring further improvement in the material well-being of the workers, collective farmers, intelligentsia, all the Soviet people . . .
> . . . Today, on the basis of the progress we have made in the development of heavy industry, we have all the necessary conditions for bringing about a sharp rise in production of consumer goods. . . . The Government and the Central Committee of the Party consider it necessary to increase significantly the investment of resources . . . and to set things right in the direction of a significant increase in the program for the production of consumer goods.[5]

The military retorted by insisting on the continued importance of heavy industry. Its views appeared in the October issue of *Voennaia mysl'*, the authoritative publication of the General Staff:

> Heavy industry is the foundation of foundations of our socialist economy. Without heavy industry it is not possible to ensure the further growth of light industry and the productive forces of agriculture, and the furthering of the defense capabilities of the Soviet state.[6]

But for the time being, while it registered these traditional views on the priority of heavy industry, the military refrained from pressing its opposition more strongly. Not until late 1954 did its interests converge with those of the Khrushchev faction and the issue of heavy versus light industry erupt once again in public discussions.

The opening shot in the second round against the Malenkov faction and the proponents of a shift in emphasis away from heavy industry was fired by Khrushchev, in a speech delivered on December 7 but withheld from publication until December 28:

> . . . Only on the basis of further development of heavy industry will we be able successfully to promote all branches of the national economy, steadily raise the well-being of the people, and ensure the inviolability of the frontiers of the Soviet Union. That is the main thing. *The further development of heavy industry*. . . .[7]

In the weeks following, the conflict between the two factions in the Party—one centered around Khrushchev, who was aligning himself with the views of the military, and the other around Malenkov, who

[5] *Pravda*, August 9, 1953.
[6] Colonel I. N. Nenakhov, *Voennaia mysl'*, No. 10, October 1953, p. 8.
[7] *Pravda*, December 28, 1954. (Italics added.)

sought to modernize and balance the budgetary allocations and investment policies—continued behind the scenes. The sharp divergence of views became evident in the disparate editorials that appeared on the same day, December 21, in *Pravda* and *Izvestiia*, one supporting Khrushchev's line and the other Malenkov's. The struggle was resolved at the meeting of the Central Committee (January 25-31, 1955), where the decision was made to relieve Malenkov of his duties as Premier.[8] Official announcement of this decision was made on February 8, several days after a hastily convened Supreme Soviet had approved the new budget, which clearly emphasized the primacy of heavy industry.[9]

The chorus of opinion from Party and military in stressing the importance of heavy industry represented a clear and impressive victory for the military. Khrushchev's caustic criticism of Malenkov,[10] supported by Shepilov's blunt condemnation of "calico industrialization,"[11] was echoed by the major military figures, who forcefully articulated the interests of their establishment.[12]

[8] The military actively promoted its views in the days prior to the Central Committee's decision to oust Malenkov. On January 15, 1955, about a week before the CC decision, *Krasnaia zvezda*, under the heading "Heavy Industry—Foundation of the Might of the Soviet State," argued that "the material basis of the defense capability of the Soviet state, the integrity of its borders, was and is heavy industry."

[9] Malenkov gave as reasons for his "resignation" his inexperience in affairs of government and his responsibility for the unsatisfactory state of agriculture. By forcing Malenkov to admit failure in managing the agricultural sector, Khrushchev exacted his pound of flesh, since Malenkov had in the past criticized and even ridiculed Khrushchev's agricultural schemes and proposals. See Victor Frank, "The Unsolved Crisis," *Bulletin of the Institute for the Study of the History and Culture of the USSR*, Vol. 2, No. 2, February 1955, pp. 3-9.

[10] Khrushchev said in an obvious reference to Malenkov: "Such would-be theoreticians allege that at a certain stage of socialist construction the development of heavy industry ceases to be the central task, and that light industry can and must outstrip all other branches of industry. These speculations are erroneous. . . ." Cited in Frank, "The Unsolved Crisis."

[11] *Pravda*, January 24, 1955.

[12] The statements of the military leaders all repeated or elaborated on the theme that "heavy industry is the foundation of the indestructible defense capabilities of the country." Cf. Marshal Bulganin, *Pravda*, February 10 and February 19, 1955; Marshal I. S. Konev, *Pravda*, February 23, 1955 ("The January Plenum . . . stressed that the general line of the Party in the economic sphere, which foresees the development of heavy industry by every conceivable means, will be firmly continued"); Marshal Zhukov, Order of the Day, February 23, 1955, and also his speech to the Twentieth Party Congress in which he said, "The growing potentialities of the Soviet economy, including above all the major achievements of heavy industry, have permitted us to rearm our army, air forces, and navy with first-class military matériel"; Marshal Sokolovskii, *Izvestiia*, February 23, 1955; and General of the Army V. Kurasov, Radio Moscow, February 21, 1955.

2. The Assessment of International Tension

In August 1953, when introducing his program, Malenkov struck a tone of reasonableness and moderation with reference to international affairs, presumably to provide the rationale for the proposed curtailment of military allocations:

> The international situation at present is characterized first and foremost by the great successes achieved by the Soviet Union and the Chinese People's Republic . . . in the struggle to ease international tension, strengthen peace, and prevent war.[13]

The following spring, Malenkov introduced another aspect of this moderate and nondogmatic view of international relations by stating that a thermonuclear war would result in a "new world slaughter . . . [and] would mean the destruction of world civilization."[14] This new trend of thought, which on the one hand asserted that international tension had eased and on the other hand presented future war as a futile exercise since it would destroy all combatants, constituted a sharp departure from traditional Soviet attitudes on war and also deeply undermined the views and interests of the military establishment. By stressing the deterrent power of nuclear weapons in a world aiming toward détente, Malenkov was denying the *raison d'être* of huge conventional arms and the need for large military budgets. (The military position on these problems had been summed up by the author of an article in *Voennaia mysl'*, in October 1953, who, after stating that the Soviet Union had both atomic and hydrogen weapons, maintained that possession of such weapons by both sides did not guarantee peace.)

Malenkov's views on the effectiveness of mutual deterrence, in which he was supported by Mikoyan, were undoubtedly strongly condemned not only by the military but within the Party. At any rate, in April 1954 Malenkov reversed himself and returned to the orthodox line, with the statement that a new world war would lead to the

[13] *Pravda*, August 9, 1953.

[14] *Pravda*, March 13, 1954. Mikoyan at the time maintained similar views, which he expressed in a speech delivered on the same day. However, the salient remarks were deleted from the official text published the following day in the central press. They were: "The danger of war was to a great extent lessened in connection with the fact that we now have not only atomic but also hydrogen weapons [which] in the hands of the Soviet Union are a means for checking the aggressors. . . ." (*Izvestiia*, March 12, 1954.) *Kommunist* (Erevan), March 12, 1954, carried the full text; *Pravda*, March 12, 1954, contained the abbreviated version.

"collapse of the whole capitalist system."[15] As time went on, the military was to become more and more outspoken in its rejection of the heretical idea of détente and mutual deterrence, and both military and political spokesmen expressed strong opinions on that score after the ouster of Malenkov.[16] The sentiment of the military was summed up finally by Bulganin, then Minister of Defense, who said in late December of 1955: "It is incorrect to assert that, inasmuch as both East and West possess hydrogen weapons, the possibility of a thermonuclear war is automatically excluded. Assertions of this kind can in fact lull the vigilance of peoples. . . ."[17]

With Malenkov out of office, Party leaders went on record as supporting the orthodox line, which coincided with that of the military. Molotov said that, in the event of a new world war, "what will perish will not be world civilization . . . but the decaying [capitalist] social system with its imperialist core soaked in blood. . . ."[18] And the Party's theoretical organ, *Kommunist*, gave this as the official opinion: "No matter how severe the consequences of atomic war, they cannot be identified with the fall of world civilization."[19]

3. *Budgetary Allocations*

The direction of the Malenkov regime, so unsatisfactory from the military's point of view, became clear with the announcement of the 1953 budget, which was approved late in August 1953. Whereas the 1952 budget had provided for 113.8 billion rubles in budgetary allocations and showed 108.6 billion rubles in actual expenditure, the 1953 budget reduced allocations to 110.2 billion and actual spending to 102.9 billion. The 1954 budget showed an even sharper decline

[15] Malenkov, *Pravda*, April 27, 1954. Mikoyan also was forced to retract his original views. He did so in the same issue of *Pravda* which carried Malenkov's reversal.

[16] To the military, Malenkov's original assertions about the easing of international tension and reliance on nuclear deterrents were most disturbing. Already in May 1954, Marshals Malinovskii, Vasilevskii, and Timoshenko forcefully set forth the opposite military views. When Deputy Premier Saburov, Malenkov's associate, pointedly played down the interests and the role of the defense establishment in a speech of November 6, 1954, the military took the offensive the following day. Marshal Timoshenko demanded greater concern with the improvement of the armed forces, because "the easing of international tension should not be overestimated." (Radio Minsk, November 7, 1954.) Marshal Bulganin closely echoed the same line. (*Pravda*, November 8, 1954.)

[17] Interview with Charles E. Shutt, head of the Washington Bureau of Telenews Agency, *The New York Times* and *Pravda* of January 1, 1956. See also "Observer" in *Pravda*, November 9, 1955, for the military's viewpoint.

[18] Molotov, *Pravda*, February 9, 1955.

[19] *Kommunist*, No. 4, April 1955, pp. 16-17.

in allocations for defense (from the previous 110.2 to 100.3 billion rubles).[20]

In addition to his consistent stress on the need to shift investments from heavy to light industry, and his cuts in the defense budgets, Malenkov alarmed the military by using funds from the state reserves to speed up the consumer program, although these reserves are intended to be kept for emergencies, and especially against the eventuality of war. It is uncertain how far he went toward depleting them, but after Malenkov's ouster the military was assured that the state reserves would be replenished. Bulganin, who made that statement, added:

> Reserves comprise our might and strengthen the defense capability of our country. It would therefore be an unforgivable mistake to slacken our attention to this important cause, or to yield to the temptation to solve individual current problems at the expense of the state reserves.[21]

While the Party leaders were secretly debating budgetary allocations for 1955, the military continued to take a hard line and to advocate a policy less geared to détente. This coincided with the beginning of the Khrushchev faction's open espousal of the views held by the military. The fate of Malenkov was thus sealed, since his sole remaining source of support now was the bureaucracy, against a united opposition representing the crucial Party machinery and the military.

C · THE REIGN OF MARSHAL ZHUKOV: RETURN TO PROFESSIONALISM

Having aligned themselves with the victorious Party faction that fought their own opponent, Malenkov, the military leaders were allowed to taste the fruits of victory upon the ouster of the Premier. The rapidity of the events and the extent of the measures that met the interests of the military were remarkable.

Most notable among the events was the nomination of Marshal Zhukov as Minister of Defense, the day after Malenkov formally "resigned" from the government. Marshal Bulganin, a champion of military interests despite the fact that he was a "political" general, became Premier. On March 11, in a long-overdue promotion, the

[20] Cited in R. L. Garthoff, *The Role of the Military in Recent Soviet Politics*, The RAND Corporation, RM-1638, March 1956, p. 9.

[21] Marshal Bulganin, *Izvestiia*, February 10, 1955.

Supreme Soviet elevated eleven generals to the rank of marshal.[22] The military press began to publish articles that stressed the military's need for greater command and professional authority. Prominent military leaders wrote commemorative pieces on the anniversary of the Red Army, expressing themselves in a self-confidently military tone, without the customary obsequiousness toward the Party leadership. Indeed, the festivities and events associated with the Day of the Soviet Army and Navy (February 23, 1955) and the tenth anniversary of the victory over Germany (May 8, 1955) reflected the renascent self-assertion of the military. Leading articles in the central newspapers, written by prominent military men, were self-congratulatory and lacking in deference to Stalin and the other Party leaders.[23] During the ceremonies at the Central Theater of the Soviet Army in Moscow, there was a significant departure from the tradition of electing the entire Politburo to the honorary Presidium *in absentia*: in 1955, instead, the Presidium consisted of the head of government, the head of the Party, the Minister of Defense, and a number of military officers and civilian heroes. Zhukov's title, "Marshal," was capitalized, while the other marshals were cited with lower-case initials. (Western analysts have at times interpreted such orthographical anomalies as presaging the rising power of the men thus singled out.)[24] Finally, articles by Sokolovskii[25] and Konev,[26] as well as Zhukov's interview with three American journalists,[27] placed great stress on the military commanders, their abilities, and their crucial

[22] It is of interest to note that in recent years the military has tended to gain major promotions after important changes in Party leadership. (a) After the arrest of Beria, ten prominent military leaders received promotions in mid-1953: Kuznetsov was restored to his former rank of Admiral of the Fleet; Zhigarev rose to Marshal of Aviation; Colonel General Nedelin became Marshal of Artillery; and six members of the Stalingrad Group (Biriuzov, Moskalenko, Grechko, Krylov, Popov, and Malinin) became Generals of the Army, while one (Vice-Admiral Fokin) rose to Admiral—their first substantial reward for having aligned themselves with Khrushchev. (b) There were further promotions on March 11, 1955. (c) Late in the summer of 1955, five military officers (Luchinskii, Fediuninskii, Gorbatov, Zakharov, and Zhadov) rose to the rank of General of the Army.

[23] See footnote 12 above; also, among many others, Marshal Vasilevskii, *Izvestiia*, May 8, 1955; Marshal Sokolovskii, *Krasnaia zvezda*, May 8, 1955; Admiral Kuznetsov, *Sovetskii flot*, May 8, 1955; Marshal Bagramian, *Oktiabr'*, No. 5, May 1955; Marshal Chuikov, *Pravda Ukrainy*, May 9, 1955; Marshal Moskalenko, *Slaviane*, No. 5, May 1955; Marshal Biriuzov, *Molodoi Kommunist*, No. 5, May 1955.

[24] See Rush, *The Rise of Khrushchev*.

[25] *Izvestiia*, February 23, 1955.

[26] *Pravda*, February 23, 1955.

[27] *Neue Zeit*, No. 8, February 19, 1955; *Pravda*, February 13, 1955. The interview took place on February 7.

role in the winning of the war. In sum, the homage paid to the army and its leaders on the occasion of the two anniversary celebrations were clearly indicative of the growing importance of the military in internal Soviet politics.

Having prevailed in its views on the primacy of heavy industry, its advocacy of high defense allocations, and its assessment of the international situation, the military went on to press its demands on the internal front. It now sought greater freedom to practice its profession unencumbered by excessive political controls; it asked for a freer hand in the shaping of military strategy and theory; and it tried to render the historical image of the military more positive through the unmasking of Stalinist legends and lies. The pressure used to attain these objectives, however, was to create strong opposition in the Party for a number of reasons. While the advocacy of heavy industry, high military budgets, and continued international tension had in the past led to division in the Party, it had not been a threat to the Party as a whole but only to some of the special interests of a single faction. After all, an efficient and effective defense establishment, even though achieved at the expense of the consumer's welfare, was a distinct asset. On the other hand, the military's opposition to Party scrutiny, its desire for extensive autonomy and an elitist officer corps, its suggestion that the Party make public admission of atrocities committed against officers, and its demands for participation in the shaping of new military doctrine (and for freedom to reject accepted orthodox thought)—these generated a growing fear that the military might become a powerful political rival and an institutional counterweight to the Party in the Soviet state. For the time being, however, the Party leadership had little choice but to tolerate the military's growing voice, in the hope of reasserting the Party's dominance at that point in the future when the ineffective collective leadership would have been replaced by a single, strong leader.

Under the firm and self-assured rule of Marshal Zhukov, the military establishment entered a new era in the Soviet state: old ideological-political shackles were found to be outmoded and abandoned; military officers raised issues that had been taboo in the past; the traditional deference to the Party gave way to professional pride and greater independence; and military leaders became public figures for the first time since the early 1930's.

Having gained in institutional stature, confidence, and strength, the military began to address itself to some sensitive problems, hoping to reverse the patronizing attitude toward the military characteristic of the Stalin period, and to emancipate itself from the confining embrace of the Party. These objectives were far removed from any conscious attempt to secure a direct political role in the state. But from the Party's point of view, though they fell short of outright Bonapartism, they tended in that direction, and the military leaders' aspiration to greater professional and institutional independence, notwithstanding their unswerving loyalty to the Party, was viewed by the Party *apparat* as a mounting challenge to the Party's hegemony.[28]

In trying to loosen the Party's hold on the armed forces, Marshal Zhukov and others struck out at the three main obstacles: (a) the Party's corrosive political controls, under which the commanders were forced to share authority with political officers and collective bodies in the units, (b) the *rigor mortis* hold of Stalinist military dogma and strategic doctrine, which was impeding urgently needed modernization, and (c) the Stalinist heritage in Soviet historiography and popular legend, which deflated the role of the military and assigned the credit for many victories and for military and political wisdom and foresight to the dead dictator and the Party.

The present chapter describes the military's efforts to remove, or at least reduce, the political control structure and to erase political dogma from military thought. (The attempt to establish the military's historical role will be treated separately.) It must be stressed that, while we are concerned with the divergent views of Party and military, the protagonists were not so clearly dichotomized. Party leader Khrushchev, having established close personal relations during the war with a number of ranking officers, the Stalingrad Group, manipulated their great dislike of Marshal Zhukov and their career ambitions to his own advantage and prevailed on them either to remain neutral in the growing conflict between the Party and the military's institutional interests or to lend him their public support. Gradually, this conflict came to express itself in a dialogue between the Zhukovites in the military, who sought greater independence for the officer corps and emancipation from the Party, and Party leaders and their supporters within the military, who challenged the Zhukovite heresies. This dialogue between two military factions, and its significance for the relationship of the military and the Party, is

[28] The nearly hysterical outbursts of anti-Bonapartist views in the wake of Zhukov's dismissal, in October 1957, reflect this pent-up frustration and fear which the Party *apparat* had to tolerate during the brief but remarkable rule of Marshal Zhukov in the Ministry of Defense.

described at length in a later chapter.[29] However, the eventual blurring of a single "military viewpoint" by the emergence of various factions does not in any way invalidate the purpose and the conclusions of the present chapter, which describes the clash of institutional interests between the Party and the military. The subsequent alignment of some officers with the Party leadership may be seen as a natural result of the Party's consistent policy of *divide et impera,* and its practice of exploiting the personal ambitions and passions of members of the military to the point where they prevail over institutional interests and professional loyalties.

1. The Issue of Strategic Doctrine

In February and March 1955, two prominent military officers, Marshals Sokolovskii and Rotmistrov, published articles denouncing the orthodox thesis of the originality of Soviet military theory and criticizing its isolation from military thought outside the Soviet Union.[30] Both authors rejected the Stalinist notion of the subordinate, "temporary" value of strategic surprise. They thought it useful to retain certain elements from bourgeois strategic writings that were adaptable to the Marxist-Leninist teachings.

The two articles were widely discussed within and without the Soviet Union, since they publicly challenged what had come to be regarded as a fundamental Soviet truth: Stalinist military science. To appreciate the significance of this, we must first realize the various purposes, functions, and objectives that "military science" has in Soviet political and military affairs. Under Stalin it became (a) a body of knowledge adding to the systematic and comprehensive understanding of the phenomena of war, i.e., a means toward studying war and arriving at firm proposals based on full understanding; (b) an extension of the scientific fetishism of Stalin and other Party *apparatchiks* into the domain of military theory and practice; and (c) an attempt to usurp the authority to define military doctrine and strategy as well as the measures necessary to their implementation by including military science in the amorphous area of "Marxism-Leninism," the body of dogma best interpreted by the head of the

[29] See Chapter VII, for details of the Stalingrad Group.

[30] Sokolovskii in *Izvestiia,* February 23, 1955; Rotmistrov in *Krasnaia zvezda,* March 24, 1955. Rotmistrov's article was nominally directed against two books on military strategy recently published by M. Taranchuk and V. Petrov, respectively. For an authoritative treatment of the evolution of Soviet strategic thought in the post-Stalinist years, see H. S. Dinerstein, *War and the Soviet Union,* Frederick A. Praeger, Inc., New York, 1959.

Party (that is, by Stalin) and, after him, by other civilian Party leaders.

This kind of military science finds very few adherents among responsible professional officers. It introduces burdensome, sterile formulas into military thought; it serves the Party leaders' narcissistic purposes; and its operational uses, in the three aspects listed above, place limits on the military's participation and influence in the development of military theory and policy.

Stalinist military science was marked by deterministic rigidity, formalistic tautology, and the pseudo-scientific apparatus characteristic of much Marxist-Leninist teaching. Stalin divided the main principles of military science into those that determine the course and outcome of war—the "permanently operating factors"—and those that have only secondary influence—the "temporary factors." Among the former were (a) the stability of the rear, (b) the morale of the army, (c) the quantity and quality of divisions, (d) the armament of the army, and (e) the organizing ability of the command personnel. Among the latter, Stalin listed specifically only the factor of strategic surprise.

The dictator's vanity and autocratic powers were such that the Soviet officer corps was forced to rely on these principles as the sole guide in the evolution of a military theory. Moreover, the military had to derive all its insights and lessons from the events of World War II. A recent Soviet assessment of the postwar Stalin period describes the growing contradiction between the technological revolution (which began to change radically not only weaponry and equipment but also the dynamics of future war) and the persistent conservatism in Soviet military thinking and planning:

> During these years, major changes took place in the organization of the Soviet army and in the weapons and the combat equipment supplied to it. . . . The development of Soviet military theory during this time was influenced negatively by the cult of personality. . . . Historical truth on the war was twisted to Stalin's advantage. He alone was credited with all military successes, and the role played by the generals was reduced to simple executive functions. At the same time, the failures in the war were written off as errors by the executors—commanders of fronts or armies. . . . Such apologetics led to dogmatization of the principle of the five permanently operating factors which supposedly determined the outcome of

the war. The doctrine of the factors was peddled as a first-rate theoretical discovery.[31]

The sterility of the Stalinist tenets might have troubled the military less had it not been for the fact that strategic surprise was not classified as a decisive factor in war. This view, which had served Stalin as a convenient rationalization of his mistakes early in the Russo-German war, was becoming a dangerous handicap to military planning and theory in the early and middle 1950's, when military leaders realized that, in the event of an all-out nuclear attack, the initial period of the war could well be decisive.

In addition to this particular point, the military began to oppose the intrusion of Marxist dogma into the vital fields of military art and science, and it also initiated steps that would enhance the military's role in the formulation of strategic doctrine and lessen that of the Party leadership. However, neither of the last two efforts became serious issues until the 1960's. During the Zhukov era, the military concentrated its criticism on the anachronistic view of strategic surprise as a "temporary" factor and went on to draw some startling conclusions from the new importance of surprise in a nuclear war. Marshal Rotmistrov, a strong champion of modernization with respect to the concept and the importance of strategic surprise, began by saying that "history has shown that skillful employment of surprise brings true success not only in battles and operations but also in war." He then extended this statement to its logical conclusion: If a surprise attack could determine the outcome of war, then it was crucial to avoid being surprised by the enemy by surprising him in a "preemptive" attack.[32]

2. *Search for a Positive Social Image*

In the mid-1950's, the military also sought to enhance its social role by asking that history be rewritten and by bringing pressure to bear

[31] Colonel I. Korotkov, "O razvitii sovetskoi voennoi teorii v poslevoennye gody" (The Development of Soviet Military Theory in Postwar Years), *Voenno-istoricheskii zhurnal*, No. 4, April 1964, pp. 39-50. For an analysis of this article and its greater relevance to Soviet strategic debates, see Kolkowicz, *Soviet Strategic Debates*. Still more recently, Marshal A. A. Grechko, the First Deputy Minister of Defense, has expressed the same views; cf. *Iadernyi vek i voina* (The Nuclear Age and War), Izdatel'stvo "Izvestiia," Moscow, 1964, pp. 3-12.

[32] "O roli vnezapnosti v sovremennoi voine" (On the Role of Surprise in Contemporary War), *Voennaia mysl'*, No. 2, February 1955, p. 14. For a comprehensive analysis of this problem, see R. L. Garthoff, *The Soviet Image of Future War*, Public Affairs Press, Washington, D.C., 1959, Chapter III.

on artists, writers, and other cultural groups to depict the military in the best possible light. These objectives became apparent at the All-Union Conference of the Union of Soviet Writers, which met in Moscow from May 27 to 31, 1955, for the purpose of improving the literary treatment of military subjects and creating a highly favorable image of the officer.

Three important articles, by Lieutenant General S. Shatilov, Aleksandr Kron, and Vladimir Rudnyi, appeared during the proceedings of the conference and set its tone. Shatilov criticized the "primitive, distorted, and incorrect" way in which the initial period of World War II had been portrayed in Soviet literature, and demanded a more truthful and realistic description of that period.[33] Kron complained that ". . . little has been written about officers and hardly anything about soldiers and sailors."[34] The most noteworthy of the articles was that by Rudnyi, who, with remarkable candor, instructed Soviet playwrights and other writers to create this idealized picture of the military professional, the commander:

> . . . it is necessary to show in what way he differs essentially from the people around him, who obey him without contradiction, not only because they are formally subordinated to him, but from deep inner respect. The high moral qualities of this man must be shown, his courage and bravery . . . as a commander, that is, in relation with his equals and the high command.[35]

In addition to these three articles, which stressed the need to improve the image of the officer, we should note a film script by K. Simonov published in the spring of 1955. Its significance lies in the fact that the author set a precedent by portraying Soviet prisoners of war in a positive manner, and not as traitors to their country, as they had previously appeared in literature and film. By his favorable presentation Simonov removed a further taint from the historical record of the Soviet army.[36]

3. *Professional Autonomy vs. Political Integration*

It would be useful to reiterate briefly the essential issues which converged in the sensitive problem of the military's opposition to political controls. First of all, we must recognize that, before 1955,

[33] *Literaturnaia gazeta*, May 28, 1955.

[34] *Ibid.*, June 2, 1955. [35] *Ibid.*

[36] K. Simonov, "Bessmertnyi garnizon" (The Undying Garrison), *Novyi mir*, No. 5, 1955.

the military at no time asked or even dared hope to see the elaborate control system completely abolished.[37] In view of the institutional power arrangements that the Party maintained within the Soviet state, the maximum practicable objectives were to confine the controllers to their official sphere of activity—political education and morale-building—and to keep them out of the professional orbit of the officers and personnel. Furthermore, the military wished to keep morale-building activities subordinate to military processes in order to prevent their interfering with strictly military duties. And, finally, the military sought to subordinate the political control organs within its units to the authority of the commanders. To be sure, at no time before the Zhukov regime in the Ministry of Defense did the military come close to attaining these objectives. For a short while prior to the purges of 1937, military commanders treated their political officers with open disdain and, owing to Stalin's feverish effort to build up his armed forces, managed to gain broad concessions of professional autonomy, but this brief period of self-assertion ended in the bloody purges. The military also gained some respite from oppressive political supervision during World War II, when Stalin, facing the possible collapse of his empire, wooed the officers with appeals to their patriotic and soldierly virtues. However, wartime concessions were rapidly rescinded at the end of hostilities, and the military was once again subjected to very rigid controls.

The period here under discussion was markedly different from previous years. Between 1955 and 1957, the military found itself relatively free of oppressive Party domination; the Party itself was suffering from internal power struggles and the destruction of cherished myths; the traditional "persuaders," the security organs, had been reduced in role and authority, leaving the military as the only massive means of coercion; and the Soviet Union was involved in a deadly political-military game with the West, which forced the Party to deal cautiously with the military, since an open rift could have had a disastrous effect on the Soviet Union's international standing. Furthermore, in the person of Marshal Zhukov the military had a spokesman who was the embodiment of military virtues and a

[37] The only evidence to the contrary is a demand made by General V. N. Gordov, Commander of the 33rd Army, who allegedly wrote to Stalin and Zhukov in June 1943, asking them to "liquidate the Military Council of the army as an organ that is unnecessary and one that does no good" and to transform the political departments into headquarters departments. See Iu. P. Petrov, *Partiinoe stroitel'stvo v Sovetskoi Armii i Flote, 1918-1961* (Party Development in the Soviet Army and Navy, 1918-1961), Voenizdat, Moscow, 1964, p. 377, fn. 3.

popular hero. Thus, the Party had no choice but to entrust the restoration of its powers to a future showdown, while the military pressed its demands and gradually brought about the withering of the political control machinery in the armed forces. The acquiescence of the Party is the more readily understood if one keeps in mind that the conflict was essentially one between two institutions serving the same state and wishing to avoid a collapse of the government or any other radical change in the internal *status quo.*

The changes introduced by Marshal Zhukov, during his tenure as Minister of Defense, in the formal and informal relations between the military establishment and the Party reflected the hopes and desires of the military professional for decades past. They also manifested Zhukov's professional bias in the emphasis on firm discipline, a sharp separation of ranks, and the tendency to relegate to the background the nonessential (from the professional military point of view) indoctrinational and political activities, if not to abandon them completely. The measures introduced by Zhukov would have sufficed by themselves to frighten the Party with the specter of Bonapartism. However, Zhukov went much further. He tried to sever the Central Committee's control links within the military hierarchy; he sharply abrogated the prerogatives of the MPA and its complex control elements in the military units; he greatly curtailed the military's contacts with local civilian and Party organs; he questioned the hallowed Bolshevik principle of *kritika/samokritika* when applied to commanders; he demanded the rehabilitation of purged military leaders and the punishment of participants in the purges; and he called for a thorough rewriting of history so as to restore the military to the honorable and prominent role that was its due.

a. The Attack on the Central Committee's Controls in the Military. As explained in an earlier chapter, the Central Committee of the CPSU has a number of control posts in the military establishment through which it obtains information, transmits policy and guidance, exerts pressure, and maintains the balance of tension and conflicting interests necessary to prevent collusion between various factions and groups. These links and plateaus of authority are: the Main Political Administration (MPA), which heads and administers the vast network of *zampolits*, political officers, and Party and Komsomol organizations at all levels of the military establishment, and the Military Councils, which are located at the Military District and other crucial command levels. The Military Council is a unique body, in which elements of military, political, and civilian authority maintain an uneasy balance. The Council deeply undermines the authority of the commander, as it is responsible mainly to the Central Committee and answers to the Minister of Defense only in an operational context, while the local Party organizations, whose secretaries normally participate in the activities of the military Party organizations, introduce an external, professionally uncommitted control element into the military community. After his ouster from the Ministry of Defense, Zhukov was accused of "trying in every possible way to isolate the Central Committee from the task of resolving the most important questions associated with the life of the army and navy" and of having sought to "bring the army and navy from under the control of the Communist Party and the Central Committee."[38] There is little doubt that some of the criticism reflected the actual state of affairs.

The MPA, the Party's crucial instrument of control, has always been a bone in the throat of the military. Together with its subdivisions it operates as a section of the Central Committee, responsible to the Presidium, and constitutes a vast authority structure within the military that interferes in the commanders' activities and is thus an impediment to many military objectives and interests. Zhukov began to whittle away at the authority of the MPA by limiting its operations to problems of political education:

> In September of 1955 the Party Central Committee defined the role of the Main Political Administration and the content of its activity in connection with the examination of the statute pertaining to the Ministry of Defense. The statute indicated that the Main Political Administration was the leading Party organ *on questions of Party-political work among troops.*[39]

This radical reduction of the MPA's scope of activity to morale-building and indoctrination was a major victory for Zhukov. In addition, the name of the institution was changed from "Main Political Administration of the Army and Navy" to the shorter "Main Political Administration," a mark of its closer integration with the

[38] See *XXII s"ezd Kommunisticheskoi partii Sovetskogo Soiuza: stenograficheskii otchet* (The Twenty-second Congress of the CPSU: Stenographic Record), Gospolitizdat, Moscow, 1962, Vol. 2, p. 120. See also Petrov, *Partiinoe stroitel'stvo,* pp. 462-463.

[39] Petrov, p. 454. (Italics added.)

Ministry of Defense.[40] Zhukov also added a control link between the MPA and its operational organs in the armed forces, thus weakening its authority still further.[41] And he allegedly "slighted the Main Political Administration and prohibited it from keeping the Party Central Committee informed about the state of activities of the troops."[42] A most telling indication of the low political weight of the MPA was the fact that the Twentieth Party Congress dropped MPA representatives from membership and candidacy in the Central Committee.[43]

To understand Zhukov's attack on the Military Councils, one must recall the history of these bodies and their role *vis-à-vis* the military. The Soviet army is territorially divided into a number of military districts, as well as Force Groups outside the borders of the USSR.[44] The navy is also divided into territorial entities. The commander of a military district has control over large numbers of troops and weapons as well as logistics and real estate, being in command of all forces stationed in his district except for the border guards, internal security

[40] Among the first measures undertaken by the Central Committee after Zhukov's ouster was to "make the title of the central political organ more precise and to rename it 'Main Political Administration of the Soviet Army and Navy.'" *Ibid.*, p. 469.

[41] This link was the individual Political Administration for each of the three branches of the service.

[42] Petrov, p. 462.

[43] While the Nineteenth Party Congress had had ten representatives from the MPA and security organs listed as members or candidates, the Twentieth Party Congress radically reduced their representation to three:

XIXth Party Congress	*XXth Party Congress*
Members	*Members*
Beria Col. Gen. Kruglov (MVD) Ignatev (MGB)	Serov (KGB) Dudorov (MVD)
Candidates	*Candidates*
Col. Gen. Goglidze Col. Gen. Kobulov Gen. Maslennikov Col. Gen. Serov Lt. Gen Riasnoi Col. Gen. Kuznetsov (F.F.) (MPA) Adm. Zakharov (MPA)	Lunev (MVD)

Significantly, the new head of the MPA, Zheltov, was not included in the Central Committee. General Zheltov was also the initial accuser of Zhukov at the meeting of the plenum which decided to remove him from office.

[44] There are about eighteen military districts in the Soviet Union, and three main Force Groups outside (in East Germany, Hungary, and Poland).

forces, and some special military bases. District commanders usually are prominent military officers, especially those commanding the key districts.

After 1937, when Stalin reintroduced the Military Council during the purges of the military,[45] the role of the military district commander became ambiguous. A Military Council normally is composed of the commander, his chief of staff, the head of the Political Department, a member of the security organs, and members of the local (*krai*, *raion*) Party organization. Although decisions of the Military Council are issued in the name of the commander, all decisions are passed by majority vote and are binding.[46]

Thus saddled with a collective decision-making organ in which the commander could obviously be outvoted by the "packed" Council, the military, for a number of years, was at the mercy of Stalin and the MPA. In January 1947, however, Stalin once more changed the relationship. Although he retained the Military Councils at the military district level, he turned them from "responsible collective organs" with full decision-making authority into "consultative organs subordinate to the commanders." Furthermore, the representative of the security organs was removed from the Council.[47]

However, the military was not to enjoy this respite for long. In July 1950, at the outbreak of the Korean War, Stalin reversed his previous ruling, as he had done in June of 1941, when the Nazis attacked Russia. According to Iu. Petrov, "The Military Councils of army groups, military districts, fleets, armies, and flotillas were transformed from consultative organs advising the commanding officers into responsible organs called upon to guide all aspects of life and activities of the troops," and, at the same time, "The post of Military Council member [chosen] from among the regular Party workers was restored," which meant that the security organs were once more represented in the councils.[48]

The military was certain to seize the first chance it saw to rid itself of the despised control organ and bottleneck in the military chain

[45] The Military Council, in its present form, was reintroduced by Stalin at the height of the purges of the military. On May 10, 1937, the personnel of the Military Council, the infamous troika, was defined as follows: "The Commander of the troops, the full-time cadre political worker [a euphemism for security functionary], and the head of the Political Department of the district." In July 1937, the Military Councils were further "packed" with the addition of the secretaries of *krai* and *oblast'* Party Committees and Central Committee secretaries of the national republic Parties. In May 1938, Stalin created the Supreme Military Council. Petrov, pp. 305-306.

[46] *Ibid.*, p. 468. [47] *Ibid.*, p. 447, fn. 2. [48] *Ibid.*, p. 453.

of command. There is little reason to doubt the truth of recent Soviet accusations as to Zhukov's intentions at the time:

> Zhukov was also attempting to limit the rights of the Military Councils . . . and was trying to change them into consultative organs [subordinate] to the various commanders. He insisted that the post of Military Council member [reserved for] regular Party members be eliminated, that appointments to Military Councils be made not on the basis of a Central Committee decision but by an order of the Minister of Defense. . . . He deprecated the role of the members of the Military Councils in every way and conducted conferences without their participation, despite the fact that their presence was necessary.[49]

Zhukov was accused of still other offenses against the Party: of attempting to eliminate the Supreme Military Council (the collective organ that includes members of the Party's Central Committee and the Presidium as well as military representatives), of forbidding members of the military who were Communists to communicate with the Central Committee, and of severely punishing those who did so communicate.[50] Zhukov's policies also were said to have "led to the disruptions of ties between military Party organizations and the local Party organizations" and thereby to have broken "a most important tradition of the army and navy."[51]

Early in the history of the Red Army, the Party had imbued it with a pervasive parochialism, which manifested itself in close ties between military units and their local civilian and Party organizations. This trait proved a hindrance to the centralization of the Red Army that became necessary in the 1920's, and Trotsky, and after him Stalin, had to resort to severe measures to combat it. However, while Stalin formally severed the military from local control, he frequently urged the military to cultivate informal ties with the locals. His purpose in so doing was, first, to maintain a nonmilitary source of infor-

[49] *Ibid.*, pp. 462-463. See also A. M. Larkov and N. T. Filippov, *Edinonachalie v Sovetskikh Vooruzhennykh Silakh* (*Edinonachalie* in the Soviet Armed Forces), Voenizdat, Moscow, 1960, p. 16; Marshal Malinovskii, in *Resheniia oktiabr'skogo Plenuma TsK KPSS v deistvii* (Decisions of the CPSU Central Committee October Plenum in Action), Voenizdat, Moscow, 1959, pp. 6-19; Malinovskii, in *K novomu pod"emu partiino-politicheskoi raboty v Sovetskoi Armii i Flote* (Toward a New Intensification of Party-Political Work in the Soviet Army and Navy), ed. Major General Z. S. Osipov, Voenizdat, Moscow, 1960, pp. 5-24.

[50] Petrov, p. 463.

[51] *Ibid.* See also Marshals Malinovskii, Grechko, and Biriuzov, in *K novomu pod"emu*, pp. 5-69.

mation on the affairs of the units and, secondly, to have a basis for employing military labor in the civilian economy during harvesting and other periods when manpower was scarce. The relationship was not an even one. While the military looked favorably on cultural and athletic collaboration between the locals and the garrisons, they resented the forced presence of local Party functionaries at military functions.[52] Zhukov, by trying to destroy this important informational link of the Central Committee, undoubtedly raised further fears of Bonapartism, for the Party believes the importance of such civil-military ties to lie in their helping "soldiers and officers better to understand the general national interests and *prevent* [*the development*] *of caste systems*."[53]

b. The Ascendance of Military Professionals over Political Functionaries. By thus limiting the role of the MPA, the Military Councils, and the local Party organizations, Marshal Zhukov had sought to restrict, or even to cut off, the influence of the upper echelons of the Party *apparat* within the military. The next step was to throttle the authority of the many subdivisions of the MPA and the Party in the individual units: the Political Departments and Sections at command levels below the Military Districts; the *zampolits* (assistant to commanders for political affairs) at those same levels; the Party committees, primary Party organizations, and their various bureaus and secretaries; and the Komsomol organizations.

Most officers view the intrusions of these political functionaries into the military sphere as a nuisance of limited usefulness. Zhukov, therefore, reduced the scope of their function to the practical tasks of education and morale-building, and stipulated furthermore that these activities were not to interfere with military tasks and were to take place chiefly during off-duty hours. In this way he sought to give the commanders full authority to carry out their duties without interference from functionaries.

The power of the Party organizations had varied considerably over the years. In 1943, Stalin sharply limited their authority by depriving them of the right to examine the personal affairs of members of their

[52] For some negative aspects of these ties between the military and the local organizations, see R. Kolkowicz, *The Use of Soviet Military Labor in the Civilian Economy: A Study of Military "Shefstvo,"* The RAND Corporation, RM-3360-PR, November 1962.

[53] Lieutenant Colonel Rtishchev, in *V pomoshch' ofitseram izuchaiushchim marksistsko-leninskuiu teoriiu* (An Aid to Officers Studying Marxist-Leninist Theory), Voenizdat, Moscow, 1959, p. 125. (Italics added.)

military units. In 1947, he reversed that ruling, and the July 1953 plenum of the Central Committee enhanced the role of the primary Party organization still further. In 1954, however, the military began to press for a reversal of that trend and achieved its first victory when the lowest level of the Party organization was moved from the company up to battalion and regiment.[54] Political functionaries thereby lost the opportunity for direct supervision of military personnel. In May 1956,

> . . . without the knowledge of the Party Central Committee, Zhukov issued an order which introduced bureaucratic rule in the management of Party organizations, set off commanders against the political workers, and spread unhealthy relations and disparity among them.[55]

As *Pravda* later put it, Zhukov forced these organs to perform "narrow educational work" and "ignored the Instructions . . . that directed the Party organizations to deal with all aspects of the military training of the troops."[56]

In addition to the Party organizations, every Soviet commander has had to endure, throughout most of the Red Army's history, the presence on his staff of a political officer, whose authority has fluctuated with the political vagaries between that of an actual superior (under the military commissar system) and that of an equal or even, to a slight degree, a subordinate. Each rise in the political officer's authority has decreased the authority and independence of the commander. The desire of every commander is to achieve in his unit what in Russian is called *edinonachalie*, the vesting of full military and political authority in a one-man command. Though the Party claims that Soviet commanders have enjoyed *edinonachalie* since World War II, this is not the case.

Having restored the institution of the military commissars at the outbreak of the Russo-German war, Stalin abolished it once more in the fall of 1942, when the excesses of powerful but inexperienced commissars became a hindrance to his immediate objectives. Seeking to appeal to the military's interests and loyalty, Stalin now declared full *edinonachalie*. In January 1950, he reinstituted the *zampolit* system at the company level, and took some steps to streamline the cumbersome control apparatus in the military.[57]

[54] I. Orlov, *Partiinaia gruppa v podrazdelenii* (The Party Group in the Subunit), Voenizdat, Moscow, 1957, p. 2.

[55] Petrov, p. 463. [56] *Pravda*, November 3, 1957. [57] Petrov, p. 452.

Zhukov, as Minister of Defense, abolished the company *zampolit* altogether, and moved the battalion *zampolit* up to the regiment, where he performed his limited duties.[58] Not only did Zhukov restrict the authority of the political organs, but he severely reduced the scope of their functions. He curtailed their right to supervise the leisure-time activities of military personnel. Also, officers were given the right to substitute combat training for political education, and their study of ideology and Party history was put on a voluntary basis. In an even more striking departure from previous practice, the time allotted to the study of Marxism-Leninism was greatly shortened, and the crucial institution of *kritika/samokritika* was severely curtailed.

This last ritual, which has been described earlier, has been a very sensitive issue in Party-military relations, and the occasion of considerable conflict, since it subjects the commander to the open criticism of his peers and subordinates. As military men, the officers strongly resent this unique and unmilitary phenomenon, but as members of the Party they must submit to the statutes that do not exclude the commander from their provisions. Zhukov, however, now emphasized the importance of exempting the commanders' professional activities and decisions from Party criticism. He also introduced strong military discipline and a strict separation of ranks, practices which the Party *apparat* opposes as fostering Bonapartism.

> Various effective forms of political work with the personnel were repealed. The Marxist-Leninist training of officers, for example, was excluded from the command training program, while political courses . . . were decreased to one-hour sessions on current affairs during off-duty hours, and political information sessions were abolished completely. Bureaucratic administration and rude treatment of subordinates were introduced into the army and navy. This distorted the essence of Soviet military discipline, which is based on the method of persuasion.[59]

Finally, Zhukov urged the political organs not to waste their time on ideological lectures and other abstract instruction, useless from the military point of view, but to keep their indoctrination closely related to the practical tasks of the military:

> . . . our political organs, and above all the MPA, [must] reorganize the content and especially the methods of propaganda. . . . It is

[58] *Ibid.*, p. 457, fn. 2. [59] *Ibid.*, p. 463.

necessary resolutely to abolish the aimlessness and abstract instruction of which we still have a great deal in educational work.[60]

The military's drive for greater autonomy and professional independence took place against the background of revolutionary changes in the Party's mythology, in its relations with the satellite regimes in Eastern Europe, and in its *modus operandi* for maintaining social controls. The Twentieth Party Congress destroyed the myth of Stalin and simultaneously indicted the reign of terror of the past, thereby raising popular hopes for the future. The upheavals in Poland and Hungary in 1956 resulted in the weakening of Moscow's control over its satellites on one hand and in the political leadership's greater dependence on the Red Army on the other. As Party leaders beat their breasts, and as their hold within and without the Soviet Union was further weakened by the continuing division in the Party hierarchy, the military intensified its drive toward emancipation.

It benefited in this effort by the great honors and offices that were being heaped on Marshal Zhukov, the popular hero feted, applauded, and decorated by Party and press, for, in the unique circumstances of the totalitarian state, Zhukov's elevation was understood to reflect the rise into power of the whole military establishment. As this belief was shared by the military rank and file itself, military virtue and command authority became acknowledged values, while the restrictive functions of the political organs subsided into the background. But Zhukov, though brilliant and brave as a military officer, proved to be no match for the cunning and patient Party leaders when it came to political maneuvering.

4. *The Party Counterattacks*

Seen in retrospect, the developments after the Twentieth Party Congress were a long triumphal march of Zhukov and the military toward institutional autonomy and real political power. Zhukov had been praised by Khrushchev at the Congress, and he became a candidate member of the all-powerful Presidium. On his sixtieth birthday, in late 1956, he received the kind of public accolades and awards usually reserved for the Party leader.[61] In January 1957, he went

[60] *Krasnaia zvezda*, April 16, 1956. For early signs of pressure from the military to obtain broader authority to pursue its profession without interference from the political organs, see *Krasnaia zvezda*, March 3, 4, 11, 16, 18, 22, and 31, 1955.

[61] On December 2, 1956, Zhukov was awarded the fourth Gold Star of the Hero of the Soviet Union, the only Soviet citizen to achieve this singular honor, and the Central Committee and the Council of Ministers sent him a public letter that was extremely laudatory.

on an official state visit to India, a mark of his high status. And the peak of his public career came during his triumphal visit to Leningrad on July 13, 1957, after he had thwarted the anti-Party group's coup against Khrushchev and been promoted to full membership in the Presidium.

By helping Khrushchev defeat the opposition and thereby consolidate his hold on the Party, Zhukov, ironically, had prepared his own downfall. The Party *apparat* was not likely to tolerate for long such a popular, powerful military leader, who aimed at separating the Party from the armed forces and would be in an excellent position to bargain with the Party for whatever advantages he was seeking.

The first signs of rising antimilitary pressures in the Party began to appear as early as 1956. More precisely, these pressures were directed against Zhukov and the "separatist" military interests and objectives he personified. Sizable opposition to the moves by which Zhukov tried to separate the military from the Party came from within the military itself, from members of the Stalingrad Group whose loyalty was divided between their professional establishment and their benefactor, Khrushchev.

The first major measure of the Party against the growing separation of the military was the announcement, in May 1957, of the "Instructions to the Organizations of the CPSU in the Soviet Army and Navy." The Central Committee had agreed on April 27 to issue these new Instructions to the military and political personnel in the armed forces. Two weeks later, when the Central Committee's decision was made public, *Krasnaia zvezda* carried an editorial on the event.[62] Although the text of the Instructions was never published in full, enough citations and commentary are available to convey its theme and intent. Thus,

> The Central Committee of the Party demands further growth in the activity and militancy of Party organizations, [and] the strengthening of their influence over all aspects of the life and activity of the troops.[63]

The political organs' authority was to be extended to all facets of military life (as it had been prior to 1955), and was to be equal to that of the commanders.[64] However, before the Party could succeed

[62] *Krasnaia zvezda*, May 12, 1957. Since the Central Committee held no plenary meeting at the time, and the document is not called a "decision," it is probable that the Instructions were drawn up in the Secretariat.

[63] *Voennyi vestnik*, No. 6, 1957, p. 2.

[64] "Secretaries of Party organizations and the *partbiuro* should maintain the most

in enlarging the role of the political organs, it had to break down the officers' claim to special status by which the military in effect raised itself above the Party and resisted its self-policing and self-regulating mechanism, the sacred ritual of *kritika/samokritika.*

> The Party Central Committee considered criticism and self-criticism an important condition . . . [and] the Instructions indicated that military Party organizations must reveal inadequacies in the training and education and in Party-political work on the basis of criticism and self-criticism.[65]

Even before the public announcement of the Instructions, there were harbingers of the stiffening attitude in the MPA and its organs toward the military's opposition to Party rules.[66] On April 25, two days before the Central Committee issued the Instructions, Vice-Admiral Komarov publicly demanded a larger role for the political organs.[67] At the same time, the conflict over the issue of *kritika/samokritika* was growing sharper and more open, as the MPA tried to assert its previous authority over the officer corps[68] and the military offered strong resistance to that effort. The MPA's campaign was briefly interrupted by an event of more urgent concern to the Party, when the anti-Party group attempted to oust Khrushchev in June 1957 and found itself outmaneuvered by its intended victim, who succeeded in destroying the intra-Party opposition with the aid of the military.[69] However, as soon as this crisis was over, the MPA renewed its attack on the military with vigor and at times with barely concealed vindictiveness.

From June 1957 on, the campaign against the military centered around the question whether or not all Communists are equal. Several articles signed by MPA generals interpreted the Instructions as meaning that commanders are Communists first and officers

---

intimate active relations with the staff, so as to be constantly abreast of all problems in the units and become acquainted at the right time with the orders and instructions of the commander. On the other hand, the commander of the unit . . . and his chief of staff must at all times make sure that the leaders of Party organizations are involved [*v kurse*] in the tasks at hand." *Ibid.*, p. 4.

[65] Petrov, p. 458. See also *Krasnaia zvezda*, May 12, 1957.

[66] E.g., *Sovetskii flot*, April 3 and 4, 1957.

[67] *Ibid.*, April 25, 1957.

[68] Petrov, p. 456.

[69] For details and speculations on the role of the military in the anti-Party affair, see Shelepin's speech at the Twenty-second Party Congress, *XXII s"ezd: stenograficheskii otchet*, 1962, Vol. 2, p. 405, as well as Conquest, *Power and Policy*, pp. 320-345.

second, and as Communists are subject to *kritika/samokritika.* Lieutenant General A. G. Rytov, a ranking functionary of the Main Political Administration, wrote:

> The commander must understand that he and his subordinates stand in one Party, a voluntary military union of like-minded Communists, and as members of this Party enjoy equal rights and bear responsibility to it. . . .[70]

Major General M. Kh. Kalashnik, another high-ranking MPA representative, made the same point even more sharply and specifically:

> The Instructions provide precise and clear rules about the direction which criticism and self-criticism must take at meetings of army and navy Party organizations. Nevertheless, in some places attempts have been made to interpret these precise and clear rules of the Instructions in a way which is not altogether correct. In individual organizations there are attempts to distinguish between Communists who may be criticized and those who may not be. Such posing of the question is fundamentally incorrect. In the Party there is no division between the "chosen" and the "unchosen"; there are not two disciplines, one for the the leader and another for the rank and file. In the Party there is one discipline; to the Party all members are equal. . . .[71]

Kalashnik also sounded a warning note when he described the Party organization as a guarantor of the Central Committee's continued supremacy: ". . . the Party organization in the armed forces was, is, and will be the dependable support of the Central Committee in the struggle with any type of deviation from the general line of the Party."[72]

Despite these overt manifestations of the Party's challenge to military autonomy, Zhukov continued to play the role of the self-confident popular figure, seemingly unconcerned by the events. After the June plenum of the Central Committee, he even began to demand the rehabilitation of the military leaders whom Stalin had purged in 1937.[73] At the very moment that the press was beginning to stress the Party's role in World War II[74] while playing down the military's

[70] *Vestnik vozdushnogo flota,* No. 7, July 1957, p. 27.

[71] *Krasnaia zvezda,* July 31, 1957.

[72] *Ibid.* See also other items concerning the need for wider use of *kritika/samokritika* in *Krasnaia zvezda,* August 9, 1957, and September 1, 1957.

[73] Boris Meissner, *Russland unter Chruschtschow,* R. Oldenbourg Verlag, Munich, 1960, p. 59.

[74] *Krasnaia zvezda,* September 26, 1957.

contribution to victory, Zhukov was making preparations for a prolonged visit to Yugoslavia. There can be little doubt that Zhukov's enemies in the Party and in the military had planned his ouster with some care, and that Zhukov's absence from Moscow was the needed occasion for the final act. Khrushchev may have remembered how near he came to being defeated by the anti-Party group partly because he was away from Moscow when they sprang their trap.

5. *The Ouster of Marshal Zhukov: The End of a Brief Triumph*

On October 4, 1957, Marshal Zhukov, accompanied by a formal naval escort, left Moscow for a visit to Yugoslavia that was given prominent coverage in the press. On October 17, the press reported that the naval squadron had been ordered to return to Sevastopol but that Zhukov was continuing his journey with an unscheduled side-trip to Albania. The next day, editorials in the military press gave hints of intensified pressure on the military by the MPA, as they stressed the need to enlarge the role of the political organs and to "use more extensively . . . the bolshevik method of *kritika/samokritika.*"[75]

The plot against Zhukov seemed to tighten on October 19, when the head of the MPA, Colonel General A. S. Zheltov, delivered a report to the Presidium of the Central Committee on Zhukov's activities in the military. The Presidium thereupon "adopted a resolution concerning Party-political work in the Soviet Army and Navy" and, "in view of the seriousness of the inadequacies revealed in Party-political work," took a number of measures by which to widen the role of the political organs and the Party in the armed forces.[76] On Octover 26, upon Zhukov's return to Moscow, TASS announced his dismissal from the Ministry of Defense and his replacement with Marshal Malinovskii, Khrushchev's loyal associate. Not until November 3, however, the day that the second Sputnik was launched, did the press carry details of the Central Committee plenum that had ousted Zhukov.[77]

The most remarkable aspect of Zhukov's dismissal was the ease with which it was accomplished. In retrospect, it seems hardly surprising that, in a showdown, the heroic but politically naïve Marshal should have commanded so little support. In Zhukov's absence from Moscow, Khrushchev, who had on his side the members of the Stalingrad Group, in effect controlled not only most of the military estab-

[75] *Sovetskii flot*, October 18, 1957.

[76] Petrov, p. 461.

[77] *Sovetskii flot*, November 3, 1957.

lishment but also the bulk of the military's representation on the Central Committee.[78] Nevertheless, to guard against untoward events, Khrushchev launched the action against Zhukov in the Presidium, where no military personnel was present, and subsequently presented the plenum of the Central Committee with a *fait accompli.* Indicative of the care with which the plotters proceeded was the precaution of sending Marshal Rokossovskii, an old associate of Zhukov, away from Moscow during the fateful days[79] by assigning him temporarily to the command of the Transcaucasian district. He returned from that assignment in time to join in the condemnation of the Marshal.[80]

With the ouster of Marshal Zhukov the Soviet military had lost a charismatic leader, a fearless spokesman, and, even more important, an officer who embodied the military virtues cherished by the officer corps and whose primary loyalties lay with the military establishment. During his brief tenure as Minister, Zhukov had imbued the officers with pride in their profession and a feeling of distinction and authority. Upon his departure, the military again had to submit to the dreary catechisms of Marxism-Leninism and the schizoid performances of men who were both military officers and Party zealots.

D · ASCENDANCE OF THE PARTY APPARAT *IN THE MILITARY: AN ERA OF GREAT REFORMS, 1957-1960*

1. The First Stage of Military Reforms

The October 1957 plenum of the Central Committee has been presented by Soviet historians as proof and symbol of the Party's ability to crush any Bonapartist trends in the military:

[78] See Appendix A-III for military membership on the Central Committee in 1957.

[79] *Pravda,* October 25, 1957, carried a small notice, reprinted from *Zaria vostoka* (the daily organ of the Georgian Communist Party, published in Tbilisi), which stated that Marshal Rokossovskii had been dispatched from Moscow, where he served as Deputy Minister of Defense, to command the Transcaucasian military district.

[80] *Pravda,* on November 3, 1957, reported the "unanimous" condemnation of Zhukov by a number of leading military personalities who had been included in an enlarged plenum of the Central Committee. Among those listed were eight members of the Stalingrad Group (Malinovskii, Konev, Eremenko, Timoshenko, Biriuzov, Gorshkov, Zakharov, and Kazakov). Two others (Sokolovskii and Rokossovskii) came from the Zhukov camp. The last one, General Gorbatov, seems not to fit into either category. Rokossovskii and Sokolovskii may well have been included to suggest the unity of the military in supporting Khrushchev. Their seeming abandonment of Zhukov was perhaps the result of their instinct for survival.

> This is the logic of the old-time Party moral: anyone who attempts to oppose the Party, to take over its functions, loses its trust no matter what the achievements of such an individual.[81]

The impact of that meeting cannot be overestimated. Numerous Soviet military and Party leaders have echoed the view of Marshal Grechko, who stated that the October plenum "was a decisive event in the life of the Party, country, and the Soviet armed forces [which] . . . launched a significant new stage in the development of the Soviet armed forces."[82]

Indeed, the plenum did more than merely remove Marshal Zhukov from office; it became a point of departure for a sweeping reform, aimed at eradicating those conditions, factors, and institutional values that favor the growth of elitism and Bonapartism in the military community. The reforms were designed formally and permanently to integrate the military with the other social institutions by breaking down artificial strictures and barriers that separated it from Party and society. Moreover, they sought to establish the Party's dominance at all levels of the military hierarchy and thus to prevent the emergence of another Zhukov.

The charges against Zhukov in the wake of his removal, laced as they were with the usual propagandistic hyperbole, would seem exaggerated. Yet there is little reason to doubt that the specter of a separatist military establishment had frightened the Party leaders and prompted them to initiate the massive social, political, and military reforms in the armed forces. Zhukov himself, by his swaggering, impolitic behavior, offered them the opportunity and justification for shaking up the officer corps and implanting very firm controls in the armed forces.

The function of prosecutor at the October plenum was entrusted to the ascetic ideologue Suslov, who emphasized that "we were dealing in this case not with isolated mistakes but with a system of mistakes, with a definite line followed by the former Minister of Defense . . . that was leading to a dangerous isolation of the armed forces from the Party [and] was tending to keep the Central Committee out of decision-making on crucial matters affecting the life of the army and navy."[83] In 1961, the Twenty-second Party Congress recorded this detailed indictment of Zhukov:

[81] Petrov, p. 464.
[82] Grechko, in *K novomu pod"emu*, p. 26.
[83] Cf. Marshal Golikov in *XXII s"ezd: stenograficheskii otchet*, 1962, Vol. 3, p. 67.

A dangerous anti-Party line and the Bonapartist policy pursued by ex-Minister of Defense Zhukov were nipped in the bud by the decisions of that plenary session. How serious the situation was can be seen from the extent to which the role of the military councils, political agencies, and Party organizations had been undermined and vitiated; absolutely all Party criticism of shortcomings in the behavior and performance of communist commanders of all grades was forbidden in the army; the Party basis of one-man leadership was thrown overboard; arrogance, rudeness, arbitrariness, and intimidation were rife in the treatment of subordinates; dissension between commanding officers and political workers was cultivated. Party life and the work of political agencies were administered by fiat and were reduced to purely educational activity. The Main Political Administration was slighted and downgraded. . . . There was a growing drift toward unlimited authority in the army and the country.[84]

The reforms introduced by Khrushchev were keyed to each of the charges listed in this bill of particulars. They rested on the "restoration of Leninist norms in Party life,"[85] which were in direct opposition to the Stalinist policies in the military. While the former implied a view of the military as nonmilitaristic, egalitarian, and collectivist, the latter were based on Stalin's belief that "the Army is a closed organization that is built from above."[86] Stalin had indeed shaped the military into a closed and disciplined professional organization, whose officers shared the trappings and functions of military professionals elsewhere. Although he also maintained a large network of controllers and informers in the military, he did not encourage these to meddle in the affairs of the officers except during

[84] *Ibid.*

[85] See the resolution of the Central Committee plenum that castigated Zhukov, in *Resheniia oktiabr'skogo Plenuma*, p. 4. See also Malinovskii's detailed analysis of the meaning of the October plenum in the military establishment in *ibid.*, pp. 6-19; Malinovskii's speech at the Twenty-first Party Congress, in February 1959, in which he accused Zhukov of opposing Leninist principles in the armed forces and added that the Central Committee had dealt sharply "with this newly emerged 'Bonaparte.'" *Vneocherednoi XXI s"ezd Kommunisticheskoi partii Sovetskogo Soiuza: stenograficheskii otchet* (Extraordinary Twenty-first Congress of the CPSU: Stenographic Record), Gospolitizdat, Moscow, 1959, Vol. 2, p. 127; and Petrov, p. 456.

[86] Article by Stalin, published in December 1923, cited by Petrov, p. 450, fn. 2. See also Stalin's repeated attempts to create a professional officer corps, free from collectivist interference but controlled by political organs, as described in Chapter III, pp. 73-75 above.

the severe crises of the purges and the war. An autocrat himself, Stalin appreciated the value of formal authority and had little use for collective decision-making in the military units or for a forced equality among the ranks.

The specific objectives of Khrushchev's reforms would seem to have been as follows:

(a) To break down barriers between ranks; to make the military Party organizations (collective bodies in which rank and position are of little importance) into centers for deliberation, criticism, and decision-making; to engage the Komsomol more actively in many of the units' tasks; and to inhibit any elitist tendencies in the commanders by reducing their disciplinary powers and transferring many of these powers to collective bodies.

(b) To establish Party supremacy in the military by introducing a dual principle at the command level. With the decision-making authority in the units lodged in the collective body of the Party organization, the commander who was a member of the Party had direction of the collective and thus, in effect, retained commanding authority. Commanders who were not Party members and therefore were disqualified from directing the Party organization had to submit to the collective wish. By this principle, the commander's authority derived, not from his position as commander, but from his prerogatives as head of the Party organization in his unit.

(c) To revitalize and greatly strengthen the Party's channels of control and authority by enhancing the role of the MPA and its subordinate bodies.

(d) To involve members of the military in local Party and social organizations so as to combat any tendencies toward exclusiveness.

(e) To establish the Party's authority to define military theory, doctrine, and strategy, by subordinating this crucial function to the Central Committee.[87]

[87] In timing, substance, and purpose, as well as in the opposition they encountered, the Khrushchevian reforms in the military correspond so closely to military reforms undertaken by the Chinese Communist Party that one is tempted to view the Soviet reforms as modeled on the Chinese. The lesson that the experience of the Chinese with their officer corps may have taught the Soviets is that, sooner or later, institutional and professional loyalties, interests, and values begin to conflict with those of the Party and the official ideology, and that such conflicts have to be solved by drastic means.

Until the mid-1950's, the People's Liberation Army (PLA) of Communist China was an egalitarian, nonprofessional force whose traditions were still those of revolutionary warfare. In February 1955, the government issued the "Regulations on the Service of Officers," and the impact of this measure was immense. The professionali-

With the Resolution on the Improvement of Party-political Work in the Soviet Army and Navy, the October plenum of the Central Committee had laid down the new line. The Party now began to implement this general resolution with a number of specific regulations, orders and directives.

Statute on the Military Councils: In April 1958, after a "cooling-off" period, the Central Committee passed a number of decisions that ushered in the military reforms.[88] The Military Councils, previously subordinate to the military commanders, were reorganized in such a way as to place them under the domination of Party spokesmen. Their size was increased, most likely to permit their being "packed" with loyal Party men and control functionaries. Their function was defined as follows: "The statute adopted by the Party Central Committee stressed that Military Councils are to resolve all the most important questions concerning the life and activity of the troops and that they are responsible to the Central Committee, the CPSU, the government, and the Minister of Defense. . . ."[89] The authority and scope of activity of these important collective bodies, which essentially control the three arms of the Soviet forces, were thus greatly enhanced and formally delineated.

> Resolutions were adopted by a majority vote. The resolutions were binding on all members of the Military Council and were implemented through the orders of the commanding officer. In cases of disagreement with an adopted resolution, a member of the Military Council had the right to forward his opinion to the Party Central Committee, the government, or the Minister of Defense. The Military Councils . . . became true organs of collective

---

zation and formal separation of the ranks, including the introduction of insignia of rank, accelerated the inevitable evolution toward institutional separateness. The officer corps now began to press for greater professional freedom and other prerogatives, which created deep concern in the Party and led to the ouster in September 1959 of Minister of Defense Marshal P'eng Teh-huai, whose position had been weakening for some time. As in the Soviet military, the main sources of conflict were: (a) military professionalism vs. political integration, (b) elitism vs. egalitarianism, (c) institutional autonomy vs. political penetration and excessive controls, and (d) the use of military forces for nonmilitary tasks. For details, see Ellis Joffe, "The Conflict Between Old and New in the Chinese Army," *The China Quarterly*, No. 18, 1964, pp. 118-140; David A. Charles, "The Dismissal of Marshal P'eng Teh-huai," *ibid.*, pp. 63-74. See also Marshal Chu Teh's article in *Pravda*, August 3, 1958, in which he outlined the essential characteristics of a "good" communist military establishment, and in so doing implicitly criticized the Soviet officer corps.

[88] See Malinovskii, in *Resheniia oktiabr'skogo Plenuma*, p. 7; Petrov, p. 469.

[89] Petrov, p. 469.

leadership. . . . Members of the Military Councils were confirmed by the Party Central Committee.[90]

In August 1958, the Central Committee fixed the composition of the new and enlarged Military Councils at the district and army group levels in an order that clearly showed an attempt to surround the military people on the councils with a majority of Party-political functionaries, who, if they thought it necessary, could veto undesirable actions and initiate successful moves of their own.[91]

Statute on the MPA: Another statute issued by the Central Committee in April 1958 sought to centralize in the MPA all authority over Party activities in the military, and to make that vital organ more independent of the Minister of Defense than it had formerly been by severing some of its organizational connections with the Ministry and emphasizing its status as a section of the Central Committee. The Central Committee "also considered it necessary to increase the role of the MPA in the management of the Military Councils and in the selection of the members of the Councils."[92] Thus, the MPA was to extend its tentacles into those central, authoritative bodies, having been instructed to supervise and "examine their practical activities . . . and report the results to the Central Committee and government."[93] The deputy directors of the MPA were named as members of the Military Councils of the different branches of the armed forces.

Statute on the Political Organs in the Soviet Army and Navy: In October 1958, the Central Committee adopted a statute which increased the role and authority of the political organs in the armed forces and restored them to prominence by instructing them to enter into all activities of the military, to strengthen the ties with the civilian population, and to introduce "Leninist norms" into military life. The time allotted to the political organs for indoctrination and political education was increased significantly. This statute in effect

[90] *Ibid.*

[91] The importance attached to Party domination of the Military Councils may be seen in the high rank of Party representatives appointed to membership in the Councils; they included Kalnberzin, Mazurov, Mzhavanadze, Podgornyi, and Snechkus, all of them secretaries of CC/CPs of Union republics, as well as Kirilenko and Efremov. *Ibid.*

[92] Malinovskii stated: "The role of the Military Councils has been strengthened. They are now even more highly authoritative organs that carry full and complete responsibility before the Party and government for the status of the forces. . . ." *Partiinaia organizatsiia chasti, korablia* (The Party Organization of *Chast'* and Ship), Voenizdat, Moscow, 1960, pp. 7-8; also, Petrov, pp. 470-471.

[93] Petrov, pp. 470-471.

removed the strictures imposed on the political organs during Zhukov's tenure in the Ministry.[94]

Changes in the Instructions to the Party Organizations in the Soviet Army and Navy: A major change was introduced in April 1958 in Paragraph 2 of the original Instructions, issued in April 1957, which distinguished between commanders who were active Party members and those who were inactive or not members of the Party at all. With the change in the Instruction, it became imperative for a commander who wanted to retain his commanding authority not only to join the Party but also to take an active part in the work of the Party organization in his unit. If he failed to do so, he faced the possibility of an unsympathetic, uncooperative Party collective with veto power, over whom he would have much less control than formerly.[95]

The effect of the changes was a startling intensification of the commanders' participation in the affairs of the Party organizations:

> The political activity of the commanders showed a noticeable increase [since] . . . it was regarded by them as a component and an organic part of their work in commanding troops. The number of commanders and directors elected to Party organs increased sharply. In 1959 there were fourteen times more communist regimental and ship commanders in Party bureaus than in 1957, and in 1960 twenty-six times more.[96]

[94] For detailed analysis of this statute, see Colonel General F. Golikov, head of MPA, in *Resheniia oktiabr'skogo Plenuma*, pp. 20-35.

[95] Malinovskii stressed that "it is necessary to understand the great importance of the newly revised second paragraph of the Instructions" (*Resheniia oktiabr'skogo Plenuma*, p. 14). Petrov describes the purpose of this change as "to prevent possible occurrence of bureaucratism in Party work and a decrease in the role of the Party organizations. The relationships between the commander—whether or not he was a Party member—and the Party organization of the unit or subunit, were determined. . . . The new edition of the Instructions pointed out that a commander . . . who is not a member of the Party will rely on the Party organization in his work, while a commander . . . who is a Party member will not only rely on the Party organization but also manage its activities" (p. 473). The effect of these strictures was reflected, in 1962, in the remarks of a general who complained that "Officers know very well from their own experience that without the active and constant involvement of Communists and Party organizations [in the commander's activities] the commander is simply unable to carry out his assigned duties." Lieutenant General of the Guards Kh. Ambarian, "Edinonachalie—vazhneishii printsip stroitel'stva Vooruzhennykh Sil" (*Edinonachalie*—the Most Important Principle in Developing the Armed Forces), *Voennyi vestnik*, No. 8, August 1962, pp. 12-15.

[96] Petrov, p. 476.

As a result of the above statutes and other changes, military commanders became very dependent on the political functionaries in their units, and *edinonachalie*, the ideal of the officer corps, became a meaningless fiction. The Party propagated the idea of the "Party basis of one-man command," and frequently cited Khrushchev's dictum that "true *edinonachalie* is inconceivable without reliance on the Party organization, on the masses of soldiers, . . . [and] without a correct, Party-oriented understanding of his duties on the part of every commander."[97] The political organs began actively to press for intensification of *kritika/samokritika*, which now was "no longer limited to the sphere of Party work but was applied also to the military sphere."[98] One can guess at the impact that this intensified use of a despised practice must have had on the commanders as one reads these remarks of Marshal Grechko:

> The communist commanders who were subjected to criticism at Party meetings and conferences for rudeness, bureaucracy, detachment from the masses, and undervaluation of Party-political work began to reorganize their activities, to listen to the voices of those under their command, to consult with them, and to show concern for them.[99]

Little by little, however, the military community began to resist the massive onslaught of changes, reforms, purges, and renewed controls.

2. *Military Opposition to the Reforms*

The public condemnation of Zhukov at the October plenum of the Central Committee was interpreted by many Party functionaries in the military as a call for a massive settling of scores with the officer corps, which they answered with a campaign of intimidation, blackmail, dismissals, and other coercive devices. Khrushchev and his associates probably had not intended to unleash this vindictive campaign, a reaction to the frustrations of the political functionaries that had built up during Zhukov's tenure. More likely, Khrushchev would have preferred a gradual process by which to rid the military of the undesirables and introduce his sweeping reforms in an unobtrusive way. Certainly, the nomination of General (later Marshal)

[97] *Pravda*, June 27, 1963.

[98] Petrov, p. 476. This was a sharp departure from the practices established by Zhukov, which strictly limited the rights of the Party organization to criticize professional activities of the military.

[99] Grechko, in *K novomu pod"emu*, p. 35.

Golikov as head of the MPA points to his desire for such a moderate course. Furthermore, Khrushchev can hardly have wanted the military to be alienated by the political control organs at the very moment that he was launching an ambitious program of military reforms intended to modernize and improve the Soviet military establishment in firepower, mobility, readiness, and general effectiveness. And finally, though he had prevailed over the anti-Party group in June and over Zhukov in October of 1957, one would assume that Khrushchev had no desire to risk a conflict with the military so soon after he had achieved dominance of the Party. However, the momentum of the antimilitary feeling among Party *apparatchiks* in the military that had been unleashed by the October plenum continued well into 1958 before it was temporarily arrested.

The Party's wrath against Zhukov, his elitism, and his efforts toward independence from political controls, which had first been revealed at the October plenum and in editorial comments on that event, was reflected also in statements of his military rivals.[100] The new hard line was expressed in a number of articles that urged the political control organs to be militant, vigilant, and detached in executing the Party's will in the military. One of these stated bluntly:

> The political functionary must not keep quiet, he must fight. . . . Each problem must be solved not on the basis of personal advantage, or friendly relations, but from the point of view of the interests of the Party and the State. A bad political functionary is the one who closes his eyes to errors and offenses of people, and who is afraid to speak of their mistakes with Party "directness."

The author cites some revealing quotes from Kirov:

> We have never, in our bolshevik experience, had completely relaxed relations. . . . Each of us becomes a criminal who considers that it would be most painful at a given moment to open one's mouth, and that it would be better not to criticize but rather to keep quiet. . . . It is necessary to . . . look the Communist directly in the eye and say: "My dear man, you have spoken a lot of nonsense and you are confused. If you cannot help yourself, then I will help you. And if I cannot pull you up by your hands, then I will pull you up by your hair. . . . But, if you do not want to improve yourself, then it is your own fault, and it would be better that you get out of here."

100 See especially Marshal Konev's personal attack on Zhukov in *Pravda*, November 3, 1957.

The article goes on to complain that some political functionaries "do not show the necessary hardness and toughness" in their dealings with the military.[101]

This intensified activity of the political control organs continued well into the spring of 1958 without signs of any serious military opposition. The first stirrings of the military's effort toward reassertion came in March 1958. The February issue of *Voennyi vestnik* carried a prominent article by Major General V. Loboda, known as a defender of officers' prerogatives and interests, in which Loboda dealt with the development of the commanding cadres in the Soviet armed forces and stressed the major role that Soviet officers had played in the Party's struggle with its various enemies. Significantly, Loboda pointedly omitted Zhukov's name in references to the October 1957 plenum while including it in several highly favorable allusions to victorious military leaders of World War II. He also spoke of the 1937 military purge and its destructive effects on the armed forces.[102]

Shortly afterward, Colonel General of the Guards V. Pen'kovskii, an associate of Khrushchev, stressed the need to develop in officers "boldness and initiative in making decisions" in view of the more exacting demands upon commanders created by the conditions of modern war.[103]

During the summer of 1958, the Soviet military press began to reflect the widening rift between the commanders and the political organs. In August, *Krasnaia zvezda* reported on specific instances of rude treatment of commanders by their political "assistants" and the latter's disregard of their direct military superiors, emphasizing that such occurrences were widespread. The correspondent, Colonel M. Erzunov, reported also on the deterioration of discipline in the units, implying that it was caused by the political organs' misinterpretation of the Party's broad directives on the intensification of *partiinost'* in the military:

[101] Naval Captain I. Baidak, *Krasnaia zvezda*, March 18, 1958. About a week later, *Krasnaia zvezda* carried another article, by a Colonel Zakharov, which was the most candid description of the events and problems associated with the ouster of Zhukov. Other articles on the Zhukov affair by prominent military leaders, which had appeared in the same paper in preceding weeks, were more cautious: e.g., Marshal Chuikov, February 2, 1958; Marshal Biriuzov, February 13, 1958; Marshal Grechko, February 16, 1958; Marshal Sokolovskii, February 22, 1958; Marshal Timoshenko, February 23, 1958; General Talenskii, February 26, 1958; and Admiral Gorshkov, February 20, 1958.

[102] Major General V. Loboda, "Komandnye kadry v razvitii Vooruzhennykh Sil SSSR" (Commanding Cadres in the Development of the USSR Armed Forces), *Voennyi vestnik*, No. 2, February 1958, pp. 12-21.

[103] *Krasnaia zvezda*, March 2, 1958.

The absence of friendly cooperation in the activities of the commander and the head of the political section has had a negative influence on the conduct of Party-political work. . . . Communists . . . do not set an example in carrying out the orders of the commander. But this does not alarm the leaders of the Party organization and the functionaries of the political section. . . . All of these facts indicate that the problem of strengthening *edinonachalie*, of supporting the authority of commanders, demands great attention.[104]

One of the major sources of friction was a massive attempt by the political organs to replace commanders with political officers. This action, by which the Party sought to strengthen its influence within the military, was no doubt facilitated by the vacancies that resulted from the resignation of officer commissions in the wake of Zhukov's dismissal. At every opportunity and under any pretext, the functionaries of the political organs now began to replace commanders with their own men.[105] The unfortunate effects of these arbitrary replacements, especially in combination with the general decline of morale and discipline, were such that in November 1958 Marshal Malinovskii felt impelled to rebuke the political officers:

It is necessary [for you] to assist them [the commanders], but not by replacing battalion, company, or platoon commanders just because you have presumably more experience. If you interfere with the commander's work, if you go over his head, the result will be destructive and will end in disorder, and where there is disorder, there is conflict, struggle, and catastrophe.[106]

At about that time, the military was beginning to reassert itself, strongly supported by leading military personalities. In the fall of 1958, *Sovetskii flot* published a large number of articles, subsequently issued in book form, by Admiral Chalyi and other ranking officers[107] who openly attacked all the sacred cows of the Party's control devices and practices in the military.[108] The main theme of

[104] *Ibid.*, August 9, 1958.

[105] *O samostoiatel'nosti i initsiative ofitserov flota* (On the Independence and Initiative of Naval Officers), Voenizdat, Moscow, 1959 (sent to the printer in November 1958), pp. 11-16.

[106] *Krasnaia zvezda*, November 1, 1958.

[107] Among the supporters of Chalyi's views were Vice-Admiral G. I. Shchedrin, Rear Admiral D. K. Iaroshevich, Rear Admiral N. F. Boguslavskii, Rear Admiral F. Ia. Akimov, Major General V. I. Popkov, and Admiral A. G. Golovko.

[108] A common practice of Party leaders, political organs, and Party organizations

the attack may be stated as follows: Modern warfare will be dynamic; it will require complex technical equipment and weapons; and both large and small units will frequently be separated from the main force, so that commanding officers will have to conduct their own movements and minor operations on the basis of independent decisions that may have critical influence on the conduct of the larger operations. Given these changed conditions, commanders and other officers must possess broad authority; they must be self-reliant, trained, and permitted to take risks independently. To allow him enough time to practice his craft and improve his training, the officer must be freed from the burden of indoctrination and other Party requirements. He must also be spared the constant harassment of political and Party organs that are subjecting him to unnecessary inspections, challenging his authority in front of his subordinates, and arbitrarily dismissing his plans and procedures and supplanting them with *ad hoc* solutions.[109]

On November 1, 1958, Malinovskii officially acknowledged the deterioration of military discipline and the damage done by the Party-political organs, and demanded that commanders be given authority to carry out their duties and that the political organs cease their destructive activities:

> All activities of commanders, political organs, and Party organizations aimed at carrying out the decisions of the October plenum must be viewed in the light of their inseparability from those practical tasks which are carried out by our forces at the present stage

---

is the "setting of examples." Thus, the political officer, on finding errors or deficiencies, admonishes the responsible or guilty officer to model his future behavior and that of his unit on some exemplary communist unit. The practice also involves relentless inspections and amateurish meddling in military plans for the unit. See *O samostoiatel'nosti*, pp. 5-18.

[109] The following are excerpts from *O samostoiatel'nosti*: "We have brought up excellent commanding cadres upon whom the Party and the government have placed total responsibility for training brave and able defenders of the socialist fatherland. It is necessary to give these cadres more independence, more scope for showing initiative." (Major General V. I. Popkov, p. 56.) "We feel that, if the commander is kept in fear because of possible undesired consequences of his bold and well-intentioned activities, there will be no way to imbue him with the necessary self-reliance." (Vice-Admiral V. F. Chalyi, p. 8.) "The honor of the officers becomes damaged when a superior, on finding faults, often imaginary ones, right away begins to replace them. . . ." (*Ibid.*, p. 11.) "Sometimes superiors tell even the most experienced commanders whom to include in duty rosters, and who among the pilots should participate in specific missions and who should not, even though the squadron commander is better able to decide all this himself, since he knows better the level of training of his own subordinates." (Popkov, p. 56.)

. . . of strengthening the combat capability and readiness of the army and navy.

Malinovskii, in setting forth this new policy, spoke of the changed nature of warfare and the higher demands it placed on the commanders. He referred to the recent maneuvers in various military districts, which he described as successful, although they most likely had revealed effects of the lack of discipline in the military. He also urged caution when placing political officers in commanding positions:

> Of course, this problem cannot be approached mechanically; rather, it is necessary in each concrete case to proceed from [an evaluation of] what this or another worker is capable of in view of his professional and political qualities.

Malinovskii next took up the problem of the deterioration of military discipline since the October plenum. Having criticized Zhukov for imposing an "alien" disciplinary regime, the Party apparently had convinced the rank and file in the military that it desired the opposite of such firm discipline. It could not hope to preserve true military discipline after abrogating the commanders' authority and subjecting them to the open criticism of subordinates. Malinovskii acknowledged the situation by referring to widespread insubordination among enlisted men and to their growing rejection of the military virtues and military discipline. He expressed himself as dissatisfied with what had been achieved, since the October plenum, in the effort to strengthen discipline: "Measures undertaken to this end are very inadequate, far less than is necessary. . . . Many military personnel behave shamefacedly [*stydlivo*] toward drill and military smartness, identifying it with 'alien drill' [*mushtra*], which recalls all the terrors of the czarist army." Pointing out the difference between the older instrument of oppression and the new army, he stated that in the Soviet army, drill and smartness were signs of high morale and inner qualities and as such were very necessary.

Addressing himself to the problem of *edinonachalie*, Malinovskii described *edinonachalie* as the best and indeed the only way of military life, and requested the political organs and Party organizations to strengthen the commander's authority and aid him in the enforcement of orders.[110]

[110] *Krasnaia zvezda*, November 1, 1958.

3. Temporary Reconciliation of Conflicting Interests

The excesses of the political control organs having generated this surprisingly strong reaction in the military, the Central Committee was forced to moderate its reforms and the tempo of their implementation. The officer corps had become deeply disturbed, and opinions came to be aired and exchanged more and more freely both at formal meetings of the military community and outside such official meetings.[111]

The Twenty-first Party Congress, which took place in February 1959, would seem to have been the point of departure for a modified policy toward the military, which was to include (a) a curbing of the political organs, especially when their control functions clearly interfered with the training and readiness of the troops; (b) greater stress on collectivist methods of military administration, with strong emphasis on the role of the Party collectives in the units; (c) the upholding of "Leninist principles," with their stress on egalitarianism, the rejection of elitism, curbs on the disciplinary rights of officers, and a breaking down of barriers between the ranks.

Already on January 20, 1959, the Central Committee had issued a statute that introduced some important changes in the structure of the political organs. It provided that the Political Departments at military academies and other institutions, in the central organs of the Ministry of Defense, and in research institutes and arsenals be transformed into Party Committees with the rights of *raion* committees. Though the avowed aim of the measure was to liberalize Party-military affairs, the true purpose was to expose the breeding grounds of elitism and professionalism (especially the academies and the Ministry of Defense) to constant scrutiny and criticism and to create division in them, while enabling the Party to maintain that the rights of the political organs had been curbed.[112]

In September 1960 the government issued new disciplinary statutes, which proscribed the use of harsh disciplinary measures and

[111] Cf. Admiral Golovko, in *O samostoiatel'nosti*, p. 89.

[112] See A. Epishev, "Tverdo provodit' v zhizn' politiku partii v Vooruzhennykh Silakh" (Firmly Carry out the Party's Policies in the Armed Forces), *Kommunist Vooruzhennykh Sil*, No. 19, October 1962, p. 6. The Political Departments are subunits of the Main Political Administration located at the level of divisional headquarters and above. Each is administered by a full-time Department head assisted by a professional staff. Khrushchev, undoubtedly to soften the military's resistance to the increased authority and role of the MPA, had these Political Departments transformed into the more "democratic" Party Committees. However, since the full-time staff of the Party Committee consists largely of MPA professionals, the change has done little, if anything, to reduce political controls over the military.

advocated instead the practice of "persuasion" and "encouragement." They stipulated also that collective groups ("comrades' courts") were to participate in the handling of disciplinary and morale problems. Finally, the statutes limited the disciplinary rights of officers below the regimental level and raised those of officers at the upper levels.[113]

The most portentous innovation, however, was a policy depreciating what are known as the "conventional" forces (the Ground Forces, the Forces of the Rear, the surface navy, and tactical aviation). Although the new, discriminatory policy was not to become a crucial public issue until the early 1960's, its incipient stage went back to early 1959, the period after the Twenty-first Congress. The policy was based on several propositions: (a) Large standing forces were expensive and of limited use in the event of a nuclear war; (b) if they could not be reduced outright (something that was in fact attempted the following year), they must be utilized productively in the economy, which was suffering from a manpower shortage; (c) the conventional forces were the most "military" of all service branches in that they adhered strongly to the traditional virtues and values; (d) the conventional forces, burdened with a vast corps of officers who had had little professional or technical education and whose prospects for a successful adaptation to civilian life were therefore bleak, had a large stake in preserving their status in the military and thus became susceptible to manipulation by the Party; and, finally, (e) the standing forces might serve to divide the military community, which would be a way of weakening the officer corps' opposition to the military reforms.

As the Party was laying the groundwork for the extensive modernization of weapons and equipment in the military and for an overhauling of Soviet strategic doctrine that would bring the doctrine into harmony with these technological changes, it was preparing for sharp reductions of the traditional forces with respect to size, role, and allocations.

This effort was to be delayed, however, by the fact that 1959 was a year of great activity and many improvements in the military. Large amounts of new weapons and equipment were being introduced into the units, and the commanders, having gained at least temporary concessions from the MPA, were enjoying more freedom to prac-

[113] See Marshal A. Grechko, "Novye ustavy Vooruzhennykh Sil SSSR" (The New Statutes of the Armed Forces of the USSR), *Krasnaia zvezda*, September 7, 1960.

tice their profession than they had since the year of Zhukov's ouster. Even though they had to spend more time on Party affairs than formerly, they could use the time to their own advantage. There ensued a period of relative tranquillity in the relations of Party and military, when the main issues concerned not the frictions between the two institutions but rather the ways of improving technical expertise in the units and of introducing officers and men to the modern weapons, equipment, and processes. This peaceful phase, however, was not to be of long duration. The Party, as we now realize, never intended to abandon the reforms in the military, though it was willing to moderate some and postpone others, whereas the military was arriving at an ever better position for dealing with the rising pressures and controls of the Party and the MPA. The next stage of the conflict began in 1960.

E · THE DIALOGUE ON POLITICAL CONTROLS RESUMES: 1961-1963

On January 14, 1960, at the Fourth Session of the Supreme Soviet of the USSR, Nikita Khrushchev announced a series of measures of great importance to the Soviet Union. Of special interest were those parts of his lengthy speech that dealt with the problems of defense and their relationship to economic policies. The central thesis of Khrushchev's statements was in many ways similar to that of Malenkov's policy speech of August 1953. Thus, Khrushchev said that (a) "the general trend is toward reduction of tension in international relations";[114] (b) "under present conditions war is no longer completely inevitable";[115] (c) "modern means of waging war do not give any country the advantage of surprise attack";[116] (d) "war would begin differently . . . and it would develop differently [from heretofore]";[117] and (e) "never in the whole history of the Soviet state has the defense of our country been so reliably secured against any chance incidents and encroachments from the outside as at present."[118] Having affirmed that "reduction of the numerical strength of the army will not prevent us from maintaining the country's defense capabilities at the necessary levels,"[119] he proposed reducing the Soviet armed forces by 1.2 million men (from 3,623,000

[114] Address published in *O vneshnei politike Sovetskogo Soiuza, 1960 g.* (On the Foreign Policy of the Soviet Union in 1960), Gospolitizdat, Moscow, 1961, Vol. 1, p. 17.

[115] *Ibid.*, p. 28. [116] *Ibid.*, p. 38. [117] *Ibid.*, p. 48.

[118] *Ibid.*, p. 28. [119] *Ibid.*, p. 48.

to 2,423,000).[120] Khrushchev justified this measure by pointing to the changed dynamics of warfare, which had enlarged the role of strategic missile forces and correspondingly decreased that of the large conventional forces. And he argued that such a reduction in armed manpower would bring about substantial savings, which could benefit other sectors of the economy:

> Our state has at its disposal powerful rocket equipment. The military air force and navy have lost their previous importance in view of the modern development of military equipment. . . . In the navy the submarine fleet assumes great importance while surface ships can no longer play the part they once did. . . . The armed forces have been to a considerable extent transferred to rocket and nuclear arms.[121]

> In our time the *defense potential of the country is determined, not by the number of our soldiers under arms* [*and*] *the number of persons in naval uniform* . . . [but] by the total firepower and the means of delivery available. . . .[122]

> . . . the reduction of the Soviet armed forces will save approximately 16 to 17 billion rubles per year. . . . This is a large additional amount for the fulfillment and overfulfillment of our economic plans.[123]

Khrushchev's announcement of the massive cut in the armed forces, the formal change in Soviet strategic doctrine, and the reduced role of many of the conventional forces, which he seemed to view as obsolete, had a shocking impact on the military and hastened the deterioration of its relations with the Party leadership. These radical changes also caused a schism within the ranks of the Soviet High Command, which manifested itself in long debates between the chief exponents of the conflicting viewpoints and attracted wide attention in the West. The gradual alienation of some members of the Stalingrad Group, coupled with the spreading opposition within the larger military community to the new policies pursued by Khrushchev, accelerated, if it did not actually bring about, the latter's ouster in 1964.[124]

What could have prompted Khrushchev, in January 1960, to embark on a series of measures that were bound to create conflicts? His motives must be sought in the economic imperatives of the Soviet

[120] *Ibid.*, p. 33. [121] *Ibid.*, p. 36. [122] *Ibid.*, p. 37. (Italics added.)
[123] *Ibid.*, p. 50. [124] See Chapter VIII, *passim.*

state as well as the political and diplomatic dynamics of the Party leadership. At the Twenty-first Party Congress, he had embarked on an ambitious policy of economic development, embodied in the Seven Year Plan, and this required substantial amounts of investment capital, which could be obtained only if allocations to other sectors were reduced. Also, Khrushchev had become convinced of the effectiveness of nuclear deterrents, as well as of the unlikelihood of an unprovoked attack from the West, and was drawing the logical conclusions from this assessment. Capitalizing on the West's overestimate of Soviet nuclear capabilities and its erroneous notion of a "missile gap," Khrushchev was seeking to cut allocations to the conventional forces, presumably so as to be able to divert some of these funds to the development of the strategic forces and some to the civilian economic sector. Also, he was eager to reduce manpower in the conventional forces, whose vast fixed numbers were tying down many young men who were urgently needed in the civilian economy.

Khrushchev undoubtedly expected the implementation of his policies to be easy and uneventful and to meet with little opposition from the military. The top of the military hierarchy, so he must have reasoned, consisted mainly of his trusted associates from the Stalingrad Group; the officer corps had been largely renewed after the ouster of Zhukov and was likely to be loyal to the new regime; and the military community as a whole had been so thoroughly cowed by the controls and indoctrination imposed since 1957 that it could not be expected to offer any opposition to directions from the Central Committee. Furthermore, Khrushchev was probably counting on the goodwill and gratitude he was earning among the officer corps by his strong military posture *vis-à-vis* the West and his exaggerations of actual Soviet capabilities; for these were not only proving politically useful in international relations but were flattering to the Soviet military and satisfied its traditional desire for a militant posture.[125]

Yet Khrushchev underestimated the inner resilience of the officer corps, and his overt and covert attempts to diminish its role and its authority and to cut allocations met with stubborn resistance. Departing from the Party's traditional policy of ruling the military by keeping it divided, he relinquished an effective operational control when he threatened the interests of several military sectors and thus

[125] For an authoritative analysis of Khrushchev's political uses of his military capabilities, see Arnold Horelick and Myron Rush, *Strategic Power and Soviet Foreign Policy*, University of Chicago Press, Chicago, 1966.

caused them to unite in the common objective of opposing his policies and reforms and, if necessary, his personal leadership. Opponents of strong political controls and egalitarianism joined critics who objected mainly to the denigration of the conventional forces, who in turn joined those whose chief objection was to Khrushchev's and the Central Committee's usurpation of the authority to define strategic doctrine and conduct high-level military planning.

The Party's new policy, as outlined in Khrushchev's speech of January 1960, represented a serious change in allocational policies, in social planning, and in the assessment of the international situation and the role of the Soviet Union in it. To anticipate any opposition to the implementation of those parts of the policy that affected the military most severely, the Party made a three-pronged effort to overwhelm the officer corps and suppress any resistance in the High Command: political controls in the military, with all their abuses, were greatly intensified; the announced reduction of the forces, in which 250,000 officers were to be severed from active service, provided the opportunity for a "cold purge" through the release of the most undesirable elements; and Khrushchev's strategic-doctrinal pronouncements were given respectability by being presented as based on scientific doctrine and derived from Lenin's teachings. At the same time, the Party apparatus began actively to promote the heroic legend of Khrushchev as a war leader and hero of great military genius.[126] Notwithstanding these various efforts, the Party found itself facing serious tension and opposition in the military as a result of the massive reduction of the armed forces, and particularly of the officer corps.

1. Social Problems of Mass Demobilization

The manpower cuts had the most immediate and severe impact upon officers in the conventional forces. The release of a quarter-million officers caused sharp resentment among the military intelligentsia, for it cast out into an unfriendly social environment a large number of men who had become used to a relatively good standard of living, high social status, and a sense of professional as well as economic security. As civilians, they now faced a bleak future, in which it would be difficult for them to earn a livelihood and support their families in an environment that had no need for their craft and and did not encourage their way of life. Demobilization thus meant

[126] See Chapter V.

demotion from a privileged social group to the lowest class of workers.[127]

Marshal Malinovskii acknowledged the problem when he said, in his speech of January 19, 1960, that, while the enlisted men would find little difficulty in adjusting themselves to civilian life, "the demobilization of more than 250,000 officers will be accompanied by various difficulties."[128] He urged officers to face up to these difficulties and make the best adjustment possible. Having cited dismaying examples and statistics, from which it appeared that of the 70,000 officers released in the preceding six years only 27,000 (35 per cent) had found work comparable to their previous military positions, while the rest had had to take jobs at the lowest level of ordinary workers, Malinovskii impressed on the officers now facing demobilization that "it does not become our Soviet people, Soviet officers . . . to be discouraged because of the necessity to change profession, or because one has to leave the armed forces without having served the requisite period for a pension."[129] After describing the government's provisions for easing the transition period, he placed the burden of success on the officer himself:

> The officers themselves . . . must show care about acquiring a skill. In the past it often happened that persons leaving the army spent a long time seeking an especially remunerative position while time passed.[130]

127 A very candid description of the socio-economic problems of officers in "socialist" countries who have been released from active service appears in J. J. Wiatr's excellent essay, "Niektore problemy socjologiczne armii socjalistycznej" (Some Sociological Problems of the Socialist Army), in *Studia Socjologiczno-Polityczne*, No. 14, 1963, pp. 29-32. Referring to such former officers as "marginal social people," Wiatr maintains that many officers transferred to the reserves are incapable of obtaining positions equivalent to those they had in the army, or of adapting themselves to the social positions which they occupied before their military service.

Another specialized study, cited by Wiatr, which sought to describe the problems of officers transferred to reserves found that "for the great majority of those interviewed, the army represented a channel for rapid social advancement. The entrance into a social group of high prestige was viewed by many of them as a permanent achievement upon which they based their future life plans. The officer's transfer into the reserves and the return to the social group from which he had entered the military was viewed by many of those interviewed as a social degradation. . . . The majority . . . were dissatisfied with their present social position and would eagerly return to active service." From E. Olczyk, *Przystosowanie sie do zycia cywilnego oficerow politycznych rezerwy* (The Adaptation to Civilian Life of Reserve Political Officers), p. 31.

128 *Krasnaia zvezda*, January 20, 1960.

129 *Ibid.* 130 *Ibid.*

The plight of the demobilized officer is reflected in a candid report, published in *Literaturnaia gazeta*, of an "interview" with a major, a former battalion commander without special skills, who had recently been released. He complained:

> I am forty-six—that's the trouble. . . . What pleasures are ahead of me? Am I to eat up my pension and wait until I die? Too soon for that. And work does not come easily for me. I need a place in life, do you understand? I need active service.

When assured that he would find work, he exclaimed: "What do you mean, work? I am an old platoon officer. Where does a company officer belong in a civilian job?"[131]

2. *Degradation of the Conventional Forces*

Another consequence of the new military policy was the use of members of the conventional forces for work in the civilian economy. The resumption of this old practice, which the Party had largely suspended since the 1930's, was most likely attributable both to the pressing need for manpower[132] and to the decline in the importance of these conventional forces.

[131] *Literaturnaia gazeta*, May 24, 1960. *Krasnaia zvezda* of February 3, 1961, reported the case of an undisciplined young soldier cynically exclaiming to his commander, who was trying to give him some fatherly advice: "I don't need any teachers. I was Grade 6 in the plant and had a former major as a metal worker apprentice working under me." See also Marshal Malinovskii's remarks to the personnel boards making the selections among the officers for demobilization and discharge, admonishing them not to discriminate against unskilled older officers (*K novomu pod"emu*, p. 12).

[132] The birth rate in the Soviet Union had suffered considerably during the war years 1941-1946. It was therefore expected that the number of Soviet citizens reaching working age between 1959 and 1965 would be low in proportion to the total population. Academician A. Kurskii (*Voprosy ekonomiki*, No. 9, 1948, p. 22) speculated that "This factor will necessitate an even greater enrollment of available urban and rural manpower resources into . . . production and a search for new ways of raising labor productivity." The extent of the impending manpower shortage for the period after 1959 can also be inferred from statistics in *Narodnoe khoziaistvo SSSR v 1956 godu: Statisticheskii sbornik* (The National Economy of the USSR in 1956: Collected Statistics), Gosstatizdat, Moscow, 1957. The following table (p. 224) shows an over-all decline of about one-third in the population of the first four school grades between 1940 and 1956.

Enrollment in Soviet Grades One Through Four, 1940-1956 (in percentages of 1940 enrollment)

	1940-41	*1950-51*	*1954-55*	*1955-56*
Urban areas	100	115	96	107
Rural areas	100	84	47	49
Total	100	92	60	66

The use of military labor was referred to in the Soviet press by the euphemism *shefstvo* (patronage). Ostensibly, a *kolkhoz*, *sovkhoz*, or factory became the "patron" of the local military unit and occasionally participated in its cultural activities, sports events, and various festivities, and the unit reciprocated the interest by assisting the "patrons" in a variety of tasks. Actually, however, the Party's designs went far beyond such sporadic mingling of civilians and soldiers during holidays, as can be seen from the many reports on *shefstvo* that appeared in the military press. The most objectionable aspects of *shefstvo*, from the military's point of view, were its arbitrariness and its disregard for timing. Since the political organs in the military units made the dispositions, they frequently used soldiers for *shefstvo* without concern for established military schedules and plans. Also, the busiest time in agriculture, and therefore the greatest demand for military labor, coincided with the most active period in the military, the field training of late summer and early fall, and in this conflict of priorities the military tended to be the loser.[133]

The importance of the issue is reflected in the frequent references to *shefstvo* by members of the High Command and other military leaders.[134] While many of these references were perfunctory, others betrayed intense partisanship. Not surprisingly, spokesmen for the technical and strategic forces strongly favored the practice of *shefstvo*, while members of the conventional forces were markedly unenthusiastic about it.[135]

3. *The Growth of Military Opposition*

In May 1960, the Party convened in Moscow a vast All-Army Conference of Secretaries of Primary Party Organizations, the first such gathering since 1938, and thus symbolic of the importance that the

[133] See Kolkowicz, *The Use of Soviet Military Labor*, *passim.*

[134] At one time or another, almost every member of the High Command expressed his approval of military *shefstvo*. However, while officers in the political organs and representatives of the privileged technical services spoke with great enthusiasm and encouraged its wider application, other officers either referred to it perfunctorily, as one of several recent Party measures, or even obliquely criticized it by stressing the constant need of the conventional forces to keep military training in the field their primary objective. See the 600-page collection of articles and speeches by various military officers concerning the recent upsurge of military *shefstvo*: *Narod i armiia—ediny* (The People and the Army Are United), ed. Lieutenant General M. Kh. Kalashnik (Deputy Head of MPA), Voenizdat, Moscow, 1959. See also *Narod i armiia—edinaia sem'ia* (The People and the Army Are One Family), Lenizdat, Moscow, 1961, and references to military *shefstvo* by the top military leaders in *K novomu pod"emu*, *passim.*

[135] See Kolkowicz, *The Use of Soviet Military Labor*, *passim.*

Party leaders attached to the pending implementation of their new military policy and to the intensification of the Party's influence in the armed forces. The main purpose of the conference was to set down the new line, and to instruct the Party secretaries on the nature and the use of the indoctrination and control mechanisms that were to accompany the military reforms and were designed to strengthen the Party's influence in the officer corps with their renewed stress on Marxist-Leninist precepts.[136]

That same month, the Party announced the mass promotion of over 450 generals. The aim of these promotions was partly to replace officers who had been released in the course of the recent reductions in force, and partly to rejuvenate the higher echelons, where superannuated ranks were blocking the advancement of younger, well-trained officers who were known to be loyal to the Party.[137]

A vast majority in the military was beginning to see in Khrushchev's policies toward the armed forces a major threat to many of their traditional prerogatives, interests, and objectives. With each new regulation, statute, and decree it became clearer that Khrushchev envisaged, ultimately, a severely truncated military organization, shot through with a network of political organs and divided between the strategic forces, to be given preferential treatment, and the conventional forces in a greatly reduced role. This vision included an officer corps divested of meaningful professional authority, in which commanders were at best *primi inter pares* in their own commands, dependent on collective decision-making bodies and subject to harassment from the Komsomol at the bottom, the MPA and Political Departments at the top, and civilian Party *apparatchiks* on the outside.

For the time being, Khrushchev still had the support of the top layer of the military and thus could risk alienating the middle and lower echelons, whose officers had neither spokesmen at the highest Party levels, who might have articulated for them their grievances and demands, nor any protectors within the military establishment against the pressures of the MPA and the political organs. Furthermore, the Party leadership, through deliberate inequality in the assignment of priorities to the various branches of the military, created an internal dissension that, it hoped, would prevent a single "military" viewpoint from crystallizing. Gradually, however, as

[136] *Krasnaia zvezda*, May 15, 1960.

[137] *Pravda*, May 9, 1960. The distribution of the promotions was as follows: 19 to colonel general, 140 to lieutenant general, 295 to major general.

Khrushchev's new military policies began to affect strongly the upper layers of the military hierarchy as well as the middle and lower ones, they provided a common bond of dissatisfaction throughout the military.

The new strategic doctrine was based on the premise that a future war would take the form of a sudden, brief nuclear exchange between the two major powers. With this assumption, Khrushchev was narrowing the range of strategic-doctrinal possibilities and opportunities to a single option, and effectively preventing the military from developing and planning for other strategic variants.[138] Also, he was consigning the traditional branches of the military, where much of its elite still resided, to the historical scrap heap and in the process was destroying a number of institutional empires and individual careers as well as cherished doctrines and tenets. Finally, in Khrushchev's doctrine the role of the military in affairs of state and in the formulation of policy had been greatly reduced. Deterrence became nearly automatic and thereby regulatory, keeping international relations in an uneasy but workable balance of terror and obviating the need and justification for the large defense budgets that in the past had been associated with high levels of international tension. Faced with the specter of their growing expendability, some members of the High Command began to question, though timidly at first, the wisdom or usefulness of the new strategic policy. Rather than oppose it outright, they began by seeking to expand it beyond the limits laid down by Khrushchev. Others, however, strongly criticized the ill effects that various Party policies were having on the motivation, discipline, and readiness of the troops.

In December 1960, the political organs reported alarming signs of a growing inertia, deterioration of discipline, and bureaucratic excesses in the military.[139] The following year, they themselves became

[138] Criticism of such strategic-doctrinal narrowness came out early in 1964, in an important polemical article by Colonel I. Korotkov, "O razvitii sovetskoi voennoi teorii v poslevoennye gody" (The Development of Soviet Military Theory in Postwar Years), *Voenno-istoricheskii zhurnal*, No. 4, April 1964, pp. 39-50. Korotkov said (p. 48): "We must admit that our military thought . . . paid insufficient attention to the study of limited [local] wars even though imperialist powers have frequently, in the postwar period, made use of them to achieve their objectives through force. Only in recent times has this shortcoming begun to be corrected." For an analysis of this and related articles, see Kolkowicz, *Soviet Strategic Debates: An Important Recent Addendum.*

[139] Colonels E. Tarasov and S. Il'in, "Vsemerno sovershenstvovat' rabotu partiinykh komitetov akademii" (Constantly Improve the Work of the Party Committees in the Academies), *Kommunist Vooruzhennykh Sil*, No. 5, December 1960, pp. 26-32; General of the Army F. Golikov, Head of the MPA, "O nekotorykh vo-

the subject of highly critical comments. In September 1961, a very candid article by Marshal Krylov attacked the fundamental tenets of Khrushchev's new policy toward the military; it condemned the principle of *kollegial'nost'* (collective initiative), the practice of *kritika/samokritika,* and the omnipresence of the political control functionaries, and strongly advocated widening the authority of the commanders. Krylov wrote:

> Lenin taught us that military affairs, more than anything else, demand the strictest unity of action of large masses of people and the subordination of the wills of thousands to that of one man—the single commander (*komandir-edinonachal'nik*).

He also warned against uncontrolled use of *kritika/samokritika*:

> . . . it is necessary to use this sharp instrument very skillfully. V. I. Lenin frequently stressed that criticism of failings must not be used just for the sake of criticism. . . .

Arguing strongly for the commander's authority and freedom to undertake decisions without interference from "assistants," Krylov attacked the political organs for hampering the officers in the performance of their tasks:

> *Edinonachalie* presupposes full independence of the commander within the limits of rights granted to him. That is why I would especially like to single out the *exceptional importance of* [*allowing*] *the officer to develop the ability and habit of independently undertaking appropriate decisions* concerning various problems which may face him in his daily duties as well as in combat. [Italics in original.]
>
> There is no doubt that *the growing role of mobility in military operations sharply elevates the importance of firm and uninterrupted control of the forces.* [Italics in original.] That is why it is necessary to have at the head of a subunit, regiment, and *soedinenie* [a force group larger than a regiment, usually a division] a commander who is able to use his full authority boldly, decisively, *without looking back over his shoulder.* . . . [Italics added.]
>
> [Many officers] waste a lot of time while making a decision or when giving orders because they feel it is their duty to consult ahead of

---

prosakh propagandistskoi raboty" (On Some Problems of Propaganda Activities), *ibid.,* pp. 16-25.

time literally all their assistants [the Russian word here is *zamestiteli*, an obvious reference to the political officers, whose full title is *zamestiteli po politicheskoi chasti*, commonly abbreviated to *zampolit*] and helpers, and to listen to their opinions and suggestions.

Finally, Krylov challenged the Party's advocacy of collectivism (*kollegial'nost'*) in military affairs; by citing in support of his position Lenin's statement that "collective deliberations must be kept down to the absolute minimum and must never be an obstacle to quick and firm decisions," he made it difficult for the political organs to refute him.[140]

Marshal Krylov's bluntness in criticizing the Party for emasculating the officer corps, and his warnings of the ill effects that such policies could have on the military's performance and discipline, clearly reflected the growing schism within the Stalingrad Group and in the military as a whole. Being a close associate of Malinovskii and Zakharov, Krylov no doubt spoke for the moderate wing of the High Command, which was becoming deeply concerned over the situation. The focus of the military's gathering opposition gradually narrowed to two main issues: the restrictive strategic doctrine of Khrushchev, and the meddling of the political organs.

a. Attack on Khrushchev's Strategic Doctrine. The first public criticism of Khrushchev's doctrine appeared in late November 1960, in an article by Lieutenant General S. Krasil'nikov. The writer took issue with those who would view a future military conflict as "a push-button war, which could be conducted without mass armies. . . . In the new war, massive multimillion armies would without a doubt be participating, which would require large reserves of commanding personnel and vast contingents of soldiers." Despite the fact that surprise attack would have serious effects, it would "not be a decisive factor determining the conduct and outcome of the war." Furthermore, said Krasil'nikov, while missile forces were becoming the central element of the Soviet military, this did "not at all mean the minimization of our ground forces."[141]

The following spring, the military opposition made its second thrust. Writing in *Voenno-istoricheskii zhurnal*, the forum of the

140 "Vsemerno ukrepliat' edinonachalie" (Strengthen *Edinonachalie* in Every Possible Way), *Krasnaia zvezda*, September 27, 1961.

141 "O kharaktere sovremennoi voiny" (On the Character of Modern War), *Krasnaia zvezda*, November 18, 1960.

traditional elements of the armed forces, General of the Army V. Kurasov launched into a detailed, though oblique, critique of Khrushchev's military doctrine.[142] Leaning heavily on the writings of Lenin for ideological support of his views, General Kurasov forcefully stated the case of the military opposition. His main points were that (a) mass armies, far from becoming obsolete in modern warfare, were still a factor indispensable to victory;[143] (b) investments in heavy industry and in the machine industry must be maintained at high levels, since these industries constituted the backbone of the country's defense and the civilian economy;[144] (c) monistic theories in the development of concepts of warfare were dangerous; and (d) it was absolutely necessary to have large, modern armies and weapons systems *prior* to the outbreak of a war.[145] Kurasov's polemic was an unmistakable attack on the ideas of Khrushchev, whose strategic doctrine and economic policies contradicted the general's position on every one of the above points.

One further point in the article may be indicative of the extent of the military's dissatisfaction. Citing Lenin on the importance of having an offensive doctrine and not relying on a defensive one, Kurasov strongly advocated developing an aggressive, dynamic strategy that did not renounce the prerogative of striking first at the enemy. He also emphasized the need to destroy, rather than merely defeat, the enemy's military forces.[146]

Several weeks after the appearance of the article, the Khrushchev faction in the military responded to it without mincing words. In the main organ of the MPA,[147] Colonel S. Kozlov, a well-known military writer and an apologist for Khrushchev and the Party,[148] sharply at-

[142] "Voprosy sovetskoi voennoi nauki v proizvedeniiakh V. I. Lenina" (Problems of Soviet Military Science in the Works of V. I. Lenin), *Voenno-istoricheskii zhurnal*, No. 3, March 1961, pp. 3-14.

[143] *Ibid.*, pp. 6-7. [144] *Ibid.*, p. 7.

[145] Kurasov cites Lenin to bolster his case for large, combat-ready conventional forces in addition to other branches of the military: "If we do not possess all means of warfare, we may suffer a critical—even a decisive—defeat. . . . By possessing all means of warfare, we will surely succeed" (p. 9). "Victory in modern war will go to that side which will better dispose of the means of warfare already available in the armies" (*ibid.*). This stress on "already available" means of warfare (i.e., available prior to the outbreak of hostilities) has been echoed by many supporters of the conventional forces and those who desire larger allocations to the defense sector. Malinovskii, Grechko, and others used that formula in 1962.

[146] Kurasov, pp. 11-12.

[147] Colonel S. Kozlov, "Tvorcheskii kharakter sovetskoi voennoi nauki" (The Creative Character of Soviet Military Science), *Kommunist Vooruzhennykh Sil*, No. 11, June 1961, pp. 48-56.

[148] Some of Kozlov's more recent writings include a clever essay entitled "Voen-

tacked the traditionalists in the armed forces, whose "dogmatism and conservatism" he found destructive to military progress:

> Adherence to past experience (or rather to that which is becoming or has become obsolete) is inevitably accompanied by an overappreciation and fetishism of former models, in particular the methods and forms of armed struggle, especially if they led to victory.
>
> Supporters of tradition, for example, do not want to recognize the changed roles of the various branches and arms of the armed forces, while dogmatically expounding the well-known thesis from Soviet military theory about their harmonious development.
>
> Obsolete, dogmatic conceptions of the circumstances attending the preparation and initiation of a war, the character of its initial stages, the possibility and duration of mobilization . . . can only interfere with progress in each of these areas, since the situation has undergone such changes that thoroughly new and unbiased decisions are needed, free from worship of the old ways.[149]

Despite rebuttals such as these, dissatisfaction in the military with the new strategic doctrine continued to grow, and found expression at the Twenty-second Party Congress in October 1961. From that august forum, Marshal Malinovskii, after praising the virtues and genius of Khrushchev and the Party, went on to say: "The Presidium of the Party Central Committee and the Soviet Government have called upon us to pay special attention to the initial phase of a possible war."[150] The chief premise of the strategic doctrine laid down in January 1960 had been precisely that the initial stage of the war would be decisive, an assumption that sharply reduced the need for large conventional forces while strongly increasing the importance of the strategic missile forces. Most noteworthy, therefore, was this statement in Malinovskii's speech, in which he clearly dis-

---

naia doktrina i voennaia nauka" (Military Doctrine and Military Science), *Kommunist Vooruzhennykh Sil*, No. 5, March 1964, in which he attempts to justify and legitimize the Central Committee's absolute power over all phases of military activity by creating a complex typological matrix of the various aspects of military life (science, doctrine, art, theory, etc.), in which the military itself retained only a very narrow margin of authority and professional freedom. See also Kozlov's article in *Kommunist Vooruzhennykh Sil*, No. 2, 1961. In addition, Kozlov figures as the general editor of S. I. Krupnov, *Dialektika i voennaia nauka* (Dialectics and Military Science), Voenizdat, Moscow, 1963.

149 *Kommunist Vooruzhennykh Sil*, No. 11, June 1961, pp. 52-53.

150 *Pravda*, October 25, 1961.

sociated himself from the narrow Khrushchevite doctrine of January 1960:

> Although nuclear weapons will hold the decisive place in a future war, we are nevertheless coming to the conclusion that final victory over an aggressor can be achieved only through combined operations by all branches of the armed forces. . . . We also believe that under modern conditions any future war would be waged, despite the enormous losses, by mass armies of many millions.[151]

During 1962, Malinovskii continued to press a moderate line that admitted and integrated the less extreme proposals of both schools of military strategy: the "radical" Khrushchevite school, which stressed the suddenness and finality of future war, whose outcome would be decided largely by strategic missile forces, and the "conservatives" in the military (centered mainly in the conventional forces), who continued to see a great role for the conventional forces in a future war, since they maintained that only a combined-arms operation would bring final victory. "Our defense capabilities," said Malinovskii, "must be such as to keep the enemy in uncertainty about the outcome of his planned war . . . and, when finally the war becomes a fact, to destroy the aggressor decisively."[152] He also repeated that, no matter how important strategic missile-nuclear weapons and the initial period of war might be, the role of mass armies and the harmonious cooperation of all branches of the armed forces still remained a crucial factor. Views to the contrary notwithstanding, he pointed out, a regular cadre army continued to be indispensable in repulsing an aggressor at the beginning of a war, and the need for such a standing army was enhanced by the complex technology of modern weapons and equipment, with which only a regular army of well-trained soldiers and officers could cope.[153]

The important work *Voennaia strategiia* (Military Strategy), edited by Marshal Sokolovskii, which appeared in the summer of 1962, added further fuel to the debates on military strategy and policy. It reflected predominantly the views of Malinovskii and the moderates, and thus provoked the wrath of the extremists in both strategic schools.[154]

[151] *Ibid.*

[152] Marshal Malinovskii, "Programma KPSS i voprosy ukrepleniia Vooruzhennykh Sil SSSR" (The CPSU Program and Problems of Strengthening the Armed Forces of the USSR), *Kommunist,* No. 7, May 1962, p. 15.

[153] *Ibid.*, p. 20.

[154] For a detailed analysis of the various strands and sources of conflict in the

Throughout 1962, the attitude of the "radical" sector of the military remained detached and rather silent,[155] while the "conservatives" and "moderates" continued to press their point of view with remarkable vigor and candor.[156] The failure of the "radicals" to assert themselves publicly might have been due in part to a compromise between the military and the Party, in which both factions would have agreed to modify and moderate their views. But such an explanation does not satisfactorily account for the continuing, and indeed worsening, conflict of opinions and interests between the military conservatives and the moderates on one hand, and the radicals and the MPA on the other. A more plausible theory is that, in 1962, Khrushchev was plan-

---

military and the Party, see T. W. Wolfe, *A First Reaction to the New Soviet Book "Military Strategy,"* The RAND Corporation, RM-3495-PR, February 1963. Wolfe maintains that the authors of *Voennaia strategiia*, faced with two authoritative guidelines—Khrushchev's theses of January 14, 1960, and Malinovskii's speech at the Twenty-second Party Congress (followed by his May 1962 article in *Kommunist*)—"appear to have taken their guidance mainly from the Malinovskii theses outlined at the 22nd Party Congress . . ." (pp. 26-27). Wolfe also views the public debates on strategy and the softening of Khrushchev's strategic views as the result of a possible compromise between the military and Khrushchev. He states: "Perhaps the basic feature of this compromise . . . is that Khrushchev's January 1960 doctrine with its preeminent stress on *deterrence* has since been modified to deal more fully and explicitly with requirements for *waging* a nuclear war should one take place" (p. 30).

155 The "radicals" who thus abstained from public expressions in 1962 had fairly dominated the discussions in 1961. Aside from the aforementioned writings of S. Kozlov, who exemplified the radical school's pseudo-scientific approaches to military strategy, and rejected older doctrine on the grounds that the new missile-nuclear technology had "cancelled out all previous concepts of the character of war," a number of other military writers expressed the radical viewpoint, including Colonel P. Sidorov (*Kommunist Vooruzhennykh Sil*, No. 12, June 1961) and Colonel N. Sushko (*ibid.*, No. 18, September 1961).

156 After the Twenty-second Party Congress, the moderates and conservatives launched a vigorous campaign to make their views public. See Malinovskii's speech at the Congress itself and his important article in *Kommunist*, No. 7, May 1962; Colonel General N. Lomov in *Kommunist Vooruzhennykh Sil*, No. 10, May 1962; Colonel I. Sidel'nikov in *Krasnaia zvezda*, May 11, 1962; General of the Army P. Kurochkin's review of *Voennaia strategiia*, in *Krasnaia zvezda*, September 22, 1962; and Marshal P. Rotmistrov's forceful argument in support of the important role of armor in nuclear warfare, *Izvestiia*, October 20, 1962. Interestingly enough, Colonel General A. I. Gastilovich, who is generally associated in the West with the radicals and whose role on the *Voennaia strategiia* editorial board, where he has expressed dissident views, has been cited to support such an assumption, was singled out for some very damning criticism by a ranking member of the MPA just prior to the publication of *Voennaia strategiia.* This may bespeak an effort by the Khrushchevites to dissociate themselves from Gastilovich's rather dissonant views on military strategy, similar to the military's pointed emphasis on the fact that Gastilovich was the author of Chapter VII, which contained these rather radical views. Or, it may indicate that the MPA leadership itself was divided on the issue.

ning the Cuban venture, which, if successful, would have silenced his opposition; for, by sharply reducing the strategic disparity between the Soviet Union and the United States, it would have shortened the costly road to parity by way of an arms race, and this saving, in turn, would have enabled Khrushchev to shift allocations more freely from the strategic to the conventional forces. A successful emplacement of strategic missiles in Cuba would, with one blow, have vindicated Khrushchev's policies *vis-à-vis* the United States, stilled some of the vitriolic harangues from Peking, and enhanced Khrushchev's position in his own Party, thereby giving him a stronger hand in dealing with the military.

b. Attack on the Political Controls. While the military's dissatisfaction with Khrushchev's strategic doctrine was carefully followed and widely analyzed in the West, little attention was being given to the growing resistance of the military community to Khrushchev's socio-political reforms of the officer corps, which had equally grave implications for Soviet politics. After the military's unexpected opposition to the egalitarian reforms in 1958, which had temporarily frustrated the attempt, Khrushchev waited until the early 1960's to resume the effort. However, as before, the military community, though it stopped short of open disobedience, interposed numerous obstacles designed to slow down the momentum of these "Chinese reforms" through bureaucratic guerrilla tactics and inertia. Thus, it met the attempt to impose firm Party controls in the armed forces with various forms of resistance by letting discipline deteriorate drastically; by obstructing political appointees in commanding positions in the performance of their duties;[157] by neglecting political indoctrination; and by openly questioning the skills, wisdom, and

[157] The head of the Cadres Department in the MPA, Major General L. Vakhrushev, reported on the problems involved in the attempts to place political officers in commanding positions and commanders in political positions. He stated that "43% of all political personnel have previously served in command positions" and described the resistance of both the professional officers and the political organs to having "outsiders" forced down their throats: "As in the past, the appointment of political functionaries to command positions at the regimental and higher levels proceeds in a timid fashion. Even those who went through special training are not willingly appointed as commanders. Usually, officers of the cadre organs explain this [unwillingness] by stating that political functionaries do not have proper command experience." He added that "Some political departments of military districts and fleets . . . give little assistance to those comrades who are appointed to political work from command duties." "Vsemerno uluchshat' rabotu s kadrami politsostava" (Improve Work with the Political Cadres in Every Possible Way), *Kommunist Vooruzhennykh Sil*, No. 23, December 1962, p. 27.

authority of the nonprofessional political functionaries in the officer corps and the political organs.

Signs of the military's resistance to the reforms and intensified political controls first appeared in the summer and fall of 1961 and became more frequent after the Twenty-second Party Congress. The MPA reported serious deterioration of discipline and morale in the military districts of Turkestan, Transbaikal, Siberia, Belorussia, and Leningrad.[158] Though the trappings of the Party Congress temporarily covered over the schism between the Party and broad sectors of the military community, both sides returned to their previous positions in the months following, and the conflict grew deeper.

The extent of the military's opposition to the Party's reforms was such as to leave little doubt that its intransigent stand was being encouraged, or at least quietly approved, by the hierarchy of the Ministry of Defense.[159] The line of attack that the Party and the MPA followed after the Twenty-second Party Congress concentrated, therefore, on the central offices of the Ministry, many of

[158] *Ibid.*, No. 22, November 1961, p. 58.

[159] An important source of the officer corps' dissatisfaction with the military policies of the Party was the new law regulating the procedures for promotions, attestations, transfers, and appointments. Colonel General A. P. Beloborodov, the former head of the Cadre Board (which deals with promotions and other personnel matters), subsequently commander of the Moscow Military District, has described the changes as follows: "A new procedure was introduced in 1959 for the attestation of officer personnel. . . . Attestation Commissions are created before each scheduled attestation . . . which include the heads of the political organs, the secretaries of the Party committees and of the Party *biuro*. The old methods used in special purpose attestations were changed, since they frequently failed to define the correct political and professional characteristics of the officers." Beloborodov states that "before appointing or transferring an officer, the commanders must consult with their assistants [clearly a reference to the political officers], chiefs of staff, and secretaries of the Party committee and Party *biuro*." Beloborodov then addresses himself to the root of the difficulty about the promotions, transfers and attestations of officers, namely the fact that the officers' careers depend on the opinion of the political officers and Party functionaries: "The principle of *edinonachalie* in connection with the appointments of cadre personnel does not obviate, but rather makes more imperative, the need for . . . superiors to consult the opinions of the political organs and the Party organizations about the practical activities and the growth potential of every officer." From "Rabotu s ofitserskimi kadrami—na uroven' trebovanii XXII s"ezda KPSS" (Work With Officer Cadres—On the Level Defined by the Twenty-second Congress of the CPSU), *Kommunist Vooruzhennykh Sil*, No. 2, January 1962, pp. 19-26.

It should be noted that the military's rejection of political controls coincided with its firm resistance to the Party's strategic guidelines as well as to attempts to create a historical image of Khrushchev as the hero of Stalingrad. Its demands for greater participation in the formulation of military doctrine and for a more prominent historical role were different aspects of the officers' self-assertion in the face of the Party's attempt to subjugate them.

whose high officers belonged to the moderate and the conservative factions. Since the Party's main instrument of control within the military is the MPA, Khrushchev used it to lay the groundwork for changes which most likely were intended to bring the MPA more directly under his personal control and to sharpen its bite for the pending power struggle with the military.

In March 1962 the MPA reported that it had "uncovered serious deficiencies" in the central apparatus of the Defense Ministry.[160] Among these it listed (a) the throttling of *kritika/samokritika* rituals, (b) "serious breaches of discipline," (c) obstruction of Party functionaries in their indoctrinational and control activities within the Ministry, and (d) the use of paid propagandists to deliver political and educational lectures in place of ranking members of the Ministry's staff.

In April, the Central Committee, which presumably was becoming deeply concerned about the military's opposition, ordered the MPA to call a meeting of the chief political personnel in the military with a view to taking firm steps toward strengthening the Party's role in the military.[161] The proceedings of the meeting were remarkable in their vehement criticism of the officer corps, whose members were accused of a large number of faults and actual offenses. They were said to be "full of deviousness" (*ochkovtiratel'stvo*) and insidious loyalty to one another, which made them practice *krugovaia poruka* (covering up for one another); high officers, including generals and admirals, allegedly were abusing their rank and authority for socio-economic advantage; instructions from the MPA and the Ministry were said to be disregarded; and men at the highest levels were cited as having tried to protect their comrades from criticism by preventing the Party organs from seeing their files. The meeting instructed the political organs to involve themselves more closely with the military community, to wipe out arrogance and conceit among officers, and to promote *kritika/samokritika.*

In May 1962, General Epishev replaced Marshal Golikov, a military moderate, as head of the MPA.[162] A close associate of Khrushchev, with a long career in the security organs and a deep involvement in political control activities, Epishev was clearly the man to break the officer corps' resistance, and his appointment suggested that a showdown was imminent.

[160] *Kommunist Vooruzhennykh Sil*, No. 5, March 1962, pp. 55-57.

[161] See a report by Major General A. Bukov, head of the Party Organizational Department of the MPA, *ibid.*, No. 10, May 1962, pp. 22-28.

[162] *Krasnaia zvezda*, May 22, 1962.

At about the same time, Marshal Malinovskii published two important articles, in which he set forth the moderate point of view on a variety of issues, particularly on matters of political education, its relationship to military training, and its bearing on morale.[163] His main points were: (a) the relationship between superior and subordinate should be strict and correct, without familiarity (*panibratstvo*); (b) while political education was important, it was no more important than military training and education; (c) political education had been too theoretical and esoteric, and it needed to be reduced in scope and related more closely to the pragmatic problems that concerned the military;[164] and (d) to maintain high morale, military personnel should be given adequate food and clothing.

Epishev, while making verbal concessions in response to the military's demands for better economic conditions,[165] began to tighten his hold on the armed forces. He initiated review procedures, instituted controls, and exposed segments of the military to scathing public criticism. Within a month of assuming his new office, he attacked the military academies, the traditional breeding ground of military professionalism and élan.[166] Again, their alleged sins were indifference to Party criticism, "covering up" for members of the officer corps, and resistance to the Party's demands for greater egalitarianism.

In August, the MPA finished a thorough survey of the activities and the personnel of the central apparatus of the Defense Ministry and made public its findings.[167] The report was a wholesale indictment of the military hierarchy within the central administrations of the Ministry. The ground forces, which had been the central target of Khrushchev's strategic and socio-political reforms as well as the major source of military opposition, were the main object of the indictment. The personnel of the General Staff and the administrative apparatus were said to ignore the directives of the Central Com-

[163] *Kommunist*, No. 7, May 1962; *Krasnaia zvezda*, May 24, 1962 (an expanded version of this article was also published in *Kommunist Vooruzhennykh Sil*, No. 11, June 1962).

[164] This, it should be noted, had been Marshal Zhukov's line when he was Minister of Defense, and had earned him the wrath of the political organs.

[165] *Krasnaia zvezda*, June 4-9, 1962.

[166] Cf. the MPA report in *Kommunist Vooruzhennykh Sil*, No. 12, June 1962, pp. 40-43.

[167] "O rabote partkoma i partiinykh organizatsii shtaba i upravlenii Sukhoputnykh voisk" (About the Work of the Party Committee and Party Organizations of the Staff and Administrations of the Ground Forces), *ibid.*, No. 15, August 1962, pp. 38-41.

mittee, to "cover up" for one another, to resist *kritika/samokritika*, and to have tolerated the deterioration of ideological and political education and a decline in military training and readiness. The report was accompanied by Epishev's strong admonition to the staff of the Ministry that in their future activities they take into account the criticism and recommendations of the MPA commission created for the purpose of furnishing such advice.

This gross encroachment of the MPA on the private preserves of the military could not but aggravate the situation, since it undermined the authority and role of the military commanders and administrators at the highest levels, including the Minister of Defense. And at the very moment that the top echelon of Party and military were planning the Cuban venture, the military community and the political organs were attacking each other with growing boldness and intensity. *Krasnaia zvezda* carried an unusually large number of articles and letters to the editor with complaints about the low living standards of the officer corps, demands for wider authority for commanders, and sharp criticism of the political control organs for their excessive intrusions into military activities.[168]

In October 1962, the Party called an unpublicized meeting of MPA functionaries from all branches of the armed forces. Both Epishev and Malinovskii participated in this extraordinary gathering, which presumably was intended to relieve tensions and improve the situation. From the subsequently published expressions of these two protagonists, however, one can only conclude that the meeting did not achieve the desired adjustment of central objectives and that the Cuban fiasco shortly thereafter further alienated the broad military community from Khrushchev and the MPA. The meeting, whose avowed purpose was to "improve the Marxist-Leninist and military-theoretical training of officers and generals"[169] as well as the role and authority of Party organizations in the military, was also attended by the head of the Central Committee Section on Administrative Organs, N. R. Mironov, and the deputy head, N. I. Savinkin.[170] Their presence underlined the importance and gravity of the occasion.

Krasnaia zvezda chose the tense period of the Cuban crisis to publish Malinovskii's remarks to the MPA gathering. Malinovskii, far

[168] See Chapter VII, p. 268, fn. 126.

[169] *Krasnaia zvezda*, October 25, 1962.

[170] For details on Mironov's position and background, see Appendices A-VI and A-VIII. Among other participants in this important gathering were: Marshals of the Soviet Union M. V. Zakharov, K. S. Moskalenko, V. D. Sokolovskii, and S. K. Timoshenko.

from yielding to the MPA's pressure, reaffirmed the need to leave the military as free as possible to perform its main task, which was to ensure the readiness and effectiveness of troops and equipment. He accused the political organs of amateurishness and ignorance in military matters, and rejected in particular their criticism of the young people then entering the military, whose low morale was being blamed for the grave disciplinary problems in the armed forces. As for *kritika/samokritika*, Malinovskii cautioned the political organs "to use that sharp weapon sensibly. We do not need criticism for its own sake, but only that which is principled and helps us strengthen our armed forces."[171]

Epishev's speech was published in the October issue of *Kommunist Vooruzhennykh Sil*, the chief organ of the MPA. Significantly entitled "Firmly Carry out the Party's Policy in the Armed Forces," it stressed again and again the Party's supreme jurisdiction in the armed forces, whose commanders were said to exercise their authority only on the sufferance of the Central Committee. Epishev warned the military:

> We think it is a very important task to explain to the military cadres the essence of *edinonachalie* in the Soviet armed forces. . . . *It is absolutely necessary that all officers, generals, and admirals clearly understand that the indispensable condition for achieving edinonachalie*, and for successful mastery of the tasks of regiments, ships, and divisions, *is the constant support given to the commanders by Party and Komsomol organizations*, the ability to direct their activities. . . .[172]

Epishev then urged the MPA functionaries to eradicate from the military "any manifestations of rudeness, swagger, and haughtiness," and pointed to *kritika/samokritika* as a "well-tried means for dealing with all negative phenomena, including perversions of *edinonachalie*."[173]

[171] *Krasnaia zvezda*, October 25, 1962.

[172] "Tverdo provodit' v zhizn' politiku partii v Vooruzhennykh Silakh" (Firmly Carry out the Party's Policy in the Armed Forces), *Kommunist Vooruzhennykh Sil*, No. 19, October 1962, p. 9. (Italics added.)

[173] *Ibid.* Epishev's assistant, Lieutenant General M. Kalashnik, elaborated on his boss's views in an article entitled "Krepit' edinstvo ideologicheskoi i organizatorskoi raboty v voiskakh" (Strengthen the Unity of Ideological and Organizational Work Among the Troops), *Kommunist Vooruzhennykh Sil*, No. 22, November 1962, in which, among other accusations hurled at the military, he cited the low levels of ideological awareness and education in the officer ranks. He said: "There still are recidivists who underestimate the importance of [ideological training]. How else could one explain the fact that the political administration of the Leningrad

In the aftermath of the stunning experience of the Cuban missile crisis, the Party was to try to use the military as its scapegoat, while the military community in turn took advantage of the unsettled situation to press its case and strengthen the opposition.

4. *After the Cuban Missile Crisis*

Despite the attempts of Khrushchev and his lieutenants to paint the fiasco in Cuba not as a failure but rather as a mutual accommodation of interests by the United States and the Soviet Union,[174] the event undoubtedly dealt a great blow to Soviet political and military policy and the country's pride.[175] Furthermore, it destroyed whatever hopes the Party and the military may have had of approaching strategic parity with the United States through the emplacement of strategic missiles close to the American borders. The Party now faced difficult policy decisions, as well as the humiliating comments of Peking and, presumably, some of its own military leaders.[176]

To the Soviet military, the Cuban debacle spelled the end of all hopes of catching up with the American strategic buildup in the near future. Worse than that, it most likely meant that Khrushchev,

---

Military District has for two years failed to bring to the attention of the Military Council problems of ideological activities? This was rectified only after an inspection by the MPA in September 1962" (p. 17). It should be noted that the head of the Leningrad Military District at that time was Marshal Krylov, a most outspoken opponent of the political organs' excessive intrusions into military affairs. (See above, pp. 159-160, for some of his views on the subject.)

[174] Khrushchev's explanations were not very convincing. At the Sixth Congress of the Socialist Unity Party of Germany (cf. *Pravda*, January 17, 1963), he said:

"There are people who claim that Cuba and the Soviet Union suffered defeat in the Caribbean conflict. But such people have a strange logic: How can it be that we suffered defeat, when revolutionary Cuba exists and is growing stronger? Who really retreated and who won in this conflict?

"We are told: If you removed the missiles from Cuba, you retreated. . . . Yes, this was our concession in exchange for a concession by the other side; this was a mutual concession. The imperialists were compelled to make a concession and renounce invasion of Cuba. And it was to protect Cuba from invasion by the imperialists that we installed the missiles. Consequently, our missiles performed their role."

[175] For an authoritative analysis of Soviet policy and behavior pertaining to the Cuban affair, see A. Horelick, "The Cuban Missile Crisis: An Analysis of Soviet Calculations and Behavior," *World Politics*, No. 3, April 1964.

[176] Several weeks after the Cuban fiasco, Khrushchev took the Red Chinese to task for accusing him of having retreated weakly: "Even those who claim that he is now 'a paper tiger' know that this 'paper' tiger has atomic teeth. . . . Some people, when the serious developments took place in Cuba, resorted only to abuse. The imperialist forces did not become weaker from these noisy shoutings. . . ." *Krasnaia zvezda*, December 13, 1962.

chastened by American firmness in the Caribbean, would shift from a militant to a détente-oriented foreign policy, which would destroy the military's chances of larger defense budgets and a prominent role in Party councils.

Events during the months following the Cuban crisis would seem to indicate that the Party leadership attempted to silence military criticism of Khrushchev's handling of the operation;[177] Party spokesmen repeatedly stressed the fact that the Central Committee and the Party possessed both the right and the instruments to guide all military affairs,[178] and they impressed upon the military that military means served political ends, which in turn were determined solely by the Party.[179] Most likely, the Party also tried to persuade the military that current political ends were best achieved by a shift from militancy to détente.

It was to be expected that military professionals would not be sympathetic to these arguments, and events between November 1962 and March 1963 suggest that they strongly resisted the Party's pressures. Challenges and counterchallenges, warnings and counterwarnings, and mutual accusations filled the pages of the Soviet press, but in February and March the two sides apparently reached some form of accommodation. Marshal Biriuzov, the most loyal champion of Khrushchev among the marshals, became the new Chief of the General Staff, and his appointment symbolized the beginning of a new phase in Soviet military politics.[180]

One can only surmise the nature of the *modus vivendi* between Party and military. The only victim of the conflict had been Marshal Zakharov, who was removed as head of the General Staff to make room for Marshal Biriuzov, and even his eclipse proved to have been only temporary.[181] The Party leadership, through the MPA, abandoned its rigid position in matters of strategic doctrine, and embraced the

[177] See Marshal Chuikov's interview in *Krasnaia zvezda*, November 17, 1962.

[178] *Ibid.* See also General Epishev in *Kommunist Vooruzhennykh Sil*, No. 19, October 1962; an editorial in *Krasnaia zvezda*, December 8, 1962; Epishev in *Politicheskoe samoobrazovanie*, January 1963; *Voprosy istorii KPSS*, No. 2, February 1963; and a series of essays on Party supremacy in the military in *Krasnaia zvezda*, February 12 and 20, 1963.

[179] *Ibid.*

[180] For details, see R. Kolkowicz, *Conflicts in Soviet Party-Military Relations: 1962-1963*, The RAND Corporation, RM-3760-PR, August 1963.

[181] Remarkably enough, when Biriuzov was killed in an aircraft accident in Yugoslavia, immediately after Khrushchev's ouster from power, Marshal Zakharov was reinstated in his old post as Chief of the General Staff, and his rehabilitation may have been symbolic of the military's return to a more influential status.

strategic view of the conservatives and moderates. Moreover, it lifted controls and reduced indoctrination in the military enough to meet at least some of the military's objections. On the other hand, the Party established its authority to speak for the military establishment in matters of strategic doctrine and policy, and apparently secured the military's assurance that it would cease its severe criticism of many Party measures. The truce, however, did not last long, and events in the year 1964 were once again to bring about radical changes in the relations of Party and military.[182]

[182] These events are treated separately in Chapter VIII, which focuses on the motives, reasons, and events behind the ouster of Khrushchev.

VI · The Dialogue on Historical Roles: A Forum for Claims, Grievances, and Demands

> The historian is not only a detached narrator who only describes events . . . within a scientific schema. He is a fighter, whose goal is to use the history of past events in the struggle for Communism.
>
> B. N. Ponomarev, ranking Party historian, in *Voprosy istorii*, No. 1, 1963.

The Communist Party uses many means of persuasion and coercion to politicize and control the citizens within the Soviet state. The main reason for this vast effort is the Party's desire for a harmonious polity in which internal contradictions either cease to exist or become "non-conflicting" and where all social efforts are planned, controlled, and executed under the Party's guidance.

However, the Party's ideals of public consent and social harmony are not easily attained. During the long years of Stalin's rule, Soviet society came close to conforming to such a model, but after Stalin's death, with factions in and outside the Party vying for power, dissonant voices were heard in public to question, and even to oppose, certain policies of the Party and the views of some of its leaders. To be sure, doubts and opposition rarely were expressed unequivocally, in keeping with the etiquette for Party members which demands that such disagreements be transmitted through esoteric, indirect, and politically "neutral" media. To maintain the fiction of a harmonious society and avoid posing a direct challenge to the Party leadership of the moment, the questioners and dissenters abide by this etiquette; although the fiction fools no one, it serves its purpose as long as the external forms are preserved and dissent is contained within the Party.

Very frequently, criticism of certain Party policies or personalities is disguised in polemics on historical issues. Such historical dialogues commonly serve as the proper context in which to dispute certain historical claims of the Party. They are also used to express disagreement with current Party policies, and at times to settle differences between the Party and the military.

History, in general, plays a major role in the Party's control mechanisms within the state. To begin with, the philosophical, ideological premises on which the political system rests are historical in the sense that world communism is assumed to be the final stage in the conflict between socio-economic classes. Moreover, the Party constantly adjusts the presentation of historical events in such a manner that past failings and mistakes are ascribed to particular personages while the ideology remains correct and the Party unsullied. Finally, as pointed out above, debates on historical events often take the place of discussions of current events when there is need for an exchange of opinions on sensitive problems without disturbing the fiction of internal harmony.

Among the greatest sins of a Soviet historian are professional objectivity and political detachment. The Party regards him as a propagandist whose main concern is to further its immediate objectives, and its vigilance over the "correctness" of historical writing is constant:

> Soviet historians rely in their research on communist *partiinost'* as a methodological principle that permits the only objective—correct understanding of social history. . . . The essential methodological importance of this principle consists of the fact that, while it does not supersede the professional skills and qualifications of the historian, it provides him with a correct general point of view. . . .[1]

When the Party leadership is torn by internal power struggles, it may happen that writers and editors get their signals mixed, or side with the losing faction, or deliberately take advantage of the absence of uniform guidance and vigilance to depart from the rigidly prescribed historical subjects and attitudes. Such indulgence in historical objectivity usually draws the wrath of the winning Party faction, which is likely to resent the public airing of embarrassing historical truths except where a particular event makes it mandatory. And even where a major disclosure is desirable, it is usually filled with political implications and therefore is left to the top leadership.

Soviet historical writings are clearly political, a fact that is reaffirmed by their close relation to current events. For example, each major political event in the Soviet Union during the past decade has been accompanied by changes of tone, stress, and attitude in Soviet historiography. The death of Stalin freed the military from silence, and a dialogue with the Party ensued. In 1953-1954, the dialogue was dominated by the Malenkov wing of the Party, while the military

[1] G. M. Smirnov, in *Voprosy istorii,* No. 12, December 1962, p. 25.

and the Khrushchev faction played only a minor role in it. With the departure of Malenkov and the rise in the fortunes of Khrushchev and Zhukov, the views and interests of these two men took over the historical dialogue in an uneasy balance, until, after the ouster of the anti-Party group and of Zhukov, only the views of the Party functionaries and of Khrushchev's adherents in the military remained, and the dialogue became a monologue.

In 1961, the dialogue resumed. The main forum for the military point of view was supplied by *Voenno-istoricheskii zhurnal* and *Krasnaia zvezda.* In addition, there appeared a large number of military memoirs, which generated disapproval both in the Party and in the military.

In 1962 and 1963, the deterioration of relations between some military elements and Khrushchev and his adherents was reflected in the growing heat of the debate. This correlation served to support several contentions: (a) the historical argument is essentially a political dialogue between the Party and broad sectors in the military; (b) through this dialogue the military can challenge the Party on vital issues; (c) the dialogue offers a useful index to perennial tensions and conflicts between the Party and the military; and (d) the military's forceful argumentation, and the Party's tolerance of it, indicate the growing assertiveness of the military and its larger political role. (The last contention finds support in the fact that in the past, whenever the Party was firmly in control of the military, it did not tolerate any public challenges from the military; it suffered them only at times when it was internally divided or when it needed the good will of the military against an external threat.)

It has been suggested that the Party's tolerance of the military's questioning of certain historical interpretations indicates its strength and lack of concern. But this argument does not hold up in the face of the great importance that the Party has always attached to the uniformity and "purity" of historical writings. Nor does it provide a satisfying theory in view of the prominence of the chief protagonists in the dialogues, the sharpness and directness of their mutual criticisms, and the sensitivity of the issue involved. The historical debates may be said to constitute a continuing effort of the major power centers in the state to prove their wisdom, strength, and indispensability and deny past failures and mistakes. The dialogue thus takes the place of an open forum in which each of these two bureaucracies, the Party and the military, can state its claims.

Dialogue on Historical Roles

A · THE ISSUES AND THE PROTAGONISTS

The historical dialogue deals with a general range of issues that nominally pertain to World War II and to the roles that the Party and the various military groups and personalities played in it. The issues, and the positions taken in the dialogue, reflect the perennial conflict of interests between the military and the Party. Thus, the military has demanded to have the armed forces' contribution to victory described in a more favorable light, partly in an effort to set the record straight, but above all to impress upon the Party that the military is the indispensable institution which not only saved the communist system from catastrophe during the war but is continually doing so. Ancillary to this position is the demand that the Party acknowledge the military's role in society, that it rehabilitate the military victims of purges, and that it refrain from interfering in military affairs.

The historical dialogue revolves around four basic questions: (1) the disastrous initial period of the Russo-German war; (2) the relative significance of the battles of Moscow, Stalingrad, and Berlin; (3) the effect of Stalin on strategy and military doctrine; and (4) the military purges of 1937.

(1) Military spokesmen maintain that it was Stalin's, and by extension the Party's, fault that the Red Army suffered the defeats of the early part of the war. They argue that the Party, for fear of provoking the Germans, had prevented any preparations from being made against the eventuality of an attack, and that total concentration of military authority in Moscow and the powerlessness of the ranking field commanders to undertake any independent action in the face of the enemy's moves led to ill-fated military operations. At the same time, they resent the fact that Stalin, the *Stavka* (the Supreme Command Headquarters), and the political generals have claimed the lion's share of credit for successes and victories and have either ignored or belittled the contributions of the military as a whole. They deny the Party's allegation that, despite the rapid German invasion of western Russian territories, the military continued to be provided with sufficient equipment, weapons, and logistics to carry out operations. On the contrary, so the military claims, in 1941-1942, the most critical period of the war, it opposed a superior enemy and succeeded in repulsing him despite very inadequate provisions for military supplies.

(2) In the historical dialogue, the battles of Moscow, Stalingrad, and Berlin have taken on a symbolic meaning greater than their actual significance. Those who claim that the battle of Moscow was the major, decisive operation during the initial stage of the war tend to be followers of Marshal Zhukov and the *Stavka.* Those who claim that the decisive battle of World War II was Stalingrad are adherents of Khrushchev and the Stalingrad Group. These two battles have been a bone of contention between the Khrushchevites and the Zhukovites in the military, and have been exploited by each side for political purposes. The conflict over the battle of Berlin arises from the opposing claims of Marshal Konev and Marshal Zhukov, who both aspire to be credited with the main role in the achievement of victory there.

(3) Obliquely, and at times openly, the military argues that Stalin, by his rigid and sterile hold on strategic-doctrinal thinking, hampered the conduct of the war and later on ossified military thought so as to whitewash his mistakes.

(4) Military historians tend to dwell on the military purges of 1937 as a most unfortunate period in Soviet history, when the senseless slaughter of thousands of officers weakened the Red Army (thus leading to the military failures, first, of the Russo-Finnish war and, later, of the beginning of the Russo-German war) and alienated much of the military from the Party leadership. Since Stalin's death, and especially since the Twentieth Party Congress, the Party has admitted the criminality of the purges, but it has placed much of the blame for them on the dead Stalin and his henchmen in the police, and has absolved the present ruling elite from all involvement.

The Party, of course, is compelled to reject the above contentions, since to accept them would be to acknowledge its dependence on the military in crisis situations and thus to place in question the premise that its power rests on doctrine and ideology. The Party therefore counters the military's views with the following assertions of its own:

(1) The "foundation of foundations" of the military's strength lies in wise guidance by the Communist Party.

(2) While the defeats early in the war were caused mainly by a combination of capitalist duplicity and Stalin's mistakes, the military bears part of the blame.

(3) In the achievement of final victory the efforts of the Party and the people in the rear (as reflected in the industrial and agricultural

output of the economic front, created and guided by the Party) were at least equal to the contributions of the military at the front.

(4) The military's lack of experience and ability in dealing with a large-scale war and a highly mobile and powerful enemy led to several major disasters in World War II. Morale and discipline in the armed forces were low, and only the Party's intercession prevented an even larger disaster in the initial stages of the war.

B · THE BEGINNING OF THE HISTORICAL DIALOGUE BETWEEN PARTY AND MILITARY: 1953-1955

Between the death of Stalin in 1953 and the ouster of Malenkov in 1955, the military made only a few tentative efforts to open a debate on historical issues. This circumspection may have been due to its realization that such a discussion was a Pandora's box, which would force the Party to make some admission of its role in the military purges of 1937, in the subsequent oppressive treatment of the military, both during and after the war, and in the biased historical presentation of the initial disasters of the war. The military at that time was not in a good position to press such a sweeping public reexamination of the historical record. The only prominent Party member to seek an alliance with and support from the military was Khrushchev. Most of the other Party leaders, including Malenkov, viewed the military with distrust, and resisted any attempts by military circles to initiate the kind of public indictment of Stalin and the Party from which the military stood to gain the most.

The main forum for the expression of authoritative views on the role of the Party and the military in the war and during the early post-Stalin period was the journal *Voprosy istorii.* In an editorial of September 1954, its editorial board reported that at two conferences, held on the previous June 25 and 28, respectively, and attended by leading historians from various parts of the Soviet Union, it had been decided "to transform the journal into the leading organ of Soviet historical science."[2]

One of the first signs of the new direction and political alignment of the journal after the announced reorganization appeared toward the end of 1954. In an editorial entitled "The Great Successors to Lenin's Work," the editors used the occasion of Stalin's seventy-fifth birthday to heap unlimited praise on the dead dictator. In the process, they quoted Stalin in a manner suggesting that he viewed the

[2] *Voprosy istorii,* No. 9, September 1954.

role of the military as a secondary factor in Soviet victories: "Only childish people think that the laws of artillery are stronger than the laws of history."[3]

The antimilitary position of *Voprosy istorii* came fully to light in its December issue, in a review by E. G. Bor-Ramenskii of B. S. Tel'pukhovskii's *The Great Victory of the Soviet Army at Stalingrad.*[4] This book, one of the first post-Stalin attempts to set straight the military's record in the war, was criticized in the journal with a sharpness that was not in proportion to Tel'pukhovskii's moderate claims on behalf of the military. Both in form and substance, the review merits closer analysis, for it proved to be the prototype of subsequent antimilitary arguments by Party historians. These are some of the reviewer's critical comments:

> . . . not a word is said about the activities of the Party and Soviet organizations of Stalingrad during its defense.[5]
>
> The book does not show sufficiently the heroism of Soviet people in the battle for the city. . . .[6]
>
> [The author] barely describes the difficulties and, what's more important, how the Soviet people overcame these difficulties.[7]

Several other remarks suggest that the reviewer's bias was not only antimilitary but anti-Khrushchev as well. Thus he complained that the author had omitted any description of the "serious military failures in military operations of Soviet units . . . in the summer of 1942" and had failed to point out that some Soviet commanders "did not understand the characteristics of modern war."[8] He also rejected the author's views of the importance of the Stalingrad counteroffensive for the outcome of the war, and mentioned other battles as having added substantially to final victory. He objected to the author's great emphasis on the role of General Chuikov in the Stalingrad battle, and suggested that other generals contributed at least as much as Chuikov. And he also complained that the writer had overstressed the activities of the Partisans in the Ukraine while barely describing those of partisans elsewhere.

Each of the reviewer's arguments against Tel'pukhovskii was actually an attack on Khrushchev and the military. The "failures in

[3] *Ibid.*, No. 12, December 1954.

[4] *Velikaia pobeda Sovetskoi Armii pod Stalingradom*, Gospolitizdat, Moscow, 1953.

[5] *Voprosy istorii*, No. 12, December 1954, p. 136.

[6] *Ibid.* [7] *Ibid.* [8] *Ibid.*, p. 137.

the summer of 1942" referred to disastrous operations at Kharkov, where Khrushchev had acted as political supervisor. The belittling of the Stalingrad counteroffensive, of Chuikov, and of the Ukrainian Partisans all were slights aimed at Khrushchev, who viewed the Stalingrad battle (in which he claimed a leading role) as the crucial operation of the whole war, who was close to Chuikov and later furthered his career, and who had organized and been responsible for the Ukrainian Partisans.

In February 1955, Malenkov was forced out of the premiership, Zhukov became Minister of Defense, and a number of Khrushchev's close associates from the Stalingrad Group were promoted to leading positions in the armed forces. This change in the top leadership and the growing prominence of the military in Party politics were reflected in the historical dialogue. *Voprosy istorii* shifted its editorial position in favor of the military in general and Zhukov in particular. The debate as such changed to a more open and direct expression of views and became a triangular exchange, in which the Stalinists in the Party continued to adhere to old positions, while the Zhukovites pressed for a broad reassessment of history and a more prominent role for the military in public affairs, and the Khrushchevites, supported by spokesmen of the Stalingrad Group, argued sharply with Zhukov and tried to minimize his achievements while emphasizing their own. The position of Khrushchev at this stage was difficult. On the one hand, he could not afford to alienate Zhukov, on whose support he presumably counted in the continuing conflict with his opponents in the Party; on the other hand, he was naturally eager to further the careers of his own adherents in the military, and had to do so without arousing Zhukov's suspicions.

C · THE DIALOGUE SHARPENS: 1955-1957

With the ouster of Malenkov, Khrushchev moved one step closer to dominating the Party. However, he achieved this gain at the price of making concessions to Zhukov and his supporters in the military. For the next two-and-a-half years, until Zhukov's dismissal from office, the two military factions dominated the historical debate. The Stalingrad Group, led by Marshal Konev, claimed most of the credit for victory, with great stress on the importance of the Stalingrad battle and extravagant claims on behalf of Khrushchev and other Party people for their performance at the front. Zhukov, in turn, with support from some ranking officers, stressed the significance of the Moscow battle, took personal credit for various successful operations, and belittled or entirely ignored the activities of Khrushchev and other Party people. The expressions on both sides were of an unprecedented sharpness and frankness.

This new phase in the debate began in February 1955, with an article by Lieutenant General A. Rodimtsev which stressed the decisive importance of the Stalingrad battle in the outcome of the war and, for the first time since Stalin's death, referred to Khrushchev as a significant contributor to that victory.[9] A few days later, Zhukov gave an interview to several American journalists in which he repeatedly emphasized his own central role in a number of crucial battles of the war.[10] Two weeks after that, Konev stated the views of the Stalingrad Group in a prominent article in *Pravda*.[11] While Zhukov's interview was strongly promilitary, Konev's article, which was an implicit rebuttal of Zhukov's statements, closely adhered to the Party line and to Khrushchev's views. Konev restated his arguments in two leading articles he wrote on the tenth anniversary of victory in Europe.[12] (Zhukov on that occasion rated only a small article.)

The clash between Konev, a spokesman of the Stalingrad Group, and Zhukov had important consequences. First of all, the public airing of sensitive historical and political issues made it acceptable and proper for military historians to submit such questions to open analysis. Secondly, the split between Zhukov and the pro-Khrushchev faction in the military was a signal to Khrushchev's rivals within the Party that the right moment had come for them to widen that split by siding with Zhukov against the Khrushchevites.

Voprosy istorii entered editorially into the fray. With a clear bias in favor of Zhukov, it listed as "valuable" sources to be used by historians of the war the names of Molotov, Voroshilov, Bulganin, Kalinin, Zhdanov, and Shcherbakov.[13] The pointed omission of

[9] *Pravda*, February 2, 1955. The only other reference to Khrushchev in connection with the Stalingrad battle was found in an article in *Voprosy istorii*, No. 5, May 1950, written by A. Samsonov. The author, writing in the prevailing Stalin-oriented manner, stressed that the Stalingrad counteroffensive was worked out by the *Stavka* and that the battle was unequaled in the history of wars.

[10] See Boris Meissner, *Russland unter Chruschtschow*, R. Oldenbourg Verlag, Munich, 1960, p. 46.

[11] *Pravda*, February 13, 1955.

[12] *Pravda* and *Krasnaia zvezda*, May 9, 1955. Publication of these articles coincided with Konev's appointment as Commander-in-Chief of the Warsaw Pact Forces.

[13] *Voprosy istorii*, No. 5, May 1955, p. 3.

Khrushchev was a slur that was sure to be obvious to Soviet readers, well attuned as they are to the Aesopian language and symbolism of Party literature.[14] To make the point still clearer, the editorial criticized historians for "glossing over" (the word used was *lakirovat'*—to varnish or veneer) the early disasters with the explanation that the "original military operations of the initial period of the war were classical forms of active defense . . . while, in reality, Soviet forces were conducting difficult defensive operations and retreated deep into the country under fierce enemy pressure." The editorial went on to attack Konev's and, by implication, Khrushchev's claims about the central significance of the Stalingrad battle, complaining about those who created the impression that the battle at Stalingrad decided the outcome of the war, ". . . as if the Soviet forces subsequently met with no serious opposition and their military operations consisted of a continuous victorious march. Such a description of events does not conform to reality."[15] Finally, the article demanded that historians pay attention to the names of military leaders and include them in their writings, and that they give greater prominence to the importance of the "anti-Hitler coalition, the military cooperation of the USSR, the USA, and England, in the destruction of the enemy. . . ."[16]

The same issue of the journal that contained this ill-concealed criticism of the Khrushchevites and the Stalingrad Group also carried a long article by the military historian E. A. Boltin, which stressed Zhukov's contribution to the final victory at Berlin and thus undermined Konev's claim to the central role in conquering the German capital.[17]

Zhukov continued to press the hard military line, presumably enjoying the confusion and division in the Party hierarchy that enhanced his own position, until the Twentieth Party Congress, which met in Moscow in February 1956 and was to have a vast impact both on world communism and on internal Soviet affairs. By destroying the Stalin myth, Khrushchev was able to make Stalin into a symbolic scapegoat for most of the ills of communism. While the reverberations and side-effects of de-Stalinization probably exceeded Khrushchev's intentions, its immediate and practical rewards lay in his gain in personal power and prestige, and in the discrediting of

[14] The omission of Malenkov from that list may be explained by the fact that he had recently been dismissed from power and prominence.

[15] *Voprosy istorii*, No. 5, May 1955, pp. 5-6.

[16] *Ibid.*, pp. 6-7. [17] *Ibid.*, p. 16.

many of his rivals in the Party because of their association with Stalinist excesses.

The Twentieth Party Congress had also an immediate impact on the relations between military and Party. In a clear bid for his support, Khrushchev bestowed accolades on Zhukov in his "secret" speech.[18] At the same time, he added to his power base in the military through military and political promotions among his own men from the Stalingrad Group.[19]

However, if such public honors and conciliatory gestures had been expected to mollify Zhukov to the point of making him give up the public role and become once more a "good general," there was to be disappointment in the Party ranks. Far from relinquishing his role of vociferous defender of the military establishment and critic of the Party, Zhukov continued the public debate with members of the Stalingrad Group who, in fact, were speaking for Khrushchev. A major clash between these factions occurred soon after the Party Congress. It followed directly upon an article by Marshal Konev, in February 1956, which once again stressed the great contributions that the Party and the field commanders had made to the Soviet victory in World War II.[20] In April, an editorial in the military periodical *Voennyi vestnik* addressed itself to the sensitive issue of the reasons for the devastating defeats suffered by the Red Army during the early period of the Russo-German war, the question that was to be at the center of the controversy.

It will be recalled that during Stalin's lifetime no mention had been made of the possibility that the Soviet Union might have shared in the responsibility for the crisis. Instead, the combination of Western imperialism and the excellence of the German army were blamed for the success of the surprise attack. Furthermore, Stalin devised the myth of the "active defense" concept so as to represent the rapid, disorganized retreat of the Red Army under the relentless blows of the Germans as part of a brilliant Soviet plan. But it did not deceive the military, who chafed under the humiliation of those early defeats. The public renunciation of Stalin at the Twentieth Party Congress broke the dike of that long-repressed bitterness, and the military now began to ask for an accurate presentation of the initial phase of the war, and to place the blame for the defeats on

[18] See *The Anti-Stalin Campaign and International Communism,* Columbia University Press, New York, 1956, pp. 53-54.

[19] See Chapter VII, pp. 248-249.

[20] *Krasnaia zvezda,* February 23, 1956.

Stalin while crediting itself with having averted worse disaster. The *Voennyi vestnik* editorial which touched off the controversy attributed the early defeats to the unpreparedness of the Red Army. While it blamed Stalin for this state of affairs, it also criticized military commanders for lack of ability in the conduct of military operations.[21]

Several weeks later, the *Voennyi vestnik* editorial provoked a direct rebuttal from *Krasnaia zvezda*, the central newspaper of the Ministry of Defense. In it, the editors of *Voennyi vestnik* were accused of "harmful judgment" in stating that "our army had to retreat and conduct difficult defensive operations because of supposed failure to bring the forces to combat readiness." The article added:

> Especially strange and unconvincing are the journal's opinions about certain uncoordinated activities of certain military groups which were supposedly caused by the lack of readiness of the Armed Forces of the USSR. . . . The authors of the article in *Voennyi vestnik* have, intentionally or unintentionally, belittled the importance of our victory in the past war. They have belittled the decisive role of the Soviet people and their armed forces in the achievement of that victory.[22]

This attack on *Voennyi vestnik* by the organ of the Defense Ministry, with its strong denial of any responsibility on the part of the military for the initial defeats, must have placed Khrushchev and his followers in a dilemma; for they could neither afford to attack the Zhukov faction directly nor quietly tolerate an outburst from *Krasnaia zvezda* which, at the very least, would be a dangerous precedent.

The Party resolved the dilemma with the publication of a reply in *Kommunist*, the organ of the Central Committee.[23] The article, while striving to sound conciliatory, firmly asserted that the Party and the Stalingrad Group had played the key role in achieving victory, but gave some credit also to Zhukov and his followers.

Thus, the authors stated unequivocally that the "political organs and Party and Komsomol organizations played a powerful role in

[21] It is noteworthy that the editorial in *Voennyi vestnik*, No. 4, April 1956, treated the operations of the Central and Voronezh Fronts at Kursk in a very favorable manner. These two Fronts were staffed and commanded by many members of the Stalingrad Group, including Konev and Khrushchev.

[22] *Krasnaia zvezda*, May 9, 1956.

[23] "Glubzhe izuchat' istoriiu Velikoi Otechestvennoi voiny" (Study More Profoundly the History of the Great Patriotic War), *Kommunist*, No. 10, July 1956. The authors were V. Evstigneev, B. Zhilin, and S. Roginskii. (Evstigneev was to receive some scathing criticism from the Zhukovites about one year later.)

the training of our soldiers," and that, in the early days of the war, "contacts between many units were often damaged and command of the forces was impeded."[24] They described the extremely critical situation at the front and the rapid advance of the enemy, who was moving across the shattered Soviet armies at the rate of 20 to 30 km a day. Having thus set the stage by giving the Party-political organs much of the credit for the development of the army and painting a dramatic picture of the chaos in the military and the crumbling of Red Army defenses at the initial German thrust, the authors proceeded to the main points.

Characterizing the *Voennyi vestnik* editorial as "basically correct," they criticized *Krasnaia zvezda* for labeling as "incorrect and harmful" its analysis of some of the causes of Soviet failures at the beginning of the war, and for failing to provide an answer to the question of why the Soviet forces had to retreat far into their country. "How did it happen," the article asked, "that our army, on whose preparedness many efforts were expended, fell into a critical situation during the initial months of the war and had to retreat?"[25]

The authors answered their own question by pointing to some of the Red Army's difficulties at the time of the surprise attack—among them reorganization, the introduction of new weapons, and the absence of mobilization—as having given the enemy the advantage. Although this did not contradict or diminish their implicit criticism of the military, the authors showed conciliatory intentions by placing the lion's share of the guilt on Stalin. Their unreserved praise, however, went to Party leaders Khrushchev, Molotov, Zhdanov, and others, and to the Party as a whole:

> . . . the Party, while under difficult conditions, did not shirk its duties, did not lose its head under the pressure of the perfidious and cruel enemy, and managed to inspire the people's masses to mobilize their efforts to oppose the invaders and radically to change the fate of war and achieve victory.[26]

The authors also referred to the battle of Moscow, but they gave it only cursory treatment, whereas they pulled out all the stops in describing the battles of Stalingrad and Kursk, thereby supporting the interests and claims of Khrushchev and the Stalingrad Group.

The exchange of criticisms between Party and military in the spring and summer of 1956 might seem, on the surface, to have been an exercise in vagueness and innuendo. Only Stalin was clearly identi-

[24] *Ibid.*, pp. 60 and 63. [25] *Ibid.*, p. 63. [26] *Ibid.*, p. 65.

fied as a villain, and all were united in condemning him. Who, then, were the other villains? Actually, it is not very difficult to identify the protagonists. Given Zhukov's professional pride and his insistence on military autonomy, and in view of his high position as Chief of the General Staff at the beginning of the war, any attack on the officer corps and any charge of military unpreparedness was an implied criticism of him.[27] By the same token, attempts to defend the military and to absolve it of any responsibility in the initial failures would also point to him. Seen in this light, the foregoing exchange would appear as a dispute between the military professionals around Zhukov, whose point of view was expressed by *Krasnaia zvezda*, and the Party faction around Khrushchev, supported by the Stalingrad Group, speaking through the article in *Kommunist*.

Far from chastened by the Party's criticism, Zhukov continued his campaign for greater professional freedom and institutional prestige for the military and his demand for a revision of the historical record that would take due account of the military's central role in World War II. For a while, there was little to suggest that his star was dimming. On the anniversary of the battle of Moscow, in December 1956, Zhukov was given accolades and expressions of public adulation that were almost unprecedented for a professional officer. The only four-time recipient of the medal of Hero of the Soviet Union, he received the congratulations of the Party leaders on the occasion of his sixtieth birthday, and the well-wishing statements were prominently displayed in the press.[28] Marshal Sokolovskii made references to Zhukov's prominent role in the battle of Moscow,[29] and Zhukov was accorded the unusual honor of being sent on an official state visit to India.[30] Finally, he was given credit for the victory at Stalingrad in historical accounts that barely mentioned Khrushchev and members of the Stalingrad Group.[31]

[27] These hints at Zhukov's role in the initial period of the war became direct accusations after his ouster.

[28] See Meissner, *Russland unter Chruschtschow*, p. 49.

[29] *Ibid.*, p. 48.

[30] This was a singular honor to be accorded to a Soviet military leader, the only two precedents having been Frunze's and Tukhachevskii's official state visits abroad, both of which took place at times when the military was asserting itself strongly against the Party.

[31] In a Radio Moscow broadcast in January 1957, Colonel Shatagin, a prominent military historian, referred as follows to the battle of Stalingrad: "The victory at Stalingrad was achieved because of the correct strategy of the *Stavka*, which was directed by Stalin, and the talented military leadership of the prominent Soviet military commanders Zhukov, Vasilevskii, Vatutin, Rokossovskii, and others."

Not only did the Zhukovites assert themselves against the claims of the Khrushchevites, but they also began to settle scores with Stalinist and other Party historians. A most remarkable exchange between Party apologists and champions of the military professionals took place in the pages of *Voprosy istorii.* It began with a letter to the editor from the authors of *Ocherki istorii Velikoi Otechestvennoi voiny* (Essays on the History of the Great Patriotic War), which had been published in 1955. The letter, by A. Samsonov *et al.*, objected to a review of their book by E. A. Boltin and A. S. Filippov, which had appeared in *Voprosy istorii* in May 1956. Along with the letter from the authors of *Ocherki* the journal carried a rebuttal from the reviewers.[32]

The authors of *Ocherki* were known Party apologists, and their book seems to have given the standard version of the events of World War II, assigning all credit to the Party, omitting reference to Stalin's role in the initial disasters, and slighting the contribution of the Red Army.

Boltin and Filippov had initially criticized the book for minimizing the hardships of the Red Army, exaggerating the production rate of Soviet industry during the war, not putting due stress on the importance of the Soviet-Western alliance for the outcome of the war, and glossing over the early part of the war without showing the real causes of the initial disasters. Each of the objections reflected the military's views in general and Zhukov's in particular.

In their letter to the editor, the authors of the *Ocherki* admitted some of these weaknesses; they tried to defend their failure to go more deeply into the causes of the initial disasters by explaining that they had no access "to documents on the history of the Great Patriotic War kept in the archives and unavailable for publication . . . owing to the secrecy surrounding archive documents."[33] General

[32] "Ob 'Ocherkakh istorii Velikoi Otechestvennoi voiny' " (Regarding *Essays on the History of the Great Patriotic War*), *Voprosy istorii*, No. 1, January 1957, pp. 210-220. The authors of the book are hard-core Party hacks. A. Samsonov has written more on the battle of Stalingrad than any other Soviet author. Before 1953, he gave all credit for the victory to Stalin; since then, he has attributed the victory to Khrushchev and his military protégés, to the Party, to the people, and only in a small measure to the military. V. Evstigneev was one of the authors of the article in *Kommunist* (July 1956) which sharply criticized *Krasnaia zvezda*, and implicitly the military in general, for having attempted to correct the historical record by removing the blame for the initial disasters in the Russo-German war from the military and thus indirectly shifting it to the Party. B. Tel'pukhovskii has become an apologist for Khrushchev and the Party in the ongoing historical dialogue between Party and military.

[33] *Ibid.*, pp. 211-212.

Boltin destroyed this feeble defense by stating that, although *Ocherki* appeared before the Twentieth Party Congress, "Soviet historians had already had access to important Party documents and materials (beginning with the materials of the July plenum of the CC/CPSU of 1953) which dealt with the question of overcoming the cult of personality. . . ."[34] He also reiterated the points of the original review with great force. He demanded that historians pay greater attention to military personalities, and that, for example, they mention individual names instead of listing such persons collectively. He seemed to be implying that, while Party personalities received unceasing publicity, military leaders were only perfunctorily mentioned in the press and in historical works.

Boltin's co-reviewer of *Ocherki* raised an even more serious problem by demolishing the claims of Party *apparatchiks* regarding industrial and agricultural production early in the war. Sacrosanct fiction had it that, despite the rapid German march into Russia, the Party leadership was able to construct a powerful industrial base deep inside the country and thus to provide the Red Army with the matériel and weapons necessary to its defense. Filippov now dismissed the Party's statistics as unreliable and false, and cited different figures in support of his case. His attack was remarkably sharp and sarcastic:

> In our review we stated that *Ocherki* has "varnished" history. Haven't real events been "varnished" when the authors maintain that "evacuation of many industrial establishments from Moscow did not cut down the supplies of military products to the front directly from the capital"?[35]

Filippov's own statistics showed that by the end of 1941 the output of the *Mosenergo* electro-station, which supplied Moscow with electric energy, had dropped to 46 per cent of the prewar level, and that even in January 1946 it was back only to 78 per cent of the prewar period. As for the authors' contention that the Soviet government allocated 14 billion rubles for capital investments in 1944 and that this was 4 billion more than in a typical year of the prewar Five Year Plans, Filippov called their statistics false, and quoted his own figures, which proved, among other points, that from 14.1 to 16 billion rubles had been invested in a typical prewar year.

The authors of *Ocherki* were taken to task also for having omitted the fact that in 1939 defense production increased 46.5 per cent over

[34] *Ibid.*, p. 215. [35] *Ibid.*, p. 219.

1938; the objection implied that they had used the smaller production base of 1938 for a more dramatic comparison with the defense industry's rate of production during the war. Charging that *Ocherki* "contains serious mistakes which result in a false picture of the activities of Soviet industry during the war years," Filippov, having supplied some of the missing data, invited readers "to judge for themselves how correct the authors of *Ocherki* are."[36]

This attack on fundamental communist shibboleths was a serious challenge to the Party. Implied in the criticisms was the view that, despite the Party's bungling of economic policy, despite Stalin's cruel and purposeless crippling of the command cadres in 1937, and despite the various obstacles that the Party placed in the way of the military, the latter nevertheless succeeded in warding off a superior enemy, saving the Party and the country from collapse.

Of special significance was a postscript to the foregoing exchange in which the editorial board of *Voprosy istorii* openly sided with the "military" position of reviewers Bolton and Filippov,[37] an unusual and gratuitous gesture that emphasized the line between the opposing factions and thus helped pave the way for a showdown.

The entire incident undoubtedly caused grave concern about Zhukov's intentions *vis-à-vis* the Party leadership. If nothing else, the unorthodox military demands and gestures would have confirmed and deepened the Party *apparatchik*'s traditional distrust of the military, which borders on the paranoid. As developments were to show, *Voprosy istorii* and some of its contributors apparently had overestimated how far the de-Stalinization and policy of moderation initiated at the Twentieth Party Congress would be allowed to go. Political and military developments such as the uprisings in Hungary and Poland dictated a curbing of the effort at political and social moderation. Also, faced with what they may have regarded as a direct challenge from Zhukov and the military, the Party leaders may well have sensed a threat of Bonapartism and therefore decided to consolidate their antimilitary efforts, careful, however, not to overplay their hand lest they precipitate a coalition between Zhukov and rival elements in the Party. Certainly, the ensuing months appeared to bring a consensus in the Party on the need to limit the military's

[36] *Ibid.*, p. 218.

[37] *Ibid.*, p. 220. The note read: "From the Editorial Board: Having published the letters of the authors and editors of *Ocherki istorii Velikoi Otechestvennoi voiny* and the reply of E. A. Boltin and A. S. Filippov, the editors associate themselves with the basic opinions maintained by the reviewers of *Ocherki*."

autonomy and institute firmer Party controls in the armed forces. The editorial board of *Voprosy istorii* was one of the first to pay the penalty for its promilitary fervor: After it had been criticized by the Central Committee, its membership was reshuffled and its organization tied more closely to the central Party organs. As explained in the March 1957 issue of the journal itself, the editors had gone too far in the public "blackening" of Stalin; they had shown lack of political wisdom in permitting debates on issues better left alone, and "most of all . . . the Party's interests often suffered in such discussions." Thereafter, the journal was to be organizationally subordinated to the historical section of the Academy of Sciences, "while in the past it had been only formally connected with one of its scientific institutes."[38] The chastened and reorganized editorial board also admitted the justice of the criticism directed at them by *Pravda*, *Partiinaia zhizn'*, and *Kommunist*, all of them important organs of the Central Committee.[39]

The historical dialogue continued unabated throughout the winter and spring of 1957. In February, on the thirty-ninth anniversary of the formation of the Red Army, a number of prominent military leaders published articles, most of which reflected the views of the Stalingrad Group. Typical of them was Moskalenko's piece, which used familiar Party formulas and clichés to praise the Party's decisive and superior role in the military establishment:

> The most important sources of victory of our Army and Navy were the Soviet socialist state system and the wise leadership by the Communist Party. Only because of the Soviet socialist system and

[38] *Voprosy istorii*, No. 3, March 1957, pp. 3-19. It should be noted that the disagreements between the editors of *Voprosy istorii* and the Party leadership involved a number of issues other than that of the military.

[39] A major measure aimed at curbing Zhukov's and the military's self-assertion and authority was a revision of the statutes governing the relations between the political organs and Party organizations and the commanders in the armed forces. This revision, in the form of "Instructions to the Organizations of the CPSU in the Soviet Army and Navy," issued in the name of the Central Committee, unmistakably challenged Zhukov and the military. However, its implementation was delayed by the cabal of the so-called anti-Party group against Khrushchev, which the latter successfully countered in June 1957 with the aid of the military and from which he emerged as the dominant figure in the Party. What Zhukov's reasons were for siding with Khrushchev against Molotov, Bulganin, and the other dissidents is not known. He may have remembered that Khrushchev had in the past made a great effort to mollify the military; that he had supported their institutional and professional objectives; and that he was aligned with many other prominent military leaders. Also, by siding with the anti-Party group, Zhukov would have split the High Command, thereby weakening his own position as the main spokesman for the military.

> the leadership by the Communist Party have our Armed Forces become a first-class army now possessing most modern weapons. . . .[40]

After the June 1957 plenum of the Central Committee, which resulted in the ouster of the anti-Party group, Zhukov, now a full member of the Presidium and seemingly riding the crest of unusual personal power, continued to press the old demand of the military for the rehabilitation of purged military leaders and the punishment of the guilty, which had long been an irritant to the Party *apparat*. On July 15, Zhukov addressed a large gathering at the "Bolshevik" factory in Leningrad and issued strong, though indirect, warnings to those who were implicated in the purges of 1937. On August 10, *Krasnaia zvezda* published a brief biography of Marshal Bliukher, followed by the rehabilitation of Marshal Tukhachevskii.[41] However, now that Khrushchev's rivals in the Party had been removed from power, it was only a matter of time before this association of expediency between Khrushchev and Zhukov would dissolve.

The October 1957 plenum of the Central Committee, which met while Zhukov was in Yugoslavia and Albania, ended Zhukov's career. With the ouster of Zhukov, who was replaced by Marshal Malinovskii, the historical dialogue gave way to a monologue; for the next few years, the Stalingrad Group dominated all historical writing and sought to apotheosize itself and Khrushchev by creating the legend of the battle for Stalingrad.

D · *THE DIALOGUE SUBSIDES*: *1957-1961*

The ouster of Zhukov left the field to the Party. While historical appraisals of World War II continued to appear in various publications, these were solely organs of the Party and reflected its views and interests. In November, historiographers were given new guidelines:

> A most important task [of historians] is the scientific analysis of the role of the Communist Party of the Soviet Union as the organizer of the national struggle with the enemy, of its many-sided activity in directing the front, the partisan warfare behind the enemy lines, and the economic and political life of the country. The research

[40] *Krasnaia zvezda*, February 23, 1957. The other major contributors were Marshal Malinovskii (*Pravda*, February 23, 1957); Admiral Fokin (*Sovetskii flot*, February 23, 1957); General Kurochkin (*Trud*, February 23, 1957); and Marshal Meretskov (*Izvestiia*, February 23, 1957).

[41] In *Boevye podvigi chastei Krasnoi Armii, 1918-1922* (Battle Feats of Red Army Units, 1918-1922), published by Voenizdat, Moscow, in the summer of 1957, and reviewed in *Komsomol'skaia pravda*, August 23, 1957.

work must thoroughly portray the superiority of the socialist economic system, the Soviet social and state systems. . . .[42]

In this context, the historians were informed also that a special military historical commission had been entrusted with the vital task of writing the definitive military history of World War II. The project was to be under the supervision of P. N. Pospelov, candidate member of the Presidium, secretary of the Central Committee, and a friend of Khrushchev. Although it would be administered by the Institute of Marxism-Leninism of the Central Committee, the instructions stipulated that the project "cannot and must not remain within the confines of the Institute of Marxism-Leninism or limit itself to the boundaries of Moscow only."[43]

The creation of the editorial commission was one of the first steps taken by Khrushchev and his supporters after Zhukov's departure. Ironically, it was the military that had been demanding such an undertaking since Stalin's death, arguing that, while Soviet historians were content with popularized and fragmentary accounts of the war, Western historians were producing large and misleading studies of that period.[44] But the deep-seated disagreements among sectors of the Party and within the military on some crucial aspects of the war had prevented a comprehensive study from being initiated. Khrushchev's assumption of full power finally cleared the way for such an enterprise. As mentioned in the introductory pages of the completed work, the commission was advised that its task was not to be "a narrow professional military-historical work, but a political-military work. . . ."[45] Indeed, the very choice of the commission's personnel,

[42] *Voprosy istorii*, No. 11, November 1957, p. 22.

[43] *Ibid.*, pp. 220-221.

[44] After Malenkov's ouster and Zhukov's assumption of the office of Minister of Defense, *Voprosy istorii* (which, as noted, shifted its editorial position from anti-military to pro-Zhukov) published an editorial (No. 5, May 1955) which included the following statements: "Ten years have passed since the end of the war. Nevertheless, the monographical research of the history of the Great Patriotic War has not been developed properly. As yet, certain works of military historians as well as many dissertations dealing with the Great Patriotic War have not appeared [literally, 'seen the light']. . . . The authors of the majority of books and brochures do not describe the mass heroism of Soviet soldiers at the front and the working exploits of workers, peasants, and the intelligentsia in the rear in a sufficiently vivid and thorough manner." The editorial hinted that more accurate descriptions of the early period of the war were to come, which would deal with Soviet failings, including the mistakes of the Party: "In characterizing the conduct of the war, the authors frequently embellish events, minimize the difficulties of the war and the strength of the enemy. . . ."

[45] *Voprosy istorii KPSS perioda Velikoi Otechestvennoi voiny* (Problems of

the views they expressed in advance of publication, and finally the contents of the volumes themselves made it obvious that the ambitious six-volume military history of World War II was intended to be, and was, heavily biased in favor of Khrushchev and his military coterie. Although the work contained a wealth of useful historical data, it whitewashed Khrushchev and the Party, while stressing the mistakes of the *Stavka* and its responsibility for some major disasters and blaming Stalin for the initial failures of the Red Army. The ultimate victory was attributed to Khrushchev's military genius and to the Party's crucial role.

The stress in the original instructions on the participation of historians outside Moscow and the Institute could have been perfunctory, but there is evidence to suggest that it was more than that. In August 1959, the editorial commission publicly announced that work on the basic structure and contents of the study had been completed. Prior to this announcement, the Shevchenko University in Kiev and the Ukrainian Ministry of Higher Education had called a conference of leading Ukrainian historians, a number of military leaders, members of the editorial commission, and historians from most of the other Soviet republics. Marshal Chuikov had addressed the conference, which dealt with various problems connected with the study of World War II then in preparation. Although the main stress was on problems of the Ukraine, the conference also concerned itself with questions of larger, national significance.[46] It is very likely that Khrushchev was giving the Ukrainian Party apparatus and its historical sections a vital role in the conception and organization of the study so as to assure himself of a group of historians even more favorable to him and more controllable than those of Moscow and the central apparatus, since the Ukraine in general and Kiev in particular were his old political haunts, from which he had risen to national prominence.

There was other evidence, too, that the Party and the Stalingrad Group were monopolizing military-historical writing on the war between 1957 and 1961. In January 1958, N. I. Shatagin, a member of the editorial commission for the forthcoming military history, published a highly tendentious article on the history of the Red Army, in which he gave the Party most of the credit for the military victories, and suggested that, in times of crisis, the military tended to

---

CPSU History During the Great Patriotic War), Izdatel'stvo Kievskogo Universiteta, Kiev, 1961, p. 9.

[46] *Ibid., passim.*

panic, and only the activity of the highly disciplined Party prevented the harm that came of such demoralization. Reaffirming also the vital role of the political organs in the military, Shatagin quoted Lenin, who had said about the success of the Revolution that "Only because the Party was on guard, because the Party was strongly disciplined . . . could the miracle take place. Only because of that, regardless of the several onslaughts by the imperialists of the Entente and from all over the world, were we able to succeed." With regard to the Party's role in the Second World War, Shatagin repeated the familiar formula: "The Party organizations and the political organs in the army and navy played a decisive role in training soldiers and officers, molding staunch, loyal, and disciplined defenders of socialism."[47]

In February 1958, B. S. Tel'pukhovskii, another editor of the projected history of the war, set down the new Party line on the historical assessment of World War II and on the respective roles in it of the Party and the military.[48] In an article significantly entitled "The Communist Party—Inspirer and Organizer of the Victory of the Soviet People," he included all the formulas that were subsequently adopted by Party historians and were repeated not only in the *History of the Great Patriotic War* but also in the *History of the CPSU*, which appeared in 1959. The salient points of Tel'pukhovskii's article were:

(1) Before the war, the Party was successfully raising the level of the economy in both the civilian and the military sectors.

(2) The German attack caught the military in a highly dis-

[47] *Voprosy istorii KPSS*, No. 1, January 1958, p. 27. It should be noted that the Communist Party has evolved a startling method of announcing drastic changes in official policy or attitude on certain issues. It uses persons previously identified with the policy, leader, or doctrine that is about to become obsolete, as spokesmen through whom to present the details and merits of the new policy or official line. The device presumably serves several purposes: (a) it humiliates and punishes those who miscalculated which among the warring factions in the Party would be the winner; (b) it suggests the excellence of the new viewpoint or person, which makes advocates even of former opponents; and (c) it discourages possible resistance among adherents of the old order as they see their former spokesmen preach the virtue of the new. And so we see A. Samsonov, the historian, praise first Stalin, then Khrushchev, and presently, after Khrushchev's ouster, Zhukov. General Boltin, initially a fervent Zhukovite, was used by Khrushchev after 1957 to collaborate on the legend of the Stalingrad battle, only to return again to his initial position, and much the same applies to B. S. Tel'pukhovskii and N. I. Shatagin. One moral to be drawn from these examples is that the lot of the scribe in the Soviet Union, while it may be hard on his nerves, is more durable than that of the heroes he extols.

[48] "Kommunisticheskaia partiia—vdokhnovitel' i organizator pobedy sovetskogo naroda v Velikoi Otechestvennoi voine" (The Communist Party—Inspirer and Organizer of the Victory of the Soviet People in the Great Patriotic War), *Voprosy istorii KPSS*, No. 2, February 1958, pp. 34-56.

advantageous position. It was in the process of modernization and was only partially prepared for war. Also, the Germans were numerically superior in soldiers, tanks, and airplanes, and had had more combat experience than the Red Army. Only a part of the Soviet forces was deployed along the borders.

(3) One of the basic reasons for the initial disasters was Stalin's false assessment of the political and military situation prior to the outbreak of war between Germany and the Soviet Union. He had assumed that Germany was not planning to attack the USSR in the immediate future, and therefore opposed any attempts to improve Soviet preparedness lest they be construed by the Germans as a provocation.

(4) Another cause of the initial defeats was to be found in the purges of 1937, which destroyed most of the commanding cadres of the army and led to the promotion of younger and less experienced officers to high commanding positions.

(5) Marshal Zhukov bore part of the blame for the early failures because he had at his disposal information on the growing threat of a German attack which he failed to pass on to the Central Committee.

(6) The Party took heroic measures to evacuate industrial establishments and move them deep into the country. Within six months, production was adequate, and by the first half of 1942, military production was exceeding the prewar levels.

(7) The Stalingrad battle was decisive for the outcome of the war, and the subsequent battle for Kursk dealt the Germans a blow from which they never recovered.

(8) The October 1957 plenum of the Central Committee (the meeting that dismissed Zhukov and reestablished the authority of the Party in the military) decisively affected subsequent developments in the military. In Tel'pukhovskii's words, its decisions emphasized "that the main source of strength of our army and navy consists of the fact that its organizer and leader is the Communist Party, the leading and guiding force of Soviet society."

In one stroke, Tel'pukhovskii's article had thus vindicated the Party, placed the blame for all mistakes on Stalin and the deposed Zhukov, reaffirmed the Party's central role in military affairs, and submerged the contribution of the military in a host of efforts by other groups of Soviet society, while managing at the same time to make conciliatory gestures toward the military.

Having laid down the general historical line, the Khrushchevites in the military proceeded to create the legend of the Stalingrad battle, and their description of the battle, and of the performance of Khrushchev and his Stalingrad Group in it, now became a central issue in the dialogue between Party and military. By awarding to Khrushchev and to the military commanders under his political supervision most of the credit for the victory in that crucial battle, while casting the *Stavka* generals, and especially Zhukov, in an unfavorable light, the Party historians created the myth of Khrushchev's military genius. Not only did their efforts aim to establish Khrushchev's strategic brilliance (for, unlike Stalin, he could lay no other legitimate claim to military experience), but they also enhanced the standing of those military commanders who served loyally with Khrushchev at Stalingrad and in subsequent campaigns on the southern sector of the front.

One of the first statements on the central importance of the Stalingrad battle to appear after Zhukov's dismissal came from a well-known apologist for Khrushchev, Marshal of the Soviet Union A. Eremenko, who had commanded the Stalingrad front, with Khrushchev as political supervisor, and whose subsequent career was greatly furthered by Khrushchev. In an article in *Kommunist*,[49] Eremenko first began to build up the heroic image of Khrushchev as a brilliant military leader, though he also stressed the vital role played by members of the Stalingrad Group during the war. These were the main points of his argument:

(1) The enemy was numerically vastly superior to the Soviet forces in the southern sector of the front, which had to bear the main brunt of his onslaught.

(2) The *Stavka* bore sole responsibility for the critical situation at the approaches to Stalingrad, because of its destructive interference with the field commands, its frequent changes in command and personnel, and its failure to understand the rapidly changing situation, which it allowed to worsen through its unwillingness to take advice from the field commanders.

(3) Khrushchev played a central part in turning the tide in favor of the Soviets: he averted panic among the people, built up morale among the troops, and helped plan the counteroffensive that destroyed the German army and brought victory to the Soviets. (These claims on behalf of Khrushchev were to seem modest in comparison with Eremenko's more sweeping claims later on.)

(4) Of the military commanders who participated in the battle for Stalingrad, Eremenko singled out Chuikov, Moskalenko, Tolbukhin,

[49] *Kommunist*, No. 1, January 1958.

and several less-known personalities; significantly, he omitted the names of Malinovskii, Zakharov, Krylov, and Golikov, who had played prominent roles in the battle.[50] Moreover, he listed with favorable comment a rather large number of political commissars and NKVD commanders who had operated on the front lines, but omitted all personal reference to such prominent officers as Rokossovski and Vatutin, who also had fought in the battle for Stalingrad in adjacent force groups.

A month after Eremenko's article appeared, another military adherent of Khrushchev, Marshal I. Bagramian, stated his views on the same subject. More moderate than Eremenko, he did not insist on the overriding importance of the Stalingrad battle. He named Zhukov among prominent military leaders, and mentioned Khrushchev as one of the Party dignitaries (listed in alphabetical order) who had served at the front. Bagramian did reiterate the Party's formula on the causes of the early reverses, but he did not put the blame on the military.[51]

Although the Party's views dominated the field of military history after Zhukov's ouster, several events broadened the scope of the debate between Party and military. They included the appearance, in 1959, of two new military journals: *Kommunist Vooruzhennykh Sil* (Communist of the Armed Forces) and *Voenno-istoricheskii zhurnal* (Military-Historical Journal). The first is the central military organ of the MPA and generally follows the line of the Party and the political control organs. The latter, being the military-historical organ of the Ministry of Defense, tends to express the views and support the objectives of the professional military in the theater forces. These two journals may well owe their existence to the organizational separation of the MPA from the Ministry of Defense that followed Zhukov's dismissal, and to the fact that the former organs of these two institutions (*Voennyi vestnik* for the military and *Voennye znaniia* for the MPA) were not prominent enough to serve as vehicles for authoritative statements. An analysis of the contents of the new journals over the past few years indicates that *Kommunist Vooruzhennykh Sil* became the mouthpiece not only of the political control organs but of the pro-Khrushchev elements among the military, while *Voenno-istoricheskii zhurnal* continued to speak for the theater forces and the traditionalists in the military.

[50] Eremenko's presentation of the Stalingrad battle foreshadowed the subsequent schism within the Stalingrad Group.

[51] *Kommunist*, No. 2, February 1958.

During 1958-1960, years of strong Party controls in the military, the Stalingrad Group and the Khrushchevites monopolized Soviet military historiography. Though members of the military community began by opposing as excessive some of the political controls that were interfering with training, readiness, and discipline, they did so because of and with the support of ranking members of the Stalingrad Group. The latter, however, did not at that time have any interest in challenging the accuracy of the historical record, since the recent revision of Soviet history placed them in a most favorable light. The result was a period of tranquillity in the dialogue of Party and military with respect to the historical issues. This temporary calm was to be shattered, in the years to come, as a result of renewed conflicts and tensions between Khrushchev and some ranking members of the military hierarchy.

E · REVIVAL OF THE DIALOGUE

As was pointed out earlier, historical writings in the Soviet Union, like most other creative expressions and media of communication, are "political" in the sense that they are either related to politics in subject matter or are exploited for political ends. Not surprisingly, therefore, the important changes that took place in Soviet politics in the 1960's, especially in the Party's policy *vis-à-vis* the military, were reflected in the historical dialogue, which had been in abeyance since the ouster of Marshal Zhukov.

After 1960, the relatively tranquil relations that had prevailed between Khrushchev and the military for three years were jarred by several developments which reintroduced many of the factors that had disturbed the relationship during the Zhukov tenure in the Ministry of Defense. The cause was to be found in a number of Khrushchev's new policies that affected the military community: (a) a drastic cut of the conventional forces, which meant sudden déclassement for many thousands of elite officers; (b) a far-reaching reform of the officer corps that threatened the rights and prerogatives of the commanders by its egalitarian intent, and the corollary strengthening of the political control organs in the armed forces; (c) the introduction of practices that debased the status of the conventional forces, including, above all, the large-scale use of soldiers in the civilian economy; and (d) a new strategic doctrine that generated widespread resentment in the military.[52]

[52] See Chapter VII, especially pp. 259-261, for details.

These innovations precipitated the deterioration in Party-military relations. Initially, the renascent historical dialogue did no more than reflect this disturbance. As time went on, however, it became itself a contributing factor in the worsening relationship. Though members of the military community had many compelling reasons for disliking Khrushchev's military policies, they were bound to be particularly offended by Khrushchev's rewriting of the history in which they had taken part. The appearance of the first volumes of the *History of the Great Patriotic War*, and of numerous military memoirs and essays, gave currency to a biased version of historical events, in which Khrushchev and the Stalingrad Group were uniformly represented as heroic and humane. This apotheosis of Khrushchev and his associates greatly irritated many of the military, and their resentment burst into the open in 1961.

The alienation was strongest in the ground forces and in the academies, the areas that had been the main object of intensified political controls and budgetary restrictions, and whose importance had been reduced in the revised strategy. Using the journal *Voenno-istoricheskii zhurnal* as their main forum, spokesmen of these circles began to protest against the gross falsification of history, emboldened, most likely, by a widening schism at the top of the military hierarchy between adherents and opponents of Khrushchev's military reforms.

Thus, in April 1961, a lengthy article dealt with the sensitive issue of political controls in the army during the war and presented the political commissars and the Party in an unfavorable light. In discussing the period of the war when the function of the political commissars in the military was once again abolished, the author described at length the commissars' opposition to this step, which meant the loss of their positions of power:

> . . . intensive, laborious, and daily efforts of the military councils and fronts and armies, commanders, and political organizations were needed to make *edinonachalie* a fact . . . to explain the crucial importance of the given measure for the achievement of victory over the German-fascist occupiers. . . . Some of the political workers (among the commissars) were perplexed and their attitude expressed itself as "What will we be doing now? Only agitating?" In practice this led to an unwillingness to remain in political work and to seeking tranfers to commanding or administrative functions.[53]

[53] Lieutenant General A. Pigurnov, "Deiatel'nost' voennykh sovetov, politorganov

After the removal of the commissars, the author reported, the Party organizations in the military were given broader authority, which sometimes caused "damage to *edinonachalie* and direct interference in the duties of the commanders." He went on to describe cases of cowardice among ranking political officers, mentioning by name the heads of *politotdel* (Political Sections) of the 206th and the 62nd divisions, Samartsev and Sanin, who were "severely punished" (probably a euphemism for being shot). The article brought up some highly sensitive problems in Party-military relations, which in the post-Zhukov calm had been carefully avoided in Soviet publications.

The first sign that the Party's monopoly of military historiography on World War II was weakening appeared in an article in *Voenno-istoricheskii zhurnal* by Marshal Bagramian, an adherent of Khrushchev and a moderate among members of the Stalingrad Group.[54] Bagramian reviewed certain operations of the First Baltic Front in 1944, with favorable descriptions of the *Stavka* in general and Vasilevskii in particular. Referring to a meeting of the *Stavka* which was attended by Stalin, Zhukov, and Vasilevskii, among others, and which discussed a planned encirclement operation of the German Force Group "Center," he stated that "on this specific subject as well as on other general topics there developed a lively exchange of opinions among the participants in the meeting, as a result of which the main concept of the entire operation became clearly defined."[55] Bagramian recalled Vasilevskii as "a very talented and wise, though cautious, military leader," who was willing to listen to, and accept, advice from the field commanders.

Marshal Bagramian's article was most likely an attempt by the moderate wing of the Stalingrad Group to mollify the dissidents in the ground forces and to bring greater objectivity to historical writing. However, attempts to placate, or to throttle, the critics met with little success.

---

i partiinykh organizatsii po ukrepleniiu edinonachaliia v period Velikoi Otechestvennoi voiny" (Activity of Military Councils, Political Organs and Party Organizations in Strengthening *Edinonachalie* During the Great Patriotic War), *Voenno-istoricheskii zhurnal*, No. 4, April 1961.

[54] *Voenno-istoricheskii zhurnal*, No. 4, April 1961.

[55] *Ibid.*, p. 15. Bagramian's description of the relaxed and cooperative spirit that prevailed between field commanders and *Stavka* members sharply contrasted with the version given by the Party hacks and the more conservative members of the Stalingrad Group, who depicted the *Stavka* as an aloof and totally uncooperative institution, which only issued orders to the field commanders and rejected their advice.

The May issue of *Voenno-istoricheskii zhurnal*, which carried the second part of Bagramian's piece, reported at length on a most interesting conference held in the journal's editorial offices on February 14. The conference was attended by a number of prominent military historians, writers, and editors, and the discussion turned on an article by Lieutenant General I. Prochko, an ardent champion of the military and a fearless critic of Party hackwork among historians. Prochko's article itself was published, undoubtedly over strong objections, in the same issue of *Voenno-istoricheskii zhurnal*.

The course of the conference brought to light the extent of the dissatisfaction that prevailed over the Party's and the Stalingrad Group's domination of the historical presentation of the war and the apotheosis of Khrushchev and his associates. In his article Prochko dealt rather sharply with several issues that arose from the growing number of military memoirs published since the ouster of Zhukov. He strongly defended the professional military against accusations that they had brought on the disasters of the early period of the war; he criticized the tendency of some Party writers to belittle the German enemy; and he openly attacked several prominent defenders of Khrushchev and the Stalingrad Group while speaking favorably about a number of "outsiders," that is to say, leading officers who did not belong to the inner circle of Khrushchev's military associates. The forcefulness and directness of Prochko's article, and also of the statements of several others present at the meeting, may indicate that these critics were not acting on their own but had at least tacit support from high-ranking military personalities.

Prochko stressed the fact that most commanders of forces deployed along the Russo-German border were very well aware of the growing threat of an attack, but he pointed out that they "had strict orders from the center not to give in to provocations, not to get involved in conflicts which could result in war."[56] He also said that Soviet commanders "never forgot the basic requirements of military statutes, [which were] to be vigilant and to remain in constant military readiness. . . ."[57] Citing from relevant memoirs, he described the reluctance of field commanders to exercise initiative; he quoted the commander of the 6th Army, Lieutenant General I. N. Muzychenko, as saying about certain actions he had found it necessary to take in the

[56] Artillery Lieutenant General I. Prochko, "Memuarnaia literatura o Velikoi Otechestvennoi voine" (Memoir Literature About the Great Patriotic War), *ibid.*, No. 5, May 1961, p. 97.
[57] *Ibid.*

face of the enemy's threatening operations: "I am not too eager to report to my superiors. They would call me a panic-monger." Prochko commented that it was "too bad that such necessary measures had to be undertaken on local initiative."[58]

Having cited passages from Marshal Krasovskii's memoirs[59] to the effect that Soviet flyers early in the war had to operate under highly disadvantageous conditions, Prochko added that, despite these and "other problems," Soviet flyers had managed successfully to oppose the enemy. He singled out Chuikov's memoirs[60] for some sharp criticism, qualified only by the usual perfunctory pat on the back. "Chuikov's book," he said, "adds little to the known factual description of events . . . at Stalingrad." And he rebuked Chuikov for exaggerating his role at Stalingrad at the expense of other commanders and forces:

> [There are] books which create the impression that the regiments and larger units described in them operated without any connection with other forces of the Soviet Army and that major successes were achieved only in places where the author of the memoirs was present. The book by Marshal of the Soviet Union V. I. Chuikov is not completely free of such failings.[61]

Prochko also sharply criticized a known Khrushchev apologist, Lieutenant General N. K. Popel', who served as political commissar of an army during the war and who, in two recent memoirs,[62] had tried to create an image of Khrushchev as a heroic, selfless, fearless, and engaging personality by drawing a series of flattering vignettes of him, together with members of the Stalingrad Group, at the front. Some authors of memoirs, said Prochko sarcastically, "'confer' on their heroes military rank which they did not possess at that time." And he concluded his article with the admonition that "we must struggle . . . against [the tendencies] to transform memoirs into novels and tales."[63]

[58] *Ibid.*

[59] Marshal S. A. Krasovskii, *Zhizn' v aviatsii* (Life in Aviation), Voenizdat, Moscow, 1960.

[60] Marshal V. I. Chuikov, *Nachalo puti* (Beginning of the Road), Voenizdat, Moscow, 1959.

[61] *Voenno-istoricheskii zhurnal*, No. 5, May 1961, p. 103.

[62] Lieutenant General N. K. Popel', *V tiazhkuiu poru* (In Difficult Times), Voenizdat, Moscow, 1959; and *Tanki povernuli na zapad* (The Tanks Turned West), Voenizdat, Moscow, 1960.

[63] *Voenno-istoricheskii zhurnal*, No. 5, May 1961, p. 104.

The only important commentator on the Prochko article not present at the February meeting was Marshal of the Soviet Union A. I. Eremenko, the major architect of the Khrushchev legend at Stalingrad, who sent in his statements on the issues under discussion. He strongly disagreed with Prochko's point that authors of memoirs should abstain from rendering detailed conversations and describing people's moods and expressions because in most cases there were no precise data on which to base such accounts. "Eremenko felt that memoirs ought to describe details, even daily details; they ought to include dialogues, excerpts from letters, etc. . . . Comrade Eremenko does not agree that a dialogue can be included only if it is based on diaries or stenographical notes."[64] (Eremenko himself was guilty of the practices that Prochko condemned, having described long dialogues between Khrushchev and himself and others, from which emerged a most favorable picture of Khrushchev and his military associates at the front.)[65]

The military historian Major General E. A. Boltin, who had at one time been a defender of Zhukov but who, after Zhukov's ouster, became associate editor of the six-volume military history of World War II, took issue with Colonel Derevianko, the perfect type of the MPA man, who had said that "memoirs must first of all be Party-oriented and must show the great heroism of the people, typical events, and the leading role of the Party." Boltin argued that, although Party orientation was necessary, one should not forget that military memoirs dealt with a specific subject and should confine oneself to it.[66] Lieutenant General P. G. Kuznetsov stated that it would be better "if writers of military memoirs approached the events described by them as military commanders. . . ."[67] Colonel P. A. Zhilin stressed that "the events described by the author's memoirs should be authentic, and should be presented in the manner in which the author of the memoir perceived them at the time, not transformed through the prism of the present."[68]

Lieutenant General A. A. Lobachev said: "It is necessary to describe events truthfully, to write in such a manner that the reader believes that what is written actually took place." He then singled out Chuikov's memoirs for this acid comment: "Memoirs should be

[64] O. Fel'dman and V. Cheremnykh, "Ser'eznyi razgovor" (A Serious Conversation), *ibid.*, p. 106.

[65] Marshal A. I. Eremenko, *Stalingrad*, Voenizdat, Moscow, 1961.

[66] *Voenno-istoricheskii zhurnal*, No. 5, May 1961, p. 106.

[67] *Ibid.*, p. 105.

[68] *Ibid.*, p. 107.

written in a lively, attractive, and interesting manner, and not, for example, like V. I. Chuikov's *Beginning of the Road.*"

The conference on General Prochko's article in the offices of *Voenno-istoricheskii zhurnal* was an important event in itself, because of the professional stature of some of its participants.[69] Its greatest significance, however, lies in the nature of its proceedings, during which several lesser military writers publicly took to task a number of military and political personages of the Khrushchev regime and also, implicitly, rejected the Party leader's claim to military genius.

Against the background of major policy differences between Khrushchev and broad sectors in the military, the historical dialogue gained in intensity and scope, reflecting the growing disenchantment brought on by the crude methods by which Khrushchev tried to subjugate and divide the military community and also by his efforts to glorify his role during the war.

In May 1961, Marshal of the Soviet Union and Chief of the General Staff M. V. Zakharov wrote two articles on World War II. Zakharov, who was a member of the Stalingrad Group and a close associate of Marshal Malinovskii, stated that the Soviet Union had suffered the greatest human and material losses of any country in the war,[70] and that the victory over Germany had been achieved through "united efforts of many countries [a reference to the Anglo-American allies], though mostly through the efforts of the Soviet people and its Armed Forces."[71] He placed the blame for the Red Army's lack of preparedness entirely on Stalin, thereby departing from the formula

[69] The participants were: Chief Marshal of Artillery N. N. Voronov; Lieutenant Generals P. G. Kuznetsov, A. A. Lobachev, and I. S. Strel'bitskii; the editor-in-chief of the memoir literature administration for Voenizdat, Colonel M. M. Zotov; K. M. Simonov; the MPA representative, Colonel P. M. Derevianko; three members of the editorial board of the journal, Colonel General of Artillery F. A. Samsonov, Major General E. A. Boltin, and Colonel P. A. Zhilin; and the editor-in-chief, Major General N. G. Pavlenko. Marshal Eremenko did not attend the meeting but sent in his remarks. The importance of the conference was underlined by the presence of K. M. Simonov, the most prominent Soviet writer and a Khrushchev favorite. Simonov did indeed try to shield the Khrushchevites, by criticizing Prochko for attempting to review a large number of memoirs in a brief article, and by maintaining, in defense of the Eremenko position, that the author of memoirs "is perfectly correct in including subjective views." *Ibid.*, pp. 107-108.

[70] *Krasnaia zvezda*, May 9, 1961.

[71] *Ibid.* The military professionals have traditionally maintained a certain historical objectivity in stressing the fact that the war against Germany was won by a coalition, in which the Western allies also fought the mutual enemy bravely. The Party historians habitually gloss over this fact and stress the West's duplicity and political machinations against the Soviet Union.

of Party writers who were ascribing part of the responsibility for the early disasters to Zhukov.[72] He also referred to the expansion of Soviet power and influence as having been made possible by the military victories of the war.[73] Though Zakharov made the customary bow to the Party, the general tenor of his articles was to stress the importance of the military factor in the Party's policies.

In November 1961, Marshal V. D. Sokolovskii reopened the issue of the battle of Moscow when he wrote as follows:

> In the battle at Moscow the Soviet Armed Forces achieved a victory which had world-wide historical importance . . . and brought the enemy a defeat, unprecedented in its scope and consequences, which sharply changed the conduct of the war on the Russo-German front.[74]

Sokolovskii also stressed the overriding contribution of the Western Front to the victory at Moscow, an implied tribute to Zhukov, who had been the commander of that front.

The Twenty-second Party Congress, in October 1961, was intended to be a major showcase of Khrushchev's personal power and a spectacle of world communism under Moscow's leadership. It was the occasion of a significant speech by Marshal Malinovskii on various military and political problems. One of Malinovskii's statements had a special poignancy that must have aroused the attention of the Party *apparatchiks*:

> We, the military, have a special account to settle with the members of the anti-Party group. I see in this room prominent military leaders who have been innocently jailed and tortured. All Communists in the military unanimously and with special fervor approve of the destruction of the anti-Party group . . . and are heartily grateful to the Central Committee of our Party for the hard Leninist line in the struggle with the anti-Party group, and most of all to Nikita Sergeevich Khrushchev. . . .[75]

While according Khrushchev major credit for the destruction of the anti-Party group, whose membership and activity he linked to the military purges of 1936-1938, Malinovskii was clearly reiterating

[72] *Voennyi vestnik*, No. 6, June 1961, p. 5.

[73] *Krasnaia zvezda*, May 9, 1961.

[74] *Voenno-istoricheskii zhurnal*, No. 11, November 1961, p. 15.

[75] *XXII s"ezd Kommunisticheskoi partii Sovetskogo Soiuza: stenograficheskii otchet* (The Twenty-second Congress of the CPSU: Stenographic Record), Gospolitizdat, Moscow, 1962, Vol. 2, p. 120.

the military's long-standing grudge against the Party for having destroyed so much of the higher officer corps during those years.[76]

In February 1962, three months after the Twenty-second Party Congress, the editors of *Voenno-istoricheskii zhurnal* recommended a reappraisal of historical accounts of the war. The main points of the editorial reflected the military's dissatisfaction with the Party's presentation of the military's role during the war (presumably, in particular, with the idealized image of the Stalingrad Group and of Khrushchev), and proposed new approaches to various problems.

First, the editorial demanded that all remnants of Stalinism be eradicated from military-historical writings; it described at great length the ill effects of the cult of personality on recent military historiography: "Stalin's mistakes were . . . whitewashed, and to that end various 'theories' were developed; prominent military leaders were described as mere executors of Stalin's 'brilliant' ideas and plans, various periods of the war, especially the initial period, were 'glossed over,' various mistakes and failings were omitted."[77]

Second, the editorial writers objected to the tendentiousness of some historical writings, though they admitted the need for a Party-oriented approach: "We must eradicate . . . [and] expose to sharp critical fire those works in which false, incorrect, tendentious, and, especially, subjective conclusions of authors have been tolerated." The particular targets of this criticism were "authors of memoirs who sin against historical truth, who dwell on trivial, immaterial facts and omit the main historical events."[78] (It will be recalled that Generals Prochko and Boltin had accused three prominent apologists for the Stalingrad Group and Khrushchev of these same sins.)

Finally, the editorial demanded that a new "fundamental and scientific history of the Soviet Armed Forces" be published on the occasion of the fiftieth anniversary of the Soviet army in 1967. The six-volume study of the military history of the war was thought "quite useful," but "it cannot answer all questions on the development of Soviet military art during the world war period."[79]

In March 1962, General of the Army P. Kurochkin reviewed the third volume of the military history of the war.[80] He singled out for special praise the operations of the 2nd Guard Army under the command of Malinovskii. He also made some ambiguous references

[76] Malinovskii's statement closely echoed that made by Zhukov on July 15, 1957, at the "Bolshevik" factory in Leningrad.

[77] *Voenno-istoricheskii zhurnal*, No. 2, February 1962, p. 6.

[78] *Ibid.*, p. 10. [79] *Ibid.*, pp. 9-10. [80] *Ibid.*, No. 3, March 1962.

to the unsuccessful operations of the Southwestern and Voronezh Fronts, which had caused the Soviet forces to retreat between 150 and 220 km in that sector. (The two fronts had been under Khrushchev's political control at the time.) And he complained that "the authors did not pay sufficient attention to the activities of the Don Front [under Rokossovskii] in the Volga operations [at Stalingrad] in November 1942."[81]

In June, Chief Marshal of Artillery N. Voronov described the encirclement (*kol'tso*) operations at Stalingrad. In so doing, he omitted even the standard bows to the Party and Khrushchev. Not only did Voronov make no mention of Khrushchev, the Party, and the Stalingrad Group, but he pointedly singled out Rokossovskii for praise, and also presented his own activities as a *Stavka* coordinator of the Stalingrad battle in a favorable light.[82]

The growing military opposition to the glorification of the Stalingrad Group—and, by implication, of Khrushchev—in the historical dialogue was clearly apparent in General Prochko's review[83] of the second book of memoirs by General Popel', *Tanki povernuli na zapad* (The Tanks Turned West). The subject of the review, its timing, and the identity of the reviewer are significant. Though the book had been published in 1960, *Voenno-istoricheskii zhurnal* waited two years before reviewing it. By then, the political climate was such as to permit an attack on the author, a defender of Khrushchev and the Stalingrad Group. The reviewer, it will be recalled, through his criticism of Chuikov, Eremenko, and Popel', among others, had become identified as being opposed to the domination of the historical dialogue by the Stalingrad Group.

Prochko in his review accused Popel' of belittling the role of the commanding officers (who were "nameless, and who supposedly did not permit firing on the enemy for fear of exciting him . . .") while mentioning many of the political workers by name and characterizing them individually.[84] He spoke sarcastically of the writer's account of the important role of the Military Council of the Army: "An impression is created that the operations of the regiments and divisions of the 1st Tank Army were not directed by their commanders and staffs, but as if all had been done under the direction of

[81] *Ibid.*, p. 90.

[82] *Ibid.*, No. 6, June 1962. Voronov's contentions were strongly criticized by a Colonel Vorob'ev in the November issue of the same journal, after there had been a general tightening of political controls in the military.

[83] *Ibid.*, No. 7, July 1962.

[84] *Ibid.*, pp. 85 and 86-87.

the brigade commanders with the approval of the Member of the Military Council of the Army." Prochko criticized Popel' for "at times idealizing his heroes" and for describing things in "a completely unmilitary way."[85] His biting remarks were clearly directed not only at Popel' but at the rapidly proliferating military memoirs with their obsequious eulogies of Khrushchev and the Stalingrad Group. Without a doubt, the candor and directness of this review surpassed anything that had been written even during the military's golden age, when Zhukov was Minister of Defense.

In October, *Voenno-istoricheskii zhurnal* published a review by Colonel E. Sulimov of G. D. Komkov's *The Sources of the Soviet People's Victory in the Great Patriotic War.*[86] It contained a sharp and undisguised refutation of Party claims and a reiteration of the military point of view on the failures and successes of World War II. Komkov apparently had described the bases of the Soviet victory in the hackneyed fashion of a Party *apparatchik* (to judge by the point-by-point rebuttal of the reviewer), slighting the contributions of the military and underlining those of the Party. Referring to the conditions listed by Komkov as the causes of victory (ideological strength, a superior socio-political system, and advanced economic development—in other words, the standard Party formula), Sulimov said that these "are all obviously indispensable in achieving victory over enemies, but are not sufficient by themselves. *In order for victory to be achieved, they must be converted into military might of the army and navy.*"[87] He also demanded that accounts listing the causes of victory be careful to describe them so that "the specific characteristic of each force that influenced the achievement of victory can be recognized." Denying claims of high industrial and agricultural productivity, he refuted some of the author's statistics on that score. Sulimov asked sarcastically: If the Soviet socio-political and economic system was superior to others, why then was it in mortal danger in the initial stages of the war?[88] And he excoriated the author for having omitted any reference to Stalin's cult and

[85] *Ibid.*, pp. 87-88.

[86] *Istoki pobedy sovetskogo naroda v Velikoi Otechestvennoi voine*, Izdatel'stvo Akademii nauk SSSR, Moscow, 1961.

[87] *Voenno-istoricheskii zhurnal*, No. 10, October 1962, p. 91. (Italics added.)

[88] This could well be a long-delayed reply to the notorious chastisement of the military in the *Kommunist* article of July 1956, where the question asked was: "How did it happen that our army, on whose preparedness many efforts were expended, fell into a critical situation during the initial months of the war and had to retreat?" See p. 186, above.

to his part in the initial failures. But the reviewer's basic point was probably summed up in this paragraph:

> We must view as a serious omission of the author that he did not consider it necessary to show in a special section the heroic struggle of the Soviet Armed Forces against fascist hordes. . . . *The book refers to the selfless struggle of the Soviet Army and Navy only in passing*, in connection with other problems, specifically problems concerned with the Party's struggle to strengthen them.[89]

The Cuban missile crisis of October 1962 had a far-reaching effect on the relations between Party and military. Though much about that period remains vague, the substance of their dialogue after the crisis indicates that certain military circles opposed Khrushchev's handling of the affair.[90]

In the months after October, political controls over the military were intensified, and MPA head Epishev was conspicuous on a number of occasions on which the military was rebuked for various failings.[91] Despite the fact that Epishev and others obliquely threatened the military and urged them to keep their place, the latter continued to express opposition. A striking example of military intransigence occurred in a debate on the anniversary of the battle of Stalingrad. Neither the issues under discussion nor the disagreements expressed were new; they reflected the familiar deep-seated conflict of interests between the professional officers in the theater forces on the one hand and the Party leadership and its adherents in the military (the Stalingrad Group) on the other. The special significance of the exchange on this occasion lay in the prominence of the authors, in the striking polarity of their views, and in Malinovskii's seeming departure from the Stalingrad Group's custom of heaping unqualified praise on Khrushchev.

The key issue of the Stalingrad debate seems to have been the role that Khrushchev (and the high military commanders under his political supervision at the front) played in the planning of the counteroffensive, which resulted in the victory at Stalingrad and thus greatly

[89] *Voenno-istoricheskii zhurnal*, No. 10, October 1962, p. 94. (Italics added.)

[90] To be sure, the causes and manifestations of the deterioration of Party-military relations at the time went far deeper and were more extensive. The historical dialogue had become the appropriate forum for the views and criticisms of the protagonists.

[91] See R. Kolkowicz, *Conflicts in Soviet Party-Military Relations, 1962-1963*, The RAND Corporation, RM-3760-PR, August 1963.

influenced the outcome of the war. The authors of articles written in celebration of the anniversary seemed to be evenly split on this issue: Marshals Rotmistrov,[92] Voronov,[93] and Kazakov[94] (members of the ground forces) omitted Khrushchev's name entirely and stressed instead the part of various military leaders, and especially of Malinovskii, in bringing about the victory at Stalingrad. Marshals Biriuzov,[95] Chuikov,[96] and Eremenko,[97] all members of the Stalingrad Group, repeatedly referred to the central role of Khrushchev, who almost alone, in their description, conceived the plan for the counteroffensive and had to persuade the *Stavka* and Stalin to accept it.

It was Malinovskii's article, however, that contained the chief surprise. First, it methodically destroyed the claim, made by several Marshals from the Stalingrad Group, that Khrushchev had played a key role in planning the counteroffensive at Stalingrad. Secondly, Malinovskii pointedly included Marshal Zhukov among those who participated in planning and executing the operation.[98] The challenge of the myth of Khrushchev's military genius, together with the reference to the popular and talented Marshal whom Khrushchev had ousted, clearly reflected the growing division between the Party leader and a large segment of the military community, including the moderate wing of the Stalingrad Group. To be sure, Malinovskii's article observed the rules of etiquette with perfunctory kudos for Khrushchev and the Party.

92 Chief Marshal of the Armored Forces P. Rotmistrov, in *Krasnaia zvezda*, January 16, 1963.

93 Chief Marshal of Artillery N. N. Voronov, in *Pravda*, January 31, 1963.

94 Marshal of Artillery V. I. Kazakov, in *Izvestiia*, February 1, 1963.

95 Marshal of the Soviet Union S. S. Biriuzov, in *Politicheskoe samoobrazovanie*, No. 2, February 1963.

96 Marshal of the Soviet Union I. V. Chuikov, in *Izvestiia*, February 2, 1963.

97 Marshal of the Soviet Union Eremenko, in *Pravda*, January 27, 1963. In his book, *Stalingrad*, Eremenko bluntly asserts in the first sentence of the chapter on the counteroffensive that "the idea for the counteroffensive at Stalingrad first occurred to me while I was still in Moscow [August 1-2, 1942]. It matured and grew during the defensive battles for the city and gradually became converted into a concrete plan, into a practical preparation for the counteroffensive. This preparation began during the most difficult period of the defense of Stalingrad, in August-September, when N. S. Khrushchev and I headed the [Stalingrad and Southeastern] Fronts." Eremenko relates a telephone conversation with Stalin some time in September, in which he suggested to Stalin that it was time to start preparing a counteroffensive. Stalin answered: "Very well, comrade Eremenko, we will think [the problem] over." Eremenko, though he does say that the final plan was the result of contributions from a large number of people from various military commands, nevertheless tries to impress the reader with the fact that he and Khrushchev were its originators.

98 Marshal of the Soviet Union R. Malinovskii, in *Pravda*, February 2, 1963.

The following are excerpts from salient passages in the articles written on the Stalingrad anniversary. They have been juxtaposed so as to illustrate the essential differences in bias between the two categories of authors.

PRO-MILITARY	*PRO-KHRUSHCHEV*
It is necessary to state that the great victory on the Volga [Stalingrad] was the result not only of high levels of Soviet military art, but also of the boundless bravery, courage, and heroism of Soviet soldiers . . . those soldiers, officers, and generals of the Soviet army who, without sparing their lives, carried out their debt to the Motherland. . . . (Rotmistrov)	The battle on the Volga and the whole Great Patriotic War have shown with great clarity the superiority of the Soviet social and state system, of our economy, of the moral-political unity of our nation guided by the Communist Party and the Soviet military art. These are the deciding factors which determined the outcome of this battle too. (Chuikov)
A large collective of Soviet military commanders—the Supreme Command, the General Staff, and representatives of the branches of the armed forces and of the Military Councils at the fronts—took part in developing [the plan for the counteroffensive]. I would like to introduce some clarifications in this matter [the origin of the plan]. In the first half of September, at the height of the defensive battles in the South, Comrades A. M. Vasilevskii and N. N. Voronov, Headquarters [*Stavka*] representatives, were sent to the Volga combat area with the task of studying the conditions of the troops on the spot. . . . After their return to the *Stavka* . . . a conference was held [where] the	The idea for the counteroffensive appeared at the height of the defensive struggles. On the 6th of October, the Military Council forwarded to the *Stavka* its proposals on the organization and conduct of the counteroffensive. The basic ideas of the proposals . . . were accepted. (Chuikov) . . . the strategic skill, iron will, and organizational talent of N. S. Khrushchev were shown [in his choice of a variant of the proposed counteroffensive]; the only alternative variant would have resulted in defeat. The *Stavka* agreed to [Khrushchev's proposal]. . . . Khrushchev has shown vast energy and wisdom in the working out and execution of the plan for the defeat of the enemy. (Biriuzov)

general outlines of the counter-offensive plan were sketched and the contours of the plan were fixed. . . . During the first days of October the Military Councils and headquarters of the fronts were drawn into the preparations of the counteroffensive. . . . Also taking part in these conferences was G. K. Zhukov . . . who came to the combat area. (Malinovskii)

The concept and plan of the counteroffensive were brilliant. They were the fruit of collective creativity. Our offensive operation was developed by the generals and officers of the *Stavka* and the General Staff, and the commands and headquarters of the branches of the Armed Forces and the fronts. (Voronov)

It was extremely fortunate that in this critical period Nikita Sergeevich Khrushchev was a member of our Military Council. . . . The idea for the counteroffensive was many times brought to the attention of the *Stavka*. . . . At the head of the Communists who risked their lives on the shores of the Volga was the loyal Leninist, the outstanding leader of our Party and government, N. S. Khrushchev. (Eremenko)

The Stalingrad anniversary debate came at a time of an acute conflict, the precise nature of which remains unclear, when Khrushchev and his followers in Party and military were facing the bulk of the military community, including formerly close associates from the Stalingrad Group. This conflict, however, with its unevenly matched protagonists, probably could not have expressed itself in a public medium, or reached the proportions that it did in the anniversary debate, if the promilitary faction had not had some support in the upper ranks of the Party. Though it is indeed difficult, as of now, to substantiate such an assumption, we may speculate, along with a number of astute observers of Soviet affairs,[99] about the existence of such a division within the Party.

The debate, however, marked the apogee of the recent cycle in the

[99] For speculations on a conflict between "reformists" and "conservatives" in the Party, and on the factions supporting each, see R. Lowenthal, David Burg, and Herman Achminov, "Nach Chruschtschow," *Osteuropa*, No. 11, 1964; Boris Meissner, "Chruschtschowismus ohne Chruschtschow," *ibid.*, Nos. 1, 2, 3, and 4, 1965; "The Coup and After," article in two parts, *Problems of Communism*, January-February and May-June 1965, contributors including M. Fainsod, R. Lowenthal, R. Conquest, C. Linden, and A. Ulam.

military's assertion *vis-à-vis* the Party and the height of its expression of institutional vigor and independence.[100] Whatever internal wounds may have remained as a result of this near-rupture in the relations of Party and military, they were at least covered up. By the spring of 1963, a *modus vivendi* seemed to have been established, and the historical dialogue was muted. This calm was shattered once again in the wake of Khrushchev's ouster, in the fall of 1964.

F · *AFTER KHRUSHCHEV*

After the Cuban missile crisis, as Khrushchev tightened the Party's controls in the military, the historical dialogue was suspended, and the year 1963 produced few historical publications that would merit special interest. By 1964, however, Khrushchev's *modus vivendi* with the military proved to have been tenuous: the Party's policy toward the military hardened, and one of the results of the development was the revival of the public historical discourse.

In the spring of 1964, Khrushchev's loyal supporter Marshal Chuikov wrote several articles on the battle for Berlin (1944-1945), in which he leveled serious accusations at the commanders of the First Belorussian Front.[101] He accused these officers, Marshals Zhukov and Sokolovskii among them, of having delayed taking Berlin for lack of skill and initiative. His charges implied that, if Zhukov had not dragged his feet at the time, the Soviet Union would now be controlling a much larger part of Europe.[102] Chuikov also reiterated the old claim that Marshal Konev had played a vital role in the battle of Berlin. The articles were to embarrass Chuikov the following year.

Khrushchev's renewed campaign against the military was evident also in an attack by the Central Committee's organ *Kommunist* on

[100] For additional articles dealing with the historical dialogue, see "Neotlozhnye zadachi istorikov KPSS" (Immediate Tasks of Historians of the CPSU), *Voprosy istorii KPSS*, No. 2, February 1957; General of the Army A. Zhadov, "Na strazhe zavoevanii Velikogo Oktiabria" (On Guard Over the Achievements of the Great October), *Voennyi vestnik*, No. 10, October 1957; General of the Army A. Zhadov, "O nasushchnykh zadachakh voenno-istoricheskoi raboty" (The Urgent Tasks in Military-Historical Work), *Krasnaia zvezda*, January 25, 1963; A. M. Samsonov, "Volgogradskaia partiinaia organizatsiia v period oborony goroda-geroia" (The Volgograd Party Organization During the Defense of the Heroic City), *Voprosy istorii KPSS*, No. 2, February 1963; V. K. Pechorkin and A. M. Samsonov, "Mezhdunarodnoe znachenie pobedy na Volge" (International Significance of the Victory on the Volga), *Novaia i noveishaia istoriia*, No. 2, February 1963.

[101] *Oktiabr'*, Nos. 3-5, 1964.

[102] He reiterated these views in *Novaia i noveishaia istoriia*, No. 2 (March-April), 1965, especially p. 6.

Voenno-istoricheskii zhurnal, which in the past had served as a forum where the military could criticize and correct the distorted accounts of its war record.[103] In another article, written for a Polish military-history quarterly, a spokesman for the Stalingrad Group restated the argument about the primary importance of the Stalingrad battle as compared with the battle for Moscow. Even before this article appeared in print, however, Khrushchev had been removed from power.[104]

The ouster of Khrushchev started a chain of events whose pattern showed the chiaroscuro characteristic of the aftermath of such changes in the past. As the deposed leader became an unperson, his former enemies began to reappear in public offices or as public personalities. As historians, propagandists, and editorial writers erased Khrushchev's name from Soviet history, they began to repopulate the past with personages who had suffered disgrace under Khrushchev. In the renascent historical dialogue within the military and between the military and the Party, the most important developments were: the reinstatement of Marshal Zhukov as a prominent figure who played a vital role in the war; the debunking of the historical claims of the Stalingrad Group and, implicitly, of Khrushchev; and a more objective treatment of Stalin's role in the war. Thus, the battle of Moscow was brought forth from historical obscurity and presented as a turning point in the Russo-German war. The first to rehabilitate it was the head of the MPA, General Epishev, formerly a vociferous exponent of the Khrushchev legends at Stalingrad, and hardly a friend of Zhukov.[105] Reaching far afield for his authority on the battle of Moscow, Epishev cited General MacArthur as saying that the scope and intensity of the Soviet operations there had made it "the greatest military victory of all times."[106] Epishev himself used many superlatives to describe the events at Moscow, while treating the battle of Stalingrad with restraint.

Epishev had opened the floodgates, and the historical debate was

[103] *Kommunist*, No. 12, August 1964, pp. 123-127. In the usual fashion, Khrushchev chose a thorough military professional, Marshal P. Rotmistrov, to sign the attack on the journal. Rotmistrov has been known in the past as a staunch defender of the military's prerogatives against encroachments by the Party, and he was thus the last person who could be expected to argue against the military's freedom to defend its historical role.

[104] Major General (and Professor) E. Boltin, in *Wojskowy Przeglad Historyczny*, No. 4, 1964, pp. 206-219.

[105] General of the Army A. A. Epishev, *Istoriia uchit* (History Teaches), Izdatel'stvo "Znanie," Moscow, 1965.

[106] *Ibid.*, p. 16.

on once more, with the Zhukovites in the attack and the former Khrushchevites in the Stalingrad Group in retreat. In March 1965, Academician A. Samsonov published a scathing rebuke to those who, in the past, had engaged in the game of deciding "which of the major battles of the Great Patriotic War played the greatest role," and he urged historians to note both differences and similarities, especially "in the battles of Moscow and on the Volga."[107] Samsonov also criticized as false certain presentations "in some recent works of history of the Great Patriotic War—for example, the description of the planning process for the counterattack of Soviet forces on the Volga and the defenses at Kursk."[108] This was an unequivocal attack on the claims that had been made by the Stalingrad Group and Khrushchev. However, this revival of the argument over the relative importance of Stalingrad and Moscow was only preliminary to the main bout to come, which took the form of a debate on the battle of Berlin, on the twentieth anniversary of Germany's defeat.

Whereas the public statements about the battles of Moscow and Stalingrad were merely the latest in an old argument and thus of rather parochial interest, the Berlin debate, surprisingly, introduced new factors into the historical dialogue between the chief protagonists and added new information to it. In the past, the intensity and vituperativeness of the exchange of views on the battle for Berlin between the Zhukovites and members of the Stalingrad Group, especially on the part of Konev, had suggested the existence of a strong antagonism, but little was known about actual events and the possible causes of this animosity. Some recent Soviet publications have now provided us with new insights into this historical chapter. If nothing else, they recreate for us an intimate sense of the unique universe of the absolute dictator and his Kremlin cabals. More important, however, these revelations enable us to understand better than before the schism in the military between the Zhukovites and the Stalingrad Group; they cast light on the way that decisions were made during the war at the very top of the Soviet hierarchy and on the relations between Stalin and his generals; and they illuminate some hitherto obscure facets of Soviet policies and intentions with respect to postwar Europe.

A remarkable feature of this most recent, post-Khrushchevian, phase of the historical dialogue is the seeming confluence of views between the Zhukovites and the dissidents in the Stalingrad Group.

[107] *Voenno-istoricheskii zhurnal,* No. 3, March 1965, pp. 21 and 22.
[108] *Ibid.,* p. 20.

Thus, Marshal Zakharov, who had been dismissed from his position as Chief of the General Staff after the Cuban missile crisis, published an article in February 1965 which strongly attacked those "historians who, in the assessment of various operations of the Great Patriotic War, were guided not by the actual military, political, and strategic significance of these operations but by the posts held by some individuals who were ordered to carry out these operations." Indeed, said Zakharov, "the higher the post held, the more strongly was it necessary to . . . 'overemphasize' the operation and to 'boost' its significance."[109] There is no doubt that Zakharov's reference was to the sycophants around Khrushchev, the more so as his entire article was devoted to the criticism of "subjectivism" and "harebrained scheming" that has become the officially sanctioned way of condemning Khrushchev.

Closely upon these statements of Zakharov followed the counterblast of the Zhukovites against Chuikov's criticism of Zhukov the previous spring. To appreciate fully their rebuttal of the Marshal's main indictments, it will be well to recall briefly the historical background of the battle for Berlin.[110] In October and November 1944, the Soviet General Staff prepared the plans for the final assault on Berlin, and Stalin decided that only the forces of the First Belorussian Front, under Zhukov's command, would conduct the Berlin operation. In January 1945, when the Soviet winter offensive got under way, Marshal Konev, extremely unhappy over being deprived of the chance to participate in so momentous an operation, pressed the General Staff for permission to have his First Ukrainian Front take part in the assault on the main Berlin axis. While the professionals in the General Staff were sympathetic to his pleas, for they envisaged a bitter and costly struggle in and around the city,[111] the *Stavka*, which was Zhukov's domain, was not. The conflict resulted in a compromise, which offered Konev a means of saving face but still denied him access to the main Berlin axis.

With the growing German pressure from the right flank in Pomerania, the Soviet advance on Berlin slowed down and eventually was

[109] *Krasnaia zvezda*, February 4, 1965.

[110] For some details on the historical background of the Berlin offensive and the Konev-Zhukov feud, see Chapter VII, pp. 235-238.

[111] For statistics on forces, logistics, and command personnel involved in the Berlin operation, see "Berlinskaia operatsiia v tsifrakh" (Data on the Berlin Operation), *Voenno-istoricheskii zhurnal*, No. 4, April 1965, pp. 79-88. See also Boltin, in *Wojskowy Przeglad Historyczny*, p. 219. According to these sources, the Soviet losses in that operation, which lasted from April 4 to May 8, 1945, were 304,887 officers and men killed, wounded, or missing in action.

halted. While Zhukov was using this lull to regroup his forces and bring up the rear, Stalin, concerned about the rising tempo of the Western Allies' eastward movement, ordered the Berlin offensive to be resumed on April 16. The decision was taken on April 1-2 in a remarkable meeting of the *Stavka*, where Stalin, faced with the two victorious and ambitious marshals, Zhukov and Konev, who were participating in the planning of the operations, shrewdly played them off against each other. He established an arbitrary line about 60 km southeast of Berlin, and indicated that whichever of the marshals got to this point first would be allowed to take Berlin. As it turned out, it was Zhukov who was given the nod, but he encountered such stiff resistance from the Germans that Konev's forces had to be called in to help him out.[112]

In March 1965, Zhukov's defenders opened their attack on the historical claims of Chuikov and other Khrushchevites in the Stalingrad Group. Lieutenant General N. Antipenko, who had been Zhukov's commander of the rear during the war, accused Chuikov of falsifying the facts and citing data to which he could not have had access, and he refuted Chuikov's allegation that he had criticized faults in the Berlin offensive as early as 1946.[113] In April, another member of Zhukov's wartime command, Lieutenant General K. Telegin, began his attack with a clear reference to the fact that Chuikov's benefactor Khrushchev was not around to protect him ("Now we can analyze the whole problem peacefully, without getting excited, and after having armed ourselves with facts . . ."), and went on to dispose patronizingly of Chuikov's claims to military foresight and strategic brilliance.[114] That same month, Konev himself publicly defended his position. He spoke of his strong desire to take part in the storming of Berlin, and hinted that Stalin's arbitrary line, 60 km from Berlin, had been a ploy favoring Zhukov, whose forces in April 1945 were much closer to that line than Konev's.[115]

In May, the Berlin dialogue was in full swing, as a number of ranking military personalities published their views in *Voenno-istoricheskii zhurnal.* The most interesting of these articles was by Colonel

[112] For historical descriptions of these developments, see the contributions of Major General P. Zhilin, Marshal of the Soviet Union A. Grechko, Lieutenant General V. Pozniak, Marshal of the Soviet Union K. Rokossovskii, Colonel General M. Kalashnik, and Colonel General S. Shtemenko in *Voenno-istoricheskii zhurnal,* No. 5, May 1965, pp. 3-72.

[113] *Ibid.*, No. 3, March 1965, pp. 69-79.

[114] *Ibid.*, No. 4, April 1965, p. 63.

[115] *Krasnaia zvezda,* April 16, 1965.

General Shtemenko, now the Chief of Staff of the Ground Forces, who had headed a section of the General Staff during the war. Under the guise of objectivity, Shtemenko slanted his historical narrative in favor of Konev, stressing Zhukov's preferential relationship with Stalin and the arbitrary manner in which both men interfered with the professional planning operations of the General Staff.[116]

In June, Marshal Zhukov himself joined the fray. In his first public statement since his ouster by Khrushchev in 1957, he revealed his particular anger at Chuikov for asking, "Why did the command element of the First Belorussian Front, after reaching the Oder in the first days of February, fail to secure permission from the *Stavka* to continue the offensive toward Berlin without stopping?"[117] and for maintaining that "Berlin could have been taken as early as February" and that this would have brought an earlier end to the war.[118] Zhukov, therefore, chose to be relatively generous toward Konev and to concentrate his attack on Chuikov, whom he lectured on elementary aspects of strategy and accused of misrepresenting Zhukov's role in the Berlin offensive; in defense against Chuikov's main charge, Zhukov presented the reasons for slowing down the winter offensive of 1945.[119]

Thus, the recent dialogue on historical roles continues both within the military and between the military and the Party, reflecting the changes in political alignments since the departure of Khrushchev, much as earlier phases of the dialogue reflected the political conditions of other periods. While it might appear as though in the Soviet Union *plus ça change, plus c'est la même chose*, there can be little doubt that military leaders have gained some important insights from this recurrent pattern. The chief lesson they owe to the cumulative effect of political changes followed by periods of military assertiveness is that it is safer and more profitable for the military professionals to remain politically aloof, with primary loyalty to their own institution, than to serve the ephemeral idols of the Party.

[116] Shtemenko, in *Voenno-istoricheskii zhurnal*, No. 5, May 1965, pp. 56-72.

[117] Marshal of the Soviet Union G. K. Zhukov, in *ibid.*, No. 6, June 1965, p. 15.

[118] *Ibid.*

[119] Chuikov had claimed that he was present in the headquarters of the 69th Army on February 4, 1945, when Stalin called Zhukov to the telephone and persuaded him to cease planning for offensive operations against Berlin, despite the fact that the consensus of the frontal commanders, including Zhukov, favored continuing the operation. Zhukov denies that he was at the headquarters that day and that such a conversation ever took place. *Ibid.*, p. 18.

VII · The Rise of the Stalingrad Group: A Study in Intramilitary Power Politics

The Party leader's constant concern about the military is reflected in the elaborate control machinery, geared to prevention as well as coercion, which the Party maintains within the military establishment. The main purpose of political control and indoctrination is to instill Party loyalty in the military and to prevent anti-Party action. However, the Party leader is also anxious about the personal loyalty of the military; he needs a reliable military elite on whose support he can count in the perennial intra-Party power struggles as well as in cases where the Party's policy meets with opposition from military circles. He seeks to assure himself of such support by cultivating a personally loyal military elite, whose careers depend directly on his own fortunes.

The Party leader stands to gain important advantages from his encouragement of a loyal elite. Specifically, he acquires thereby a body of professionally reliable military decision-makers whom he can trust to offer military advice attuned to his own preferences, to execute his military policies, and to deal with any intramilitary opposition to such policies. Moreover, the existence of such a loyal group assures the Party leader of stability at the highest levels of the military hierarchy, since admission to this elite occurs through cooptation of politically reliable officers. At the same time, by cultivating an elite, the Party leader injects an element of division into the military which hinders the coalescence of a unified military point of view and the emergence of a single military spokesman.

Both Stalin and Khrushchev were substantially aided in their rise to power by the support of personal followers in the military, and both used their Trojan horses to control the military. Indeed, the striking similarity in the two dictators' operational code *vis-à-vis* their preferred elites within the military invites closer comparison.

(1) Though decades apart, both Stalin and Khrushchev created their own personal following in the military from among disaffected officers in the field commands. Acting as the protectors of the field commanders' interests against the encroachments of the central authorities based in Moscow, they gained the commanders' loyalty, and made it possible eventually to combine resources and to link the careers and fortunes of the commanders to the figure of the emerging dictator.

Stalin began to gather future military allies around him during the battle of the southern Ukraine, especially during the defense of Tsaritsyn (later Stalingrad, now Volgograd) between August and October 1918. He exploited the field commanders' strong dislike of Trotsky, and of the central Party-military organ (the *Revvoensovet Respubliki*) that Trotsky headed, as the common denominator of their varied interests and objectives. To the field commanders, thin-skinned former NCOs now in command of vast armies, Trotsky was an arrogant intruder from the distant capital, who arbitrarily appointed and demoted as he went along, and who criticized them humiliatingly for their military mistakes, while claiming their victories for himself.[1]

Khrushchev acquired his future military associates during World War II, mainly during the battles in the southern Ukraine that culminated in the battle of Stalingrad. Using the field commanders' strong dislike of Marshal Zhukov and of the Moscow-based *Stavka* (of which Zhukov was the most dominant member, next to Stalin),

[1] The conflict between Trotsky and the field commanders, who included Stalin and Voroshilov, centered on Trotsky's forceful promotion of the idea that military specialists from the old army should be given command of major forces at the front. At Tsaritsyn, Stalin and Voroshilov carried on what amounted to a private war with Trotsky. D. Fedotoff-White, in his excellent study on the Red Army, states that the opposition from the field commanders was generated by their resentment of "the centralized control of military affairs from Moscow . . . the appointment of commanders by central military organs and the direction of military operations by former czarist officers." *The Growth of the Red Army*, Princeton University Press, Princeton, N.J., 1944, p. 65.

This growing animosity between the field commanders and Trotsky was given further momentum by the establishment of the *Revvoensovet Respubliki* (Revolutionary Military Council of the Republic), which had near-absolute powers in matters of war and was headed by Trotsky. Stalin also served on it for a short period, but was removed from it after he began to oppose Trotsky. The opposition to the *Revvoensovet Respubliki* served to unite field commanders and political commissars around the *revvoensovets* of the field commands. Among the most prominent members of these field command *revvoensovets* were such Stalinists as Voroshilov, Bubnov, Gusev, and Kirov. *KPSS i stroitel'stvo Vooruzhennykh Sil SSSR, 1918-iiun' 1941* (The CPSU and the Development of the Armed Forces of the USSR, 1918-June 1941), Voenizdat, Moscow, 1959, p. 134.

Leonard Schapiro also views Trotsky's drive toward centralization of military authority in the Red Army as the main source of friction between the field commanders and Trotsky. "The Birth of the Red Army," *The Red Army*, ed. B. H. Liddell-Hart, Harcourt, Brace and Company, New York, 1956, pp. 28-29.

S. I. Gusev conveyed the flavor of the prevailing dislike of Trotsky and the latter's arrogance in his letter to E. D. Stasova, the secretary of the Central Committee: "Trotsky sets the tone for the whole system. Frequent changes of the political workers and commanders, crowding the Southern Front *Revvoensovet* with a great number of Party members and Trotsky's princely journeys along the front. . . ." See G. V. Kuz'min, *Grazhdanskaia voina i voennaia interventsiia v SSSR* (The Civil War and Armed Intervention in the USSR), Voenizdat, Moscow, 1958, p. 236.

Khrushchev became the protector of the field commanders and established with them an alliance of long duration.

(2) After the civil war, Stalin and his military associates faced a military establishment that was dominated by Trotsky and his appointees. But gradually Stalin replaced the latter with his own candidates, aided in this effort by a number of developments. Trotsky, through his arrogance and his call for a return to revolutionary principles in the creation of the Red Army, had alienated broad, unrelated interest groups within the military and Party: (a) the victorious Red Commanders, who had defeated the counterrevolutionary forces as well as the Polish army and were in no mood to listen to Trotsky's plans for dissolution of the professional standing army and a return to a territorial militia; (b) the military commissars, most of whom resented Trotsky's views of their functions as temporary and subsidiary; and (c) various splinter groups in the Party and military who became angered by Trotsky's high-handed dismissal of their views during the 1918-1921 period. Among these last factions were the proponents of *partizanshchina* (guerrilla warfare), the Bukharinites, and the Military Opposition, all of them opposed to orthodoxy in the emerging Soviet military establishment and in favor of a loosely organized and disciplined decentralized structure.

Remarkably, Trotsky managed to alienate utopians, conservatives, and moderates alike. As long as he had Lenin's support, however, he retained his dominant position. After Lenin's death, Trotsky was ousted from the *Revvoensovet Respubliki* and forced to witness the ascent to power of Stalin and his military associates.

Khrushchev's postwar situation was roughly similar, with Stalin relegating most of Khrushchev's wartime military associates from the Stalingrad Group to political and professional obscurity, while retaining in central military positions his own former associates from the civil war days and also a group of younger military commanders assumed to be protégés of Zhukov. After Stalin's death, however, Khrushchev, with the support of the military, succeeded in ousting Malenkov in 1955 and the so-called anti-Party group in 1957. In October 1957, he was able to remove Marshal Zhukov from the Ministry of Defense, supported in this move by his followers in the Stalingrad Group, who by then had become entrenched in the military establishment.

(3) The parallel between Stalin's and Khrushchev's relations with their respective military associates extends to the eventual conflict between the dictator and his loyal elite. Stalin caused widespread re-

sentment among the Soviet High Command by his retention of the dual command principle and by the brutality associated with collectivization. The resultant tensions led to the military purges of 1937, in which the more professional among the dictator's military associates were destroyed, while the "political" officers were retained and promoted. Thus, the Tukhachevskii group and the Far Eastern Command suffered destruction, while Voroshilov, Budennyi, and Timoshenko survived the purges unscathed.

The Stalingrad Group, whose members came to dominate the military establishment after the rise of Khrushchev in the Party, eventually became internally divided, as the more professional and sophisticated officers found themselves at odds with Khrushchev on a number of major issues, while an inner clique of politically oriented and less distinguished officers followed their benefactor blindly. The issues that caused this polarization of loyalties and interests in the Stalingrad Group were Khrushchev's sweeping reforms of strategic doctrine and of the socio-political structure of the officer corps, as well as his economic policies, which effectively discriminated against the less important sectors of the military establishment in favor of the strategically vital ones. The split in the Stalingrad Group was essentially a crisis of primary loyalty in which members had to choose between their professional and institutional interests as military people concerned with the welfare of country and Party, and unquestioning loyalty to their benefactor and Party leader.

Thus, both Stalin and Khrushchev created personally loyal military elites by manipulating the alienation of groups of officers from the central military authorities; both dictators were aided considerably by these military elites in their rise to power; and both rewarded their supporters with the highest military and political positions. Yet, in the long run, despite the preferential position of these elites, professional and institutional interests and loyalties tended, with some exceptions, to overrride personal loyalties to the benefactors and to cause divisions and crises.

In this chapter we shall describe the origins and development of the special relationship that has united a number of military officers now occupying the highest positions in the Soviet military establishment with the faction of the Party most closely identified with Khrushchev. The relationship goes back to World War II, to the battle of Stalingrad in the fall and winter of 1942-1943 and the military operations that followed it. The name "Stalingrad Group" is most appropriate, because members of this military elite first met and became close to

Khrushchev during the battle of Stalingrad, and that battle was to become the symbolic rallying point for the group and its benefactor (while the battle of Moscow became associated with Zhukov and his supporters). The special relationship between Khrushchev and his military followers has had a striking impact on their careers, and thus on internal Soviet politics and on international affairs.

A · *THE FORMATIVE STAGE*: *1941-1945*

The suddenness, swiftness, and momentum of the German advance that followed upon the attack of June 22, 1941, confronted the Communist Party with the greatest crisis it had faced since its assumption of power. Among the first measures with which Stalin sought to deal with the deteriorating situation at the front was the creation, on June 30, of the State Defense Committee (*Gosudarstvennyi Komitet Oborony*, or GKO), a small extraordinary body in which were concentrated military, political, economic, and police powers.[2] The GKO consisted of from five to eight members of the Politburo and was headed by Stalin. (It was abolished only on September 19, 1945.) In a further effort to concentrate all power in himself, or in men directly subordinate to him, Stalin assumed the position of People's Commissar of Defense on July 19, and in August took the title of Supreme Commander-in-Chief.[3]

Immediately under Stalin and the GKO was the *Stavka* (short for *Stavka Verkhovnogo Glavnokomandovaniia*, or Supreme Command Headquarters), created at the very beginning of the war, which consisted of about a dozen top military officers whose basic functions were to develop strategic plans and to advise Stalin on the conduct of the war. The General Staff was subordinated to the *Stavka*, and the Chief of the General Staff became a member of the *Stavka*. Prominent members of the *Stavka* were frequently assigned to coordinating, and sometimes to directing, complex, large-scale military operations. Marshals Zhukov, Vasilevskii, Timoshenko, and Voronov, for example, who were *Stavka* members, personally led various frontal operations.[4]

[2] *Ideologicheskaia rabota KPSS na fronte (1941-1945)* (Ideological Work of the CPSU at the Front [1941-1945]), Voenizdat, Moscow, 1960, p. 23.

[3] *Ibid.*

[4] The function and role of the *Stavka* and its relations with the field commands were recently described by Major General N. Pavlenko in *Voenno-istoricheskii zhurnal*: "The *Stavka* of the Supreme Command was created at the very beginning of the war, and the General Staff became its operational organ. The *Stavka* directly commanded the operations of the Fronts and the fleets. Rapid developments of events, and frequent destruction of communications between the General Staff and

The basic Soviet field command during World War II was the Front, which usually consisted of from five to seven armies, one or two tactical air armies and special artillery, and supporting armored formations. The range of initiative left to the Front command tended to vary with the size of the Front, the importance of the operation, and Stalin's reliance on the command. Usually, the Front command received instructions from the *Stavka* and operated within the plan of battle thus transmitted from above. The army command was given less initiative than the Front, and at the divisional and regimental levels initiative was almost nonexistent.

In addition to military representatives from the *Stavka*, Stalin also dispatched to the various Fronts and armies prominent members of the communist hierarchy, including Politburo members A. Zhdanov, K. E. Voroshilov, D. Z. Manuilskii, A. S. Shcherbakov, and N. S. Khrushchev.[5] These men provided Stalin with control, from the top, of the decisions and activities at the front. For control from the bottom, Stalin reintroduced the political commissars in all military units.[6]

It was in his capacity as political supervisor of various Fronts (the official description of the function was a "Member of Military Council of the Front") that Khrushchev came into contact with the general officers with whom he subsequently established close ties. The high centralization in Moscow of initiative and control over all military activities, and the frustrating lack of authority of army and Front commanders, placed Khrushchev in the highly advantageous position of an intermediary between Moscow and the field commanders. In that capacity he exerted strong influence on the selection of commanding

---

the Front, in July 1941 dictated the creation of an intermediate level of strategic command, the Main Command of Theaters, upon which was placed [nominally] the direct leadership of combat operations at the Front. Available data show, however, that the Main Command of Theaters was not in fact entrusted with the necessary authority or means to carry out its functions." (No. 11, November 1961, pp. 93-103.) See also R. L. Garthoff, *Soviet Military Doctrine*, The Free Press, Glencoe, Ill., 1953, pp. 192-199. On June 23, 1941, Stalin created the *Stavka* of the Soviet High Command (*Stavka Glavnogo Komandovaniia Vooruzhennykh Sil SSSR*) which functioned as GHQ. On July 10, the *Stavka* was transformed into the *Stavka Verkhovnogo Glavnokomandovaniia*, whose members were Stalin, Molotov, and Marshals Shaposhnikov, Voroshilov, Budennyi, Timoshenko, and Zhukov.

[5] *Istoriia Velikoi Otechestvennoi voiny Sovetskogo Soiuza, 1941-1945* (The History of the Great Patriotic War of the Soviet Union, 1941-1945), Voenizdat, Moscow, 1961, Vol. 2, p. 57.

[6] I. F. Pobezhimov, *Pravovoe regulirovanie stroitel'stva Sovetskoi Armii i Flota* (Legal Regulation of the Development of the Soviet Army and Navy), Gosiurizdat, Moscow, 1960, pp. 93-94.

personnel, on decisions regarding military operations, on settling disputes among field commanders, and on the relations between the military commands and the local Party organizations.

On July 10, 1941, Stalin divided the front line into three major theater commands, and assigned commanding and political personnel to these as follows:

(1) The Main Command of the Northwestern Theater, which was to direct the Northern and Northwestern Fronts (along with appropriate naval commands), to be commanded by K. E. Voroshilov, with A. A. Zhdanov as political supervisor.

(2) The Main Command of the Western Theater, which was to direct the Western Front and some naval commands, to be commanded by S. K. Timoshenko, with N. A. Bulganin as political supervisor.

(3) The Main Command of the Southwestern Theater, which was to direct the Southwestern and Southern Fronts and some naval commands, to be commanded by S. M. Budennyi, with N. S. Khrushchev as political supervisor.[7]

Thus did Khrushchev, who was given the rank of Lieutenant General, become involved, under the direct authority of Stalin, in the extremely vital task of whipping up the patriotic fervor of the retreating Soviet armies and maintaining political control over the generals in the field. His authority was substantial, despite his very limited military experience.

In the course of various defensive operations during 1941, Budennyi and Khrushchev earned the displeasure of Stalin and of Marshal Shaposhnikov, the Chief of the General Staff. After the disastrous defeat at Kiev, Budennyi was replaced by Timoshenko on September 12, 1941, but Khrushchev continued for the moment to serve as political supervisor of the Southwestern Theater.[8] Toward the end of September, however, Stalin abolished the Southwestern Theater as such, and Timoshenko and Khrushchev retained the command of only the Southwestern Front.[9] In that position, Khrushchev moved eastward with the retreating Red Army. In May 1942, the Southwestern Front under Timoshenko was badly defeated at Kharkov, when several Soviet force groups found themselves encircled and then routed by a superior German force. In the middle of July, the

[7] *Boevoi put' Sovetskikh Vooruzhennykh Sil* (The Battle Path of the Soviet Armed Forces), Voenizdat, Moscow, 1960, p. 264.

[8] *Istoriia Velikoi Otechestvennoi voiny*, Vol. 2, p. 107.

[9] *Ibid.*, p. 111.

German military dealt another blow to the Soviet forces of the Briansk and Voronezh Fronts, and their 1st, 4th, and 6th Tank Armies rolled over the Soviet defenses in the Voronezh area and pushed through toward the great bend of the Don. The forces of the Southwestern Front, which were bypassed from the northeast, were too exhausted and disorganized from previous battles to offer much resistance to the advancing German forces. This development placed the vital strategic area of Stalingrad in great danger, since the Germans, if they took Stalingrad, would be able to destroy the last remaining communication lines between the central regions and the Caucasus.

On July 12, to deal with the rapidly deteriorating situation at Stalingrad, the *Stavka* created the Stalingrad Front, made up of the 62nd, 63rd, and 64th Armies, which were transferred from the strategic reserves; later, it added the 21st, 57th, and 8th Air Armies. In addition to the military forces, the Party also mobilized 183,000 civilians in Stalingrad and set them to building defenses around and within the city.[10] The defense of Stalingrad was to become the central endeavor in Soviet military operations of 1942; in a special directive of August 9, the *Stavka* stated that "the defense of Stalingrad and the defeat of the enemy, who is approaching Stalingrad from the south and west, is of decisive importance to the whole Soviet-German front."[11]

As the situation at Stalingrad continued to deteriorate, Timoshenko, who had proved incapable of halting the German advance, was dismissed on July 22 and replaced by Lieutenant General V. N. Gordov.

Furthermore, on August 5, the *Stavka* divided the Stalingrad Front in two (the Southeastern Front and the Stalingrad Front), in the hope of thereby stemming more effectively the two main thrusts of the German advance.[12] However, when the situation remained critical and there were signs of panic among the Soviet forces, the *Stavka*, on August 14, ordered the two Fronts unified again and placed under the command of General Eremenko and the political supervision of Khrushchev.[13] Lieutenant General Golikov took over command of the Southeastern Front, as Eremenko's deputy.[14]

Toward the end of August, Stalin dispatched General Zhukov to

[10] *Vtoraia mirovaia voina* (World War II), ed. Lieutenant General S. P. Platonov, Voenizdat, Moscow, 1958, pp. 310-311.

[11] *Ibid.*, p. 316.

[12] A. M. Samsonov, *Stalingradskaia bitva* (The Battle of Stalingrad), Izdatel'stvo Akademii nauk SSSR, Moscow, 1960, p. 154.

[13] *Ibid.*, p. 159.

[14] Marshal of the Soviet Union A. I. Eremenko, *Stalingrad*, Voenizdat, Moscow, 1961, p. 87.

the Stalingrad Front.[15] On September 3, he sent Zhukov a telegram to the effect that the situation in Stalingrad was deteriorating. ("Stalingrad may be taken today or tomorrow.") The telegram empowered Zhukov to take all necessary measures to halt the German advance and advised him that "procrastination of any officer at the front will be viewed as a crime."[16]

The arrival of Zhukov at the Stalingrad Front set off a chain of events which was to have a lasting effect on his relations with the Stalingrad Group. As the direct representative of Stalin and empowered with wide authority, Zhukov proceeded to shake up the field command and to make major changes in the disposition of the forces, with little concern for the views or advice of the field command. Eremenko notes in his memoirs that he and Khrushchev were "disappointed" after Zhukov's arrival in their headquarters,[17] because he ignored their pleas to reinforce the southern sector of the Stalingrad Front with troops from the northern sector. While this may have been one of several reasons, a more likely cause of "disappointment" would seem to have been Zhukov's criticism of the breakdown of communications and control between Eremenko's headquarters and his units, for, despite massive fresh forces placed at Eremenko's disposal at Stalingrad, the Germans kept advancing on the city. Eremenko blamed this condition on the frequent changes ordered by the *Stavka* in the Stalingrad Front command, which, he said, led to confusion and the loss of valuable time.[18]

When Zhukov rejected their demands for reinforcement of the southern sector, Khrushchev and Eremenko went over his head and, on September 23, complained to Stalin over the telephone. According to Eremenko, Stalin sided with them and promised changes in the near future.[19] Events, however, belie this assertion and suggest that Stalin accepted Zhukov's point of view against that of the field commanders. On September 30, one week after the telephone conversation, Stalin ordered the Stalingrad Front divided once more and renamed. The former Stalingrad Front became the Don Front, and the former Southeastern Front now was called the Stalingrad Front. Eremenko and Khrushchev found themselves in command of the new Stalingrad Front, the smaller of the two, while the new Don Front was placed under the command of Lieutenant General Rokos-

[15] *Ibid.*, p. 209.

[16] *Ibid.*, p. 163. See also Eremenko's article in *Kommunist*, No. 1, January 1958, p. 30.

[17] *Stalingrad*, p. 209.

[18] *Kommunist*, January 1958, p. 28.

[19] *Stalingrad*, p. 210.

sovskii and the political supervision of Major General Zheltov.[20] Thus, the scene was set for the growing conflict between the field commanders and Khrushchev on the one hand, and Zhukov and the *Stavka* generals in Moscow on the other.

Although he had failed to sway Stalin against Zhukov, Khrushchev continued to enjoy a position at the front advantageous to his own interests. The Soviet field commanders had very little freedom to act without first checking with the *Stavka* in Moscow. Given the poor communication systems between the fronts and Moscow, they sometimes failed to take the most necessary actions for fear of misconstruing instructions and earning the wrath of Stalin.

Their lack of authority had a corrosive effect on the field commanders, who feared and disliked the emissaries from the *Stavka.* They also resented their political supervisors, who had authority to intervene in military-political affairs of the units without bearing the responsibility for military losses, and who, moreover, possessed sources of information on military plans, whereas the commanders often were kept in the dark until the last possible moment.[21] The extent of the field commanders' frustration at their lack of authority is reflected in this passage from a recent Soviet publication:

> . . . the top leadership of the war theaters was not, in fact, entrusted with the necessary authority or means to carry out their functions and could not undertake or independently carry out important decisions.
>
> . . . the *Stavka* [frequently] rejected correct decisions of Theater Commands; it gave directives to the fronts over the heads of the commanders-in-chief of the Theaters, did not take into consideration their opinions, and, moreover, during the first period of the war, abolished, created, and again abolished Theatre Commands. Consequently, this important strategic command level became transformed into a sort of information center and did not become a superior instrument . . . of rapid operational command.[22]

Into the power vacuum of the field commands Khrushchev injected his extensive authority. Recognizing the opportunity afforded

[20] Samsonov, *Stalingradskaia bitva*, p. 237.

[21] Marshal Chuikov complains in his memoirs about the fact that he was kept uninformed about operations intended by the *Stavka* for his 62nd Army at Stalingrad until just prior to the beginning of the Stalingrad counteroffensive, and that he had to guess the *Stavka*'s intentions and plans from personal observations and on the basis of information coming in through the "soldiers' heralds," i.e., the grapevine. Marshal V. I. Chuikov, *Nachalo puti* (Beginning of the Road), Voenizdat, Moscow, 1959, p. 221.

[22] Pavlenko, in *Voenno-istoricheskii zhurnal*, No. 11, November 1961, p. 102.

him by the uneasy relationship between the field commanders and the *Stavka* representatives and political commissars, he displayed his adroitness in handling interpersonal relations. Instead of playing the narrow *apparatchik*, he took the part of defender of the field commanders' interests, and succeeded in gathering around him the loyal military following that was to play such an important role in his future career.

A recent Soviet study of the war describes the relationship between Khrushchev and Marshal Vatutin, with whom Khrushchev served for a period as political supervisor. In dealing with *Stavka* representatives who came to Vatutin's headquarters during the battle of Kursk, "Khrushchev . . . always supported Vatutin with his authority as a prominent governmental and Party figure." Vatutin, says the author, "whom Nikita Sergeevich knew for many years in the Ukraine, when he was chief of staff for the Kiev military district," always "felt more self-assured and relaxed whenever Khrushchev arrived at the front."[23]

Marshal Eremenko also relates several incidents in which Khrushchev used his authority to protect and support the field commanders against *Stavka* interference. He describes a heated dispute with Vasilevskii at the Stalingrad Front on the merits and demerits of an operational plan involving the 2nd Guards Army. Eremenko concludes that "Khrushchev's support of this [Eremenko's] proposal played a decisive role in its being accepted [by Vasilevskii]."[24]

Marshal Chuikov describes a number of occasions when Khrushchev intervened in his behalf or when Khrushchev's name was invoked as a threat. At one time, Chuikov was involved in a heated argument with the NKVD garrison commander of Stalingrad, a Colonel Saraev, until he threatened to call the Military Council (i.e., Khrushchev) of the Front, whereupon Saraev readily agreed with Chuikov's point of view.[25] On several occasions, including a dispute with the artillery commander of the Front[26] and another with the commander of the rear,[27] only Khrushchev's personal intervention brought about the results desired by Chuikov.

In conflicts between commanders and the political commissars attached to their units, Khrushchev often sided, at least outwardly, with the commanders. That the relations between commanders and

[23] Aleksandr Voinov, *Trevozhnaia noch'* (An Alarming Night), Voenizdat, Moscow, 1960, p. 82.

[24] *Stalingrad*, pp. 411-414.

[25] Chuikov, *Nachalo puti*, p. 100.

[26] *Ibid.*, p. 127.

[27] *Ibid.*, p. 234.

political commissars usually were far from cordial is apparent from many military memoirs published in the Soviet Union.[28] Marshal Chuikov describes one political officer attached to his 62nd Army, a man by the name of Abramov, as a thief.[29] And he resentfully observes that, while the commanders were kept in the dark on the crucial issue of the target date for the planned counteroffensive at Stalingrad, and consequently were in a state of virtual paralysis for many days, the political commissar of his army, General Gurev, had had the information all along.[30] Chuikov recalls that he often had to rely "on the soldiers' grapevine" for information relating to pending operations: "Through various little tiny channels news came to us about the movement of large forces to Stalingrad and about the arrival of Comrades Vasilevskii, Voronov, and other representatives from the *Stavka*."[31]

Khrushchev also showed personal courage and laid great stress on appearing in the front lines with the soldiers and officers, in sharp and probably calculated contrast to the behavior of other Party dignitaries, who sought the safety and comforts of the rear headquarters.

Zhukov's treatment of the field commanders under his command, in contrast to Khrushchev's, seemed designed to alienate them. This description of Zhukov's arrival at the front around Kursk conveys the aura of fear, mixed with expectation, that he created:

> The commanders looked after the Marshal with fear and hope. With fear, because they knew that it was a rare visit of Zhukov that did not bring with it . . . dismissals from commanding positions and sharp criticism, and with hope, because the authoritative representative of *Stavka* could [get things done] since he knew the situation well and could make appropriate decisions.[32]

The same work contains this account illustrating the effect of Zhukov's arrogance and personal rudeness: "General Getman [the commander of an army visited by Zhukov], who only five minutes ago was a tough, self-assured man, was now falling apart." When Getman attempted to intercede in behalf of some unfortunate commander whose

[28] General of the Army I. I. Fediuninskii is among those who have described their unpleasant relations with their political assistants. He speaks of his as cold-eyed and pale, "a face upon which neither sun nor wind will leave a mark" and who, he hints, rose to prominence during the military purges of 1937-1938. (*Podniatye po trevoge* [Roused by the Alarm], Voenizdat, Moscow, 1964, p. 114.) Colonel General A. L. Getman (cited in Lt. General N. K. Popel', *Tanki povernuli na zapad* [The Tanks Turned West], Voenizdat, Moscow, 1960, pp. 277-288) has similar recollections.

[29] *Ibid.*, p. 66. [30] *Ibid.*, p. 243. [31] *Ibid.*, p. 221. [32] *Ibid.*, p. 164.

unit had been surrounded by the Germans despite valiant efforts, Zhukov burst out that, if the officer should return to the unit, he was to be court-martialed. And when the army commissar spoke up in the man's defense, he was dismissed with the sneer: "Bah, member of the Military Council, intercessor!"[33]

Khrushchev, like Stalin during the civil war years, sensed the widespread dissatisfaction among the ranking field commanders and used it to unite these officers, with himself as the focal point. That he possessed the sense of the politician and the practical psychologist who understands a given situation and knows how to manipulate it to his own interest is indicated by the manner in which he selected the commanders who were to serve with him and subsequently to throw their lot in with his. Thus, in several instances, Khrushchev singled out commanders who were in disfavor, presumably with the thought that their feelings of gratitude and loyalty would be particularly strong.[34]

The selection of commanding personnel played a key role in Khrushchev's relationship with the Stalingrad Group. The importance of that function, and the great stress placed by the Party on the thorough and careful choice of ranking military personnel, are reflected in Eremenko's description of the selection of Chuikov to command the 62nd Army. He states that "Stalin was always quite strict in the selection of cadres" and that only after Khrushchev and Eremenko had assured him over the telephone that Chuikov was the right man did "Stalin agree with our recommendation."

Chuikov was Khrushchev's personal choice to succeed Krylov as commander of the 62nd Army at Stalingrad. He had already achieved a relatively high position before the war, when he commanded the 4th Army stationed in former Polish territories.[35] During

[33] *Ibid.*, p. 169.

[34] A recent military memoir affords a glimpse into this Khrushchevian tactic. Having come upon an incident at a divisional staff headquarters in which an officer was being arrested for having "shown too much initiative" in the front lines, Khrushchev took a deep interest in the affair and an immediate liking to the officer (Podgorbunskii), who despite his unfortunate situation and deep head wounds remained self-possessed and fearless. Outside the room, in answer to someone's explanation of the affair, Khrushchev said: "His obstreperousness is only on the surface, it will go away, it doesn't count. But he seems to be an excellent man. It would be a good idea to get to know him better. Wait for me here." Khrushchev then returned to Podgorbunskii and took him outdoors, where "they walked up and down, disappearing behind the hill, then appearing again." Later, according to the witness, "Nikita Sergeevich ordered the release of Podgorbunskii and lay down with us in the damp grass." *Ibid.*, p. 127.

[35] Colonel General L. M. Sandalov, *Perezhitoe* (The Past), Voenizdat, Moscow, 1961, p. 41.

the war, his career until Stalingrad was not very promising, for he was removed from his command as a result of unsuccessful operations in the initial stages of the war. At Stalingrad, however, where he was deputy commander of the 64th Army before receiving the command of the 62nd Army, his activities, under Khrushchev's tutelage, raised Chuikov to great prominence among military officers.

But Chuikov was only one of a number of Soviet officers who owe their distinguished careers to having been singled out by Khrushchev for important commands. R. I. Malinovskii, for example, arrived at the Stalingrad Front with a tarnished reputation. He had commanded the Southern Front in the Caucasus during the summer of 1942, but had been relieved of that command after some spectacular defeats there. He was subsequently selected, presumably by Khrushchev, to command the newly formed 66th Army. In the Caucasus, Malinovskii had earned the great displeasure of the *Stavka* and Stalin (whose henchman Beria once hurled grave accusations at him and threatened him with arrest).[36] But at Stalingrad he quickly regained his good reputation, and became one of the most prominent military leaders in the Soviet Union.

Another protégé of Khrushchev, K. S. Moskalenko, arrived at Stalingrad with a bare remnant of his 38th Army. He initially was included in the staff of the newly organized 4th Army, but under Khrushchev's auspices he became famous as commander of the 1st Guards Army and, later, of the 38th Army.

S. S. Biriuzov had served in a unit of Chuikov's 4th Army before the war. At the time of the Stalingrad battle, though only a minor officer, he was appointed chief of staff in Malinovskii's 66th Army, which he subsequently took over. He later served with Malinovskii as his chief of staff in the 2nd Guards Army.

A. A. Grechko did not serve directly with Khrushchev at Stalingrad, although he commanded forces on the southern sector of the front line. At the time that Malinovskii was commanding the Southern Front in the Caucasus,[37] he had commanded the 18th Army, which he subsequently lost. In the winter of 1942-1943, he was given the command of the 56th Army, which operated directly southward of the Stalingrad Front, then under Khrushchev's political supervision. Grechko came into direct contact with Khrushchev toward the end of 1943, during the battle of Kiev, when he served as deputy com-

[36] General of the Army I. V. Tiulenev, *Cherez tri voiny* (Through Three Wars), Voenizdat, Moscow, 1960, p. 196.

[37] Brezhnev served as political commissar of the 18th Army.

mander of the 1st Ukrainian Front under Vatutin, under Khrushchev's immediate supervision. During the preceding six or eight months, he had been conspicuously promoted from Major General to Colonel General.[38]

The nucleus of the Stalingrad Group was formed during the battle of Stalingrad and gained in cohesion during the battles of Kursk and Kiev. Constant friction between the *Stavka* generals and the field commanders during the remainder of the war ensured a lasting schism between the Zhukovites and the Stalingrad Group. One of the irritants to the field commanders who had served at Stalingrad was the fact that, while most of them remained at their old ranks, four members of the *Stavka* (Zhukov, Vasilevskii, Voronov, and Kazakov) received promotions to Marshal soon after the end of the campaign. The field commanders' alienation was deepened by Zhukov's (and, of course, Stalin's) extravagant claims of victory at Stalingrad. Another source of friction was Zhukov's (and Vasilevskii's) close supervision of the operations on the southern sectors of the front, where Marshal Konev and other members of the Stalingrad Group commanded the forces. Given Zhukov's arrogance and arbitrariness and Konev's volatile temper and independence of mind, one can hardly doubt that their relations worsened. Still another cause of tension between the Stalingrad Group and the *Stavka* was the growing prominence of Rokossovskii, a protégé of Zhukov, who was promoted to Marshal and given much credit for the Stalingrad counteroffensive, while Eremenko and other members of the Stalingrad Group were barely mentioned. And finally, later on, Zhukov's extravagant representation of his own role in the battle for Berlin as compared with that of Konev ensured the continuance of their feud.[39]

The majority of the original group that had participated in the battle of Stalingrad continued to serve close to one another. At the battle of Kursk, in the summer of 1943, Khrushchev, Vatutin, Konev, and Malinovskii were among those who commanded various units at the front.[40] In the winter offensive of 1943-1944, Khrushchev re-

[38] Marshal of the Soviet Union R. I. Malinovskii, in *Krasnaia zvezda*, November 5, 1963. See also Lieutenant General S. P. Platonov (ed.), *Vtoraia mirovaia voina* (World War II), Voenizdat, Moscow, 1958, p. 408.

[39] See Chapter VI, pp. 181-185.

[40] In Soviet historiography of the post-Zhukov (i.e., post-1957) period, the battle of Kursk was frequently referred to as another symbolic rallying point of the Stalingrad Group and as a link in the myth of Khrushchev's military genius. However, beginning in the fall of 1963, the 1943 battle for Kiev began to take on a striking importance in historical writings as well as in the evaluations of prominent Soviet military men. Since it had previously been considered by Soviet historians

mained with Vatutin's 1st Ukrainian Front, while Konev commanded the 2nd Ukrainian Front, and Malinovskii the 3rd Ukrainian Front. Zhukov was coordinating the activities of the 1st and 2nd Fronts.

In the summer offensive of 1944, Khrushchev served at the 1st Ukrainian Front with Konev, whose chief of staff was Zakharov, while Biriuzov served as chief of staff under Tolbukhin on the 3rd Ukrainian Front. The forces of the 1st Ukrainian Front included the 38th Army under Colonel General Moskalenko, who had Major General Epishev as his political supervisor. Among the units of the 4th Ukrainian Front (directly north of the 38th Army) was the 1st Guards Army under Colonel General Grechko.[41]

The *Stavka* group headed by Zhukov and the Stalingrad Group headed by Konev may be said to have fallen out originally over the battle of Stalingrad. But the rift became more serious, and indeed permanent, as a result of events preceding and accompanying the battle for Berlin.

The *Stavka* had begun to plan for this final operation in Germany as early as October 1944.[42] The chief planners, Generals Antonov,

---

as a rather obscure battle of no major significance, this sudden reversal suggests political-military motives rather than an honest historical judgment.

What is significant about the battle for Kiev is that it was almost the private affair of members of the hard core of the Stalingrad Group. The commanders of the forces which stormed the Ukrainian capital, Khrushchev's old preserve, were Konev, Grechko, Moskalenko, and Vatutin; among the political supervisors of the forces were Khrushchev and Epishev. Cf. article by Malinovskii in *Krasnaia zvezda*, November 5, 1963. It is somewhat curious that Malinovskii, who had not participated in the battle for Kiev, should have been the one to write the article stressing its importance. There may be a direct connection between Malinovskii's authorship of the extremely flattering description of Khrushchev and his associates, and his conspicuously modest rejection, the previous January, of the claims to military genius that were being made on his behalf (and on their own) by Eremenko, Biriuzov, Chuikov, and Moskalenko during the debate about Stalingrad in the Soviet press. It is not unlikely that Malinovskii signed the subsequent article under pressure.

[41] Khrushchev left the military in the fall of 1944 to return to Party activities in the Ukraine. One of his most immediate and major tasks was to deal with the pro-Nazi, anticommunist element in the Ukraine. This problem is described as follows in a major Soviet study of the war: ". . . great attention was given to Party-political work in the Western Ukraine. It was to be expected that bourgeois agents had created hatred toward the Soviet Union." F. Vorob'ev and V. M. Kravtsov, *Velikaia Otechestvennaia voina Sovetskogo Soiuza, 1941-1945* (The Great Patriotic War of the Soviet Union, 1941-1945), Voenizdat, Moscow, 1961, p. 330.

[42] Among Soviet sources, mostly in the form of memoirs, which present the conflicting views on the roles of Marshals Konev and Zhukov in the Berlin offensive, the following are about evenly divided between the pro-Konev (i.e., pro-Stalingrad Group) and the pro-Zhukov (*Stavka*) point of view. For the Konev position, see Marshal V. Chuikov, "Konets tret'ego reikha" (The End of the Third Reich),

Grizlov, and Lomov of the General Staff attached to the *Stavka*, foresaw two offensive movements, the first of these to last fifteen days and cover from 250 to 300 km to a line touching Bromberg, Poznan, Breslau, and Vienna, and the second to take the Soviet forces into Berlin and possibly beyond it in another thirty days.[43]

On November 7, 1944, Zhukov and Konev, in Moscow to celebrate the anniversary of the Revolution, met with Stalin and the officers of the General Staff and heard Stalin announce that Berlin was to be taken by the forces of the First Belorussian Front under Zhukov's command. Stalin's arbitrary decision[44] to reserve for Zhukov the plum of all Soviet military operations and victories dismayed the planners of the General Staff and deeply offended Konev, who wanted to have a part in the conquest of Berlin.

Once the winter offensive was under way, events did not go entirely as planned. On January 26, 1945, Zhukov informed the General Staff of his decision to keep up the offensive momentum until he reached Berlin. Konev's notice to the General Staff the following day that he, too, was going to move his troops, the First Ukrainian Front, in the direction of Berlin precipitated heated debates in the General Staff over how to reconcile Konev's plans with Stalin's dictum. General Antonov recommended to the *Stavka* that Konev's First Ukrainian Front be permitted to take part in the assault on Berlin. But the *Stavka*, which was Zhukov's domain, after agreeing with the proposal in principle, recommended that a dividing line be drawn between the Fronts; using Zhukov's guidelines for the purpose, they

---

Oktiabr', No. 3, 1964, pp. 101-149, and No. 4, pp. 123-169; Chuikov, "Kapituliatsiia gitlerovskoi Germanii" (The Surrender of Hitler Germany), *Novaia i noveishaia istoriia*, No. 2, 1965, pp. 3-25; Colonel General S. Shtemenko, "Kak planirovalas' posledniaia kampaniia po razgromu gitlerovskoi Germanii" (How the Last Campaign for the Destruction of Hitler Germany Was Planned), *Voenno-istoricheskii zhurnal*, No. 5, May 1965, pp. 56-72; Marshal Konev, interview in *Krasnaia zvezda*, April 16, 1965. In defense of the Zhukov position, see Marshal G. Zhukov, "Na berlinskom napravlenii" (On the Berlin Axis), *Voenno-istoricheskii zhurnal*, No. 6, June 1965, pp. 12-22; Lieutenant General N. Antipenko, "Ot Visly do Odera" (From the Vistula to the Oder), *ibid.*, No. 3, March 1965, pp. 69-79; Lieutenant General K. Telegin, "Na zakliuchitel'nom etape voiny" (At the Last Stage of the War), *ibid.*, No. 4, April 1965, pp. 54-70. Among the more "objective" and moderate views are Academician A. Samsonov, "Za glubokoe issledovanie istorii Velikoi Otechestvennoi voiny" (For a Thorough Research of the History of the Great Patriotic War), *ibid.*, No. 3, March 1965, pp. 17-24; and A. A. Epishev, *Istoriia uchit* (History Teaches), Izdatel'stvo "Znanie," Moscow, 1965.

[43] Shtemenko, *Voenno-istoricheskii zhurnal*, No. 5, May 1965, p. 61.

[44] "The work of the General Staff in planning the final thrusts became extremely complicated by Stalin's subjective and categorical decision assigning a special role to the First Belorussian Front." *Ibid.*, p. 68.

relegated Konev to the territory south of Berlin, thereby in effect preventing his forces from gaining access to the main offensive axis.[45]

Proposals and counterproposals became academic, however, when German resistance in Pomerania stiffened and threatened the right flank of the Soviet front line, and the problem was compounded by severe shortages of fuel and other matériel and by the dangerous extension of the Soviet supply lines. When the General Staff decided to order a halt to the offensive movement, thus giving commanders time to bring up supplies and regroup their forces for the final assault on Berlin, Stalin, as described earlier, became worried about the rapid progress of the Western Allies into Germany[46] and, at the *Stavka* meeting of April 1-2, ordered the Berlin operation resumed on April 16 and to last no more than from twelve to fifteen days. To ensure the rapid success of the operation, members of the General Staff suggested a pincer movement by Zhukov's and Konev's forces, a proposal that clashed head-on with Zhukov's idea of a frontal assault by his forces alone, and with Konev's suggestion of a coordinated frontal assault by his and Zhukov's forces. Stalin resolved the impasse by walking up to the maps and drawing a line between the two Fronts which terminated at Lubben, about 60 km southeast of Berlin. According to Marshal Konev, Stalin just drew the line without comment and left the marshals to puzzle over his intentions; according to Colonel General Shtemenko, he said, "Whoever gets there first will also take Berlin."[47] Whether or not he actually stated it, even Konev agreed that this was the general understanding of the meaning of Stalin's gesture.[48] Again, as we know, the events themselves decided the outcome of this situation, when Konev's armored forces were needed to help stem the German pressure on Zhukov's left flank and so were called in to join the assault on Berlin.

Echoes of that clash between Zhukov and Konev, however, still continue to be heard twenty years later. In the aforementioned inter-

[45] "After heated debates in the office of General Antonov, the General Staff proposed to approve both decisions, with which the *Stavka* agreed. However, the dividing line between the Fronts which was used was the one recommended by Marshal Zhukov." *Ibid.*, p. 65.

[46] "There was no doubt that the Allies intended to take Berlin before us, despite the fact that according to the Yalta agreement the city belonged to the Soviet occupation zone." (*Ibid.*, p. 70.) Stalin is reported to have asked: "Well, who will take Berlin, we or our allies?" (Konev, *Krasnaia zvezda*, April 16, 1965.)

[47] Shtemenko, p. 71.

[48] Konev, *Krasnaia zvezda* interview, April 16, 1965.

view in April 1965, Konev recalled with bitterness the events of the *Stavka* meeting of April 1, 1945:

> According to all directives of the Supreme Command, only the First Belorussian Front was to move on Berlin. Its forces were the closest to Berlin. Ours were about 100 to 130 km away. . . . But what Soviet soldier would not want to storm the enemy's capital? . . . Of course, I also wanted the forces of my Front to move directly on Berlin. . . . But this was at the time merely a wish.[49]

The interviewer's comments hint at the extent to which Konev's pride was hurt at the *Stavka* meeting:

> . . . Konev, recalling it, looks out the window. His phrases are laconic, full of professional military terms. His tone of voice is even and relaxed. . . . I think, nay, I am convinced, that on that first of April 1945, he was not so peaceful.[50]

And General Shtemenko, in his account of the meeting, relates that "Marshal Konev became very angry over the dividing line . . . , because it gave him no opportunity for an assault on Berlin."[51]

In the battle for Berlin, then, and also in the Far East, which was to be the final campaign of the war, the members of the Stalingrad Group stayed close together. Thereafter, some members of the Group were transferred to remote commands, where they remained until the death of Stalin. Malinovskii went to the distant Far Eastern Command, where Zakharov and Krylov served on his staff, and the remainder either were relegated to obscure posts or, like Konev, Grechko, Chuikov, and Moskalenko, served in central positions in western Russia.[52]

The conflict between the *Stavka* and the Stalingrad Group, which had strengthened the latter throughout the war, became dormant in the immediate postwar period. It burst into the open after Stalin's death

[49] *Ibid.* [50] *Ibid.*

[51] Shtemenko, p. 70. The debate on the battle of Berlin has only recently become a *cause célèbre* in the Soviet Union and an acceptable subject for public analysis. No doubt it will continue to figure in Soviet military and historical writings. Only recently, several of Marshal Zhukov's staff members have very candidly challenged the main contention of the anti-Zhukov camp: that Berlin could have been taken earlier, most likely in February 1945, had it not been for the Marshal's vain and vainglorious drive to take the German capital alone, without assistance from Konev. (See Antipenko, *Voenno-istoricheskii zhurnal*, No. 3, March 1965, p. 75; and Telegin, *ibid.*, No. 4, April 1965.) The targets of their criticism are, interestingly enough, Marshal Chuikov and General Prochko, two of the architects of the legend of Khrushchev and the Stalingrad Group in the battle of Stalingrad.

[52] See Appendix A-V.

and greatly influenced the Party's military policies in the years to follow.

The Stalingrad Group remained loyal to Khrushchev for a long time, and its rise to power along with their benefactor reflected the close relationship between them. Eventually, however, the Group became divided into a conservative, strongly pro-Khrushchev and pro-Party faction, and a moderate faction whose members viewed their obligations and loyalty to the military establishment as paramount to others. The conservative wing included Marshals Biriuzov, Moskalenko, and Chuikov; the moderates gathered around Marshals Malinovskii, Zakharov, Grechko, and Krylov. This polarization, which later became public, seems to have begun in the war years, and to have been furthered by the geographical separation of the two factions after the war.[53]

B · *THE POSTWAR STALINIST PERIOD*

While Stalin had had to make concessions to the military during the war,[54] he severely curtailed the military's prerogatives and professional autonomy after the war, and instead encouraged the massive reassertion of Party *apparatchiks* within the armed forces. The first public statement hinting at such a policy was made by Stalin on February 9, 1946. In it Stalin said that the war had been won not only through military effort but mainly because of the superiority of the Soviet social and political system:

> It would be . . . fallacious to maintain that we achieved victory owing only to the bravery of our troops. Without bravery, of course, it is not possible to achieve victory. However, bravery alone

[53] Evidence of friction between the two factions includes Marshal Malinovskii's most uncharitable remarks about Marshal Moskalenko, made to his face in 1959, when he accused the latter of being a braggart and a superficial person. Cf. *Partiinaia organizatsiia chasti, korablia* (The Party Organization of *Chast'* and Ship), Voenizdat, Moscow, 1960, p. 8.

Chuikov's dislike of M. V. Zakharov, who served as chief of staff on the Stalingrad Front, is evident from his memoirs. He relates that "to talk with him was always a torture" because Zakharov kept nagging him over the phone, from the relative security of headquarters, about details of the disposition and condition of various units, and Chuikov says arrogantly that it was rather difficult to give detailed answers to such questions in the heat of the battle. *Nachalo puti*, p. 187.

The appointment of Chuikov to the command of the 62nd Army also caused friction between him and Krylov (who had been commanding the 62nd Army after the removal of General Lopatin from the command), as Krylov no doubt resented being replaced by Chuikov, and the ill-feeling between the two came out in an oblique way in Chuikov's memoirs. *Ibid.*, p. 186.

[54] See Chapter III, pp. 67-68, for details.

> is not enough to conquer an enemy who possesses a massive army, first-class weapons, excellent officer cadres, and fairly good equipment.

He went on to claim implicitly all credit for the victory, maintaining that the essential factors in the Soviet victory were industrialization and collectivization, which had enabled the Soviet economy to provide the army and the people with the tools and weapons they needed to withstand the enemy.[55]

Stalin's speech set the tone, and soon events followed that corroborated this antimilitary attitude of the Party. Zhukov was removed from his position of prominence and sent to the obscurity of the Odessa Military District. In 1946, Stalin transformed the National Commissariat of the Armed Forces into the more centralized Ministry of Defense, at the same time abolishing the separate National Commissariat of the Navy and assigning its functions to the new ministry.[56] In 1947, a political general, N. A. Bulganin, took over as Minister of Defense and received the rank of Marshal of the Soviet Union.[57] That same year, the Council of Ministers approved the "Theses on the Political Organs of the Armed Forces of the USSR," which upgraded the political organs' authority while undercutting that of the commanders.[58] In the next few years, other regulations were issued that further tightened the Party's hold over the military.[59]

Khrushchev's contacts with the Stalingrad Group in the early post-

[55] See *Kommunisticheskaia partiia v period Velikoi Otechestvennoi voiny, iiun' 1941-1945 god* (The Communist Party During the Great Patriotic War, June 1941-1945), Gospolitizdat, Moscow, 1961, pp. 279-290. Compare Stalin's argument of 1946 with more recent military statements, which strongly reject such a view and stress the chaos and disorganization in the Soviet economy during the early war years. These later statements by the military, which were published mainly during the Zhukov period (1955-1957), attempted to show that the Red Army, although very poorly provided for by the Communist Party leadership, still managed to oppose and finally defeat a powerful, well-equipped enemy. For details on the heated debate between Boltin and Filippov on the one hand, and Samsonov, Evstigneev, and Tel'pukhovskii on the other, in the pages of *Voprosy istorii*, No. 1, January 1957, see Chapter VI, pp. 188-191.

[56] Pobezhimov, *Pravovoe regulirovanie stroitel'stva Sovetskoi Armii i Flota*, p. 108.

[57] Raymond L. Garthoff, "The Marshals and the Party: Soviet Civil-Military Relations in the Postwar Period," *Total War and Cold War: Problems in Civilian Control of the Military*, ed. Harry Coles, Ohio State University Press, Columbus, 1962, p. 243.

[58] *Ibid.*

[59] Pobezhimov, p. 108. See also Chapter III, pp. 73-75, above for details on the Party's oppressive treatment of the military during that period.

war period were sporadic. Since these years were marked by intense conflicts between Zhdanov, Malenkov, and others, with Zhdanov in the ascendance, Khrushchev's own career seemed in danger, and it was not until Zhdanov's death that he emerged among the top contenders for Stalin's mantle. For the Stalingrad Group these early years may be described as a period of holding the line, of preserving the wartime gains in promotions and military assignments. Thus, Grechko stayed on as commander of the important Kiev Military District, where he came into frequent contact with Khrushchev in his dual capacity of district commander and member of the Party's Central Committee. Moskalenko also held a military post in the Ukraine, and Malinovskii, Zakharov, Krylov, and Eremenko continued to serve in the Far East.

The death of Zhdanov in 1948 resulted in the reshuffling of positions among the top Party leaders, as Zhdanovites were excluded from the apparatus and others, including Khrushchev and a number of his protégés, moved into central positions in Moscow. As a result of these realignments within the Party, the military seemed to have gained in stature and influence: Marshal Vasilevskii replaced Bulganin as Minister of Defense; the MPA was weakened when it was divided into two parts, one for the army and one for the navy;[60] Zhukov was permitted to reappear in public; and at the Nineteenth Party Congress, in 1952, an unprecedented number of senior military professionals were coopted into the Central Committee as full members, while Zhukov, among others, was included as a candidate.[61] Moreover, Khrushchev took along to Moscow several of his close associates: Moskalenko, who became Chief of Staff of the Moscow PVO District; Epishev, who was appointed Deputy Minister of State Security under another Khrushchev follower, Ignat'ev;[62] and Mironov, who left the

[60] In 1950 Stalin once more reorganized the Ministry of Defense by again dividing it in two: the Ministry of War under Vasilevskii, and the Ministry of the Navy under Admiral Kuznetsov, who was back in favor after having been court-martialed in 1947 for allegedly conspiring with the Western allies. The most likely reason for such a division was caused by Stalin's "balancing" propensities: having brought the military professionals back into positions of authority (presumably because of the need to modernize the Red Army and adapt it to the changing nature of warfare), he at the same time sought to delimit their authority by decentralizing the highest echelons of the High Command. Significantly, one of the first measures undertaken after Stalin's death, on March 15, 1953, was the reunification of all military authority in a single Ministry of Defense. See Pobezhimov, *Pravovoe regulirovanie stroitel'stva*, p. 108.

[61] Garthoff, "The Marshals and the Party," pp. 243-244.

[62] See *Ezhegodnik Bol'shoi Sovetskoi Entsiklopedii. 1962* (Yearbook of the Large Soviet Encyclopedia, 1962), "Sovetskaia Entsiklopediia," Moscow, 1962, p. 594.

Party apparatus and entered an unspecified position in the Ministry of State Security.[63]

Of the other members of the Stalingrad Group, Chuikov was given the prestigious command of the Soviet Force Group in East Germany, and Krylov and Eremenko took over as commanders of, respectively, the Far Eastern and West Siberian Military Districts.[64]

Zakharov, who had served with Malinovskii in the campaign against Japan in 1945, remained in the Far East and eventually was given command of the East Siberian Military District. In 1947 he returned to Central Russia to become head of the Academy of the General Staff. Two years later, he took over the Main Administration of the General Staff, and in 1952 he became Chief Inspector of the Soviet Army, a position he held until Stalin's death.[65]

Malinovskii remained in the Far East, as commander of the Maritime Military District, until after Stalin's death. Konev was Commander of the Ground Forces from 1946 to 1950.

While the members of the Stalingrad Group thus slowly ascended the military ladder, their advancement was relatively inconspicuous and had little immediate impact, for the top layer of the High Command was still largely in the hands of *Stavka* people and hard-core Stalinists.[66] With the death of Stalin, Khrushchev emerged as a powerful contender for power, but his main source of influence and

[63] *Ibid.*, p. 606. In 1952 another Khrushchev associate, A. A. Aristov, took over the vital position of head of the section on Party, Trade Union, and Komsomol organs in the Secretariat, which controlled all important appointments in the Party network.

[64] Garthoff, "The Marshals and the Party," p. 248.

[65] *Ezhegodnik Bol'shoi Sovetskoi Entsiklopedii. 1962*, p. 595.

[66] Among the full members and candidates elected to the Central Committee at the Nineteenth Party Congress in 1952 were nineteen military personalities, who might be classified as follows by their origins or leanings:

Stavka Professionals	*Stalinist "Political Generals"*	*Stalingrad Group*
Vasilevskii	Timoshenko	Konev
Sokolovskii	Shtemenko	Bagramian
Zhukov	Budennyi	Chuikov
Kuznetsov, N. G.		Epishev
Bogdanov		Grechko
Gorbatov		Malinovskii
Malinin		
Meretskov		
Nedelin		
Zhigarev		

General source: *Bulletin of the Institute for the Study of the History and Culture of the USSR*, Supplement, Vol. 2, No. 5, May 1955.

authority came from his Party activities and from the positions of influence in the internal central Party apparatus. The growing influence and stature of his protégés in the military were not significant enough at first to have much bearing on events. The main tests of their relationship lay ahead, to be resolved during the power struggles of 1953-1957. The military establishment had emerged from the Stalin period still under the control of *Stavka* members, with the Stalingrad Group by and large only in the second echelon.

C · THE MALENKOV INTERREGNUM: THE MILITARY PULLS TOGETHER

The two years between Stalin's death and Malenkov's ouster from his leading position in the government were characterized by the intense maneuvers of two powerful factions for supremacy in the Party. One faction centered around Khrushchev and used the Central Committee and the Secretariat as a power base, and the other formed around Malenkov, with the governmental bureaucracy and the Party Presidium as its sources of power. The Ministry of Defense was nominally under the control of the Council of Ministers, and consequently under Malenkov's authority. But Malenkov's announced military policies,[67] and his already low standing among the military professionals,[68] caused the latter to support the pro-Khrushchev group (whose primary objective then was to unseat Malenkov). The military, whose support was essential to the objectives of both sides, was in a position to play off one Party faction against the other.

Khrushchev, though he sought the loyalty of the entire military establishment and was willing to further Zhukov's career in return for his support, at the same time continued to consolidate the positions and careers of the Stalingrad Group members. In this effort, he was aided greatly by two close associates who held vital positions both

[67] Malenkov's various policy announcements concerning the military followed logically from his general belief, which H. S. Dinerstein describes as "the idea that there would be peace in their time." (*War and the Soviet Union*, Frederick A. Praeger, Inc., New York, 1959, p. 66.) Such a view led naturally to a policy geared to a possible détente, with less stress on the military factor in international relations, and possibly therefore lower allocations and a less important internal role for the military. Such views were likely to find very few military adherents.

[68] On the seventy-fifth anniversary of Stalin's birth, *Voprosy istorii*, then closely identified with Malenkov's views, pointedly selected the following quotation from the dead dictator's writings for an obviously antimilitary emphasis: "Only childish people think that the laws of artillery are stronger than the laws of history." (No. 12, December 1954, p. 8.)

in the Party and in the military: A. Aristov, who was head of the cadre section in the Secretariat, which dealt with promotions, demotions, appointments, and other personnel matters in the Party machinery,[69] and F. Golikov, who occupied the similar position of head of the Main Cadre Board in the Ministry of Defense.[70] Since the personnel selection machinery is one of the vital sources of influence, Khrushchev therefore possessed powerful leverage, which he seems to have used with great skill, at least in the military sphere.

A brief glance at the shifts in commands and commanding personnel right after Stalin's death indicates that Khrushchev was following a divide-and-rule policy in the military. While Zhukov and his associates dominated the central military apparatus (and to a lesser extent the political stage as well), Khrushchev saw to it that his own followers in the military were moved into vital controlling positions, whence they would be able to exert a decisive influence in the event of an intra-Party or intramilitary showdown.

When Stalin died, four members of the Stalingrad Group already occupied key command positions: Malinovskii (Maritime Military District); Krylov (Far Eastern Military District); Eremenko (West Siberian Military District); and Bagramian (Baltic Military District). In addition, the following Stalingrad Group members were given new commands in 1953 and early 1954: Moskalenko (Moscow Military District); Chuikov (Kiev Military District); Zakharov (Leningrad Military District); Grechko (Soviet Force Group in Germany); Konev (Carpathian Military District); and Biriuzov (Soviet Southern Force Group in the Balkans). Khrushchev also placed his close associate L. Brezhnev in the key position of deputy head of the MPA,[71] under the ineffectual and unpopular General Zheltov.

These and other shifts and new appointments substantially strengthened Khrushchev's position in the military and, by extension, in the Party. While Zhukov and his followers were strong in the Ministry of Defense, with Zhukov as First Deputy Minister of Defense, Khrushchev's associates controlled the most important territorial commands, the elite troops in Germany and the Balkans, and to some extent, through Brezhnev and Golikov, the political apparatus in the military.

[69] Leonard Schapiro, *The Communist Party of the Soviet Union*, Random House, New York, 1960, p. 518.

[70] N. Galay, "The Significance of Golikov's Removal," in *Bulletin of the Institute for the Study of the USSR*, Vol. 9, No. 8, August 1962, p. 36.

[71] *Ezhegodnik Bol'shoi Sovetskoi Entsiklopedii. 1962*, p. 589.

To appreciate the significance of these gains, one must understand the authority and influence enjoyed by the commanders of key military districts and Force Groups. The military district commander has a dual role: he is the ranking officer in charge of all troops, logistics, and equipment in his district and directly under the Minister of Defense; he is also the ranking member of the Military Council of the military district and as such mainly responsible to the Central Committee. The Military Council has supreme authority in the district and is responsible to the Ministry of Defense only in an operational sense.[72] Zhukov strongly opposed this duality of the district commanders' role and attempted to undermine the Central Committee's direct influence at this crucial level of the military command and to keep the district commanders solely responsible to the Ministry of Defense. Though he was not very successful in this effort, he did frighten the Central Committee apparatus as well as the MPA, who began to view his activities with the greatest concern.[73]

Khrushchev's control of the chief military district and Force Group commands, achieved by the advancement of his men to key positions in the military machinery, was to be of great importance in the coming struggle with Malenkov, and still later in the conflicts with the anti-Party group and with Zhukov. For the moment, however, the Zhukovites continued to dominate the central apparatus of the Ministry of Defense, with Zhukov himself and Vasilevskii as Deputy Ministers of Defense and Sokolovskii as Chief of the General Staff.

While the two military factions were consolidating their respective positions, they both sought the removal of Malenkov, whose policies were out of step with the objectives of the military. After the long terror of the Stalinist era, the military desired greater freedom of expression and certain changes in its own thought, its practices, and its social role. But Malenkov consistently opposed any pressures from the military in such directions.[74] Whereas the professional officers

[72] See Chapter V, pp. 123-125.

[73] See Iu. P. Petrov, *Partiinoe stroitel'stvo v Sovetskoi Armii i Flote, 1918-1961* (Party Development in the Soviet Army and Navy, 1918-1961), Voenizdat, Moscow, 1964, pp. 461-464. See also Chapter V, pp. 124-126, above, for details on the changing role of the Military Councils. It is of interest to note the Party *apparatchiks'* attempts to minimize the negative effects that the near-sovereign role of the Military Council has on the military chain of command: ". . . experience . . . indicates that fully empowered Military Councils do not minimize the role and respect of the Minister or the Commander." A. M. Larkov and N. T. Filippov, *Edinonachalie v Sovetskikh Vooruzhennykh Silakh* (*Edinonachalie* in the Soviet Armed Forces), Voenizdat, Moscow, 1960, pp. 15-16.

[74] Thorough analyses of these military pressures for major revisions in military thought, internal organization, and processes may be found in H. S. Dinerstein's

thought the enforced silence of the Stalinist period to have been extremely detrimental to military expertise and capability and to Soviet strategic doctrine and were now expecting a mandate from the Party to modernize the armed forces, Malenkov apparently opposed any public debate of the failings of the Stalinist era. In 1954, on the occasion of the seventy-fifth anniversary of Stalin's birth, the Malenkov-controlled journal *Voprosy istorii* eulogized the dead dictator in the traditional manner. At the same time, however, the military was demanding some measure of de-Stalinization, especially in the training of the military:

> It is well known that in propaganda work in the military errors were permitted along the lines of lowering the role of the people, the working masses, in the social development while exaggerating the role of the personality. *Such errors must be corrected. It is necessary to explain to our soldiers the harm and inadmissibility of the cult of the personality*, and to develop and strengthen in them a Marxist-Leninist world-view . . . and *educate them in the spirit of loyalty to the Soviet nation. . . .*[75]

Moreover, while the military favored continued massive investments in the industries related to defense (especially heavy industry), Malenkov was stressing international relaxation and the need to shift investments to consumer goods.[76] In sum, Malenkov's policies seem almost to have been calculated to consolidate the military into a unified opposition.

---

indispensable *War and the Soviet Union*, and R. L. Garthoff's *Soviet Military Doctrine*.

[75] Colonel Nenakhov, in the authoritative military publication *O Sovetskoi voennoi nauke* (On Soviet Military Science), Voenizdat, Moscow, June 1954, p. 49. (Italics added.)

[76] The military's satisfaction with the removal of Malenkov is evident from Marshal Konev's statements in the weeks and months after the ouster: "The Communist Party and the Soviet government pay attention mainly to the development of heavy industry, which represents the essential basis of the national economy and indestructible defensive capability of the country. . . . The January plenum of the CC and the Second Session of the Supreme Soviet of the USSR stressed that the general line of the Party would be strictly continued in the economic sphere, and foresaw the development of heavy industry by every conceivable means." (*Pravda*, February 23, 1955.) "The war has shown that heavy industry was, is, and will be the fountainhead [*osnova osnov*, literally, the foundation of foundations] of the indestructible might of our state and its armed forces. The further development of heavy industry in our country will continue to assure in the future the power of our state." (*Pravda*, May 9, 1955.)

The removal of Malenkov in February 1955 (which had become almost inevitable after the Molotov faction joined Khrushchev's anti-Malenkov drive in the fall of 1954) deprived the alliance between Zhukov and the Stalingrad Group of much of its *raison d'être.* Khrushchev continued to deal cautiously with the Zhukovites in the military and to support them in public. But at the same time he made a strong effort to build up an independent power base in the military establishment that would be centered around the Stalingrad Group. In the wake of Malenkov's removal, therefore, and as a result of the military's enhanced role in Party politics, long-suppressed differences between the two major military factions erupted into the open.

D · THE RISE AND FALL OF MARSHAL ZHUKOV, 1955-1957: THE MILITARY PULLS APART

The two major developments that followed the ouster of Malenkov in February 1955 were the military's noticeable self-assertion and rise from relative obscurity into political prominence, and a growing factionalism within the military itself. This factionalism was not then readily apparent; on the contrary, it looked as if, for the first time since the war years, the military professionals were acting in unison, as they pressed demands on the Party, claimed rehabilitation of their purged heroes, and openly sought a larger role in Soviet politics. In retrospect, however, one can discern the growing split between the Stalingrad Group, whose membership closely adhered to Khrushchev's views and policy, and the Zhukovites, who pressed hard for greater independence of the military from Party tutelage and for the Party's public admission of its past injustices to the military professionals.

Zhukov's public image and some of his statements caused widespread concern in the Party apparatus, but the political realities of the period severely limited the power of Khrushchev and his military associates to rid themselves of Zhukov. The Khrushchev-Zhukov collaboration was essentially a marriage of convenience, prompted by Khrushchev's desire to keep the entire military establishment on his side during his struggles for power in the Party. Once this motive was removed, with the destruction of the intra-Party opposition, Khrushchev's need to conciliate Zhukov and to tolerate his personal ambitions disappeared.

Despite Zhukov's dramatic emergence on the Soviet political and military stage after Malenkov's ouster, and despite his self-assertive ways and his efforts at self-aggrandizement, his position would seem, in retrospect, to have been doomed from the outset. While Zhukov was playing the lead in the military and serving as its spokesman in high Party councils, Khrushchev continued to solidify his influence and his power base in the armed forces, thus gradually undercutting Zhukov's real sources of power. In other words, he was still using Zhukov as evidence of the identity of interests that united the Khrushchev factions in Party and military with the armed forces as a whole, while at the same time preparing the ground for his own victory in their eventual confrontation.

1. *The Promotions of 1955 and the Rising Influence of the Stalingrad Group*

One month after Malenkov's ouster, six officers received promotions to the high rank of Marshal of the Soviet Union and four to Marshal of a branch of the armed forces. Soon afterward, six other generals were promoted to the rank of General of the Army. At least thirteen of the sixteen were members of the Stalingrad Group, and, furthermore, all six appointees to the highest rank, that of Marshal of the Soviet Union, were among Khrushchev's closest military associates.[77] Thus, the promotions, though they strengthened the whole military establishment, which had enjoyed few such major promotions since the war, represented an especially important gain for the Stalingrad Group and Khrushchev.

On February 9, 1955, at about the time of Malenkov's ouster, Zhukov had taken over the Ministry of Defense. But with Vasilevskii and Sokolovskii remaining in the key positions of First Deputy Minister and Chief of the General Staff, respectively, and with several lesser men appointed to ranking positions in the central apparatus of the Ministry, Khrushchev's followers continued to make inroads into the command positions and high ranks.

One of the effects of the Twentieth Party Congress (1956), which was to have such wide repercussions in the whole communist camp, was to strengthen the role of the military in the state. By destroying

[77] Bagramian, Eremenko, Grechko, Biriuzov, Chuikov, and Moskalenko were promoted to Marshal of the Soviet Union. Sudets and Varentsov were members of the Stalingrad Group promoted to Marshal of an arm. Of the appointees to General of the Army, at least five (Krylov, Zakharov, Popov, Kazakov, and Fediuninskii) were Stalingrad Group members, some of whom were to reach top military positions in the post-Zhukov period.

the image of an invincible Stalin, Khrushchev implicitly acknowledged the fallibility of the Party leadership, and at the same time he officially acknowledged the acts of injustice committed against the Soviet officer corps in the purges of 1937 and during the war. The military's role was further enhanced when Zhukov became the first candidate to the Presidium—evidence of the growing influence of the military at the highest levels of the Party hierarchy—and a number of professional officers from the top military echelon were coopted into the Central Committee. Again, however, while these developments benefited the entire military establishment, they were further illustrations of the growing strength within the military of the Stalingrad Group faction.

Of the twenty military officers in the new Central Committee, at least three Stalingrad Group people could be counted among the full members, and seven were candidate members. As for the remaining ten, if we exclude Bulganin, Voroshilov, and Budennyi as essentially "political" generals, only five—Zhukov, Vasilevskii, Sokolovskii, Nedelin, and Gorbatov—may be regarded as representing the Zhukov faction.[78]

To be sure, the entire military representation in the Central Committee amounted to only 20 out of a total of 255, or 7.8 per cent.[79] It is significant, however, that members of the Stalingrad Group made up the bulk of this representation: first, because they thereby came into close contact with the political decision-makers, to whom they could express their needs and views; second, because CC membership symbolized their growing role; and, third, because they were able to bolster Khrushchev's influence in intra-Party affairs, since the Central Committee, after Malenkov's ouster, became the forum where most important decisions and policies of the Party were formulated.

The Stalingrad Group scored further gains during the 1955-1956 period with the promotion of several of its members to leading commands: Biriuzov was given the important command of the PVO-S (or Air Defense Command) Forces; Kazakov took over the Southern Force Group; and Malinovskii became Commander-in-Chief of the Ground Forces.[80]

[78] *Current Soviet Policies—II: Documentary Record of the 20th Party Congress*, Frederick A. Praeger, Inc., 1957, pp. 196-202.

[79] The Central Committee as constituted at the Twentieth Party Congress included 133 full members, of whom eight were military men; of the 122 elected to candidate membership, 12 represented the military. Source: *XX s"ezd Kommunisticheskoi partii Sovetskogo Soiuza: stenograficheskii otchet* (The Twentieth Congress of the CPSU: Stenographic Record), Part II, Gospolitizdat, Moscow, 1956, pp. 500-503.

[80] See Appendix A-V.

2. *The Growing Discord Between Zhukov and the Stalingrad Group*

Having been deprived of a public voice during the Stalin era and most of the Malenkov interregnum, the military, once it had been freed from these restraints and had entered the public arena, began to talk in a multitude of voices. Long-suppressed animosities came to light; "family" jealousies and squabbles found their way into the press; the imposition of Party ideologies was openly questioned and rejected. However, in the babble of self-aggrandizing claims, historical reconstruction, and demands for various reforms one could detect the sharpening polarity of views between adherents of Khrushchev and of Zhukov. Although officially still one family (at least until the June 1957 plenum of the Central Committee), the two factions were growing apart on several issues.

As mentioned earlier, their most noted rivalry and divergence of views concerned the historical claims of Zhukov, who represented the *Stavka*, and Konev, who spoke for the field commanders. While Konev and his associates were insisting on the overriding historical importance of the Stalingrad battle and the role of field commanders in it, Zhukov continued to stress the decisiveness of the battle of Moscow as well as his own and the *Stavka*'s role. The opening shot in this polemic was fired by a Lieutenant General Rodimtsev, who had served with Khrushchev during the battle of Stalingrad. Rodimtsev firmly expressed the view that the battle for Stalingrad had been the crucial operation of the war and that Khrushchev's role in it had been important.[81]

Marshal Zhukov's rejoinder came in an interview with three American journalists, who asked his opinion as to which of the battles was the decisive one, Stalingrad or Moscow. Zhukov's evasive answer was that "the breakthrough in the war was achieved by a number of successful operations during 1941 and 1942." When asked whether he personally had participated in the Moscow and Stalingrad battles, Zhukov replied in a manner which must have angered the Stalingrad Group:

> . . . I was commander of the forces during the defense of Moscow. I directed all preparatory operations connected with conduct of the Stalingrad campaign. The actual operations were conducted by Marshal Vasilevskii. I was at that time involved in the preparations for the following offensive. . . .[82]

[81] *Pravda*, February 2, 1955.

[82] The American journalists who interviewed Zhukov on February 7 were W.

Two weeks after the interview that prompted these remarks, Konev stated the views of the Stalingrad Group in a prominent article in *Pravda*:

> The organizer and inspirer in the struggle of the Soviet people against the fascist invaders was the Communist Party of the Soviet Union. Under the leadership of the Party, and thanks to its versatile organizational activities among the masses, the country became transformed into a single military camp. The most prominent [of the Soviet operations in 1941-1942] was the Stalingrad operation. . . .[83]

This reference to Stalingrad as the most important battle of the 1941-1942 period was no doubt a pointed rebuttal of Zhukov's recent statement. Konev also departed from the alphabetical order, customary in the listing of prominent Party leaders who served at the front, by placing Khrushchev's name at the head of that list. And he rejected Zhukov's claim to having played the central role in planning and executing the Stalingrad battle when he said: "The commanders of fronts and armies were the direct organizers of the operations which led to the destruction of the enemy's main force groups."[84]

Another noticeable divergence in the views publicly expressed by Zhukov and Konev concerned the role of the Party leadership and of Party ideology in military affairs. While Konev lavishly praised the Party for its crucial role in the achievement of victory in World War II, Zhukov alternately stressed his own role and that of military professionals.

The two men differed also on the desirable function of Party-political control organs in the military. Whereas Zhukov actively opposed their intrusion into military affairs, the Stalingrad Group either avoided taking a stand or spoke out in support of the political control organs and their vital role in the military.

Despite the gains of the Stalingrad Group in the defense establishment and in political life, Zhukov continued to hold the center of the military stage. As we have seen, on the occasion of his sixtieth birthday in December 1956 he received innumerable accolades, and

---

R. Hearst, S. Kingsbury, and F. Conniff. The above remarks are quoted in Boris Meissner, *Russland unter Chruschtschow*, R. Oldenbourg Verlag, Munich, 1960, p. 46.

[83] *Pravda*, February 23, 1955.

[84] *Ibid.*

the following month he embarked on an official state visit to India, which was prominently reported in the Soviet press. At the same Central Committee plenum that ousted the so-called anti-Party group, Zhukov was elected to full membership of the Presidium, the first military professional in Soviet history to be so seated. Yet even as Zhukov was enjoying the role of the popular military hero, there were signs of the Party's deep concern about his hold on the armed forces, and attempts were made to stem the growing independence of the military.

In April of 1957, the Central Committee met in an unannounced session and passed a decree intended to reassert the Party's control over the military establishment.[85] The "Instructions to the Organizations of the CPSU in the Soviet Army and Navy," which were first mentioned publicly on May 12, strongly demanded the upgrading of the political organs' role and authority in the military. The public debate that ensued on the various issues raised by the Instructions lost some of its urgency, however, in the rush of political events that attended the battle for domination of the Party, several weeks later, during the secret plenary meeting of the Central Committee in June 1957.

Details of that vital political struggle for power in the Soviet Union are still obscured from view, but it seems clear that the military played an important role in the ousting of Molotov, Bulganin, and the rest of the "anti-Party" group. Zhukov's ascendance to the Presidium, as well as his subsequent triumphant trip to Leningrad, may have been signs that he overestimated his true position in the new regime of Khrushchev.[86] For it was only a matter of time before Khrushchev and his

[85] See Chapter V, pp. 131-132.

[86] There have been various speculations on the role of Zhukov and the military in connection with the ousting of the anti-Party group. Some of these speculations center on the rapid employment of military aircraft to transport Central Committee members sympathetic to Khrushchev to Moscow, so that they could offset an impending roll-call vote engineered by the anti-Party group in the absence of Khrushchev. Of similar interest is a statement made by A. N. Shelepin, then chief of the security organs, at the Twenty-second Party Congress in 1961. According to Shelepin, Bulganin, who was being branded as one of the plotters against Khrushchev, "during the June days of 1957, when the factionists undertook the open attack against the Central Committee, deployed his own guard in the Kremlin [and] emplaced additional sentries who did not without his permission pass anyone into the Governmental building where the Presidium of the Central Committee CPSU was in session. . . . Luckily, the Central Committee discovered in good time the danger of the anti-Party group and rendered it harmless." It is not unlikely that some sort of military intervention, or threat of it, was needed to dislodge the anti-Party forces from the Kremlin. *XXII s"ezd Kommunisticheskoi partii Sovetskogo Soiuza: stenograficheskii otchet* (The Twen-

Stalingrad Group, having removed their main opponents within the Party, would put an end to Zhukov's self-aggrandizing, impolitic public behavior and relegate him to obscurity. After the June plenum, the first sign of such an eventuality was to be seen in the renascent public dialogue on the need to sharpen political controls in the military and to use *kritika/samokritika* ruthlessly at military meetings, as well as in the growing assertiveness of the political control functionaries in the military.[87] However, if Zhukov saw the signs of danger, he did not heed them. His march through Leningrad several weeks after the June plenum, his open appeal to the masses of citizens and soldiers that reportedly met with tumultuous applause, his continued stress on his own role during major battles of the war, his ominous calls for the punishment of those who had participated in the purges of the military[88]—these and other acts and statements were bound to alienate the Stalingrad Group, the Party *apparatchiks*, and ultimately Khrushchev himself, who could not but resent the growing popularity of the war hero.

Thus, while Zhukov was playing the role of public hero and central military leader, the Stalingrad Group gradually moved into most of the command posts and political control positions in the military. Zhukov's fall came quietly and had no visible repercussions. He was sent on a trip to Yugoslavia, detained further by an unscheduled side-trip to Albania, and even deprived of his naval escort, which departed from Yugoslav waters, leaving Zhukov in no position to challenge his opponents. Moreover, he had created so much animosity among many military leaders, including those of the Stalingrad Group, that he could not count on support from them. Recalled to Moscow from his trip, Zhukov was faced with the *fait accompli* of his ouster.

E · ASCENDANCE OF THE STALINGRAD GROUP, 1957-1960

Marshal Zhukov's dismissal from his leading posts in government and Party seemed to cause no disturbance and meet no opposition.

---

ty-second Congress of the CPSU: Stenographic Record), Gospolitizdat, Moscow, 1962, Vol. 2, p. 405.

[87] See Chapter V, pp. 132-133, for a detailed treatment of this problem.

[88] See Chapter VI, p. 192. While Zhukov was being given lavish coverage in the military press, the celebration of the military festivities in Moscow received only cursory treatment. The military leaders who participated in the Moscow festivities were largely members of the Stalingrad Group, including, among others, Konev, Malinovskii, Biriuzov, Bagramian, and Golovko. *Sovetskii flot,* July 14, 1957.

Although, to the public, the Party tried to convey the impression of a unanimous condemnation of the Marshal by all military leaders,[89] the ouster was quite specifically a victory for the Stalingrad Group, some of whose members took pleasure in publicly denigrating the war hero. With Zhukov deposed, the way was now open for them to the top of the military establishment. Within the next few years, Khrushchev had promoted them to leading positions, coopted them into the Central Committee, strengthened his personal relations with them, and, by a rewriting of history, retroactively credited them with a central role during World War II.

The Stalingrad Group's intense resentment of Zhukov's claim to military genius was evident in Marshal Konev's venomous outburst only a few days after the ouster of Zhukov had been announced:

> Comrade Zhukov, who is an extremely vain person, and who lacks the modesty becoming a Party member, used his position as Minister of Defense and introduced in the armed forces the cult of his personality. . . . Under his personal direction there was created an artificial aura of fame and infallibility around the person of Zhukov.

Konev then listed a number of military disasters allegedly caused by Zhukov. He also strongly rejected the latter's claims in connection with the battles of Stalingrad and Berlin, and he lashed out repeatedly at Zhukov for taking undeserved credit, either for himself or for the *Stavka*, and for belittling the role of the field commanders:

> It was, to say the least, immodest of Comrade Zhukov to brag about his achievements, to exaggerate them out of proportion. . . . Comrade G. K. Zhukov . . . falsified the actual state of affairs and belittled the role of the people, the heroism of our armed forces, the *role of the commanders and the political associates, the military commanders of fronts, armies, and fleets.*[90]

[89] On November 3, 1957, *Pravda* reported that the Central Committee plenum which ousted Zhukov included these military leaders who unanimously approved of the measure taken against the Minister of Defense: Malinovskii, Konev, Eremenko, Biriuzov, Gorshkov, Batov, Zakharov, Kazakov, Timoshenko, Sokolovskii, and Rokossovskii. The last two were not members of the Stalingrad Group, and in previous statements had supported Zhukov's policies and views in the military.

[90] Marshal of the Soviet Union I. S. Konev, "Sila Sovetskoi Armii i Flota—v rukovodstve partii, v nerazryvnoi sviazi s narodom" (The Might of the Soviet Army and Navy Lies in Its Leadership by the Party and in Its Indestructible Tie with the People), *Pravda*, November 3, 1957. (Italics added.)

The Rise of the Stalingrad Group

Little by little, men whom Zhukov had appointed were replaced by followers of the Stalingrad Group. Between 1957 and 1963, three major shifts in commands brought about the following appointments:[91]

Malinovskii	Minister of Defense, 1957
Biriuzov	Commander-in-Chief of the Strategic Missile Forces, 1962, and Chief of the General Staff, 1963
Grechko	Commander-in-Chief of the Ground Forces, 1957, and Commander-in-Chief of the Warsaw Pact Forces, 1960
Chuikov	Commander-in-Chief of the Ground Forces, 1960
Moskalenko	Commander-in-Chief of the Strategic Missile Forces, 1960
Zakharov	Commander of the Soviet Force Group in Germany, 1957, and Chief of the General Staff, 1960-1963 and 1964
Krylov	Commander of the Leningrad Military District, 1957, the Moscow Military District, 1960, and Commander-in-Chief of the Strategic Missile Forces, 1963
Bagramian	Commander of the Services of the Rear, 1959
Sudets	Commander-in-Chief of the PVO Forces, 1962
Golikov	Head of the MPA, 1957
Epishev	Head of the MPA, 1962

Once entrenched in the military establishment, the Stalingrad Group, with eager assistance from the Party apparatus, began to create an historical legend centered around the battle for Stalingrad. Its purpose in so doing was to destroy the myth of Zhukov, the *Stavka*, and Stalin as the true authors and executors of the Stalingrad counteroffensive, which had turned the tide of the war; to upgrade the role of the Stalingrad Group in that crucial battle; to reiterate the Party's central role in the country's victory in the war; and, finally, to create a new myth around Khrushchev's military genius at Stalingrad.

Thus, the Stalingrad Group gained control of the armed forces and acquired political influence through the association with Khrushchev, and its public image and historical record were strongly

[91] From 1957 to 1960, most changes in commands took place at the Military District level, where Zhukovites were replaced with Stalingrad Group members. In the command of the Ground Forces, that of the Soviet Force Group in Germany, and the vital command of the Leningrad Military District, on the other hand, one Stalingrad Group member took the place of another (Grechko replaced Malinovskii, Zakharov replaced Grechko, and Krylov replaced Zakharov). Furthermore, both Malinovskii and Grechko were awarded the prestigious order of Hero of the Soviet Union in 1958, and in 1959 Zakharov was promoted to Marshal of the Soviet Union. For Malinovskii this was the second such award. For Grechko it was the first, and obviously an attempt at political conciliation, since the Hero of the Soviet Union is usually awarded during wartime. It is of interest to note that Zhukov had received four stars of the Hero of the Soviet Union, the only military person in the Soviet Union ever to be thus honored.

enhanced by the revision of history. Soon, however, serious differences of views arose between some of its military leaders and the Party, the result primarily of active opposition to certain measures by which the Party sought to change radically the organization and processes of political controls in the military. Though initiated unostentatiously, these measures posed a threat to the authority and prestige of officers and in some measure also to internal discipline, training schedules, and combat readiness. The public debate between the proponents of full authority (*edinonachalie*) for officers and the advocates of the Party's right to dominate all aspects of military life (including the power to interfere with military procedures and authority), which broke into print in the fall and winter of 1958, reflected the turbulent mood of the officer corps.[92]

The origin of these tensions in the armed forces went back to the October 1957 plenum of the Central Committee, which ousted Zhukov. The communiqué of the plenum and various accompanying editorial statements strongly emphasized the Party's new, firm line with the military and accused Zhukov of having severely restricted the Party's role in the military community during his reign in the Ministry. Taking these statements as signals of an opportune moment to rid the officers' community of undesirables, the political control organs began to replace commanders at the slightest provocation. They interfered with military operations, procedures, and authority, with great detriment to morale and discipline in the units. In the fall of 1958, the military professionals began to reassert themselves, presumably with tacit support from some members of the High Command. Their attack on the excesses of the political organs was launched by Admiral Chalyi,[93] who was supported by a number of ranking naval and military officers. The debate ended temporarily in a formal, lengthy pronouncement by Marshal Malinovskii, the new Minister of Defense and leading member of the Stalingrad Group.[94]

The public reaction of various prominent members of the Stalin-

[92] See Chapter V, pp. 142-147.

[93] Chalyi's startlingly candid affirmation of the professional officers' criticism of the practices initiated by the political control organs in the military since the ouster of Zhukov was eventually issued in a collection of articles entitled *O samostoiatel'nosti i initsiative ofitserov flota* (On the Independence and Initiative of Naval Officers), Voenizdat, Moscow, 1959. The very sharpness and directness of Chalyi's attack, which was supported by other high officers, including First Deputy Commander of the Navy Admiral Golovko, suggests that it had the tacit blessing of some of the highest circles in the High Command. See Chapter V, pp. 145-146, for a detailed description of the military's resistance.

[94] *Krasnaia zvezda*, November 1, 1958.

grad Group to these intensified encroachments of the political organs on the officers' sphere of authority bears closer inspection, since it hinted at future strains and division among them. Although, in their public statements, all the Stalingrad Group members continued to make the requisite obeisance to the Party, they clearly differed in the stress they placed on the roles and the relative authority of the political organs and the military professional within military units. Malinovskii, Zakharov, and Grechko indicated deep concern over the negative effect of intensified political control and indoctrination on military discipline, readiness, and efficiency, as well as on the dignity of the officers. Malinovskii stressed that insufficient attention was being given to "the persistent struggle to carry out military training plans as *tasks of the state*"; and that deterioration of discipline in the units was frequently brought about by the lowered authority and prestige of the professional officers.[95]

In 1959 Malinovskii repeated these points when he warned the overzealous political organs not to disrupt military procedures and operations and not to interfere unduly with the commander's authority: "If you interfere in his work, going over his head, then the result will be negative and will lead to disorders, and where there are disorders there are conflicts, fights, and disasters."[96]

Marshal Grechko closely adhered to the Malinovskii line, stressing the changed nature of future warfare, which "raises the role of a strict single commander and demands of him exceptional decisiveness, self-reliance, and quick reaction to all changes in the situation." Grechko emphasized also that the officer must have a "thorough knowledge of military equipment and weapons and the ability to employ them under even the most difficult conditions of modern warfare."[97]

Marshal Zakharov expressed concern about the consequences of lowered discipline in the units: "Lack of discipline under conditions of rapidly changing modern warfare, when the soldier has in his hands not a sabre . . . but new powerful weapons of tremendous destructive force, can lead to catastrophe!"[98]

[95] *Ibid.* (Italics added.) It is remarkable that Malinovskii found it necessary to caution the political control organs on the distinction between these functions of the military, which are primarily the concern of the state rather than of the Party.

[96] Marshal Malinovskii, in *K novomu pod"emu partiino-politicheskoi raboty v Sovetskoi Armii i Flote* (Toward a New Intensification of Party-Political Work in the Soviet Army and Navy), ed. Major General Z. S. Osipov, Voenizdat, Moscow, 1960, p. 16.

[97] Marshal Grechko, in *K novomu pod"emu*, p. 33.

[98] Marshal Zakharov, in *K novomu pod"emu*, p. 70.

Marshals Biriuzov and Moskalenko, on the other hand, though they also referred to the deteriorating discipline, took the attitude of the Party zealots who maintained that the disciplinary rights of the officers, if used too harshly and too widely, would, in the words of General Lapkin, the Deputy Head of the MPA, "lead to the separation of commanders from subordinates."[99] Biriuzov suggested dealing with the dissatisfaction in the officer corps by strengthening the authority and the role of the Komsomol, since "the political morale of the personnel, their success in military training, and the strengthening of their discipline will depend to an overwhelming extent on the activities of the Komsomol organization."[100]

Moskalenko similarly mouthed the Party *apparatchik*'s line:

> The Soviet commander cannot separate himself from the masses, show aloofness. *Edinonachalie* does not give anyone the right *not* to consider the opinions of Party organizations and the community, and to replace educational activities with the soldiers by peremptory shouts and sheer bureaucratism.

He also touched on the sensitive issue of *kritika/samokritika,*[101] which had been widely and intensively reinstituted after Zhukov's ouster, to the great resentment of the military professionals. "Some comrades were afraid that sharpened use of *kritika/samokritika* would have a negative effect on the role of *edinonachalie* and the authority of the commander," said Moskalenko, and went on to deny the grounds for such fears and at the same time to reaffirm the Party's dominant position in the military.

Although these divergences of views showed up in print on several occasions, there was no suggestion of any deeper split within the

[99] Colonel General P. A. Lapkin, in *K novomu pod"emu,* pp. 99-100. Lapkin tried to justify the need to weaken the prerogatives of the officer by stressing the fact that Zhukov had fostered such elitism and that it had undermined Party control: "It is known that [Zhukov's] activities were falsely covered under the guise of the struggle for the strengthening of *edinonachalie.* Actually, it led to the destruction of *edinonachalie.*" Ironically, Lapkin was unintentionally describing the true nature of events.

[100] Marshal Biriuzov, in *K novomu pod"emu,* p. 67. Exhortations to raise the influence and activity of the Komsomol in military affairs are a tradition with the political organs, not with the military professionals. The latter resent the Komsomols as busybodies and frequently show irritation at their intrusion into purely military affairs. The political control organs, on the other hand, tend to urge the younger Party zealots to engage themselves fully in military affairs, and, especially during periods of tension between Party and military, encourage them to goad and criticize their military superiors at Party meetings.

[101] Marshal Moskalenko, in *K novomu pod"emu,* p. 121.

Stalingrad Group during the 1957-1960 period. Furthermore, because of the opposition from the military professionals, who had support from the highest military levels, a compromise formula was worked out that partially bridged the interests of the political control organs and the military professionals.[102] On such vital issues as strategic doctrine and the reorganization of the armed forces, Khrushchev was being supported by his associates in the military. But the period of turbulence in the officer corps, and the varying reactions of members of the Stalingrad Group to the Party's attempts to interfere with the military's professional freedom and institutional interests and autonomy, had been ominous, and the disagreements of 1958-1959 between the Party leadership and some members of the Stalingrad Group were to grow to much larger proportions in the years following.

As time went on, the marshals and generals no doubt realized that Khrushchev and the Party *apparat* basically distrusted the military establishment; the memory of the Zhukov era, when the Party's traditional hold on the military had been so drastically curtailed, was still fresh in everyone's mind. Though members of the Stalingrad Group continued to enjoy power and prestige, the renaissance of antimilitary attitudes in the Party, which recalled the days of Stalin, caused them concern and eventually led to conflicts of loyalties.

F · PARTIINOST' *VS. PROFESSIONAL LOYALTY: A CHALLENGE TO THE STALINGRAD GROUP*

Although the Party's effort to introduce sweeping socio-political reforms into the armed forces had been strongly rebuffed by the military in 1958 and resulted in a compromise between the protagonists, there could be little doubt that the Party eventually would try again to restore its control over every aspect of military life and to eradicate those conditions in the military that favored elitism. Actually, the Party *apparat*, after the ouster of Zhukov, never suspended its efforts to institute a new policy toward the military. Unobtrusively, it succeeded in introducing a number of far-reaching reforms that deeply affected the officers and men of the Soviet army and resulted in much tighter political controls over their activities. Thus, the officers' authority was severely limited by being made dependent on the acquiescence or approval of collective bodies within the various

[102] See Chapter V, pp. 148-150.

commands. Also, the disciplinary and symbolic prerogatives of commanders were considerably reduced. And the Party's use of large numbers of military personnel on nonmilitary tasks greatly affected both military readiness and morale.

While these social and political reforms were enough to cause dissatisfaction and provoke opposition among the military professionals, such tensions in Party-military relations were manageable and containable as long as the upper levels of the military hierarchy either collaborated with the Party or remained quiescent. However, Khrushchev's introduction of yet another major reform finally involved the top of the military hierarchy in the deepening conflict.

On January 14, 1960, the formal announcement by Khrushchev of a new Soviet strategic doctrine introduced a critical factor into the relations between Party and military. It was to cause a dangerous deterioration of that relationship and to alienate a number of Khrushchev's close supporters in the military. Whatever the merits of the doctrine as such, the new policy was a shock to the military community. Among other things, it involved a reduction of the armed forces by one-third, which meant the release of a quarter-million officers from their secure and comfortable life into an unpromising future and often an undesirable social environment, and constituted a blow to many vested interests and personal careers. Secondly, by stressing the central role of strategic missile forces and the crucial importance of the initial stage of a future war on the one hand, and denigrating the role, size, and mission of the conventional forces on the other, Khrushchev not only radically reversed traditional Soviet military thinking but also forcibly committed the military to a rigid and confining doctrine. It was this aspect of his reforms that aroused particular concern among the High Command and caused a rift between Khrushchev and some ranking members of the Stalingrad Group.

Khrushchev's social, political, and military reforms came at a rather inauspicious time. The armed forces were in the process of absorbing and learning to use large amounts of new weapons and equipment, and great numbers of young technicians were entering the officer ranks, which gave rise to new tensions emanating from the more traditionally minded military community. Also, the Soviet Union was then pursuing an aggressive foreign policy based to a large extent on the political exploitation of its presumably powerful military capability. The last thing the Party elite desired, therefore, was a discernible deterioration of the Soviet forces' effectiveness and readiness that would lessen their credibility as a deterrent. And the critics in the military seized precisely on this point when they opposed political controls or argued for greater institutional autonomy.

However, the Party leadership and the apparatus, having committed themselves to a major military reform on the grounds of ideology and political necessity, could not easily rescind it and admit failure. Instead, they opted once again for partial and temporary accommodation with the military, and proceeded quietly to lay the groundwork either for a more successful future showdown or, preferably, for a gradual, imperceptible implementation of the original reforms. What was subsequently to unite most members of the military establishment against the increasing pressures from the Party was the threat they perceived to their professional freedom and institutional autonomy, as much as the arbitrariness and narrowness of Khrushchev's doctrine.

In December 1960, Marshal Golikov, then head of the MPA, stated that "serious signals" had appeared which indicated, among other things, that some commanders and political workers had slipped back into apathy and bureaucratic inertia and were completely neglecting the Party's instructions as to the reforms.[103] In February 1961, Marshal Bagramian urged moderation and concern in dealing with commanders, officer-specialists, and enlisted personnel, since the new weapons and equipment were very complex and needed careful attention and professional expertise. He also advocated a higher standard of living for military personnel.[104]

The first direct attack on the political organs came in an article published in *Voenno-istoricheskii zhurnal*, the traditional forum for spokesmen of the conventional forces and military orthodoxy. The author, Lieutenant General A. Pigurnov, pointedly brought up some events of World War II, portraying in a most unflattering way the political commissars, whose extensive authority at the time, he alleged, had damaged *edinonachalie* and led to "direct interference with the duties of the commanders." He also described in detail some cases of cowardice among ranking military commissars.[105]

In the spring and summer of 1961, the military continued to assert itself, with support from several members of the Stalingrad Group. In April, Marshal Bagramian described the *Stavka* and its members

[103] General of the Army F. Golikov, "O nekotorykh voprosakh propagandistskoi raboty" (On Some Problems of Propaganda Activities), *Kommunist Vooruzhennykh Sil*, No. 5, December 1960, p. 19.

[104] *Kommunist Vooruzhennykh Sil*, No. 3, February 1961, pp. 26-27.

[105] See Chapter VI, pp. 200-201, for more details of Pigurnov's article.

in rather positive terms, stressing its moderation and its willingness to heed the judgment of the field commanders.[106] The following month, Marshals Chuikov and Eremenko, the two main military apologists of Khrushchev, were criticized by several military historians for personal vanity and for giving currency to fictitious accounts of the battle for Stalingrad.[107] Marshal Zakharov, in an historical appreciation of the war, refrained from blaming Zhukov and the military for the initial disasters, and emphasized that the expansion of Soviet influence in Europe had been made possible by military victories.[108]

In September, *Krasnaia zvezda* carried an unusually candid article by General of the Army (now Marshal of the Soviet Union) N. I. Krylov. While acknowledging the principle of the Party's supremacy over the military, Krylov made it clear that he considered undue Party-political interference with the officers' functions and authority as pernicious and dangerous.[109] Krylov's statements merit attention, partly because his career has advanced considerably in the past few years, an indication that his criticism of excessive intrusion by the political organs has not affected his standing in the military.

The first sign of a reaction by the Party to the military's growing opposition to the reforms came in an announcement from the MPA, which reported on a meeting of heads of political organs, military districts, and security organs in the spring of 1961.[110] The conference stressed the need for better discipline, stronger motivation, and greater pragmatism in the armed forces, and called for wider authority for commanders. In November 1961, the MPA issued an account of deteriorating discipline in a number of military districts, of stifling bureaucracy in the Party-political organs, and of instances in which commanders' orders had been challenged and questioned by

[106] *Voenno-istoricheskii zhurnal*, No. 4, April 1961.

[107] The critics were general officers from the conventional forces who, along with several other ranking members of the officer corps, met in the editorial offices of the *Voenno-istoricheskii zhurnal* to debate certain failings of Soviet military-historical writings. The fact that two of the most prominent historical apologists of Khrushchev's role at Stalingrad were publicly criticized by other officers may indicate a substantial opposition among the officer corps, which may have had tacit support from members of the High Command, to the Party's self-aggrandizing role in military affairs. For more details of this debate, see *Voenno-istoricheskii zhurnal*, No. 5, May 1961, pp. 95-110. See also Chapter VI, pp. 202-205.

[108] *Krasnaia zvezda*, May 9, 1961.

[109] *Ibid.*, September 27, 1961. See Chapter V, pp. 159-160, for excerpts from this article.

[110] *Krasnaia zvezda*, June 8, 1961.

Party functionaries.[111] There can be little doubt that the decline in the discipline and readiness of the armed forces had reached dangerous levels and that the Party elite, attributing this situation to the obstreperousness of the military, believed that it needed immediate correction.[112] The Party's attention, however, was temporarily taken up with preparations for the Twenty-second Party Congress and the ensuing Party-political problems (mainly the growing conflicts with Red China and Albania), and Party leaders did not address themselves to the matter until the spring of 1962.

A number of events during the spring and summer of 1962 pointed to the growing unrest in the military. In March the MPA reported that it had uncovered serious breaches of Party and military discipline in the central apparatus of the Ministry of Defense. Among them it listed the stifling of all criticism of superiors, disregard of the Central Committee's instructions concerning political education, and failure of higher officers to see to the political education of their subordinates.

The report also mentioned that not Marshal Golikov, the head of the MPA, but his deputy, Colonel General Efimov, was presiding at the meeting that was to deal with these shortcomings.[113] If this created any uncertainty about Golikov's status, the situation was soon clarified by the announcement of his replacement with General of the Army A. A. Epishev.[114] The appointment of Epishev, a former Deputy Minister of Security and close associate of Khrushchev, represented

[111] "V glavnom politicheskom upravlenii Sovetskoi Armii i Voenno-Morskogo Flota" (In the Main Political Administration of the Soviet Army and Navy), *Kommunist Vooruzhennykh Sil*, No. 22, November 1961, pp. 57-60. (The foregoing is a recurrent heading under which *Kommunist Vooruzhennykh Sil*, on behalf of the MPA, announces important changes, rules, and decisions affecting the military. After Epishev became head of the MPA, such announcements appeared more frequently than ever before, the result of the greater activity and involvement of the political control organs.)

[112] The MPA reported that "failings in the activities intended to strengthen discipline, order, and organization were exposed to a basic and sharp analysis at the meetings and conferences [of various political control organs]. Communists spoke with great concern about the fact that the CC/CPSU's instructions to improve military discipline are, in some [the Turkestan, Zabaikal, Siberian, Belorussian, and Leningrad] military districts and fleets, being carried out with extreme slowness."

[113] "O rabote partiinogo komiteta i partorganizatsii shtaba i upravleniia tyla Ministerstva oborony SSSR" (About the Work of the Party Committee and Party Organization of the Staff and Administration of the Rear by the USSR Defense Ministry), *Kommunist Vooruzhennykh Sil*, No. 5, March 1962, pp. 55-57.

[114] *Krasnaia zvezda*, May 22, 1962.

a throwback to the time when the MPA was ruled by men associated with police functions.[115] Khrushchev thereby was unmistakably putting the military on notice, and Epishev rapidly began to put his imprint on the armed forces. In June 1962 the MPA reported on a conference held at MPA headquarters and presided over by Epishev, which had strongly criticized a number of serious deficiencies in the military academies and various other military institutions and institutes—that is to say, in the traditional breeding ground of military professionalism and elitism.[116] Again the military was accused of not following the Central Committee's instructions concerning *kritika/samokritika* and the need to tighten discipline. Officers also were warned against covering up for one another and were urged to intensify the Marxist-Leninist indoctrination of their units.

Only two months later, the MPA announced that the central apparatus of the Ministry of Defense had been found badly deficient in most of its activities.[117] The August report mentioned Epishev's severe criticism of the Ground Forces headquarters, whose personnel he had found guilty of a number of malpractices, including failures to keep the MPA informed on certain matters of political activity and morale.[118]

The intensified conflict between the Party *apparat* and the military community created a dilemma for members of the Stalingrad Group. The issues and conflicting interests involved were such as

[115] See Appendix A-VI.

[116] "Sovershenstvovat' partiinuiu rabotu v akademiiakh i uchilishchakh" (Improve Party Work in the Academies and Institutes), *Kommunist Vooruzhennykh Sil*, No. 12, June 1962, pp. 40-43.

[117] "O rabote partkoma i partiinykh organizatsii shtaba i upravlenii Sukhoputnykh voisk" (About the Work of the Party Committee and Party Organizations of the Staff and Administrations of the Ground Forces), *Kommunist Vooruzhennykh Sil*, No. 15, August 1962, pp. 38-41.

[118] To soften the blow of Epishev's tightening of controls in the military, the Party made several conciliatory gestures: (a) In June 1962, it convened in Moscow a large military gathering, where promises were made to raise the standards of living of the military and their dependents. The conference also served as a "pressure valve" for military frustrations of all sorts by addressing itself to the uncovering of bureaucratic malpractices and discrimination. (*Krasnaia zvezda*, June 4-9, 1962. See also R. Kolkowicz, *The Use of Soviet Military Labor in the Civilian Economy: A Study of Military "Shefstvo,"* The RAND Corporation, RM-3360-PR, November 1962, pp. 24-26, 32-34.) (b) In the months following the June conference, the political organs made a show of prosecuting various low-ranking military and political officers for alleged wrongdoings that were said to have lowered the military's standard of living. (See Kolkowicz, p. 36.) (c) The unpopular practice of military *shefstvo* was abandoned, but it was to be resumed in the spring of 1963, after the Party had reasserted itself in the armed forces.

could not be ignored by the High Command. At stake were (a) the military's authority to participate in the planning of doctrine and strategy, (b) a measure of freedom for the military to practice its profession without pernicious political controls, and (c) the military's institutional and historical values and objectives. Members of the Stalingrad Group had to choose between the easy road of abstaining from the conflict between the Party and the military community and the more hazardous one of entering into it, either on the side of their benefactor Khrushchev and the *apparat*, or in behalf of the military and its institutional interests. The result was a polarization of loyalties in which the Stalingrad Group was split between the active supporters of Khrushchev (Marshals Biriuzov, Moskalenko, Chuikov, Eremenko, Sudets, among others) and those who, notwithstanding their public support of Khrushchev, deviated sufficiently from his military policy to constitute an opposition. The latter group included Marshals Malinovskii, Zakharov, Grechko, Krylov, Voronov, and Rotmistrov.

In May 1962, Malinovskii published two major articles. In the first, he addressed himself to Party-political problems in the armed forces; in the second, he dealt at greater length with strategic-doctrinal problems. Though essentially toeing the Party line, he deviated from it enough to make several important points: (a) discipline in the military demanded "simplicity and strictness in the relations between superiors and subordinates, a basic military camaraderie without familiarity [*panibratstvo*] and improper advances [*zaigryvanie*]"; (b) political indoctrination must be closely related to practical problems found in the daily life of the military; (c) political indoctrination should be made more modern and less hackneyed, since the majority of the younger officers and soldiers were better educated and more sophisticated than in the past; and (d) political indoctrination should be not only improved but curtailed. To bolster the last point, Malinovskii cited Lenin's dictum "Better less, but better."[119]

In his second article, which dealt with strategic doctrine, Malinovskii emphasized the following important points: (a) the Soviet Union must maintain a military capability that would credibly convey to the potential aggressor the futility of any intended aggression; (b) the primary task of the Soviet Union was the defense of the country; (c) in a future war, which would differ radically from past wars, there would still be a basic need for "massive armies," and

[119] *Krasnaia zvezda*, May 24, 1962.

victory would be achieved only through the "united efforts of all branches of the armed forces" and (d) therefore, the Soviet Union would continue to need regular cadres, since only such an army would be capable of dealing rapidly and effectively with the demands of modern warfare.[120]

Malinovskii's emphasis on the high priority of military needs was echoed by Marshal Grechko, who stated:

> . . . to build Communism does not mean to be concerned only with the development of the nation's economy, but to be concerned in every possible way with the strengthening of the Motherland's defensive capabilities and to raise the military readiness and might of the armed forces.[121]

Grechko illustrated his point about the deterrent power of a defense capability with the following parable:

> To restrain the aggressors, to halt their greedy intentions, is possible only through force. The tiger never attacks the elephant, even when he is thoroughly starved. He does not attack him because the elephant is stronger than the tiger. . . .[122]

The strategic views of Malinovskii and his followers were prominently displayed in an important volume on military strategy published in the summer of 1962. Edited by Marshal Sokolovskii, it represented the first major Soviet work on military strategy in thirty-six years. Its editorial bias was unmistakably in favor of the strategic views held by the Malinovskii wing in the military and implicitly criticized the Khrushchevian tenets. The comprehensive volume was a landmark in Soviet military writings and attracted much attention in the West. Although the committee of fifteen authors who participated in the book was said to represent a crosscut of military views, the introductory remarks identified only one of the authors as responsible for a particular chapter. It is worth noting that this author, Colonel General A. I. Gastilovich, departed very sharply from the general line followed in the other chapters. His line was the closest to Khrushchev's, in its insistence on the central im-

120 "Programma KPSS i voprosy ukrepleniia Vooruzhennykh Sil SSSR" (The CPSU Program and Problems of Strengthening the USSR Armed Forces), *Kommunist*, No. 7, May 1962, pp. 11-22.

121 A. A. Grechko, *Vysokoe prizvanie* (The High Calling), Voenizdat, Moscow, 1962, p. 5. (Approved for publication July 14, 1962.)

122 *Ibid.*, p. 8.

portance of missile-nuclear forces in future warfare, its strong emphasis on the initial period of such a war, and its deprecatory remarks about the expense and limited utility of standing conventional forces in nuclear war.[123] On the whole, the Sokolovskii volume represented a challenge to some of Khrushchev's strategic ideas and thus may be thought to have enhanced the position of his opponents in the military.

In October 1962, Marshal Zakharov gave an "interview" to *Krasnaia zvezda* on the problem of "*edinonachalie* and *edinonachal'niks*."[124] After reaffirming his close allegiance to the Party and its views regarding the military, he went on to make several points which echoed those of Krylov, Malinovskii, and Grechko: In Zakharov's opinion, the commander's authority, though bestowed on him by the Party and therefore different from the militarist's authority in nonsocialist countries, must nevertheless be unimpeded in view of the mobility and rapidity of military operations in modern war. Zakharov cited Lenin as favoring *edinonachalie* over *kollegial'nost'* (collective action) in some situations: "*Edinonachalie*, Lenin taught, ensures the best utilization of human capabilities and a realistic, and not just a superficial, control of activities." In condemning the collectivist method in the military advocated by the political control organs, Zakharov again quoted Lenin on the irresponsibility that attended collective decisions: "He called it a dangerous evil, which in the military quite often unavoidably leads to catastrophe, chaos, panic, and defeat."

Another noteworthy statement that *Krasnaia zvezda* quoted from the Zakharov interview was that, while military equipment, weapons, and procedures were becoming progressively more complex and demanding greater attention and higher specialization, many political officers

> . . . maintain that it is not their duty to become deeply and substantively involved with military affairs, with . . . tactical and operational training, with such problems as how new methods of warfare are being developed. . . . This, they maintain, is the duty of commanding personnel only.[125]

[123] See Marshal V. D. Sokolovskii (ed.), *Soviet Military Strategy*, U.S. eds. H. S. Dinerstein, L. Gouré, and T. W. Wolfe, Prentice-Hall, Inc., Englewood Cliffs, N.J., 1963, pp. 36-37.

[124] *Krasnaia zvezda*, October 12, 1962.

[125] *Ibid.* See also R. Kolkowicz, *The Impact of Technology on the Soviet Military: A Challenge to Traditional Military Professionalism*, The RAND Corporation, RM-4198-PR, August 1964.

The growing division of opinion between the MPA and at least some members of the High Command manifested itself strongly at the lower levels of the military hierarchy, and toward the latter part of 1962 *Krasnaia zvezda* began to reflect this military self-assertiveness.[126] To stem the deterioration of these relations, the Party convened a closed meeting of top functionaries of the political control organs with several ranking military personalities, including Malinovskii. The exact date of that meeting is not known, but *Krasnaia zvezda* chose October 25, the height of the Cuban missile crisis, to publish the statements that Malinovskii had made at the conference. The published speech of the Minister of Defense opened with some hard, bristling comments on the dangerous game played by the NATO powers in Europe. Next, Malinovskii addressed himself to internal military problems and to the political-military issues in the Soviet army, and developed his main point, about the central importance of military readiness under conditions of thermonuclear war:

> At the present, in the face of missile and nuclear weapons, the safety of our country and of the whole socialist system will depend, in a very direct manner, on the *level of military readiness* of the army and the navy. *I say this without any exaggeration, taking full account of the capabilities and intentions of the imperialist aggressors.* [Italics added.]

In view of the paramount need for military preparedness, Malinovskii emphasized that it was necessary "decisively to eradicate even the smallest manifestation of opposition to or delay [in attaining]

[126] An unusually large volume of letters to the editor, articles, and essays that appeared in *Krasnaia zvezda* and elsewhere in the summer, fall, and winter of 1962 reflected unrest and controversy in the military community. The authors were asserting the prerogatives and authority of officers while criticizing those of the political control organs. Their expressions of opinions focused mainly on three problems: (a) *strong criticism of the poor living conditions of the officer corps and demands for improvement* (e.g., General of the Army Kreizer in *Krasnaia zvezda*, October 23, 1962; Colonel Iashkin, *ibid.*, November 10; Marshal Malinovskii, *ibid.*, November 18; an unsigned article and several letters to the editor, *ibid.*, November 25; and an editorial, *ibid.*, December 1, 1962); (b) *insistence on wider authority for commanders*; and (c) *criticism of the political control organs* (cf. some unusually candid items in *Krasnaia zvezda*: editorial, October 3; Colonel Rybkin, October 4; report of a conference, October 11; editorials, October 12, 13, and 21, the last a strong criticism of the political organs for a variety of failings; Malinovskii, October 25; Colonel Iashkin, November 10; and, on November 14, 1962, a long report on "dead souls," the term used for military personnel carried on the active roster of units but actually used for political work). It is noteworthy that these criticisms fell off sharply after January 1963.

high levels of readiness." He pointedly reminded his readers of the ill effects of laxity in the Soviet army at the beginning of World War II. He sharply criticized orthodoxy in military thinking as an obstacle to military effectiveness and readiness, and went on to attack the political control organs as another major impediment to the desired goal: "If they [political officers] do not properly know modern military technology, they will not be able constructively to carry out political-educational work among the personnel."

Malinovskii also urged that military activities be planned in such a manner as to leave military personnel enough time not only for military training but for political training and adequate rest periods. Furthermore, he rejected the criticism of the political organs that described the younger men in the military as being of "special character" and accused them of disliking military life and having little patriotism and little respect for Marxist-Leninist teachings and authority. He then attacked the methods often used by the political control organs when inspecting the units:

> It frequently happens as follows: a group of functionaries from a higher staff or political organ will arrive in a deficient unit and will occupy themselves [solely] with the collection of information and criticism of the deficiencies. It is absolutely clear that from such a "method" of work nothing good will come.

Finally, Malinovskii advised both the military and the political organs to use the sharp tool of *kritika/samokritika* very carefully, since it could be destructive when used indiscriminately.

When Malinovskii's speech was published, the Soviet government was facing one of the most difficult situations of the decade, the Cuban missile crisis. A discernible divergence between the views of the military and those of the Party on the United States' position *during* the crisis, and the more severe attitude of the Party toward the military *after* the crisis, lead one to assume that some military circles disapproved of Khrushchev's handling of that affair.[127]

The abortive attempt to present the United States with a *fait accompli* in Cuba caused noticeable strains and disagreements between the Party and the political organs on the one hand and broad circles of the military (including some members of the Stalingrad Group) on the other. The Soviet press carried various veiled accusations of unnamed recalcitrants in the military; Epishev and his

[127] See R. Kolkowicz, *Conflicts in Soviet Party-Military Relations: 1962-1963*, The RAND Corporation, RM-3760-PR, August 1963.

assistants became increasingly bold; two ceremonial occasions were used by the main protagonists in the battles of World War II to minimize one another's claims to military brilliance and farsightedness; members of the Stalingrad Group publicly expressed dissident views on the crucial issue of the Party's and Khrushchev's historical role in the armed forces; and there was a reshuffle of personnel in the High Command.

On November 17, 1962, *Krasnaia zvezda* carried a noteworthy account of an interview with Marshal Chuikov, the Commander of the Ground Forces. Its substance forecast the Party elite's line with the military and served as a warning to those in the armed forces who opposed the Party's prerogative to direct, control, and supervise all aspects of military life. It reiterated the contention that the authority of the military commander exists only on the sufferance of the Party and may therefore be rescinded at any moment, and that the civilian authorities in the Central Committee are the ultimate decision-makers in all matters concerning military affairs. Thus, Chuikov cited this well-worn Leninist formula to assert the military's thorough subordination to the civilian authority of the Party:

> *The politics of the military department, as of all other departments and institutions, is carried out on the strict basis of general directives given by the Party through its Central Committee and under its direct control.* [Italics in original.]

To drive home this central point, Chuikov quoted from documents "not known to the general public" in an alleged exchange between Lenin and Stalin during the Russo-Polish war of 1920, when Stalin telegraphed to Lenin:

> The Politburo wastes its time on trivial matters. . . . It must be noted, in connection with the attitude of the Central Committee, which favors peace with Poland, that our diplomacy sometimes very effectively spoils the results achieved through our military victories.

Criticizing Stalin's defiance of the decisions and opinions of the Central Committee, Chuikov said about Lenin's reply to the telegram:

> Lenin stressed again the decisive role of the Party and its Central Committee in matters connected with the conduct of war. "Our diplomacy," he wrote, "is subordinated to the Central Committee and will never spoil our victories."

The apparent intent of the Chuikov "interview" was to impress upon the military community three main contentions of the Party: (a) The military man at the front cannot understand the broader aspects of warfare; (b) the view of some military people that diplomacy will deprive them of the rewards of their victories is false and narrow; and (c) the military is subordinate to the civilian Party authority and must accept and abide by its decisions.[128] In what sounded like a veiled threat to the dissidents, Chuikov also was quoted as saying that, although many officers had understood and accepted the need for the Party's dominant role in military affairs, there were still others "who do not draw the final conclusions or maintain proper attitudes and opinions."[129]

The first major statement after the Cuban crisis by the head of the MPA, General of the Army Epishev, reflected the same stiffening in the political leaders' attitude toward the military. It repeatedly affirmed the traditional dominance of the Party over the military and recalled the sobering lesson of the Zhukov period, when the Party was kept out of military matters.[130]

Having accused the military of "artificially separating ideological from organizational work,"[131] Epishev suggested that the Party-political organs begin to involve not only the military personnel but also their families in indoctrinational and other forms of political activity.[132] He cited the well-known communist zealot A. S. Makarenko, whose views on education and indoctrination were among the most radical and doctrinaire in the Party, as saying: "Go into the households and work with the children.[133] Remember that the edu-

[128] The important bearing of the Chuikov interview on developments in the Soviet Union may be gathered from the fact that four Polish periodicals (*Polityka*, *Zolnierz Wolnosci*, *Wojsko Ludowe*, and *Zolnierz Polski*) either reproduced or analyzed it.

[129] See Kolkowicz, *Conflicts in Soviet Party-Military Relations*, pp. 16 and 19, for descriptions of Kosygin's and Khrushchev's references to unnamed communist critics of the peaceful solution of the Cuban missile crisis.

[130] General of the Army A. Epishev, "Tverdo provodit' v zhizn' politiku partii v Vooruzhennykh Silakh" (Firmly Carry out the Party's Policy in the Armed Forces), *Kommunist Vooruzhennykh Sil*, No. 19, October 1962, p. 9. Epishev stated that "Well-founded alarm is caused most of all by the fact that, in a number of subunits, units [*chasti*], and *soedineniia*, the separation of Party-political work from the concrete tasks undertaken by the forces has not been completely overcome." The article obviously was written after the Cuban missile crisis, at least in its final form, since it contains references to the crisis.

[131] *Ibid.*, p. 12.

[132] *Ibid.*

[133] In November 1962, *Kommunist Vooruzhennykh Sil* (No. 22, pp. 74-75) reported on the campaign to involve military families in indoctrination and control

cational process takes place on every square meter of the earth."[134] Epishev also reported "serious deficiencies indicating that the role and importance of the organization of VLKSM [Komsomol] in the life and activities of soldiers are being underestimated," and he urged more active use of the Komsomol for the tasks ahead.[135]

The strength and authority of the MPA in the wake of the Cuban missile crisis were indicative of the growing division in the High Command, and especially in the Stalingrad Group. The military, the MPA, and the Party elite apparently were involved in tense maneuvering for position, which was reflected in public statements and in developments that were ambivalent or otherwise unclear.

The Party and the MPA seem to have taken the offensive immediately after the Cuban missile crisis and in an effort to intimidate the military or, possibly, to anticipate a feared reaction by the military to the Party civilians' clumsy handling of the Cuban affair. One of the publications dating from the tense period after October is Marshal Malinovskii's pamphlet *Vigilantly Stand Guard over the Peace.* Issued in November 1962, the pamphlet contains some contradictory and atypical views of the Minister of Defense, which have raised questions regarding its true authorship. On the one hand, Malinovskii takes a very liberal attitude on the need for extensive political control over the activities of the military; on the other hand, he sharply questions the Party's attempts to dictate strategic doctrine by excluding the military from its formulation, and criticizes the polical leaders for their denigration of military science.[136]

Malinovskii's remarks on political controls ring the more false when one compares them with statements on the same subject by Marshal Krylov, whose views in the past had closely coincided with Malinovskii's. The following juxtaposition dramatically underlines the disparity that seemed to have developed in the viewpoints of the two men, and lends support to assumptions that someone other than Malinovskii wrote all or most of the pamphlet to which he then was forced to sign his name.

---

activities in the armed forces. The report stated that initially there had been opposition, since the involvement of families was a "delicate matter," but went on to stress the official attitude that to refrain from scrutinizing "the personal and family affairs of Communists" was "an incorrect practice."

[134] See Chapter IV, p. 93, for a discussion of Makarenko's thesis on the education and control of the citizen.

[135] "Tverdo provodit'," p. 13.

[136] *Bditel'no stoiat' na strazhe mira*, Voenizdat, Moscow, 1962.

Malinovskii (*November 1962*)	*Krylov* (*September 1961*)
Edinonachalie acquires full force and gives real results when it rests on the support of the Party organizations and of all the military collective.	*Edinonachalie* presupposes full independence of the commander within the limits of rights granted to him. That's why I would especially like to single out the *exceptional importance of [allowing] the officer to develop the ability and habit of independently undertaking appropriate decisions*. . . . [Italics in original.]
It is not shameful for anyone to consult with his subordinates in order to take their experience and knowledge into consideration. Before making a decision, a commander not only may, but is obligated to, hear the opinions of his assistants, deputies, and the leaders of the Party organization.	Many officers waste a lot of time while making decisions or when giving orders because they feel it is their duty to consult ahead of time literally all their assistants. . . . It is necessary to have . . . a commander who is able to use his full authority boldly, decisively, without looking back over his shoulder. . . .

In criticizing the Party for interfering with the military's role in formulating strategy and doctrine, Malinovskii used a subterfuge: he took issue with the Party's attempt to make military science into a "type of science of sciences, somehow universal and all-embracing," one that contained "everything that predetermines victory." To broaden the scope of military science in such a way would be to render it militarily useless, he indicated, and would place it within the domain of the Party policy-makers, thereby excluding the military from participation.[137]

Sometime in November of 1962, Chief of the General Staff Marshal M. Zakharov disappeared from public view and was temporarily replaced by his deputy, General V. D. Ivanov. The mystery of

[137] The same concern had been clearly expressed earlier by the General Staff organ *Voennaia mysl'*, No. 4, 1955 ("To include in military science questions beyond its competence means to ruin military science as a specific branch of knowledge"). More recently, the same view was voiced by an advocate of military rights and authority, Colonel I. Korotkov, in *Voenno-istoricheskii zhurnal*, No. 4, April 1964, pp. 39-50.

Zakharov's whereabouts during the winter served to deepen the general uncertainty as to the nature of Party-military relations.

In the meantime, through the medium of the MPA and its head, General Epishev, the Party continued to put pressure on the central apparatus of the Ministry of Defense, in an attempt to intimidate its members and, possibly, to purge them of some of the elements undesirable to the Party. In the middle of November, General Epishev and N. R. Mironov, head of the Section on Administrative Organs in the Central Committee (which is in charge of police, security, judiciary, and some military affairs), participated in a meeting of the Party *aktiv* of the Ministry of Defense, during which demands were made "to strengthen the role and influence of Party organizations and to improve all Party-political work in the central apparatus of the Ministry of Defense, in the districts, fleets, and Force Groups." The meeting passed a resolution "to improve the activities of the Communists in the central apparatus of the Ministry of Defense" and urged that "serious attention be given to improving Marxist-Leninist education of generals, admirals, and officers."[138]

On December 8, *Krasnaia zvezda* reported another meeting of the Party *aktiv* of the Ministry of Defense, attended by Epishev and Mironov's deputy, which spoke of abuses due to the fact that "some sectors of the military apparatus remained for years outside of any controls."

Party *aktivs* normally deal with the specific problems of their own membership,[139] and this applies also to the *aktiv* of the central apparatus of the Soviet Ministry of Defense, which includes the top military hierarchy. The unusual frequency of *aktiv* meetings in the Ministry in the winter of 1962 indicated that some urgent problems involving the High Command needed to be resolved. As subsequent events were to show, these problems arose from pressure on the internal apparatus of the Ministry of Defense that was being brought by the MPA, and by the Secretariat of the Central Committee through Mironov, to restore the Party to dominance within the High Command and to subordinate the military fully to the

[138] *Krasnaia zvezda*, November 18, 1962.

[139] According to the official Party handbook on political functions in the military (*Partiino-politicheskaia rabota v Sovetskoi Armii i Voenno-Morskom Flote*, Voenizdat, Moscow, 1960, pp. 63-64), the Party *aktiv* consists of Party members who are "commanders, political workers, members of the Party *biuro*, secretaries of Party organizations, *partorgs*, members of Party commissions, leaders of Marxist-Leninist seminars with officer personnel, and other Party members who actively participate in Party activities. . . ." The *aktiv* is supposed to meet regularly every three to four months. See also Appendix E for details on Party organizations.

political control of the MPA. Military opposition, however, persisted and expressed itself in various ways. A striking example of the widening split between Khrushchev and some members of the Stalingrad Group was offered by the polemics of a number of military and MPA leaders in the pages of the press on the occasion of the twentieth anniversary of the battle of Stalingrad in late January of 1963. The key issue under discussion was the precise part that Khrushchev and the Party had played in the battle, and the role of ranking military leaders and of military professionals in general.[140] At stake was Khrushchev's claim to military genius, which a number of loyal military and Party associates had made in his behalf on the strength of his role in the crucial counteroffensive at Stalingrad. Marshals Biriuzov,[141] Chuikov,[142] and Eremenko[143] reiterated the case for Khrushchev, who, in their view, had been almost alone in conceiving the plan for the counteroffensive and had had to persuade the *Stavka* and Stalin to accept it. Marshals Rotmistrov,[144] Voronov,[145] and Kazakov,[146] on the other hand, omitted Khrushchev's name from their articles entirely, stressing the decisive role of the various military leaders, especially of Malinovskii. The most

[140] See Chapter VI, pp. 210-214, for a longer discussion of this polemic.

[141] *Politicheskoe samoobrazovaniie*, No. 2, 1963, pp. 33-41.

[142] *Izvestiia*, February 2, 1963.

[143] *Pravda*, January 27, 1963.

[144] *Krasnaia zvezda*, January 16, 1963.

[145] *Pravda*, January 31, 1963. This sharp divergence of attitudes on Party practices and Party leadership among members of the High Command is apparent also in the different reactions of Marshals Biriuzov and Voronov to the introduction of military commissars into the Red Army during World War II. Biriuzov, who was then commanding the 132nd Infantry Division, showed his slavish adherence to the Party in his enthusiastic endorsement of this feared and repugnant measure: "It was at that time that we received a report that the . . . Military Commissars had been reintroduced into the Red Army. I remember well the satisfaction with which this news was received. Every commander felt then how necessary it was to strengthen political leadership in the forces." (*Kogda gremeli pushki* [When the Guns Thundered], Voenizdat, Moscow, 1961, p. 29.) By contrast, Chief Marshal of Artillery N. N. Voronov, a straight professional officer, wrote to Stalin after having visited the Stalingrad Front in the early fall of 1942: "The time has come to make [commanders] fully authoritative [*edinovlastnymi*] leaders, so that in combat the commander could undertake independent rapid decisions. . . . This would raise discipline. . . . It is necessary to raise the authority and prestige of the commanders so that they could fully and personally be responsible for all that is good and bad. . . . There is only one way—to return to *edinonachalie*. With the reintroduction of *edinonachalie*, I am convinced, much will become improved in our army, and we will fight more successfully." (*Na sluzhbe voennoi* [In the Military Service], Voenizdat, Moscow, 1963, pp. 254-255.)

[146] *Izvestiia*, February 1, 1963.

interesting contribution to the polemic was that of Marshal Malinovskii himself, who methodically and gratuitously undermined the implicit claim of Khrushchev to having played a central part in planning and executing the Stalingrad counteroffensive.[147]

For the moment, the military's stand in the controversy over Stalingrad was to remain the strongest manifestation of its assertiveness toward the Party. As events of the following weeks suggested, the tensions between Party and military that arose from the Cuban debacle were somehow settled, and the Party and Khrushchev emerged once again as the victors.

In the latter part of February, the Soviet press carried another polemic, this time on the occasion of the forty-fifth anniversary of the establishment of the Soviet army. In sharp contrast to the preceding one, however, it was given over to the arrogant and patronizing statements characteristic of the MPA and the pro-Khrushchev members of the Stalingrad Group. The remarks of Marshals Malinovskii[148] and Zakharov,[149] on the other hand, timidly repeated the new Party line.

In the course of January and February of 1963, General Epishev published three articles,[150] in which he bluntly and repeatedly asserted the Party's dominant role in the military. He gratuitously brought up the sensitive issue of the military's responsibility for the initial disasters in World War II, while praising the Party for undoing the damage. In each article, Epishev called for the intensification of military *shefstvo.* And he also readmitted some of the strategic-doctrinal views of the conventional forces by stressing the need for large standing armies in future wars.

The Party's successful reassertion of its power over the military was reflected also in a massive propaganda campaign in the press, which reaffirmed the Party's dominance and lectured the military about learning to recognize and accept its limited, subordinate role in the Soviet state. This new, hard Party line appeared in editorials and articles in *Kommunist Vooruzhennykh Sil,*[151] the MPA's central

147 *Pravda,* February 2, 1963. 148 *Pravda,* February 23, 1963.

149 *Krasnaia zvezda,* February 22, 1963.

150 *Politicheskoe samoobrazovanie,* January 1963; *Pravda,* February 2, 1963; *Voprosy istorii KPSS,* No. 2, February 1963. Epishev's first deputy, Colonel General P. Efimov, also published a lengthy article on the occasion of the 45th anniversary of the Red Army, closely echoing his superior's hard line. *Partiinaia zhizn',* February 1963.

151 "Of the greatest importance to control is criticism, especially criticism that comes from below. . . . All activities of the political organs and Party organizations must be conducted in such a manner that the Communist feels that his

organ, as well as in a series of prominent essays in *Krasnaia zvezda* that included these passages:

> Only the Party . . . is capable of correctly solving all problems connected with the defense of the socialist fatherland, military organization, and the theory and practice of military affairs.

> The Communist Party and its Leninist Central Committee headed by N. S. Khrushchev unrelentingly and firmly maintain a policy of strengthening Party influence in the army and navy and decisively repulsing any attempts to curtail the role of the Party leadership in the armed forces.[152]

> The army is an instrument of politics and serves the political sphere of interests.[153]

The main points that were so forcefully stated and restated in this propaganda campaign were that only the Central Committee (i.e., a body of civilian decision-makers) was capable of planning for the whole of the military establishment; that the strategic-doctrinal theses propounded by Khrushchev in 1960 were the basis for the developing Soviet military doctrine; and that the Central Committee was intimately involved in all aspects of military life and nothing pertaining to military affairs escaped it scrutiny.[154]

The victory of the MPA and the wing of the Stalingrad Group

---

superiors are interested in his suggestions and critical observations, that they do not remain empty words. . . . Control is necessary over all people, regardless of their rank and formal position." (*Kommunist Vooruzhennykh Sil,* No. 1, January 1963, p. 10.) For other statements reflecting this new, hard line of the Party and MPA in the military, see *ibid.*, No. 7, April 1963, pp. 9-20; and S. Baranov and E. Nikitin, "Rukovodstvo KPSS—osnova osnov sovetskogo voennogo stroitel'stva" (The CPSU's Leadership—the Very Basis of Soviet Military Development), *ibid.*, No. 8, April 1963, pp. 17-25.

152 February 20, 1963.

153 February 12, 1963.

154 Among the various signs of the Party's reassertion *vis-à-vis* the military we may list an article by Marshal Rotmistrov in *Agitator*, No. 8, April 1963. Rotmistrov had omitted any reference to Khrushchev in his January 16 article in *Krasnaia zvezda* and in two prominent articles in *Voenno-istoricheskii zhurnal* (No. 12, December 1962, and No. 1, January 1963) which dealt with the battle of Stalingrad. Yet in April he was praising Khrushchev's brilliant role in connection with the battle of Kursk, even though the anniversary of the Kursk battle was still four months away at the time of the *Agitator* article. Paradoxically, while Khrushchev could legitimately claim a major role at the battle for Stalingrad, his part in the Kursk battle had been rather minor. It may therefore be assumed that Rotmistrov was forced to write the Kursk article as a form of apology to Khrushchev for having previously minimized his role in the Stalingrad battle.

loyal to Khrushchev became unmistakably clear with the official replacement of Marshal Zakharov by Marshal Biriuzov as Chief of the General Staff.[155] Not only was this appointment symbolic of the new power relationship in the High Command, but it also offered Khrushchev valuable leverage in the main planning body and the intellectual center of the Soviet army.

However, Khrushchev's disloyalty to some of his close associates and friends in the military, together with his dogmatic insistence on a strategic doctrine that was becoming a hindrance to the military community, was to cost him dearly. The *modus vivendi* he established with the military after the Cuban missile crisis (an arrangement that seems to have included the military's acceptance of tighter political controls and indoctrination as the price for greater freedom to explore and debate military doctrine and military science) was at best a temporary peace.

G · NOTE ON METHODOLOGY

This study of the Stalingrad Group is based on open Soviet sources, which cannot be counted on to depict the precise nature of events or to express independent personal judgments. With their monotonous sameness, Soviet communications convey the impression that private views and animosities, political passions, and struggles for power are nonexistent in the communist state. Even in matters less sensitive and vital than military affairs, Soviet secrecy is a well-

[155] Marshal Zakharov had dropped out of sight in November, his name having last appeared in the press in connection with an official function he attended on November 18. On December 7, *Krasnaia zvezda* reported a military function and in the place usually reserved for Zakharov's name (after those of Malinovskii and Grechko, and before Epishev's) Zakharov's deputy, General of the Army V. D. Ivanov, was listed. Thereafter, until December 19, *Krasnaia zvezda* placed Ivanov's name after Epishev's without reference to his official position. On December 20 and 23, the paper identified Ivanov as "Acting Chief of the General Staff of the Soviet Armed Forces." Zakharov's name, however, was retained in its former position, before Epishev's, among the signatories of obituaries for several deceased generals on December 7, December 28, January 25, and January 30. Also, while the February 24 issue of *Pravda* identified Zakharov by his full title as Chief of the General Staff and described him as the host at an official reception on the 45th Anniversary of the Soviet Armed Forces, *Krasnaia zvezda* failed to mention this reception; and it did not identify Zakharov, whose article it carried on the same day, by his title. By March 15, the controversy over Zakharov seems to have been settled. In an obituary for a General Kuprianov, published on that day in *Krasnaia zvezda*, Zakharov was not listed, and his usual place in the list of names under the obituary notice was occupied by Marshal Biriuzov. On March 28, Biriuzov was finally identified in *Krasnaia zvezda* as the new Chief of the General Staff.

known phenomenon. Therefore, before asserting the existence of a community of interests and a link in careers between a given Party leader and a particular group of officers in the military, I established a number of criteria by which to test hypotheses about the military elite.[156] Specifically, these criteria were designed to answer the basic question whether there was such an identity of interests as would permit one to speak of a "Stalingrad Group," or whether the Group was merely a random assortment of military leaders who happened to reach military and political prominence independent of any relationship to Khrushchev. Although it would be foolhardy to present the thesis of the Stalingrad Group and its special relation with Khrushchev as clear-cut and unequivocal, the evidence in support of this thesis is as strong as one can hope to find in Soviet materials. To sum it up:

(1) The Russo-German front of 1942-1943 was over two thousand kilometers long. This front line was divided for operational purposes into some thirteen frontal sectors (called "Fronts"). There were over two thousand generals in command of troops and in other positions. Yet the present Stalingrad Group comes almost without exception from the group of generals who were located at a single frontal sector (the Stalingrad Front), which was under Khrushchev's personal supervision during the six to seven months of the bitter battle for Stalingrad. (Even the two most recent heads of the MPA, Golikov and Epishev, came from that group.)

(2) After the battle of Stalingrad, various clusters of members of the Group (Konev-Grechko-Moskalenko-Biriuzov-Epishev; Malinovskii-Zakharov-Krylov-Rotmistrov; and Eremenko-Chuikov) were concentrated at other frontal sectors, commanded by prominent men of the Stalingrad Group.

(3) Several members of the Group continued to work closely with Khrushchev after he returned to head the Ukrainian Party apparatus, and still later, after he had gone to Moscow, with his close associates in the CPSU (Grechko, Chuikov, Moskalenko, Konev, Epishev, and Mironov).

156 In recent years, several Western writers—notably R. L. Garthoff, T. W. Wolfe, J. M. Mackintosh, and L. Schapiro—have drawn attention to the close relationship between Khrushchev and a number of officers from the southern front line. Though they postulate the existence of a "southern group," most of their arguments, with one exception, remain highly speculative, as they have refrained from analyzing the origins, motivations, and environmental changes and resultant conflicts that are relevant both to the history of the Stalingrad Group and to the personalities composing it.

(4) If the above facts serve to stress the close connections between Khrushchev and members of the Stalingrad Group before Stalin's death and thereby indicate the origins of their relationship, the following criteria were used to test the Group's identity during the period of Khrushchev's struggle for personal power and after he achieved it: (a) promotions of Group members (unusually rapid advancement or promotions that seemed connected with certain stages in Khrushchev's rise to power); (b) rising political stature (its coincidence with Khrushchev's rise to power); (c) preferential treatment of Group members in the Party press; (d) strong adherence to Khrushchev's views and policies in public utterances; and (e) unusual prominence and frequency of public appearances.

With few exceptions, the members of the Stalingrad Group satisfied these criteria. They were promoted to some of the highest ranks and positions after Khrushchev had deposed Malenkov and assumed dominant (though not yet dictatorial) control in the Party. After the ouster of the anti-Party group and Zhukov, which left Khrushchev the unchallenged leader in the Party, the Stalingrad Group took over the top positions in the defense establishment. In 1961, many of them were elevated to the Central Committee. Although there is also a large number of high-ranking officers in the defense establishment, most of them have a very limited public role and tend to concern themselves with their narrow professional interests rather than with those that fall into the "political-military" category.

In addition to the above factual events and developments, which are easily verified, it is well to examine several other factors, which are of a conjectural nature. The main purpose in listing them here is to anticipate a question as to the causes of the alliance between Khrushchev and the generals at the battle of Stalingrad and thereafter.

In a political system where the ruler's will is the law, secondary leaders who aspire to power seek to place trusted associates in key positions both for present protection and to secure an advantage against the day of the dictator's demise and a subsequent struggle for succession. This cabalistic aspect of power politics in the Soviet Union has been described by many Western students of communism, and specialists in such palace politics have earned themselves the name of "Kremlinologists." To select trusted lieutenants has been one of the most important and sensitive problems for every ruling elite in the Soviet Union. What, then, may have been the characteristics that qualified members of the Stalingrad Group as lieutenants, and what were the circumstances and conditions that led to their alliance with Khrushchev?

(1) *Direct contact and personal friendship*: The extreme competitiveness in all Party practices, and the pervasive distrust of almost everybody as a potential rival, cause the leaders of the elite to surround themselves with people whom they know intimately and whose views and loyalties they trust. For, as Lenin expressed it and Stalin echoed it, the fundamental criterion for action is "Who [will conquer] Whom" (*kto-kogo*).

(2) *Shared experiences under stress*: This criterion, an extension of the preceding one, emphasizes the special camaraderie that comes with fighting a common enemy under adverse conditions.

(3) *Common interests and views*: The fact that the Party leader and the military officers support each other would seem to imply *ipso facto* a community of interests. However, in view of some drastic cases in which the Party leader and certain officers whom he placed in positions of power ultimately did not share the same goals, we must distinguish between a seeming mutuality of interests (e.g., the alliance of Khrushchev and Zhukov, which was of a tactical and ephemeral nature) and the community of interests between Khrushchev and the Stalingrad Group, which was much firmer, though not necessarily unassailable.

(4) *Common antagonists*: Another possible reason for the union of out-groups in highly competitive political-social environments is the presence of a common internal adversary against whom it is desirable to marshal combined resources.

The circumstances of the relationship between Khrushchev and the Stalingrad Group as it developed during the battle for Stalingrad closely fit these criteria: Khrushchev frequently came in contact with the generals of the Group; he personally selected several and had them promoted; he shared with them some of the most dramatic and important months in Soviet history; and he sympathized with their plight in the face of the arbitrary and denigrating measures of the *Stavka* representatives.

The foregoing thesis about the rise of the Stalingrad Group and of its members' special relationship to Khrushchev thus rests largely on such empirical factors as close contacts under stress, opposition to common adversaries, and promotions to positions of influence that paralleled the Party leader's rise to power, which are supported by a number of conjectural factors based on our general knowledge of political behavior in the totalitarian state.

VIII · The Military and the Ouster of Khrushchev

> . . . Comrades, it can simply not be permitted that the authority of one person can grow to such proportions that this person imagines he can do anything, that he does not need the collective any more. In such a case, this person may cease to listen to the opinions of the other comrades who have similarly been called upon to share in the leadership, and may attempt to suppress them.
>
> Khrushchev, on the cult of the personality, at the XXII Party Congress, October 1961

> It must not be permitted that one man, even if he possesses the highest authority, removes himself from the controls of the top collectives and the Party organizations and presumes to know everything and to be able to do anything and not be in need of the knowledge and experience of other comrades.
>
> *Partiinaia zhizn'*, No. 20, October 1964, after Khrushchev's ouster

A change of leadership in the Soviet Union is not a process governed by either tradition or established rules. No Soviet Party leader has ever voluntarily relinquished his powers, and no provisions exist for the transfer of authority should the incumbent die or be removed as a result of disability or political coercion. This serves to explain why Lenin's infirmity and death, Trotsky's forced removal, and the death of Stalin proved to be such critical events. A grave leadership crisis can be expected to arise also from an intra-Party coup resulting from realignments of political relationships and loyalties among representatives of those institutions that carry the chief political weight in the state. The former leader then finds himself with a *fait accompli*, engineered by his opponents, to which he has no choice but to submit. This was the case, though to varying degrees, in the ousters of both Malenkov and Khrushchev.

Most of this book was written while Khrushchev was still in power. Even now, many details of the event, and of the machinations behind the scenes that brought about Khrushchev's ouster, are not yet available to us. But it may nevertheless be useful to extend this study of Party-military relations into the present, on the basis of what is now known or apparent, and to connect earlier events to what we know about the new regime. In so doing, we shall try, in this chapter, to find any connections that may exist between the fall of Khrushchev and his problems *vis-à-vis* the military. At the same time, this exploration of recent events will afford us a chance to test tentatively our initial assumptions about the dangers incurred by Party leaders who consistently slight and obstruct the military's institutional interests, and it will provide an opportunity for us to reexamine the thesis that the Soviet military is steadily gaining in institutional autonomy and professional freedom.

A · MAJOR CHANGES IN INTERNATIONAL POLITICS

The central characteristic of the early "cold war" period was its bipolarity: it grew logically out of the distribution of political, economic, and military power between the two major societies of the world, and it was reinforced by the deep American suspicions of Stalinist Russia's territorial designs (which had already resulted in an Eastern Europe unified behind the "iron curtain") and by the revived fear of international communism. A major factor in this bipolarity was the specter of modern war and the fact that, at the time, only the two great antagonists possessed the fearful new weapons. Thus, while a growing bloc of Eastern countries was forcibly held together by Moscow and kept divided by it from the West, other nations sought aid and protection in the Western alliance system. The peripheral and underdeveloped areas, including former colonies, had as yet little political and military value and therefore did not enter decisively into the confrontation of the two blocs.

As time went on, however, rapid developments in science and technology and the emergence of new personalities and power alignments within the blocs brought radical changes in international politics. A precarious nuclear balance gave way to the nuclear stalemate and more stable deterrents. The acute sense of terror at the possibility of a nuclear war was replaced by the belief that nuclear war had ceased to be an instrument of rational policy. Also, both camps were losing some of their internal cohesion, as member nations sought to emancipate themselves from the center and grew impatient with the continuing expectation that they subordinate their national self-interest to the larger interests of the bloc. In the Western camp, this centrifugal movement was aided by diverse, and at times almost contradictory, interests. According to the prevailing rationale, for example, the growing unlikelihood of nuclear war was making the subordination of the smaller nations' interests to the U.S.-directed objectives of the bloc less and less compelling; yet, as these nations sought to develop their own aims and to rely more heavily on their national resources, possession of a nuclear capability of their own came to appear to them as an indispensable goal. In the Eastern bloc, the momentum for decentralization was provided by the death of Stalin, which precipitated the relaxation of political controls and modification of social institutions within and among communist countries. More recently, the conflict that has arisen from Red China's challenge to the Soviet Union as leader of the bloc has severely affected a whole range of political, economic, and military interests that concern the various members of the bloc, and has contributed to some major changes in the communist camp.

At the same time that "bloc fatigue" was weakening the inner ties in both camps, the two great powers were busy building and emplacing a new generation of powerful weapons, long-range missiles with nuclear warheads. Their guiding purpose was either to make capital out of these developments or to forestall any radical changes in the *status quo* that might occur as a result of the adversary's acquiring comparable weapon systems. By the late 1950's, both sides seemed to have recognized that the new weapons, because of their speed, accuracy, destructiveness, and virtual invulnerability, had introduced a parameter for political action, which, in a sense, had stabilized the relations between the blocs. Khrushchev, in his "missile politics" of the late 1950's and early 1960's, seems to have been engaged, not so much in a militant campaign through which to secure major political or military concessions from the West, but rather in a delaying tactic intended to convince the United States that the Soviets had achieved the nuclear parity they considered necessary to international stabilization. Ironically, just as the two major powers began to desire such stabilization more strongly, the chief secondary powers in both camps, Red China and France, became sharply dissatisfied with the *status quo* and took steps to emancipate themselves from the rulers of their respective alliances. Thus, the effort toward international stabilization was severely undermined from within the two camps themselves, and the resulting imbalance was aggravated by actions on the part of "uncommitted" nations.

Khrushchev seems to have appreciated the "logic" of this development and to have sought to adjust his policies to it. A major prerequisite of stabilization, as he saw it, was a modicum of strategic parity, and, since the Soviet economy lacked the resources for an out-and-out arms race with the United States, Khrushchev gambled on the chance that placing offensive missiles in Cuba and presenting the United States with the *fait accompli* might prove an effective shortcut to parity. When the maneuver turned into a fiasco, Khrushchev abandoned all attempts at achieving strategic parity in favor of a massive campaign aimed at détente and at the peaceful, negotiated settlement of many outstanding issues. This effort was accompanied by a changed internal policy under which social priorities were so realigned as to subordinate ideological and political interests to the pragmatic objective of enhancing the material well-being of society.

B · KHRUSHCHEV'S GRAND DESIGN

Khrushchev's domestic plan envisaged a vast, long-range investment in the chemical industry, which was to provide fertilizer for agriculture and other products for the consumers. It included improved social services, larger pensions and incomes, rapidly expanding living space, and the growth of light industry.[1] At the same time, Khrushchev sought to reorganize the Party *apparat*, dividing it into two functionally oriented areas, i.e., industry and agriculture, in which the Party functionaries would be the managers and experts rather than mere *apparatchiks*.[2] With this plan, a renascence of bourgeois values made itself felt in Soviet society; the acquisition of goods and services and their consumption became once more respectable objectives. Seen together with the aims of political détente, peaceful coexistence, and the settlement of festering issues through negotiation, this was a far cry from the ascetic, revolutionary spirit of yesteryear.[3]

[1] The vision that inspired Khrushchev's Grand Design is reflected in his impassioned outcry soon after the Cuban missile fiasco, which, in a sense, had released him from the obligation to seek a détente from a position of strength, freeing his attention and energies for a different approach: "Comrades! Our country has all the requisites for moving still more confidently and rapidly along the road to communism. For this we need only one thing—peace, an opportunity to labor undisturbed, to build our big, bright house." *Pravda,* February 28, 1963.

[2] One of the first measures of the Brezhnev-Kosygin regime was to do away with this organizational split of the Party apparatus. See "Resolution of the Plenary Session of the CPSU Central Committee on Merging Industrial and Rural Province and Territory Party Organizations," *Pravda,* November 17, 1964.

[3] Among the vast volume of Western commentary on Khrushchev's ouster are: P. B. Reddaway, "The Fall of Khrushchev," *Survey,* No. 56, July 1965; Boris Meissner, "Party and Government Reforms," *ibid.*; a series of papers on the theme "Nach Chruschtschow" by David Burg, Richard Lowenthal, and Herman

Khrushchev's "Grand Design" was politically, economically, and militarily sound. Notwithstanding their many conflicting interests and objectives, the United States and the Soviet Union had much to lose from any situation in which their allies could maneuver them into dangerous political and military positions, with disastrous potential consequences, and from a relationship so unresolved and unpredictable as to leave the initiative to lesser and less responsible powers. They had to take bold steps, therefore, toward settling such unsolved problems as nuclear testing, inadequate communications, arms control and disarmament, and possibly even the German question. Economically, too, a détente promised to be most useful. It would free some resources previously allocated to defense for more productive uses; it would provide skilled personnel to be used in peaceful and constructive endeavors; it would open the way to vital and profitable trade activity between communist and non-communist countries; and it would permit the Soviet Union to tackle such perennial economic headaches as the bad state of agriculture with greater resources and larger reserves of skilled managers.

The military advantages of a détente also were apparent. Once the Soviets ceased to compete with the United States in the development of strategic arms, they would be able to challenge the American predominance by shifting the East-West competition from a militant to a peaceful plane, on which, at the very least, the American strategic superiority would be politically less useful. By adhering firmly to a military doctrine that regarded a nuclear encounter as the only possible confrontation between the two camps, Khrushchev also provided the justification for reducing the size of the conventional forces, which are so expensive to maintain. This military doctrine implied, of course, that the Soviet Union's strategic forces-in-being were adequate deterrents that would prevent such a fatal nuclear encounter.

Khrushchev's Grand Design, though apparently a sensible adaptation to the realities and one that promised to yield benefits to the

---

Achminov in *Osteuropa*, No. 11, November 1964; Boris Meissner, "Chruschtschowismus ohne Chruschtschow," *Osteuropa*, Nos. 1, 2, 3, 4, 1965; Werner Scharndorff, "Die Stabilität der heutigen Sowjetführung," *Politische Studien*, No. 161, May-June 1965; a series of articles on the theme "The Fall of Khrushchev" by Petr Kruzhin, A. Avtorkhanov, Stefan Stolte, and A. Kashin, in *Bulletin of the Institute for the Study of the USSR*, No. 12, December 1964; a series of contributions on the theme "The Coup and After" by Merle Fainsod, Richard Lowenthal, Robert Conquest, Adam Ulam, and others, in *Problems of Communism*, January-February and May-June 1965.

Soviet Union and also, to some extent, to the world at large, encountered strong opposition within the Soviet Union and in other parts of the communist camp.

C · WHY THE DESIGN FAILED

The grand designs of political leaders must be accompanied by mandates to undertake radical changes. These are not necessarily of an ideological kind. Rather, because of their large scope and visionary premise, such programs often demand priority in manpower and other resources and in the order of official social objectives, and their proponents must have the authority to allocate these accordingly. To acquire and retain such authority requires great political skill and tact. The advocates of grand designs, however, frequently become zealots who, in their relentless pursuit of distant objectives, tend to overlook the claims of established institutions and to offend many elements in the bureaucracy by ignoring vested interests and customary relationships. Thus, Khrushchev, in his zeal to bring prosperity and peace to his country, forgot this cardinal rule of politics: if you must threaten the interests of power groups in the polity, attack them one at a time, never all at once.

Khrushchev's was the case of the pragmatic reformer who made mistakes, some of which he could have avoided, and whose vision foundered on the rocks of institutional resistance. Ironically, these same institutions were not opposed to progress as such, nor even necessarily to the substance of Khrushchev's program. But they resented both the scope of the reforms and Khrushchev's style. What, then, were some of the mistakes and failings that cost Khrushchev their good will and ultimately led to his ouster?

(*1*) *The appearance of playing to the wrong audience*: Khrushchev's declaratory and actual policies designed to bring about a détente suggested that the Soviet attitude toward the West was changing and that the Soviet leadership was trying to conciliate the Western public, at the same time that Khrushchev's relations with some of the most powerful institutions in the Soviet state—the military, the Party bureaucracy, and the governmental bureaucracy—were steadily deteriorating. The impression, in certain parts of the communist camp, that Khrushchev was placating the "wrong" side was enhanced by the growing Sino-Soviet schism. Whatever the basic merits of that case, it was clear that Khrushchev's views and his personal vanities were aggravating the situation to the danger point; he seemed to be ready to sacrifice the support of Red China, the second largest communist nation, at the same time that he was eagerly seeking a genuinely peaceful coexistence with the West.[4]

(2) *The specter of one-man rule and the "cult of personality"*: Even as he was endangering his relations with the most powerful institutions in the Soviet state by demanding that they sacrifice many of their own objectives and interests in the cause of reform and progress, Khrushchev alienated them still further and heightened their mistrust of him by concentrating more and more power in himself and a small coterie of loyal followers.[5]

(3) *The uncertain trumpet*: In asking the Party, the experts, and the institutions to follow and support him in his bold policies, whose long-range benefits to the state and its citizens promised to be momentous, Khrushchev was in the embarrassing situation of having a rather unspectacular record of past achievements. Soviet agriculture, despite various crash programs and experimental schemes, was still a weak link in the Soviet economy, and the government was forced to use badly needed funds to buy grain from the West. Khrushchev's sizable commitments in foreign aid and loans to such places as Egypt and Cuba were not yielding the expected political rewards and represented a drain on the Soviet economy. Soviet control and influence in the East European countries were rapidly diminishing during Khrushchev's rule, though the responsibility for this trend was not entirely his. Finally, the Cuban missile crisis, for which Khrushchev was widely being blamed, had displayed to the whole world the hollowness of his militancy and bravado, and, in a sense, had formally established the unequal role of the Soviet *vis-à-vis* the American military.

(4) *Overestimating the power base*: One of Khrushchev's great errors lay in his cavalier treatment of the various bureaucracies, his indifference to the fact that their members were increasingly unhappy with his programs. He was undoubtedly under the impression that he could afford to incur their displeasure so long as the top leaders in these institutions were men whom he himself had placed in these positions of power and with whom he maintained close personal and professional relations. The Stalingrad Group in the military, and such handpicked lieutenants as Brezhnev and Shele-

[4] See "Das Echo auf Chruschtschows Sturz" (The Echo of Khrushchev's Fall), *Osteuropa*, No. 3, 1965, pp. 166-176, and No. 4, 1965, pp. 228-240.

[5] See Meissner, *Osteuropa*, No. 3, 1965, pp. 138-145, for data and inferences on Khrushchev's effort to concentrate power in himself, his son-in-law Adzhubei, and others.

pin in the Party and government, were among those whose primary loyalty could be assumed to be to their friend and benefactor rather than to any abstract idea of the good of country or Party. If Khrushchev suspected that they entertained any plans for enhancing their personal power, his actions did not show it.

(5) *A matter of style*: Khrushchev's manner and personality, as well as his style of ruling, were bound to irritate and offend many. His coarseness and "folksiness"; his personal vanity; his sudden departures from established norms and traditions; his "harebrained" schemes and his crash programs; and his simplistic pragmatism and vulgarized Marxism-Leninism—these might have been the prerogatives of a strong man whose power came directly from the revolutionary masses; they did not befit a ruler who owed his strength to the vagaries of collective leadership.[6]

To be sure, this list of Khrushchev's failings does not do justice to either the man or his policies. Khrushchev succeeded, in spite of bureaucratic inertia, in freeing the Soviet Union from its remote and unrealistic position in the "cold war." Like a latter-day Peter, he tried, and with some success, to liberalize and modernize, if not to "Westernize," his country. Not faulty intent and vision, therefore, but the wrong steps in their implementation, led to his downfall. By threatening simultaneously the interests of the various, mutually antagonistic, power groups in the Soviet state, he furnished these institutions with a common bond, which enabled them to unite, either by tacit understanding or by overt action, in the single effort to dispose of Khrushchev.

D · *THE FALL OF KHRUSHCHEV*

There is little evidence at present that would link the Soviet military directly with the forced dismissal of Khrushchev in October of 1964. But even a cursory look at events before and after the ouster suggests that the military may well have exerted some indirect or even direct pressure to have Khrushchev removed from office. A brief examination of the relevant developments in the two years preceding the event may help to clarify our picture of how it came

[6] This particular aspect of Khrushchev's personality and manner of ruling has come in for the most virulent criticism since his departure. As early as October 17, 1964, in announcing his dismissal, *Pravda* alluded to it: "The Party of Lenin is an enemy of subjectivism and inertia in communist construction. Wild planning, premature conclusions, hasty unrealistic decisions and actions, boasting and blather, overpreoccupation with administration, unwillingness to take account of the fruits of science and practical experience . . . are alien to it."

about. We shall not attempt to deal with the broader political implications of the Khrushchev affair; our main interest here will be to understand the military factor in it.

1. A Modus Vivendi *Between Party and Military*

The Cuban missile crisis of October 1962 was a crucial event both in the political life of nations and in the private lives of their people. The confrontation of the two superpowers suddenly conjured up for the multitudes across the globe the terrifying specter of nuclear war. As regards the relations between the two powers most immediately concerned, the impact and the reverberations of the crisis have not yet completely subsided.

The decision to risk his dangerous gamble in Cuba was undoubtedly not an easy one for Khrushchev. Most likely, he saw the Cuban venture as the necessary prerequisite to his initiating a détente with the West. Had it succeeded, he would have been able to take such an initiative from a position of approximate military parity rather than from one of military inferiority. Success in Cuba would also have allayed some anxieties in the Soviet military and in the Party.

Though many details of the Cuban crisis are still shrouded in secrecy, there is good reason to suspect that there was resistance within the Soviet High Command to Khrushchev's ready yielding to U.S. demands.[7] Later on, therefore, when Khrushchev obviously had no further need to seek strategic parity with the United States, one wondered in what manner the Party leader would deal with the military, which apparently had challenged him at the height of a dangerous crisis.

Surprisingly enough, few heads rolled. The reason that the military did not pay the high price one might have expected was most likely Khrushchev's need to get under way with his Grand Design. Not only did this commitment outweigh all other considerations, but it required, if not the active support of the various institutions of the state, at least the assurance that they would not interfere with the effort. Relations between Party and military after the Cuban missile crisis, therefore, seem to have been governed by some *modus vivendi*, which included a number of major concessions by the military. Thus, it would appear that the Party was to be the sole leader and spokesman on political, economic, and doctrinal affairs,

[7] See R. Kolkowicz, *Conflicts in Soviet Party-Military Relations: 1962-1963*, The RAND Corporation, RM-3760-PR, August 1963.

while the military ceased to question and criticize publicly, and agreed not to deviate from, the Party's guidelines on military and political affairs, and, furthermore, accepted intensive political controls and submitted to a larger measure of indoctrination. At the same time, the Party, for its part, undertook to accommodate itself to the military's demands for a more flexible military doctrine and strategy that would admit the need for mass armies and conventional weapons;[8] it left the military free to discuss and criticize those aspects of military science that had no political implications,[9] and gave assurances that there would be no purges or mass firings in the military.

The arrangement proved to be no bargain for the military. Chief of the General Staff Marshal Zakharov was dismissed, to be replaced with Marshal Biriuzov, a very loyal Khrushchev man. The head of the Main Political Administration, General Epishev, became a ubiquitous and irritating figure in the military, showering it with admonitions, exhortations, and warnings. Worst of all, however, Khrushchev's Grand Design spelled doom for many military interests and aspirations. It may be worth looking at the particular aspects of Khrushchev's policies that affected those interests most immediately, and noting the military's resistance to them.

2. *The Threat to the Military's Interests*

We have spoken earlier about the range of vital interests and objectives that large military institutions in industrialized societies have in common, regardless of their socio-political environment.[10] They may be summed up as (a) a consistently heavy investment in defense industry (in the Soviet Union this means primarily in heavy industry); (b) large standing forces and large military budgets;

[8] This concession to military demands for a less restrictive doctrine came out soon after the Cuban missile crisis in articles by Head of the MPA Epishev (see *Voprosy istorii KPSS*, No. 2, February 1963, p. 10). However, Khrushchev seems to have reverted to his original doctrinal views in 1963-1964.

[9] A well-known military spokesman for Khrushchev's strategic views, Major General S. Kozlov, performed a logical sleight of hand to rationalize the restrictions on the military's freedom of expression and dissent. By setting up a new typology of the elements that enter into Soviet military theory and assigning to them varying political and quasilegal status, he reduced military science to a very narrow functional discipline, which was open to varying opinions by the military, while removing most aspects of military theory and practice into the political field, where military disputation is restricted. See "Voennaia doktrina i voennaia nauka" (Military Doctrine and Military Science), *Kommunist Vooruzhennykh Sil*, No. 5, March 1964, pp. 9-16.

[10] See Chapter X, pp. 323-330.

(c) a certain level of international tension (maintained by depicting political opponents as aggressive and unpredictable) so as to justify the large budgets and armies. To these "external" needs must be added such "internal" interests as (d) demands for professional freedom and institutional autonomy, and (e) the cultivation of a noble image of the military in the eyes of society. How was each of these objectives affected by Khrushchev's Grand Design?

a. Investments in Defense Industry. When he first spoke about raising investments in light industry, consumer production, agriculture, and social services, Khrushchev admitted that such a policy entailed the need to reduce allocations to other sectors of society:

> It is necessary to state frankly: When the government reviews questions of the distribution of means by branches—where to direct how much of the resources—difficult puzzles often have to be solved. On the one hand, it would be desirable to build more enterprises that make products that satisfy man's requirements, to produce clothing, footwear . . . to invest more means in agriculture and to expand housing construction. We know that the people need this . . . to give more good things to the people—this is the basic goal of the Communist Party of the Soviet Union. . . . On the other hand, life dictates the need to spend enormous funds on maintaining our military power at the required level. This reduces, and cannot help but reduce, the people's possibilities of obtaining direct benefits.[11]

Having acknowledged the burdensome obligations of defense, Khrushchev then told the Party that defense allocations would be deemphasized in the coming year. Two months later, with his military-industrial audiences thus prepared for the unhappy decisions to come, Khrushchev boldly attacked the wastefulness of the defense industry and the secrecy with which it covered up this inefficient use of its resources:

> There are considerable reserves for increasing production even in the defense industry. But poor use is being made of these reserves because defense plant production is closed, and this means that any shortcomings and faults in the work of these enterprises are also closed to criticism.
>
> The defense industry is coping successfully with its tasks in creat-

[11] *Pravda*, February 28, 1963.

ing and producing modern armaments. *But these tasks could be solved more successfully with less expenditure.* [Italics added.][12]

b. Military Budgets and Size of Forces. Once the Nuclear Test Ban Treaty had been signed and a détente with the United States had begun, Khrushchev went on to the domestic phase of his program, a necessary part of which was the cutting down of the military forces and the military budget. There can be little doubt that here he encountered strong criticism of his policies both within the Party and from the military, which he refuted publicly under the guise of answering Western allegations:

> Some people in the West think that, if we develop chemistry, we will be neglecting defense. No, chemistry has its place, and so does defense.[13]

Significantly, however, he said in the same speech before the CC/CPSU:

> I want to inform the plenary session of the Central Committee that we are now considering the possibility of a further reduction in the size of our armed forces. . . . It is also planned to introduce . . . a proposal to reduce military expenditures somewhat in the budget for the next year, 1964.[14]

Details of these measures were furnished shortly afterward by Minister of Finance V. Garbuzov:

> The Soviet government considers it possible to provide for a reduction of 600,000,000 rubles in the outlays for the USSR Armed Forces in the budget for 1964. . . . Expenditures on defense are planned at 13,300,000,000 rubles, which constitutes 14.6 per cent of total budget expenditures, as against 16.1 per cent in 1963.[15]

Garbuzov gave no specific figures on the intended troop cuts, which Khrushchev was subsequently to use as bait in his dealings with the United States in an effort to make America reduce her troop commitments in Europe.[16]

[12] Khrushchev's speech to the Russian Industry Meeting on April 24, published in *Pravda*, April 26, 1963.

[13] Khrushchev's concluding remarks on December 13, 1963, at the Plenary Session of the CPSU Central Committee, *Pravda*, December 15, 1963.

[14] *Ibid.*

[15] *Pravda*, December 17, 1963.

[16] Khrushchev seems to have intended to kill two birds with one stone by making political capital out of an economically desirable move. Having decided

Although the official Soviet figures on military budgets may not be reliable, there is no disputing the psychological and functional impact that these projected reductions had on the Soviet military community.

c. International Tension. Like many military institutions, the Soviet establishment thrives in a milieu that contains elements of danger, tension, and uncertainty. Active mistrust between the Soviet Union and its major adversaries, a hesitancy about settling outstanding problems through negotiation, the existence of certain political "hot spots," and a militant foreign policy thus contribute to the Soviet Union's need for a strong military. Internally, moreover, these factors create apprehensions about external troubles. These, in turn, bring out a capacity for selflessness and self-sacrifice in the populace and its leaders. Given a national commitment to the vital interests of the state, this adds up to a nation in readiness, on the alert, and "outward-oriented."

By contrast, Khrushchev's foreign policy of détente, combined with an increasingly "bourgeois" domestic policy, had a strongly negative effect on the military. One aspect of it was the sense of frustration in the military community, whose members could hardly attack such goals as détente and peace, and could not publicly speak out against a program for raising the people's standard of living.

After the Cuban setback, therefore, the dynamic Party leader pursued with growing intensity his campaign for peace abroad and economic progress at home. Toward the West, he aimed pleas for coexistence and negotiatory approaches to unsolved problems ("The Soviet government will continue striving to convince the governments of the states that were formerly our allies of the necessity for putting an end to the vestiges of the second World War").[17] On the domestic scene, he shifted the emphasis from political ideology to economic pragmatism ("The highest calling of Soviet man, his primary duty, consists of creating, amassing wealth for the country, for a better life for society. . . .").[18]

In December 1963, he told the Central Committee that "we are

---

to reduce the standing forces, he was going to make those cuts among the Soviet forces stationed in East Germany, and to use this gesture as further proof of his desire for a détente and as a way of prompting Western troop reductions in Europe. (See Khrushchev's election speech, *Pravda*, February 28, 1963.)

[17] *Pravda*, February 28, 1963.

[18] *Ibid.*

opposed to the arms race, we do not want to pour oil on the flames"[19] and reassured his audience that "important steps have been taken toward relaxing international tension in recent months, and a foundation has been laid for solving international problems through negotiations."[20] He also distinguished between "the sane forces in the USA" and the "aggressive militarist circles" and "madmen," and appealed to the conscience of the sane element to seek peaceful solutions.[21] In January 1964, the Soviet government issued a "Memorandum on Measures Aimed at an Easing of the Arms Race and a Relaxation of International Tension," which advocated negotiations on a wide range of difficult problems.[22]

Satisfied that the détente was under way, Khrushchev turned to his domestic program, using the Party's propaganda machine to give it ideological legitimacy, while he drove the bureaucracies into high gear for the achievement of his socio-economic goals. Pulling out all the stops, he allowed Lenin[23] and Marx[24] to be used in support of "chemicalization" and the emphasis on consumer production. Khrushchev mocked those of his critics who "break their heads worrying" whether or not the decisions of the December 1963 plenum represented a deviation from the general line that accords primacy to heavy industry, a line "which the Soviet Union until now has consistently followed."[25] And he spoke out against "certain leaders of the economic councils of the economic regions and the Union republics," who, instead of "increasing the output and improving the quality of the consumer goods they produced, substantially reduced or completely halted the manufacture of these products."[26] Khrushchev's simple credo, which he was still preaching in his last months in office, was: "The chief thing in deciding the question of 'Who will win' is economic competition, economic competition. I repeat it for the third time—economic competition."[27]

[19] *Pravda*, December 15, 1963.

[20] *Ibid.* [21] *Ibid.* [22] *Pravda*, January 29, 1964.

[23] *Pravda*, February 21, 1964, published a "recently discovered" letter of Lenin, in which Lenin argued that the New Economic Policy had caused no radical changes in the social system of the Soviet Union and would not produce such changes as long as power lay in the hands of the workers.

[24] *Pravda*, February 24 and 25, 1964. In a lengthy article, the leading economist A. Arzumanian argued the ideological correctness of consumer production, citing Marx, among others, in support of his thesis.

[25] *Sel'skaia zhizn'*, February 15, 1964.

[26] Report to the Supreme Soviet on July 13, 1964, *Pravda*, July 14, 1964.

[27] Speech at World Youth Forum, *Pravda*, September 1964.

d. Internal Military Problems. While the external socio-political scene was changing in a direction that was very disadvantageous to the interests of the military establishment, the Party began to interfere more and more in the internal affairs of the military community. In May 1963, the MPA issued instructions requesting officers to intensify their ideological training, and chiding officers and even generals for avoiding indoctrination and remaining inert and aloof.[28] Political controls throughout the military were tightened in 1963 and 1964. The public statements of officers became bland and unspirited, an indication that the military was being forced to avoid controversial subjects and to fall in line with Khrushchev's drive toward peaceful coexistence.

3. *The Military Fights a Rear-Guard Action*

By 1964, the military apparently saw possibilities for defending its interests, and gave signs of a growing unrest. Marshal Malinovskii called together a meeting of Soviet writers "devoted to the military and patriotic theme in literature and the arts," and used this forum to make a number of points. Emphasizing that "the question of war and peace has great importance in our lives," he elaborated on the continuing danger of war and on the urgent need for military readiness and high morale, which, he found, were being undermined by a creeping pacifism in some sectors of Soviet society. Malinovskii also reiterated the military's view that conventional forces would play a vital role in a future war,[29] a view that Khrushchev did not share.

There is little doubt that Khrushchev sensed the wariness and tension in a military relegated to the background and forced to accept reductions and submit to a passive role. He seems to have taken some precautionary measures to consolidate his control at the top echelons of the defense establishment and thereby avert possible troubles from that quarter. Thus, three of his loyal followers from the Stalingrad Group, Ukrainians who had long been closely connected with him, were promoted to General of the Army in April 1964, a fact that could only strengthen Khrushchev's influence and authority in the military establishment.[30] And on the much-celebrated

[28] *Krasnaia zvezda*, May 24, 1963.

[29] *Ibid.*, February 9, 1964. Malinovskii stated that "each branch is important in its own place, but all of them have been called upon to solve in concert the common tasks and to display their strongest aspects."

[30] *Pravda*, April 25, 1964. The three were A. L. Getman, P. K. Koshevoi, and A. T. Stuchenko.

occasion of his seventieth birthday, in April 1964, Khrushchev prompted the military to give public and prominent emphasis to his role as "Supreme Commander of the Armed Forces."[31] He thus revealed both his continuing desire to subordinate the military to his authority and his concern over the military's possible intentions.

Developments in 1964 augured well for the military, for Khrushchev began to have trouble at home and abroad. Under the persistent sniping from Peking, and in the face of a growing U.S. commitment in Southeast Asia, Khrushchev embarked on personal diplomacy (including the use of members of his family) in an effort to settle the German problem; in the process, he deeply disturbed not only the East German regime, but the conservatives in Party and military at home.[32] Economically, Khrushchev's visions and slogans were mocked by the realities. Bad weather and poor management caused Soviet agriculture to fall short of production goals, and the Soviets had to buy gain abroad. Khrushchev's reorganization of the governmental and Party bureaucracies was causing much confusion, resentment, and waste. Yet Khrushchev hewed close to his old line. Speaking before the graduates of the military academies in July, he told them that the international situation had eased and that the main goals of society lay in the economic field. It would appear that Khrushchev had for once lost his keen awareness of danger. Or else he was choosing to ignore, blithely or fatalistically,

[31] *Krasnaia zvezda*, April 18, 1964. For some views on this development, see N. Galay, "The Significance of the Reestablishment of the Supreme Command of the Soviet Armed Forces," *Bulletin of the Institute for the Study of the USSR*, No. 7, July 1964.

[32] Speaking in East Germany on the occasion of East Germany's fifteenth anniversary, Brezhnev assured his uneasy audience that "only shortsighted politicians who are completely divorced from life, such as certain gentlemen on the banks of the Rhine, can console themselves with the hope of making some kind of decision or deal behind the back of the GDR to the detriment of its national interests and security. No, my worthies, this will not happen! You can never expect this from us!" (*Pravda*, October 7, 1964.) Compare Brezhnev's firm line with Khrushchev's rather ambiguous and less reassuring statements to a visiting Japanese delegation a month earlier: "You may ask: 'What about Germany?' I have already said more than once that the German question is not a national question but a socio-political question. . . . The ruling circles of the FRG want a single German state on capitalist foundations. The German Democratic Republic and its people want a united Germany that is socialist. Apparently, this situation will remain for a while, the question will be solved by history. . . . When will this happen? I don't know. Who will decide it? The Germans themselves must decide it." (*Pravda*, September 20, 1964.) There is little doubt that Khrushchev's personal diplomacy in 1964 *vis-à-vis* West Germany was a major factor in weakening his position in the Party.

the growing alienation of the several centers of power in the Soviet Union.[33]

The tempo of events quickened in August and September. The Sino-Soviet tensions threatened to lead to actual skirmishes, as troops were reported to be concentrating along the borders.[34] In August, the military journal *Voenno-istoricheskii zhurnal*, known for its boldness in questioning Khrushchev's historical claims and his military policies, was sharply admonished to mend its ways; characteristically, Khrushchev used a highly regarded military professional, Marshal Rotmistrov, to do the hatchet job.[35] In September, he again angered the military when, having only recently talked about some "terrible weapons" he had inspected,[36] he publicly denigrated the tank forces, questioning the utility and decrying the expenses of this vital branch of the armed forces:

> When I went out onto the training field and saw the tanks attacking and how the antitank artillery hit these tanks, I became ill. After all, we are spending a lot of money to build tanks. And if —God forbid, as they say—a war breaks out, these tanks will burn even before they reach the line indicated by the command.[37]

This was in direct conflict with the view that a number of leading military people were expressing in 1964.[38]

On October 2, as Khrushchev was departing for his *dacha* at Gagra, *Pravda* carried a summary of a speech he had made at a meeting of the Party presidium and the Council of Ministers. It was clear from the summary that Khrushchev intended to push vigorously ahead with his program:

> In drafting the long-range plan [for 1966-1970] . . . Comrade Khrushchev emphasized that it was essential to be guided by the fact that the main task of this plan is the further improvement of the living standard of the people.

[33] After Khrushchev's ouster, Gomulka acknowledged that the deposed leader had confided in him in the fall of 1963 that "he considered the possibility of giving up all of his offices." *Trybuna Ludu*, October 18, 1964.

[34] See *Pravda*, September 10, 1964 ("Mao Tse-tung also openly presented his expansionist ambitions and made unfounded territorial claims on neighboring socialist countries").

[35] *Kommunist*, No. 12, August 1964, pp. 123-127.

[36] *Pravda*, September 20, 1964.

[37] Speech by N. S. Khrushchev on September 19, 1964, at a reception in honor of participants in the World Youth Forum, *Pravda*, September 22, 1964.

[38] See Marshal Malinovskii's speech published in *Krasnaia zvezda*, February 9, 1964; and articles by Marshal Sokolovskii, *ibid.*, August 25, and Colonel General of the Armored Forces V. I. Zhadov, *ibid.*, September 13, 1964.

> . . . In drafting the long-range plan for development of our economy we must accord first place to the satisfaction of the growing material and spiritual requirements of man.

Khrushchev also was quoted as saying, "the defense of the country is at a suitable level," thus destroying whatever hopes the military may still have entertained for a significant share in Khrushchev's proposals for fiscal allocations.[39]

The relentlessness with which Khrushchev pursued his vision, his failure to adjust his objectives to the realities of power politics in an authoritarian state, his impatience with those who would not or could not keep up with his fast pace—these were the mistakes that hastened his defeat. It may be possible and useful, however, to examine his case for any institutional constants that entered into it and might similarly contribute to the downfall of a future dictator, thus delimiting the actions of any leader in the post-Stalin era who is subject to the principle of collective leadership. Our particular task here is to speculate on the extent to which the military's institutional objectives and perennial grievances may be vital factors in a change of Party leadership.

We do not intend to dwell on the presumable plot behind Khrushchev's ouster. To judge by the smoothness and precise timing of the event and the lack of visible repercussions, there can be little doubt that it was the outcome of some form of conspiracy. Very likely, such a plot would have included spokesmen of most, if not all, of the powerful institutions in the state—Party, governmental bureaucracy, security organs, and military—albeit in an uneasy coalition.[40] Upon his unscheduled return from Gagra, Khrushchev apparently was faced with a resolute Presidium and Central Committee and was compelled to submit to the will of the Party majority. As he disappeared into political and historical obscurity, he left behind him an ambitious socio-political program, toward which his successors were bound to feel somewhat ambivalent. No matter how much of the Grand Design they found useful and relevant to their own ends, they obviously had to introduce important changes, because the very reason for the anti-Khrushchev coalition was the fact that each of the disparate institutions in it was dissatisfied with some aspects of Khrushchev's program. How much, and what part, of his design will be preserved will depend on the outcome of the struggle for

[39] *Pravda*, October 2, 1964.

[40] For speculations on the event, see sources listed in footnote 3, above.

power that we can expect to take place among the several institutions.

E · AFTER THE FALL: THE MILITARY BEGINS TO REASSERT ITSELF

The ouster of Khrushchev was officially announced on October 16, 1964.[41] It gave rise to expectations of major changes in Soviet foreign and domestic policy. In the confusion surrounding and following the event, and in their ignorance of the true facts, journalists and Soviet experts speculated on such possibilities as a Sino-Soviet rapprochement; a return to stern conservatism in the Soviet Union accompanied by firmer Party control over society; and a reversal of foreign policy leading to renewed militancy. At the same time, as was to be expected, Khrushchev's successors were trying to convey to audiences abroad the impression that there had been no change in the Soviet Union's peaceful intentions. At home, they were announcing the continuation of the more popular aspects of Khrushchev's domestic program. They were clearly aware of the vulnerability of the machinery of government and Party during such a critical period of transition and leaderlessness, and were protecting their exposed position by stressing the continuity of programs and commitments and by closing ranks.

As the new regime became better entrenched, however, and as the problem of Khrushchev receded into history without serious repercussions, the anti-Khrushchev coalition became strained. Although there were no dramatic or even visible changes in the country's internal and external programs, some cracks appeared in the façade of unity and homogeneity. More important, the institutions that had joined in the common front against Khrushchev began once again to press their different interests and, through their spokesmen, express their separate views. The military establishment, in particular, having chafed under its reduced socio-political role in the last phase of Khrushchev's regime, now began to reassert itself. The form in which it did so followed a familiar pattern: It included presenting the international scene as one of tensions and dangers rather than of political relaxation and military détente; stressing the importance of giving high priority to defense needs in economic planning; demanding a larger measure of institutional and professional autonomy

[41] *Pravda*, October 16, 1964. The reasons for his resignation were given as "advanced age and deterioration in the state of his health."

along with freedom from strong Party controls; and trying to create a more positive social image of the military profession.

For a few months after Khrushchev's ouster, the military refrained from speaking out in these terms. It quietly tolerated the new regime's initial statements that domestic programs would remain essentially unchanged, of which these remarks of Brezhnev were an example:

> The national economy must develop harmoniously, it must serve the interests of achieving the highest productivity of social labor and a constant rise in the people's living standards. The development of heavy industry must be subordinated to the requirements of constant technical reequipment of the whole economy, the needs of defense, and also the interests of rapid advances in agriculture, light industry, and the food industry.[42]

Brezhnev also repeated the old Khrushchevian theme that "the Soviet people eagerly desire that the relaxation of international tension, a relaxation that has begun, may continue, and that solutions be found for the fundamental international problems. . . ."[43] After the turn of the year, however, this moderate line gave way to firmer and more aggressive expressions on the part of the military and some ranking members of the Party. The growing dissent of the hard-liners and the reiteration of the moderates' arguments may be viewed as a new dialogue of profound importance to Soviet politics.

As a preliminary to the main bout for resource allocations and a more prominent role for the military's interests in Soviet policies, the military settled an old score with deposed Party leader Khrushchev. Most fittingly, the man who led the attack on Khrushchev while insisting on the military's prerogatives in the formulation of defense policies was Marshal M. V. Zakharov, now once more the Chief of the General Staff, whom Khrushchev had dismissed from that same position after the Cuban missile crisis. The burden of Zakharov's attack was that "subjectivism is dangerous in any activity [but] it is particularly dangerous in military affairs which deal with the problems of the country's defense. . . ." He also asserted that military dilettantism in Party leaders can be very detrimental to doctrine and strategy, especially in the case of persons who claim "strategic farsightedness" but lack a "rudimentary knowledge of military strategy."

[42] Brezhnev's speech on the occasion of the 47th anniversary of the October Revolution, *Pravda*, November 7, 1964.

[43] *Ibid.*

Stressing the overriding importance of professional expertise in the affairs of modern military establishments, Zakharov attacked "leaders who are under the spell of old experiences, who turn this experience into a fetish and, by their authority and high position, obstruct the coming into being of everything that is new, progressive, and outstanding."[44]

Having thus dealt with the deposed leader, Zakharov injected himself several weeks later into the emerging debate on resource priorities by advocating continuous high investments in heavy industry and stressing industry's crucial role in the maintenance of a modern and well-equipped army. He sought to bolster his case by the well-tried technique of citing Lenin and arguing from historical analogy:

> The Soviet people have [in the past] not for a moment failed to carry out V. I. Lenin's legacy: always be on the alert, cherishing the defense capabilities of our country and our Red Army as the apple of our eye.

He also acknowledged that the "powerful heavy industry" had always been "the foundation of foundations of the whole socialist economy and of the firm defense capabilities of our country."[45]

Zakharov's public statements echoed tense private discussions in the Party and military on the subject of resource allocations, a debate that emerged into public light in the spring and summer of 1965.[46]

Briefly stated, the issues in this dispute were: What proportion of available resources should be allocated to defense? What sort of military posture should the Soviet Union seek in the next five to ten years? Can nuclear war still be viewed as a rational instrument of politics? And, how much institutional autonomy should the Party grant to the military establishment?

The growing disagreements on these issues seem to have divided the ruling Party elite. One group, including such people as N. V. Podgornyi, D. S. Polianskii, and A. P. Kirilenko, now favors giving continued priority to resource allocation for internal economic development. Another group, led by M. A. Suslov and A. N. Shelepin, is siding with the military's point of view in emphasizing the importance of further strengthening Soviet defenses.

[44] *Krasnaia zvezda*, February 4, 1965.

[45] *Ibid.*, February 23, 1965.

[46] For a more extensive treatment of the problem, see T. W. Wolfe, *The Soviet Military Scene: Institutional and Defense Policy Considerations*, The RAND Corporation, RM-4913-PR, July 1966.

Thus, in May 1965, Podgornyi stated that "priority development of heavy industry and strengthening of defense" were not realistic, since they would restrict consumer welfare and cause renewed material sacrifices by the population.[47] Several months later, Polianskii expressed similar views.[48] By contrast, Suslov asserted in June that, in view of the worsening international situation, the Soviet Union must prepare to meet the challenges of the capitalist world, which necessitate continuing "material sacrifices" by the Soviet people in order to ensure that the Soviet defense establishment is maintained at the "highest levels."[49] In the following month, Shelepin warned that "the Soviet Union has no right to ignore the constantly threatening danger of a new military attack by the predatory imperialists and that, accordingly, the Soviet government is devoting untiring attention to the further strengthening of the country's defense capabilities."[50]

The growing factional disagreements in the Party and the military undoubtedly placed Kosygin and Brezhnev in a difficult situation. Although presumably they appreciated the need to allocate a larger share of the resources to the non-defense sector, they could not disregard the mounting pressures from the military and their supporters in the Party. Eventually, the two leaders chose a middle road between the factions. In their public statements, they stressed the need to maintain the defense establishment at current levels and, if need be, to increase its allocations. In July 1965, Brezhnev said that it was necessary "to strengthen the country's defense capabilities in light of the international situation."[51] Kosygin stated that he would "be happy to devote to other branches of the national economy" parts of the "large expenditures" necessitated by the defense establishment, but that it would be unwise to do so because, "in the present situation, to economize on defense would be acting against the interests of the Soviet state and the Soviet people."[52] By the end of the summer, the hard-liners seemed largely to have prevailed. The new state budget for 1966, announced in December, far from providing for a cutback in allocations to the defense establishment, actually showed a 5 per cent increase in projected defense expenditures (13.4 billion rubles as compared with 12.8 for 1965).[53]

Along with its insistence on changes in resource allocations, the

[47] *Pravda*, May 22, 1965.
[48] *Ibid.*, November 7, 1965.
[49] *Ibid.*, June 5, 1965.
[50] *Ibid.*, July 25, 1965.
[51] *Moscow News*, July 10, 1965.
[52] *Pravda*, July 12, 1965.
[53] See R. Kolkowicz, *The Red "Hawks" on the Rationality of Nuclear War*, The RAND Corporation, RM-4899-PR, March 1966.

military also began to press the regime to abandon several of Khrushchev's strategic and doctrinal formulas and to adopt a more militant stance on the viability of nuclear deterrence, the Soviet Union's future force postures, and the "justness" and political rationality of nuclear war. Khrushchev, it will be recalled, had forced the military to accept a military doctrine built on the assumption that any future war would rapidly become a nuclear war, thus obviating the need for large conventional forces-in-being. Moreover, Khrushchev and his supporters in the military had argued that such a war would be an act of political and military madness.

A most striking example of the pressure by which the military sought to sway the government in favor of its views was displayed in an article published in a leading military organ in September 1965.[54] Its author, Colonel E. Rybkin, had gained some renown in the past with a very tough little book in which he asserted that war, no matter how destructive, "is never a useless firework, as it has been characterized" by some "bourgeois pacifists."[55] In the present article, Rybkin sharply attacked the moderate views of some prominent Soviet military strategists who in recent years had maintained that (a) nuclear deterrence was viable and effective, (b) Western leaders by and large were prudent and rational, (c) victory in a nuclear war was impossible, and (d) nuclear war would not be a "just" war. Rybkin concentrated his attack on Major General Talenskii, formerly a spokesman for Khrushchev's military views and now a mouthpiece of those moderate elements that rejected nuclear war as an instrument of policy. He likened Talenskii to the "reactionary-utopian pacifists" and "peace-yearners" in the West who maintained that "nuclear war has paralyzed itself" and that peaceful coexistence among nations was made possible by the "principle of nuclear parity." Denying the validity of Talenskii's contention that "war with the use of thermonuclear weapons has outlived itself as an instrument of politics, turning it into a weapon of national and social suicide,"[56] Rybkin maintained that nuclear deterrents could not reliably prevent war and that "an 'automatic' initiation of war has grown more likely, even under conditions of a minor international conflict," because of the complexity and automaticity of weapons and the "continuing adventuristic actions

[54] "O sushchnosti mirovoi raketno-iadernoi voiny" (On the Essence of World-wide Missile-Nuclear War), *Kommunist Vooruzhennykh Sil*, No. 17, September 1965, pp. 50-56.

[55] *Voina i politika* (War and Politics), Voenizdat, Moscow, 1959, pp. 25-26.

[56] General N. Talenskii, "Razdum'ia o minuvshei voine" (Reflecting on the Last War), *Mezhdunarodnaia zhizn'*, No. 5, May 1965, p. 23.

of the imperialists." He also deprecated the "talk about the 'self-negation' of war" of those who pointed to the terrible devastation that would result from a thermonuclear war: "An *a priori* rejection of the possibility of victory is harmful because it leads to moral disarmament, to a disbelief in victory, and to fatalism and passivity." He called for a "struggle against such views and moods." He also advocated a more realistic assessment of the comparative military standing of East and West, and proposed putting an end to the complacency and phrasemongering which, in the past, had rested "on the assumption that the objective advantages of our progressive system almost automatically assure us of speedy victory. There are hardly any notions more dangerous and ignorant, especially in military affairs."

Rybkin concluded with this admonition: "To maintain that victory in nuclear war is not possible at all would be not only untrue on theoretical grounds but dangerous from the political point of view as well." Having thus demolished the arguments of the military moderates, of the self-deluding Party hacks, and of those who put their faith in nuclear deterrence, Rybkin called for an intensive development of military technology, improvement of the military art, and the highest levels of military readiness.

Rybkin's attack on military and political moderation seems to have been only one of the opening shots in a new round of Party-military disagreements. Another recent example of the military's growing assertiveness *vis-à-vis* the Party is to be seen in a bold attempt to reopen the debate on the Red Army's heroic and brilliant contribution to victory in World War II. The military has strongly resented the support that Soviet historians have given to the Party's claims that it supplied the Red Army with a vast array of weapons, equipment, and logistics, more than sufficient to offset the losses incurred at the beginning of the German surprise attack. The military's position is that, despite Stalin's devastation of the officer corps in the purges of 1937 and the policies by which he hampered preparation against the German attack, and despite the Party's inept handling of the early stages of the war, the Red Army managed to repulse a superior enemy and thereby saved country and Party from destruction. Only during the brief period of relative military freedom under Zhukov, however, did the military's views on this issue appear in public. After Zhukov's ouster, in 1957, the military was forced once more to repeat the Party's formula.

Now, however, this touchy issue has again been raised in public, in a review of a book on the Party's role in the development of the Soviet armed forces.[57] The reviewers, Colonels Ia. Zimin and V. Morozov, summarily dismissed the usefulness of the book, accusing its authors of such faults as (a) falsifying statistics so as to give an impression of the Party's firm grasp of the war economy and able management of the war effort; (b) attempting to denigrate the military's initiative in dealing with the German invader; (c) slurring over the fact that Allied assistance was important to the Soviet war effort; and (d) overstating the Party's role in the development and guidance of the Red Army, which, the reviewers said, was not warranted by data cited.[58]

This strong challenge to the Party apparatus was taken up in a counterreview of the book, which laid the blame for the early disasters in the war firmly at the military's doorstep, and sharply rejected the notion that the Party had in any way mishandled the war effort. This review, which appeared in the Central Committee organ *Kommunist*,[59] stated that only individuals were guilty of mistakes or transgressions, thus restoring the formula of the Party's infallibility.

The military's bold provocation of the Party suggests some support from ranking members of the Party hierarchy who disapproved of the moderate policies of the present regime. Very likely, the resurgence of this debate was only a skirmish in a power struggle between the militant and the moderate factions in Soviet society, perhaps in anticipation of the Twenty-third Party Congress scheduled for March 1966. The military, whose actions often constitute a weathervane of Soviet political developments, appear to have sensed the division within the Party and to have tried to benefit by openly throwing in their lot with the militant side.

[57] *KPSS i stroitel'stvo Sovetskikh Vooruzhennykh Sil* (The CPSU and the Development of the Soviet Armed Forces), ed. Major General (also Professor) N. M. Kiriaev, Voenizdat, Moscow, 1965.

[58] It is noteworthy that their review appeared in *Voenno-istoricheskii zhurnal* (No. 8, August 1965), the traditional forum of entrenched military interests, whose pages have often been used for protecting military claims and interests against the encroachments of the Party.

[59] No. 14, September 1965, pp. 117-121.

Part Three

Dilemma of a Totalitarian Elite

IX · The New Technology and the Rise of the Technocrat: Their Effect on Party-Military Relations

A · THE TECHNICAL EXPERT IN THE OFFICER CORPS: A CONFLICT BETWEEN TRADITIONALISM AND MODERNITY

"The history of the modern military establishment," writes Morris Janowitz, "can be described as a struggle between heroic leaders, who embody traditionalism and glory, and military 'managers.' "[1] This conflict between idealism and practical self-interest also affects the Soviet military and its relations with the Party.

In recent years, Soviet military leaders have publicly stressed the growing technical and scientific requirements of military life, echoing Vauban's ancient prescription on the importance of the officer's acquiring a knowledge of the sciences: "I know hardly a profession in which it is more necessary. For the soldier who only knows his sword cannot achieve great things."[2] Marshal Malinovskii has told his officers that "without high levels of technical training, without knowing the basics of physics and mathematics, it is impossible to conduct modern military operations expertly."[3] Still more recently, the Soviet Chief of the General Staff said, in a lecture to the officer corps, that such important problems as "correlation of the types of armed forces . . . the determination of their place and role in the military potential of the country, and their role and place in a thermonuclear war [could] only be solved correctly on a scientific basis."[4] What impact has the massive influx of modern weapons, equipment, and techniques had on the Soviet military community? What changes have these developments brought about in the mili-

[1] *The Professional Soldier*, The Free Press, Glencoe, Ill., 1960, p. 21. For relevant problems pertaining to technological innovation and its impact on various military establishments, see Samuel P. Huntington, "The New Military Politics," pp. 13-16, and Philip Abrams, "Democracy, Technology, and the Retired British Officer," pp. 150-189, in Samuel P. Huntington (ed.), *Changing Patterns of Military Politics*, The Free Press of Glencoe, Inc., New York, 1962. See also Emil Obermann, *Soldaten, Bürger, Militaristen*, J. G. Cotta'sche Buchhandlung Nachf., Stuttgart, 1958, pp. 203-213.

[2] Sebastian le Prestre, Seigneur de Vauban, cited in Werner Hahlweg (ed.), *Klassiker der Kriegskunst* (Classics of Military Art), Wehr und Wissen Verlagsgesellschaft mbH, Darmstadt, 1960, p. 161.

[3] *Krasnaia zvezda*, October 25, 1962.

[4] *Ibid.*, February 4, 1965.

tary power structure and in the military's relations with the Party apparatus?

In the armed forces of the Soviet Union, as in those of many other countries, the elite, the Establishment, has traditionally come from the military academies. The graduates of the academies who assume commands enter an officer community dedicated to camaraderie, mutual support, and the other traditional military virtues.[5] The ideal Soviet officer combines bravery, manliness, and leadership skills with staff and command abilities. He is more likely to earn the respect of his men by courage and personally inspired authority than by clever staff work or technical expertise. In the past, technical expertise, though acknowledged as desirable in an officer, did not rate very high among his qualities.[6] Since World War II, however, and particularly since the launching of Sputnik, with the extensive modernization of the Soviet armed forces, large numbers of engineers and technicians have entered the officer ranks. They are to be found predominantly in such elite bodies as the air defense forces, the strategic missile forces, and the submarine navy. This influx of well-trained technical officers into the military community is changing the image of the military commander and is threatening the traditional officers' dominant positions and careers. Furthermore, the technical officers' resistance to becoming involved in Party-political activities makes for strained relations with the political control functionaries in the military. Thus, the rise of the technocrats in the military has introduced new and potentially far-reaching problems into the relationship between Party and military.

The French military writer F. O. Miksche recently observed that "Soldier-technicians are regarded less as comrades than as 'colleagues,' not constituting a unit, but a kind of community effort."[7] Miksche belittles the importance of the new *homo technicus* in

[5] As one Soviet officer has expressed it, "In an institution where each man is a brother to his fellow-man even an unknown soldier is best friend to each of us." *Krasnaia zvezda*, October 13, 1962.

[6] For an authoritative and trenchant view of various images of the Soviet officer, see the following statement by Marshal Konev, cited by Milovan Djilas in his *Conversations with Stalin* (Harcourt, Brace and Company, New York, 1962, p. 82): "Voroshilov is a man of inexhaustible courage. But—he was incapable of understanding modern warfare. . . . Budennyi never knew much and he never studied anything. He showed himself to be completely incompetent and permitted awful mistakes to be made. Shaposhnikov was and remains a technical staff officer." Konev is implying that courage, while admirable, is not sufficient, but that technical expertise alone is also a narrow virtue.

[7] *Military Review*, August 1962, p. 76.

modern military establishments and accuses him of "complex primitivism."[8] His views are not isolated; they reflect the turbulence in some military establishments that is caused by the massive influx of modern weapon systems and the accompanying growth in the number and influence of technicians in uniform.

The Soviet military establishment has been undergoing such an internal upheaval as a result of the need for modernization. While the traditionalists are fighting a rear-guard battle, the modernizers are pressing on, presumably with the support of the highest Party leaders, weeding out the technically backward and inept, and replacing them with younger and better-trained technicians. The extent and the ruthlessness of this purge among the Soviet officer corps in the past few years were such that Marshal Malinovskii felt impelled to rebuke the cadre organs:

> Cadre organs are trying to get rid of experienced technicians only because they are 35 years old, and supposedly have sat around too long in their positions and therefore have no prospect of advancement, etc. . . . Not even regimental commanders are assured of remaining in their position. If they do not have an academic education, then the cadre personnel do not even want to talk to them.[9]

Malinovskii then tried to counter the argument that older, less useful officers were blocking the way for the younger and more capable officers:

> [The retention of older officers] . . . does not mean that the road is blocked to the advancement of youth. One could not block the way to advancement of capable, diligent young commanders even if one wanted to: they "appoint themselves" to higher positions even if they do not have a higher military education.[10]

The growing emphasis on the role and importance of the technocrat in uniform is reflected in the statements of ranking military leaders. Marshal Biriuzov, the former Chief of the General Staff, has stressed the changed relationship between the professional and the technical officer:

[8] Miksche criticizes the technician for not seeming "to grasp the fact that the technical means and methods are not an end in themselves, but a means to an end." *Ibid.*

[9] Cited in *K novomu pod"emu partiino-politicheskoi raboty v Sovetskoi Armii i Flote* (Toward a New Intensification of Party-Political Work in the Soviet Army and Navy), ed. Major General Z. S. Osipov, Voenizdat, Moscow, 1960, p. 12.

[10] *Ibid.*, p. 13.

> In our army the number of engineer-technical cadres constantly grows. In the missile forces, for example, there are at the present time 72 engineers and technicians to every hundred officers. In the air defense forces [PVO] the number of engineers and technicians exceeds the number of officers who have graduated from officer schools and [higher military] academies. These facts . . . bear witness that the engineer-technical cadres in the army and navy represent a powerful force.[11]

> It can be said without exaggeration that to such officer-specialists belongs the future of our armed forces.[12]

Warning the professional military officers not to discriminate against "technical" officers, Biriuzov went on to say that "such 'classification' was inherited by us from those distant times when one could count the engineers in the military on the fingers of one hand."[13] He also stressed that "the development of our armed forces is at present at such a level that to the engineers and technicians belongs a very important role in solving literally all tasks facing our forces."[14]

Biriuzov's predecessor and successor, Marshal Zakharov, pointed out that, while "in past wars the gaps in a commander's military and technical knowledge were sometimes filled in by his native intuition . . . it is very risky to rely on intuition in nuclear warfare under conditions of rapid and highly mobile military operations."[15]

B · THE POLITICAL NEUTRALITY OF THE MILITARY TECHNOCRAT

One of the most remarkable aspects of the military technocrats' position in the Soviet armed forces is their consistent and vehement refusal to become involved in the normal political-educational activities in their units. The Soviet press frequently quotes technical officers as expressing such views as: "I am a specialist. My job is to ensure good conditions and combat readiness of the equipment; the education of soldiers and sergeants—that is the job of commanders and political workers."[16] Or: "That's not our job. Education—that's the political worker's job. We are engineers. Our element is tech-

[11] Cited in *Voennyi inzhener—aktivnyi vospitatel'* (The Military Engineer—An Active Educator), Voenizdat, Moscow, 1962, p. 5.

[12] *Ibid.*, p. 7. [13] *Ibid.*, p. 17. [14] *Ibid.*, p. 5.

[15] *Krasnaia zvezda*, October 12, 1962.

[16] *Ibid.*, March 14, 1960.

nology."[17] This reluctance, especially of the younger technical officers, to participate in Party work has generated ill-feeling among the political officers and also some of the professional officers. The latter resent the fact that they themselves must submit to large doses of indoctrination and political work, while the *tekhnary*, who enjoy greater career security and preferential treatment, are allowed to remain aloof from such time-wasting activities.[18]

The technical officers' propensity for "crawling into their technical shell"[19] has been strongly criticized by a number of leading military and political personnel, who oppose the notion that a "military engineer is a 'pure' specialist who has little time left, after attending to complex systems of contemporary weapons, to carry out other duties."[20] Marshal Biriuzov is among those who have commented on this problem:

> It is not a secret that among our military engineers, especially among the young, one finds a desire to be appointed to positions where their duties would be concentrated on servicing military equipment. Having obtained such a position they feel themselves "free" of any involvement in the education of personnel.[21]

Yet, despite the criticism leveled at them in public, the military technocrats are still resisting the various attempts to engage them more fully in political work, and the issue continues to be debated. Political functionaries such as General Epishev, the head of MPA, may state categorically that a Soviet officer "cannot be a narrow military specialist, but [must be] an organizer and expert in the teaching and upbringing of subordinates,"[22] but other military leaders stress the importance of not burdening the technical officers with too much

[17] Cited by Colonel General N. Antonov in *Kommunist Vooruzhennykh Sil*, No. 2, January 1961, p. 34.

[18] The reviewer of *Chelovek i tekhnika v sovremennoi voine* (Man and Equipment in Modern Warfare), by Colonel V. K. Abramov, finds it irritating that in the entire book the author does not once talk about "the influence of the ideological activities of the Party on the thought and feelings of the Soviet people about the Party-political work in the soldier masses." *Kommunist Vooruzhennykh Sil*, No. 11, June 1961, p. 89.

[19] General of the Army I. Pliev, *Kommunist Vooruzhennykh Sil*, No. 19, October 1962, p. 27.

[20] *Kommunist Vooruzhennykh Sil*, No. 1, January 1962, p. 72.

[21] *Krasnaia zvezda*, May 21, 1961.

[22] A. Epishev, "Na strazhe mirovogo truda sovetskogo naroda" (Guarding the Peaceful Work of the Soviet People), *Politicheskoe samoobrazovanie*, No. 1, January 1963, p. 21.

political-indoctrinational work. Early in 1963, for example, the First Deputy Commander of the Soviet Strategic Missile Forces, Colonel General V. Tolubko, criticized certain practices which overtax officers with political duties at the expense of their professional training and activity.[23]

Malinovskii has made the point that, while political involvement is necessary for officers, it is no more important than that political officers should have technical expertise and up-to-date technical training: [Thorough familiarization with science and technology] . . . applies equally to political workers. If they are not sufficiently familiar with modern military equipment, they will not be able expertly to conduct political-educational work among the personnel."[24] In the same vein, *Krasnaia zvezda* has on several occasions attacked the preferential treatment accorded to political indoctrination and political instructors and has criticized the fact that specialized education and training are being slighted.[25] And, finally, Marshal Biriuzov, while asserting the need for some political participation by technical officers, has wondered whether it "is advisable to burden a specialist who has higher training with such tasks as belong to the sphere of duties of sergeant personnel."[26]

Whatever may be the reluctance of the professional officers to accept technical innovation and the elevation of the technical officers, the demands of modern warfare have made the technocrats in uniform indispensable to the viability of the Soviet armed forces. Since the political leadership and many of the military leaders favor a strategic doctrine that assigns a crucial role to the strategic forces, which are based heavily on modern technology and must be kept at a high level of readiness, the men in charge of such weapons and equipment inevitably have become the new elite among the military.[27] The technical officers are quite aware of the importance of their role, and expressions of their self-assurance range from simple self-congratulatory observations to dire forecasts of the consequences of not heeding the technocrat:

[23] "Officers sometimes complain that they never have the opportunity to prepare adequately for their duties. In the units where such difficulties occur, it is necessary in the coming year to unburden the officer of excessive loads and do away with the unnecessary waste of time." *Krasnaia zvezda,* January 8, 1963.

[24] *Ibid.*, October 25, 1962.

[25] *Ibid.*, October 13, 1962; January 13, 1963; February 3, 1963; and March 20, 1963.

[26] *Ibid.*, May 21, 1961.

[27] See R. Kolkowicz, *The Impact of Technology on the Soviet Military: A Challenge to Traditional Military Professionalism*, The RAND Corporation, RM-4198-PR, August 1964.

> The time is coming when the technician and engineer will assume one of the central places in war. . . . If military leaders fail to understand the changes that have taken place in military technology and continue to adhere to obsolete methods, [they will bring about] disasters and grave losses on the battlefield.[28]

Military engineers, as one officer points out, perform functions that require remarkable expertise and have a high economic value, despite the fact that "the engineer has until recently often been looked upon as a narrow specialist, some sort of highly qualified 'technocrat.'"[29] A naval captain pointedly asks why seven hours a week of the officer's time are allotted for political education and only one hour-and-a-half for professional-technical training, and why military personnel who are studying political education are given two or three days to prepare for classes while those taking professional training are permitted only one day.[30]

The technical officers' open challenge of some fundamental Party practices in the military appears the more remarkable when it occurs in the face of an intimidation campaign by the political organs.[31] Their relative freedom to assert themselves arises from an important advantage they have over professional officers with lower skills in being able to command lucrative and prestigious civilian positions in the event of their dismissal from military service.[32] Moreover, because

[28] Candidate of Philosophical Sciences Lieutenant Colonel A. O. Baranov, *Voennaia tekhnika i moral'no-boevye kachestva voina* (Military Technology and the Combat Morale of the Soldier), Voenizdat, Moscow, 1961, pp. 5-7.

[29] Engineer-Captain D. Kovalerchuk, in *Krasnaia zvezda*, February 3, 1963.

[30] Naval Captain 3rd class V. Sherel, in *ibid.* Among those of the technical officer personnel who have publicly criticized the prevailing restrictive Party practices in the military are the following: Colonel General A. Podol'skii, deputy commander of the Soviet Union's Air Defense Forces (PVO), who strongly urged that all the time necessary be given to personnel desiring to improve their technical expertise (*Krasnaia zvezda*, January 4, 1963); Major General D. Smilevets of the Engineering-Technical Services, who took issue with the excessive use of the military's time for subjects not geared to technical specialization (i.e., for political indoctrination), and asked: "Is it not strange that, despite the fact that military technology is developing very rapidly, military institutes cannot increase the number of hours needed for the teaching of specialized and technical subjects?" (*ibid.*, October 13, 1962); and Lieutenant Colonel Rybkin, who criticized the political organs for making allowances for officers studying political subjects ("they gave them three full days a month and three evenings a week during which they were freed from any service duties"), while officers who tried to improve their technical-professional standards through correspondence courses "have not been given a single day for doing the homework assigned by the academy" (*ibid.*, October 4, 1962).

[31] See R. Kolkowicz, *Conflicts in Soviet Party-Military Relations: 1962-1963*, The RAND Corporation, RM-3760-PR, August 1963.

[32] See Kolkowicz, *The Impact of Technology.*

their skills are urgently needed, the technical officers enjoy some preferential treatment when it comes to participating in the drab political-educational activities. The leverage of the technical officers *vis-à-vis* the political organs inevitably leads to friction between them.

C · THE CONTROVERSY OVER THE ROLE OF THE TECHNICAL OFFICER

"As long as there are dangerous and irksome tasks to be done, an engineering philosophy cannot suffice as the organizational basis of the armed forces. . . . Heroism is an essential part of the calculations of even the most rational and self-critical military thinkers."[33] Janowitz's perceptive statement underscores an important question that is disturbing many well-ordered military communities: how to preserve a military ethos, with the ideals of heroism, bravery, dedication to duty, and personal sacrifice, and protect the authority of the commander in the age of computerized war techniques, cybernetics, and managerial procedures.[34]

The conflicts and tensions between traditionally oriented professional officers and the more progressive and pragmatic technical officers have deeply disturbed the Soviet military,[35] and there are innumerable instances of the running battle between the traditionalists and the innovators. Thus, a spokesman of the latter, Lieutenant General V. Petukhov, in an article entitled "Overcoming 'Traditional' One-sidedness,"[36] criticizes the practice of singling out only a soldier's

[33] Janowitz, *The Professional Soldier*, p. 35.

[34] Khrushchev was also sensitive to this problem. During his last reception in the Kremlin for the graduates of the military academies, he stressed that "even with automation, the individual plays the decisive role" and rejected the distorted image of the modern officer as an impersonal technician: "Today in our country an officer is frequently conceived of as a man in a white coat who sits at a control panel and pushes buttons. . . . But you military men well know what modern military operations will be like." *Pravda*, July 9, 1964.

[35] In 1961 the military press carried a running discussion, initiated by Engineer-Colonel Beloborodov in *Krasnaia zvezda*, January 27, 1961, which focused on the subject of similar, standardized service insignia for all officers, technical as well as professional. In many letters to the editor and other responses, the engineer officers overwhelmingly expressed the desire to be treated as full-fledged officers and left no doubt that they wished to be placed in commanding positions. Marshal Biriuzov entered the discussion on May 19, 1961, and stressed the growing role of the technical officers in the Soviet army. The new emphasis on the technical officers' role was underlined in the customary reception for graduates of military academies in the Kremlin, where Engineer-Colonel Samusenko was elected to speak in the name of all graduates. See *Krasnaia zvezda*, March 3, April 19, May 19, and July 9, 1961.

[36] *Ibid.*, March 23, 1964.

heroic deeds and military virtues when citing his achievements: "Frequently, on hearing stories of such heroics, a soldier thinks to himself, 'I would surely like to be such a brave and courageous man, but to study technology—that's very dull.'" Petukhov complains that these accounts will tell you that the hero "did not retreat even one step before the enemy" but usually fail to mention his professional or technical skill. And he reminds his readers that "it is not only bravery that counts but also the mastering of the equipment and skill of combat."

The gauntlet of the military professionals has been taken up by Major General Makeev,[37] the authoritative editor-in-chief of *Krasnaia zvezda.* In a rather striking departure from communist orthodoxy, Makeev stresses the historical continuity of military virtues: "The concept of military honor has existed since time immemorial; it is as old as armies. . . . Even in the old Russian army there were good traditions—bravery, selfless dedication, and military skill were revered." He goes on to distinguish between the hard lot of the officer, that is to say, of the military professional, and that of the ordinary soldier:

> There is a saying: the soldier is at war even in peacetime. But the soldier serves his prescribed time and departs into the reserves. The officer, however, is also a soldier, but he is at war for a lifetime. How many inconveniences, how many trials! But the officer withstands all, overcomes all. He does not lose courage. He holds high his honor, the honor of the officer and citizen.

Makeev also argues with those who hold that the career of the officer has little social utility. The officer's contribution, he says, is "no less necessary to the fatherland than that of the *kolkhoznik*, agronomist, engineer, teacher, or doctor." And he criticizes the unconcerned citizen (*obyvatel'*) for not caring that "while he sleeps, thousands of officers carry on their difficult duties."

Other traditionalists among the officers continue to plead their own cause, stressing the unfortunate lot of the commander and the dangers of bookishness (*shkoliarstvo*) in the technocrats. A Colonel of the Guards, G. Iashkin, gives an impassioned description of the hardships and the virtues of commanders "who spend sleepless, frightening nights in the extreme heat of summer, during the rain and frost of autumn, [and] who work in a dedicated manner with every single soldier and sergeant. . . ." He then continues with this unmistakable attack on the political officers:

[37] *Izvestiia*, February 12, 1963.

> And at times it may become necessary to enter the battle alongside those who feel that, since such is the lot of the officer, there is no need to be especially concerned about his welfare and essential needs, and about the conditions of his work.[38]

Chief Marshal of Armor P. A. Rotmistrov warns that

> Disproportionate stress on theoretical training may lead to the separation of officers from life, may transform them into scholastics (*skholasty*) who do not understand life at all but are capable only of citing the book. Such officers may become dogmatic and superficial.[39]

Relations between the traditionalists and the technocrats have been exacerbated by a development which is also causing concern in the Party and in the High Command: the growing antimilitarism of Soviet society, in particular among Soviet youth. *Krasnaia zvezda* reflected the increasing concern over this attitude when it initiated a debate in its pages on the merits and demerits of military service as a career. The discussion revealed some of the younger generation's deep disenchantment with the military, as expressed, for example, in this withering remark to a young man who was contemplating a military career: "Don't be a fool, Igor; only failures put on a gray overcoat voluntarily, and you are a bright boy."[40]

In a letter to the old war-horse Marshal Budennyi, several students of military academies broached the delicate subject of the nobility of the military profession:

> There can be no beauty [of profession] where, they say, people are training to kill others. . . . They say that there have been and are bourgeois philosophers and generals who talk of the beauty of war. . . . They say that while the officer profession is necessary at present, it is uninteresting and unromantic, and that any civilian profession is better than the military.[41]

[38] *Krasnaia zvezda*, November 10, 1963.

[39] *Ibid.*, January 30, 1963.

[40] *Ibid.*, August 26, 1962.

[41] *Ibid.*, January 13, 1963. On the issue of the conditions of military service as a profession, *Krasnaia zvezda* also carried some opinions which contradicted the official line. Among them was the following, published on December 26, 1962: "I do not believe that comrade Matukhin [an advocate of the beauty of the military profession] experiences happiness from his service. It seems to me that, if you gave him suitable conditions and a good income, he would have thrown over this 'beautiful' life and would have taken off his 'beautiful' uniform. . . . Where can there be beauty? In the daily routine where everything is figured out

The extent of antimilitary and pacifist trends in Soviet society was reflected in several other public statements, including this rebuke by Marshal Malinovskii to Soviet writers and artists:

> In recent times, mistaken tendencies in representing the last war have appeared. Motifs of pacifism and the abstract rejection of war have made themselves felt in certain works of literature and painting, and in the movies.[42]

General Epishev similarly condemned artists and writers for "a note of pacifism" which had appeared in their works and which "belittled the heroic spirit of military events." He expressed his "great concern with the ideological and artistic imperfection of certain works dealing with military life" and urged writers to produce works that would "teach youth to be brave and courageous, steadfast and firm, in the struggle with the enemies."[43]

There has been evidence also of a growing disenchantment among both Party and military leaders with the excessive stress on technical expertise at the expense of traditional "general military skills." This was reflected in a statement by the former Chief of the General Staff, Marshal Biriuzov, which served to close a public debate on the subject:

> The problems [of the debate] concern the relationship between the commander's technical abilities and his general military skills. The opinions on these are divided. Some comrades maintain that the commander must possess such a level of knowledge as will enable him to be thoroughly familiar with all types of equipment. Others maintain that the officer must primarily concern himself with general military training. . . .

Biriuzov then stated as his own view that the traditional functions of the commander are as vital today as ever, and that "sheer technicianship, separated from practical affairs, inevitably leads to narrow-mindedness."[44]

Although the technical officers are growing in numbers and authority, and although they are critical of the old-fashioned ways of the traditionalists among the professional officers, they do not, by

---

to the last minute? Or in the days which all seem alike? To see in them the beauty of life means to be a limited person."

[42] *Ibid.*, February 9, 1964.

[43] *Kommunist*, No. 5, 1964, p. 73, and *Krasnaia zvezda*, February 9, 1964.

[44] *Krasnaia zvezda*, April 28, 1964.

and large, attempt to impose a new set of values on the latter beyond their insistence on up-to-date, functional principles and methods. On the contrary, the technocrats would like to be accepted by the traditionalists in the officer corps; they want to be viewed as commanders, and they, too, seek rapport with their men.[45] In other words, the conflicts in the officer community are caused not so much by the technocrats' violation or rejection of the old military virtues as by the traditionalists' resentment at having to share authority with the intruders and at the realization that they themselves may have become expendable. If the technocrats' pragmatism were to be reconciled with the older commanders' military ethos, this could greatly strengthen the corporate autonomy of the officer corps.

D · TRENDS AND OUTLOOK

The initial impact of a changing technology and the modernization of the Soviet armed forces was such as to divide and debilitate the officer corps. Large numbers of traditional commanders were replaced by technical officers,[46] traditional military values came to count for less than technical expertise, and established strategic views yielded to the overriding emphasis of the "progressives" on strategic missile-nuclear weapons and forces[47] (a development that caused political controls in these forces to be relaxed, at the same time that they were tightened in the conventional forces).[48]

Gradually, however, the shock effect of these reforms on the military has been subsiding, and countertrends are discernible that are likely to have a unifying effect. These new and long-range developments are (a) the growing acceptance by both Party and military leaders of a war strategy that places renewed emphasis on traditional methods of warfare and the need for conventional forces; (b) the humbler attitude of technical officers toward the traditional commanders, whose values and virtues they have come to respect and

[45] See footnote 35, above.

[46] Lieutenant General Kalashnik, deputy head of the MPA, stated that "since 1945 the number of engineer technicians in the armed forces has grown three times." *Kommunist Vooruzhennykh Sil,* No. 22, November 1962, p. 15. It should be noted that, while the absolute increase of technicians was indeed threefold, the relative increase was from ten- to fifteen-fold, because in 1962, when Kalashnik was writing, the Red Army was only about one-quarter the size it had been in 1945.

[47] See Kolkowicz, *Conflicts in Soviet Party-Military Relations.*

[48] See R. Kolkowicz, *The Use of Soviet Military Labor in the Civilian Economy: A Study of Military "Shefstvo,"* The RAND Corporation, RM-3360-PR, November 1962.

emulate; (c) the bond of common opposition by all officers to the excessive control functions exercised by the political organs; and (d) the concern over pacifist trends in Soviet society which has prompted the Party to build up the military profession, and to do so partly by making concessions to the officers' demands for more authority and status.

The influence of the technocrats in the Soviet officer corps will continue to rise—though the tension between them and the traditionalists will lessen—partly because of the technical and scientific needs of the armed forces and partly because the Party elite increasingly favors the pragmatic approach, as shown in its use of managerial and administrative techniques. It is indeed remarkable, for instance, to note, in the great outpouring of official statements in the wake of Khrushchev's ouster, the almost unanimous condemnation of the deposed leader for his nonscientific and traditionally intuitive way of making and carrying out decisions, and the great emphasis on the need for scientific discipline, objectivity, and progressive methods. To quote Chief of the General Staff M. V. Zakharov:

> A revolution has occurred in military affairs which is unheard-of both in extent and in consequences, a revolution which has produced a truly profound change in the organization, training, and education of the armed forces and in the views, manners, and forms of armed struggle. . . . With the emerging of rocket-nuclear arms, cybernetics, electronics, and computer equipment, any subjective approach to military problems, harebrained plans, and superficiality can be very expensive and can cause irreparable damage. Only the thorough scientific foundation of decisions and actions . . . will guarantee the successful fulfillment of the tasks. . . .[49]

Similar views have more recently been expressed by A. N. Shelepin and L. I. Brezhnev, powerful members of the ruling elite.[50]

[49] *Krasnaia zvezda*, February 4, 1965.
[50] *Ibid.*, July 25, 1965, and July 4, 1965, respectively.

X · Assessing the Military's Role in Soviet Politics

> The Army embodies in itself its morality, its law and its mystique; and this is not the morale nor the mystique of the nation.
> R. Girardet, quoted in Michael Howard (ed.), *Soldiers and Governments*, London, 1957.

A · CRITERIA FOR GAUGING THE POLITICAL ROLE OF THE MILITARY

The Communist Party, as has been shown, does not recognize the existence in the Soviet state of any institutional values, any professional interest, and any loyalties other than those relating to the Party. Except in the rare moments of internal power crisis, it has been able effectively to prevent spokesmen of the military from revealing the military establishment to be a separate institution with distinct needs, objectives, and characteristics.

The earlier chapters of this study have presented the relationship between Party and military as essentially a history of conflicts of interest, during which the military, far from becoming an integral part of the Party or of a homogeneous society, has been increasingly intent on asserting its ideas and advancing its own cause. Persuasive though this historical evidence may seem, however, it is desirable to test by other means the proposition that the military does possess a distinct personality and seeks to pursue unique objectives in Soviet affairs.

Probably the most helpful criterion in the assessment of the military's political role is the degree of political integration to which the Soviet military establishment submits at the hands of the Party apparatus. Its usefulness derives from the fact that the Party's ideal is the total integration and politicization of the military institution. The degree to which reality falls short of this absolute thus becomes indicative of the military's success in attaining professional freedom, institutional autonomy, and socio-political influence. For we may assume that the Soviet military bureaucracy is subject to the generic endeavor of military establishments in other societies to assume a social and political role in the state, whereas, as we know, it is characteristic of autocratic, one-party regimes to aim at subordinating all institutions to the ruling elite. If we can measure the degree to which the two institutions achieve their mutually exclusive goals, we shall be able to assess their relative strength and to test the conclusions derived from the historical evidence of the military's changing role.

In this attempt at a systematic exploration of the Soviet military's position, that is to say, of the way in which it has succeeded in avoiding political integration, we shall apply several criteria that may be regarded as universal, inasmuch as both communist and non-communist writers have found them useful in testing the political awareness and institutional autonomy of military establishments. To be sure, most Communists would not acknowledge their universality; they would doubtless disagree with Westerners, who maintain that institutions develop and maintain unique characteristics and objectives regardless of their socio-political environment, and would argue that any institution emerging in a communist society would *ipso facto* be an integral part of its social and political system. They might not deny, however, that if the military establishment in a communist society were somehow to become alienated from the system, it could then behave much like the military institutions of bourgeois nations.

1. Universal Traits of Military Institutions

Most military establishments have in common a number of characteristics which reflect their natural drive toward autonomy and their inherent professionalism. They might be summed up as (1) institutional closure, (2) detachment from the rest of society, (3) an elitist value system, (4) a hierarchical structure of authority, and (5) limited possibilities for employing the soldier's professional skills in civilian life.

In the prevailing communist view, an institution that is closed to the Party's scrutiny, and whose members desire exclusiveness, cultivate elitism, and at the same time control powerful means of violence, represents a threat to the Party and to the socialist state as a whole. Marshal Zhukov, after his ouster in 1957, was accused of "Bonapartist" designs as evidenced by his policy of institutional closure, his fostering of elitism and greater detachment from the people, and his abuse of his position to restrict the Party's controls. Party leaders congratulated themselves on having destroyed in time a dangerous trend which, if left unchecked, might have had serious consequences.[1]

But the memory of the Soviet Communists is short-lived; despite the recency of these disclosures about Zhukov's and the Red Army's dangerous tendency toward institutional autonomy, they are again

[1] See *XXII s"ezd Kommunisticheskoi partii Sovetskogo Soiuza: stenograficheskii otchet* (The Twenty-second Congress of the CPSU: Stenographic Record), Gospolitizdat, Moscow, 1962, Vol. 3, p. 67.

proclaiming that the Soviet military is an integral part of the social fabric. Outside the Soviet Union, however, communist writers, less restrained than the Soviet Party hacks, are not so sanguine. Thus, the Polish Communist J. J. Wiatr, in a series of authoritative essays on the sociology of military institutions, has approached the problems of the socialist army more realistically. He writes:

> The proper functioning of modern armies—including socialist armies—necessitates the existence of people who dedicate themselves to the military profession, who acquire the necessary qualifications, and to whom military service becomes a full-time profession. Such a group is distinct from other professional social groups in society, it has specific attitudes and unique points of view. The extent of its internal cohesiveness depends on the many factors pertaining among others to its history and social make-up.[2]
>
> Even preliminary results of current research support the hypothesis that in the socialist army military professionals constitute a separate social group with certain characteristics of internal solidarity.[3]

Wiatr also stresses the dangers that grow out of the inevitable modernization and specialization process of the socialist armies. The main danger, as he sees it, lies in the "conflict inherent in the professionalization of the officer corps of the socialist army."[4] This conflict arises from attempts to stress the professional functions of the officer while doing away with the influence of political functionaries in the military. Pointing to the ouster of Zhukov as the apex of such a trend in recent times, Wiatr sees it as underlining the fact that the "process of professionalization of the officer corps generates

[2] Jerzy J. Wiatr, "Niektore problemy socjologiczne armii socjalistycznej" (Some Sociological Problems of the Socialist Army), *Studia Socjologiczno-Polityczne*, No. 14, 1963, p. 47.

[3] *Ibid.*, p. 48.

[4] *Ibid.*, p. 30. Wiatr cites historical instances of such "internal contradictions" between the military's "natural" drive toward professional freedom and primacy and the Party's opposition to such trends and its attempts to balance "naked professionalism" with political involvement and control. He states that such contradictions in socialist armies are "not new," and refers to the Red Army's difficulties in the 1920's and the Polish army's problems in the late 1940's. He adds: "Discussions of this type reflect a natural contradiction inherent in the professionalization process of the officer corps of a socialist army; the contradiction derives from a tendency—incompatible with the army's objectives—to endow the cadres with a one-sided professional characteristic. . . . Such a tendency was opposed in a very firm way by the Party. In October 1957, the CC/CPSU condemned the practice of substituting military training for political activities."

certain difficulties and dangers, which can be averted only if there is knowledge of their existence."[5] The way to avoid them is through the socio-political integration of the military with the rest of society.

2. *Political Integration of the Military as the Antidote to Professionalism*

The emergence of the modern army and of the modern military man has deeply affected the power relationships within most states. The elitism, detachment, discipline, and apolitical tendency of military professionals have bred violent distrust as well as passionate championship of the military institution. Among its strong supporters have been such bourgeois civilian writers as Carlyle, Treitschke, Nietzsche, Kipling, Theodore Roosevelt, and Thiers.[6] Among the greatest detractors of military professionalism and of standing armies have been the leaders of revolutionary movements in the United States, in France, and in the Soviet Union, to whom the separatist and elitist tendencies of the professional officer appeared dangerous on political and ideological grounds.[7] However, whereas most Western democracies have managed to contain their military in a workable relationship despite these tendencies toward exclusiveness and elitism,[8] the totalitarian one-party states of the twentieth century

[5] *Ibid.*

[6] See Alfred Vagts, *A History of Militarism*, Meridian Books, Inc., New York, rev. ed., 1959, p. 20.

[7] See Samuel P. Huntington, *The Soldier and the State*, Harvard University Press, Cambridge, 1957, pp. 143-162. James Madison expressed a strong American feeling about the large professional army when he said: "I believe there was not a member in the Federal Convention who did not feel indignation at such an institution." Cited in Michael Howard (ed.), *Soldiers and Governments*, Eyre & Spottiswoode, London, 1957, p. 14. In support of the French revolutionary opposition to military professionalism, see J. P. Marat, *Pisma wybrane* (Selected Works), Warsaw, 1951, and Saint-Just, *Selected Works*, Warsaw, 1954, as cited by J. J. Wiatr, "Militaryzm: pojecie i problematyka socjologiczna" (Militarism: Conceptualization and Sociological Approaches), *Studia Socjologiczno-Polityczne*, No. 6, 1960, p. 51, fn. 35.

[8] The American and British military establishments, though they play major roles in the foreign policies of their nations and cultivate many of the values, symbols, and interests of highly professional military institutions, have never challenged the civilian authorities and are not thought of as representing such a challenge. In Great Britain, Michael Howard observes (*Soldiers and Government*, p. 21) that "whereas in many continental countries there has often been a profound rift between civil and military interests, here there has only been a shallow depression." The difference may, of course, be explained by the fact that the leaders of the civilian government and the military have come from similar socio-economic classes.

In the United States, relations between the civilian and military authorities are more complex, but, though they contain some elements of conflict, these hardly represent a threat to internal stability or traditional political institutions.

have faced some difficult problems in accommodating themselves to their military establishments.

It is part of the ideological premises of such totalitarian states to view their environment as harboring constant threats to their power and to assume that political programs must be geared to the frequent use of violent means for the attainment of social, military, or political objectives. Such a political system allows little tolerance for an autonomous military, and the histories of the Soviet Union and of Nazi Germany illustrate these contradictory interests of the totalitarian state and its military institution. Although the military establishment in Germany was in many ways different from that now emerging in the Soviet Union, there are analogies in the relationship of the two institutions with the elite of their ruling parties.[9]

Though both Stalin and Hitler came to power, not on the shoulders of the military, but as leaders of a popular movement, they viewed

---

Despite the fears of the Jeffersonians and Jacksonians, despite the acid observations of de Tocqueville, and despite warnings of collusion between the military and industry, there is little evidence of an acute threat of militarism in the United States. For de Tocqueville's views of the dangers of military establishments in democratic societies, see "On War, Society, and the Military," in Leon Bramson and George W. Goethals (eds.), *War: Studies from Psychology, Sociology, Anthropology*, Basic Books, New York, 1964, pp. 321-336.

[9] Communist writers are very sensitive about such analogies. Wiatr takes issue with Western political scientists and sociologists who lump together communist and fascist states on the grounds that both are political systems in which the military establishment is forcibly integrated with a single party. Referring to the Seventh Conference of the International Political Science Association (1959), which dealt with the problem of civil-military relations, Wiatr points out that, while "non-Marxist" social scientists recognize three categories of civil-military relations (the three different contexts being civilian supremacy in a constitutional democracy, party rule, and military rule), they exaggerate the similarities in the party-ruled system, i.e., the analogy between fascism and communism. Wiatr starts out, by implication, to criticize as narrowly dogmatic the view of such prominent Soviet writers as Viskov and Skopin, "who are generally inclined to see in the very term militarism a phenomenon derived from capitalistic conditions," whereas, he reminds them, there are other important causative factors; thus, ". . . it is generally assumed that the militarization of the national life favors the ascendance of military types to leading positions" ("Militaryzm," pp. 40, 41). He goes on to distinguish, however, between the fascist and the socialist army: "(1) The fascist system retains the old army and seeks to win over the military as well as to obtain control (from top to bottom) over the military; the socialist army is created at the outset on the premises of a fighting organization of a revolutionary movement; (2) the socialist army represents an important channel of social advancement, and seeks to eliminate elitism and to imbue the officer corps with characteristics of the people; (3) in socialist countries there is a clear merging (ideological and personal) of the leading cadres of the military and the civilian sectors of society, which makes it difficult to talk of two mutually opposed groups" (p. 43).

the existence of a modern, professional military establishment as a *sine qua non* for the survival of their political systems and the achievement of their objectives.[10] Yet, realizing also the possible political dangers inherent in a powerful military establishment, they set out, once their own position was firmly secured, to ensure the military's political subordination to the Party by breaking down its institutional barriers, abrogating many of its traditional prerogatives, and subjecting it to *Gleichschaltung* with other institutions in the party-dominated state.[11]

Integrating the military with the general socio-political movement under the Party's hegemony thus became a central political problem for these totalitarian regimes. Though partially successful, both parties fell short of fully achieving their objectives, however, because of the military's propensity toward closure. This characteristic tendency of the military institution has been remarked on by a number of students of the problem. Thus, W. H. Morris-Jones asks: "Who would deny that in all countries the military professionals are more sepa-

[10] Hitler had to make the difficult and dangerous choice between the politically and ideologically loyal hordes of the SA under Roehm and the politically and personally distant military professionals of the old Reichswehr, which became the Wehrmacht. His decision in favor of the latter was strongly influenced by the factor of the military's strict professionalism and discipline. "The skills and abilities of the various specialists and technicians of the military profession . . . made a strong impression on the 'Führer'. . . . There was no substitute for this in the ranks of the SA. . . ." (Gert Buchheit, *Soldatentum und Rebellion: Die Tragödie der Deutschen Wehrmacht*, Grote, Rastatt/Baden, 1961, p. 25.) Goerlitz states that "it was hardly expected that the SA would reach a *modus vivendi* with the Reichswehr" and that Hitler set in motion events that were to destroy the former's pretense of serving as a military institution. "So, Hitler was compelled to make his choice, and, since the SA despite its numbers had little chance against artillery and machine guns, Hitler chose the Army." (Walter Goerlitz, *History of the German General Staff, 1657-1945*, Frederick A. Praeger, Inc., New York, 1962, pp. 284 and 287.) In the Soviet Union, Trotsky and Stalin followed a similar course of action: resisting the extremist, utopian factions within the Party, who viewed the prospect of a standing army with horror, they methodically recruited skilled officers from the old Russian army for the Red Army, crushed the "revolutionary" intra-Party opposition, and centralized the growing Red Army, doing away with the multiple parochial controls.

[11] Goerlitz views this problem as follows: "It was natural enough that Hitler should endeavor to penetrate this phalanx of the officer corps, for every totalitarian state had sooner or later come up against a similar problem." He states (pp. 278-279) that "In Germany this inner conflict was never really resolved at all. Hitler scored some partial success, but in the end the tradition-conscious part of the officer corps revolted against him." He mistakenly adds (p. 277) that "In Russia it was not solved till 1937, when the army was finally brought into gear with the one-party state at the cost of some ten thousand officers' lives." Actually, this problem has never been completely solved in Russia either.

rated from the rest of society than any other profession?"[12] Wiatr observes that "Every army is not only a part of the general social system but is also a separate, and to some extent autonomous, . . . social system."[13] Alfred Vagts notes "the natural tendency of armies . . . toward a self-government brooking no outside influences." And Bismarck once observed that "many officers considered all things outside the army 'as alien enemies.'"[14] In Nazi Germany the military professionals resisted being placed on a par with the political soldiers of the SA and SS, and rejected the "revolutionary" Nazi spirit as "having no place in an institution that is based on the principle of discipline and obedience."[15] The main spokesman for the military professionals against the Nazi Party's attempt at integration, General Fritsch, suffered disastrously for his resistance. He was accused of having "sought to oppose the injection of party-political maxims into the army."[16]

In the communist nations the problem of how to integrate the military into the political system is far from solved. Although it would be alarmist to call it acute, it is festering within the power structure of many of these states and, given the right conditions, could become very serious. This is how the communist writer Wiatr sees the problem:

> If there also exists in a socialist army a social group of military professionals, and if it is to some extent internally cohesive, then we may consider the circumstances that are conducive to, and the circumstances that oppose, the growth of elitism in the officer corps. The primary conducive factor is professional exclusiveness under circumstances where duty is carried out at the risk of the officers' lives and where it is universally viewed as honorable.[17]

Among other favorable conditions Wiatr cites military discipline, which gives the officer a unique and advantageous position as compared with superiors in civilian institutions, and also protects him, at least to some extent, against criticism from his subordinates.

[12] Cited in Wiatr, "Militaryzm," p. 49.

[13] Wiatr, "Niektore problemy socjologiczne," p. 41.

[14] Vagts, *Militarism*, p. 296. Elsewhere, Vagts quotes a British general as saying, "Politicians make us soldiers sick, soldiers being perchance too straight and honest for them" (p. 318). Compare these with an 1869 description of the Armed Forces of the Crown as "A class of men set apart from the general mass of the community, trained to particular uses, formed to peculiar notions, governed by peculiar laws, marked by peculiar distinctions." (Quoted in Howard, *Soldiers and Government*, p. 11.)

[15] Buchheit, *Soldatentum*, p. 49. [16] *Ibid.*, p. 17.

[17] Wiatr, "Niektore problemy socjologiczne," p. 47.

Wiatr next lists as the conditions that discourage elitism among the officer corps in the socialist army: (1) the political activities of the Party within the military, (2) the class principle in the selection of officers, (3) the rejection of traditions associated with the older, bourgeois armies, and (4) the possibilities for acceding to the rank of officer. He concludes that "the influence of factors that counteract elitism is, to judge by general observation, an overriding one. The socialist army struggles successfully with tendencies toward a transformation of the officer corps into a closed elite."[18]

Wiatr's arguments, though remarkably restrained and relatively unencumbered by propagandistic verbiage, do not, however, make a very strong case for the total absence of such bourgeois traits in socialist military institutions. Indeed, his formula for the political integration of the military is an implicit recognition of the failure of communist parties to create a new kind of military institution:

> The principle of the Party's dominant role in the military is the basis for solving the problems of relations between the civilian and military authorities in the socialist state. We view the solution of this problem . . . as being dependent on the application of integration principles. The principle of integration, as it is applied in practice and as it derives from theoretical pronouncements, depends on (1) the realization that the goals of the army are identical with those of the whole socialist society, while the policies of the Communist Party that rule society are the sole and determining substantiation of these objectives, (2) the striving to educate the military cadres in the same spirit and climate in which the civilian Party and governmental cadres are raised, and (3) the daily ties of military life with the civilian life of society.[19]

Wiatr states that, in contrast to the situation in many Western states, where the military's subordinate role *vis-à-vis* the civilian authorities is mainly a matter of formal arrangement, in the socialist states, "instead of such formal-legal subordination of the army, which remains a separate, isolated social system, a conscious effort is made to merge organically the civilian and military sectors of social life."[20]

While the normative formulas which the Communists use to deal with their military establishments do thus prescribe for the harmonious coexistence of the institutions, the political and social realities in their societies clearly indicate that there is a wide gap between theory and practice. The fact that the Communists do not rely on regulatory

[18] *Ibid.*, p. 48. [19] *Ibid.*, p. 32. [20] *Ibid.*

provisions of the legal or constitutional kind prevalent in Western society, but resort instead to a relentless and expensive effort at politicization and control to keep the military politically and ideologically docile and administratively manageable, suggests the Party leaders' fundamental distrust of the military. Furthermore, while the norms for the political integration of the military presuppose identical objectives for the army, the Party, and society as a whole, this is at best a formula for the future; at present, as in the past, many of the military's institutional objectives are not identical with, and frequently are in strong opposition to, those of the Party. It is this conundrum of the inherent conflict of interests between the institutions, between the military and the political professionals whose relationship is both complementary and contradictory, that lies at the root of political instability in the communist systems and is one of the major factors in the internal and external politics of the Soviet Union.

B · TRADITIONAL INDICES OF POLITICAL POWER

1. The Statistical Approach: "Head-Counting"

A generally accepted yardstick for the political power of a party or faction in most political systems is the extent to which it is represented in the decision-making political bodies. Such a statistical approach has many merits: using "hard" rather than the more subjective "soft" variables, it is probably the only one that permits quantifiable assessments, and it therefore lends itself to comparative analyses. However, if used without qualifications, this approach can also lead to certain ambiguities and fallacies. Thus, while it is very useful to compare the proportional representation of military spokesmen in the Central Committee during various periods of Soviet history, one must be careful not to relate such numbers to direct political influence or political power. Indeed, recent experience suggests quite the contrary. For example, if we look at military representation on the Central Committee after six of the seven Party congresses since 1930,[21] we notice that during two periods when the military's role in the Soviet state was distinctly inferior, its representation on the Central Committee was at its highest. Or, if we compare the proportion of military representatives on the Central Committee in 1956 (when the

[21] The seventh was the Twenty-first Party Congress, which was convened, in 1959, as an extraordinary gathering for the discussion of Khrushchev's Seven Year Plan, and did not concern itself with the organizational changes that normally result from Party congresses.

military was asserting itself most strongly and the Party was relatively weak) with the 1939 representation (in the aftermath of the purges, when the military was thoroughly demoralized and politically emasculated), we notice that the figure for 1956 was 7.8 per cent as against 10.7 per cent in 1939.[22] It might even be said that, in the past, the Party leadership has regularly increased the military representation on the Central Committee in the aftermath of some coercive or aggressive action toward the military, attempting thereby to show its good will and to effect a reconciliation with the "cleansed" military. In this sense, an increase in the number of military members in the high councils of the Party would not necessarily be a sign of the military's rising political influence, but could be interpreted rather as a token gesture by which the Party leadership sought to express its good will toward the military and its desire for better relations.

2. *The "Charismatic Index": Measuring the Military Leaders' Popularity*

A very useful approach to assessing the political standing of individual factions or leaders in the communist states has been to measure their "popularity," both quantitatively and qualitatively, by such essentially crude status symbols as, How well are they publicized? How prominent is their picture or name in the press? How many times have they been applauded during a speech? Of what rank are the accolades or superlatives associated with their names? There is little doubt that, in a society in which the ruling elite controls all channels and media of communication and considers them of crucial importance in the constant effort to politicize the populace, such indicators of social prominence and status are indeed closely related to political influence. Again, however, one must be cautious and selective in using this "charismatic index," since the Party leaders often bestow public accolades on figureheads or political nonentities for purely symbolic ends.

[22] The *Bulletin of the Institute for the Study of the USSR*, No. 1, January 1962, p. 7, lists these figures for the military's share in the membership of the Central Committee between 1930 and 1961:

Party Congress	*Total Membership*	*Total Military*	*Percentage of Total*
Sixteenth (1930)	137	5	3.5
Seventeenth (1934)	139	8	6.0
Eighteenth (1939)	139	15	10.7
Nineteenth (1952)	236	26	11.0
Twentieth (1956)	255	20	7.8
Twenty-second (1961)	330	31	9.5

3. *Political Connection: "Who's with Whom"*

Another approach to assessing the political influence of individuals or groups in the Soviet Union is to establish their links with the Party leader or other high Party personalities. This is a helpful yardstick to the extent that it takes into consideration the cliquish, stellar-satellite aspect and the essentially personal nature of Soviet Party politics, but it can lead to ambiguous conclusions and frequently tempts the observer to see more than the data warrant. At times, the links between a military personality and a given Party leader that are established by this method are not sufficiently credible, thereby casting doubt on the usefulness of the approach. Open Soviet publications and the public statements of Party and military leaders have a monolithic quality, and it is indeed rare for any public figure below the top of the Party hierarchy to make a public statement that significantly departs from the established Party line and unequivocally expresses personal, unorthodox views, preferences, policies, or objectives. In the absence of such clear-cut evidence, the researcher often resorts to elaborate deduction or inference in order to establish a causality or to demonstrate that General X is a Khrushchev man and that Marshal Y is a Stalinist and Admiral Z a Kosygin man.

To be sure, no such logical or verbal gymnastics may be needed to link the Party leader with the military group or personality in question; usually, there is enough evidence to support the thesis that the two are furthering each other's interests. For example, in the case of the "political generals," it was easy enough to establish that the Voroshilovs, Timoshenkos, Budennyis, and Bulganins were creatures and blind supporters of Stalin. The links between the Stalingrad Group and Khrushchev are also demonstrable, and they lend persuasive support to the thesis about the coincidence of their interests, ambitions, and objectives.

This methodological approach, like the preceding ones, has both a broad utility and several weaknesses. It is useful because it singles out some central and relevant factors that enable the Western observer to recognize the calculus applicable to Party politics in the Soviet state; it illuminates the symbolism of that political stage and helps to distinguish the true political actors and their real roles from the creatures of the Party press.

The weakness of the method, as of the earlier ones, lies in the danger of relying too strongly on a mechanical and statistical approach to this complex, secretive, and unpredictable political game, which may prevent the researcher from seeing the forest for the trees. Carried to its extreme, this can lead to a situation where the pursuit of minutiae becomes all-encompassing, and where description and interpretation of the larger events, developments, or issues are then glibly derived from such a large body of essentially irrelevant data. Also, this quantitative method, though adequate for purposes that call only for an understanding of short-range trends, often fails to come to grips with the broader context and the underlying issues.[23]

4. The Fever Chart of a Crisis

Many students of Soviet affairs believe that, whenever the Party's dominant hold on the Soviet state becomes weakened as a result of internal struggles for power, by an external threat, or during wartime, other institutions, previously kept in a state of submission and political impotence, will gain in stature and influence. Understandably, political analysts who share this belief therefore try to assess the political power of different groups by examining their role in such critical situations.

In the Soviet Union, a major crisis of this kind is a shock to the body politic, causing tension and confusion in a socio-political structure theretofore kept rigid and controlled by a single leader or dominant faction. If the crisis is caused by the death of a leader who had been strongly entrenched, the shock will be severe, as personalities and loyalties, the lifelines of political power, are severed and new loyalties and alignments lead to new power arrangements. The behavior of the military under these conditions will be crucial to the outcome of the crisis, because the military, with the capability to support or reject contenders for the succession, can be the balance wheel that ensures continuity and order. Although it did not play a very significant part in the crises of the Stalin era, its role became very important after the death of the dictator. In the intra-Party power struggles of 1953-1957, the military, in the absence of an effective terror machine, represented the only major instrument of coercion in the state.

By following the developments of a crisis and the fortunes of both the potential and the actual contenders for power, one can begin to recognize the shape of things to come and foresee possible solutions to

[23] For a useful exercise in soul-searching by some Western students of the Soviet Union and the communist bloc, see four articles published in *Survey*, No. 50, January 1964: Arthur E. Adams, "The Hybrid Art of Sovietology"; Robert Conquest, "In Defense of Kremlinology"; Alec Nove, "The Uses and Abuses of Kremlinology"; and T. H. Rigby, "Crypto-Politics."

the crisis. Some analysts go on to predict future crises (such as inevitable succession problems) and to anticipate the implications of the political alignments that will follow them.

This approach to Soviet politics is the more useful as it focuses on anomalous periods and situations in which the rigidly directed body politic suffers from turbulence and confusion, opening opportunities to power-seeking elements. These are also times of candid and direct statements and embarrassing disclosures. It is as if, for brief moments, the dialectical-propagandistic covers were removed to reveal the naked structure of real power relationships in the Soviet state, permitting such institutions as the military to realize their own potentialities.

C · SOCIO-POLITICAL CHANGES AND THEIR EFFECT ON THE MILITARY'S STATUS

The foregoing methods by which Western analysts try to assess symbolism in Soviet political life and to recognize actors, factions, and their interrelationships all seek to penetrate the walls of secrecy and conspiracy; to identify the leading figures and their following and ascertain their views, idiosyncrasies, and intentions; and to recognize possible challengers and opponents to these leaders and estimate not only their chances of success but their ideas for the future. Essentially, all these methodologies are attempts to arrange the phenomena of the Soviet socio-political scene in a way that reveals regular patterns and renders it predictable and orderly. Some of them, moreover, tend to treat the Soviet political scene as if it were static, that is to say, as if, while leaders and factions came and went, political power arrangements and institutional relationships remained essentially unchanged.

The Soviet political scene, it is true, has changed little from decade to decade, and the Communist Party has maintained its dominance and frozen other institutions in subordinate positions. Yet certain cumulative processes have changed the quality of the relationship of some of these institutions. In the following, we shall deal with these developments as they have affected the evolving political role of the Soviet military establishment.

1. Internal Developments

There is a growing consensus among Western observers of communist affairs that the countries of the Eastern bloc are showing broad trends toward moderation, though to varying degrees. A curbing of the secret police organs, greater freedom of expression, the loosening of travel restrictions, less militant political slogans, improved standards of living—these and other developments are frequently pointed to as significant departures from the oppressive conditions of the past. What influence, if any, do these changes have on the relations between Party and military? And how do they affect the institutional interests and objectives of the Soviet military establishment?

A most important development has been the broadening of the Party's power base within Soviet society, with the concomitant lessening of the rigid hold of the Party *apparat* and a larger role for the various professional and social groups in the state. Under the regime of Khrushchev, whose "goulash communism" tended to subordinate abstract ideological goals to the practical tasks of economic and social development, the *apparatchik* was frequently told to listen to the manager, scientist, engineer, or general and not to interfere with his useful functions. In recent years, Khrushchev had set up a program which intended to invest social and governmental bodies with authority to deal with a number of problems vital to the state and the Party, an authority formerly vested in the Party apparatus. Although the Party retained indirect control over these bodies, the program nevertheless was a major socio-political experiment.[24]

The CPSU, with its membership swollen to over twelve million, has ceased to be a "vanguard." Party leaders have gone to great trouble to recruit into this large body the most useful and influential members of Soviet society. And, though Party elite and *apparat* are still firmly in control, the inclusion of the industrial, scientific, and professional intelligentsia in the ranks of the Party leads one to speculate on what changes this massive recruitment may have brought about in the Party and its way of ruling the state.

[24] Khrushchev referred to this new feature of "collective" initiative and control at the Thirteenth Komsomol Congress in April 1958 (*Pravda*, April 19, 1958), and at the Twenty-first Party Congress, where he announced more formally the institution of this type of social control: "Problems pertaining to public order and to rules of socialist interrelations must be progressively transferred to social organizations" (*Pravda*, January 28, 1959). For a more detailed analysis of this trend, see *Sovetskoe gosudarstvo i pravo*, No. 10, 1958; N. G. Aleksandrov, *ibid.*, No. 12, 1958; and M. V. Barsukov, *ibid.*, No. 8, 1959.

An even more serious decline in the authority of the Party apparatus was caused by Khrushchev's decision to split the *apparat* into two functional groups, one industrial and the other agricultural, thereby reducing Party functionaries to the level of equals, or even subordinates, to industrial and agricultural managers and experts, and greatly weakening their power and prestige. One of the first measures of the post-Khrushchev regime was to reunify the Party apparatus. (See Chapter VIII, p. 285.)

One consequence of the Party's greater inclusiveness is a mild form of pluralism in Soviet society. As the professional groupings are gaining in prestige, remuneration, influence, and social importance (while these same attributes are becoming less apparent among the members of the *apparat*), there is a greater self-awareness among these groups and an inclination to test the Party's permissiveness in letting them pursue their institutional objectives and cultivate their own values and loyalties.

Another development related to the growing moderation and social pragmatism is the further erosion of ideology, which is ceasing to serve as a credible guide for social action. Soviet society is showing the effects of its "embourgeoisement," which manifests itself in the desire for material possessions and a widespread cynicism about communist ideology, especially among the younger generation. Furthermore, the absence of charismatic figures among present and potential Party leaders is likely to weaken whatever awe there now remains in regard to the Party rulers, and whatever trust in their omnipotence.

Although apparent, these factors do not as yet present the Party leadership with an insurmountable challenge. It is not unlikely, however, that, at some point in the future, the leaders will face a choice between trying to stem this trend toward "embourgeoisement" by some hard measures and harnessing it to modified ideological programs.

Parallel to the growing moderation that is visible in Soviet society there has been, in recent years, a more moderate trend in Soviet foreign policy. But it would be unwise to read this development as signifying a radical and final departure of the Party from the traditional course and long-range aims of Soviet foreign policy. The leaders of the CPSU continue to regard a powerful military establishment as a basic guarantee of the Party's ability to maintain itself in power, both within the Soviet Union and as leader of the bloc, and as the main deterrent to foreign aggression. Although in recent times Soviet policy, both internal and foreign, has adapted itself to conditions that call for less militancy and repression, this moderation has not substantially altered the traditional character and function of the Soviet armed forces.

We must ask, however, whether the role of the military is not likely to be severely affected by the growing pacifism and antimilitarism, and the general "embourgeoisement," of Soviet society. In the 1920's, during the period of the New Economic Policy, a similar antimilitaristic trend, together with the intensive economic development program, severely threatened the emerging Red Army. Is there any parallel between that situation and the present one? The answer to this question is that, although the military institution and the officer's profession have lost in prestige, the military's role and influence in Soviet politics are likely to continue to rise, for the following reasons:

(1) Soviet foreign policy, both *vis-à-vis* the West and as it relates to the other countries of the bloc, depends for its effectiveness on the existence of a strong military establishment. A credible military threat, or even a show of force, may eventually be needed to stem the effort of other bloc countries toward emancipation from Moscow's rule. On the international scene, even under a policy of détente, and given the conditions of a nuclear "stalemate," the balance of power can be preserved only through the maintenance of a military force strong enough to destroy, and therefore to deter, any aggressor.

(2) In view of the aforementioned diffusion of the Party's strength and authority, and in the absence of a terror machine, the military has become the main instrument of coercion, and the leaders of this highly structured and well-integrated organism may try to play a crucial role in future power struggles within the Party, as they have done in the past.

(3) The military stands to gain also from the waning ideological commitment noticeable throughout the Soviet Union and from the ascendance of manager-bureaucrats in the place of charismatic leaders, for, as a result of this development, the ideological constraints on the officer corps are likely to diminish, the commanders' professional authority will rise accordingly, and the officer-technocrat may find more sympathetic acceptance among the new kind of political rulers than he has had from the traditional elite. Moreover, the Party may find it necessary to combat the spreading pacifism and antimilitarism of the populace by enlarging the role and thus enhancing the prestige of the officer corps.

Even a moderate and conciliatory phase in Soviet internal and foreign policy need not lessen the political weight of the military. The effectiveness of the Soviet Union's commitments toward the West and within the bloc hinges on the ability to maintain a powerful military establishment, and unless Party leaders revise their basic political and ideological objectives—an unlikely eventuality—the military will continue to play a vital political role.

2. The International Context

Recent years have witnessed several major developments in international affairs: the stabilization of the nuclear deterrent and the lessened likelihood of nuclear war; a loosening of alliances, both in the Soviet bloc and in the Western camp; the United States' and the Soviet Union's growing concern over the political and military policies of some of their allies, or former allies, which they view as endangering the *status quo*; and the Soviet Union's political and diplomatic endeavor to achieve a détente through conciliatory moves and disarmament negotiations.

These developments add up to a significant change. Although the Soviet leaders' true intentions concerning détente and disarmament remain uncertain, their deep concern about the schism between Russia and Red China and about the satellites' efforts toward emancipation is quite evident. Furthermore, having failed, in 1962, to attain some measure of strategic-nuclear parity with the West through the emplacement of missiles in Cuba, and unwilling at that point to enter into an arms race that could have overcome the strategic disparity, Soviet rulers shifted the East-West competition from the militant political-military arena to the conciliatory level of diplomacy and economics. Today, though the strategic disparity is such as to prevent them from seizing the political initiative in international affairs, their weapons and forces-in-being are sufficient to deter the West from any unprovoked aggression. While this may not be an ideal state of affairs from the Soviet point of view, it is probably preferable to any change in the balance of power that would result from allowing other states to acquire a significant nuclear capability.

How does a policy which underplays the military factor and stresses the negotiatory approach and the goal of disarmament affect the role of the Soviet military establishment? On first thought, one would assume that under conditions of détente, when the military factor plays a less active part in foreign policy, the Soviet military as an institution would find its influence significantly reduced. On the grounds that the present deterrents were workable and sufficient, it might be thought, the Party leaders would want to divert resources from the military to the economic sector and seek to achieve political gains through an aggressive political-economic policy in place of the aggressive political-military policy of the past. Moreover, they might find such a change the more desirable as it would greatly reduce the potential weight of the military, which would be relegated to only a marginal social and political role.[25]

Such reasoning, however, would be hasty and short-sighted. For one thing, it would ignore the significance of the tensions and conflicts within the communist bloc, and their sharply nationalistic quality.[26] Moscow's quarrels with China, Albania, Rumania, and in the past with Yugoslavia, are more than ideological quibbling. They reflect clashes of interests between nations, and the leaders of these states are nationalists as much as they are Communists. It is not unlikely that the future will bring more and more conflicts of this kind. If it does, the Soviet leaders will have to rely more heavily than in the past on a patriotic national army capable of defending their country's interests.

With respect to the West, the Soviet Union, notwithstanding its present conciliatory policy, has not substantially changed either its long- or its short-range objectives. First among these remains the achievement of world communism, however remote such a goal may be. Nearer at hand are the tasks connected with ruling a state, preserving past gains, and finding and exploiting opportunities for advancing to the more distant goals. They include maintaining the military security of the Soviet Union; the building of communism in the former satellites and the safeguarding of Moscow's influence over those countries; propagating communism in the underdeveloped countries; and the advancement of communism in the capitalist world.

As the international balance of power is replaced by a "balance of terror," as Soviet control over the satellites weakens and ideological and political tensions between Moscow and Peking grow, and with the specter of nuclear proliferation looming ever larger, the Party leaders will most likely find the possession of a powerful

[25] Khrushchev, in fact, tried to pursue such a course. In the process, however, he threatened the military's interests and caused it to align itself with his rivals in the Party.

[26] The markedly nationalistic flavor of the ideological and political dispute between the Soviet Union and members of the socialist camp is conveyed in the heated remarks of Khrushchev's son-in-law and former editor-in-chief of *Izvestiia*, Adzhubei, in an interview with West German reporters (*Der Spiegel*, August 3, 1964, p. 18), when he was asked what the Soviet Union would do about reported claims by Red China to Soviet territory:

"Our Prime Minister [Khrushchev] has said that the borders of our country in the West, East, North, and South are sacred. We are ready to discuss border problems peacefully. However, one must know that the Soviet borders—in the West as well as in the East—are guarded not only by our total military might but also by the hearts of all our people. Our borders are inviolable."

military establishment their most indispensable guarantee of strength in the face of such challenges. Thus, far from having lost its importance, the Soviet military continues to be the *sine qua non* in the pursuit of the Party's policies, and its role as the policeman in the bloc, as the shield against external aggression, and possibly as the means to the achievement of future political gains is likely to grow.

D · POLITICAL RELIABILITY VS. PROFESSIONAL EXCELLENCE: THE PARTY'S SEARCH FOR A SYNTHESIS

The Communist Party apparatus is essentially orthodox: while superficially it adjusts, develops, and reforms the social and political processes and institutions in the polity, it continues by and large to adhere to the creed of an older time, the revolutionary and Stalinist era. One of the ways in which this heritage manifests itself is in a deep-seated reluctance to delegate authority to those professional and institutional groups—including, above all, the military—whose functions are vital to the state and the Party. It appears that the Party cannot rid itself of this heritage of distrust; the apparatus regards the tension between institutions as a necessity and cannot tolerate its relaxation.

The military represents an especially worrisome case, because it possesses the means, the organization, and the discipline for sudden organized violence. The natural tendency among the ordinary members of the Party apparatus is to distrust the officer corps, with its desire for exclusiveness and its respect for the heroic, and to view its members as potential troublemakers who must be kept controlled and subdued. At a higher level, however, the Party's relations with the military are fraught with contradictions and dilemmas.

It is one of the characteristics of cold-war politics that major political gains or losses (with the former sometimes manifesting themselves in the launching of large economic or social undertakings) may result from changes in the assumptions of both sides about the state of military parity that exists between them. It is almost as if, from time to time, the two cold-war opponents fought a "pretend war" with their available weapons, and the winner were awarded a scoring point. Indeed, this is so much a feature of the shadow war that increments in the military capabilities of one side which result in a changed balance of military potentialities sometimes seem to be automatically translated into new political advantages or disadvantages. It follows that the need to maintain the Soviet military machinery at a high level of readiness, efficiency, and destructiveness would be a very important consideration for the Party leadership.

It is not difficult to see the particular dilemma that arises for the Party out of the contradiction between its innate distrust of the military and the importance of keeping Soviet military strength both high and credible. To maintain its position as the leading communist state, to safeguard its gains and stake out new policy goals around the globe, the Soviet Union relies heavily on both the political and the military weight of its armed forces.

The political-military game between East and West through which the delicate "balance of terror" is maintained has seemed to follow a set of unwritten rules. According to these, a "scoring point," translatable into a political or propagandistic gain, goes to the side which lets it be known, and convincingly so, that it has a weapon or weapon system that is either newer and more plentiful or bigger than that of the opponent.

It might seem to be rational policy for the Party to avoid any gratuitous injury to the military's effectiveness, its morale and good will. But the Party does not behave in an entirely rational way, its distrust of the military being almost instinctive, and it is constantly forced, therefore, to balance the requirements of its external political objectives against considerations of internal political stability. The results of this ambivalent attitude and conduct might be summed up as follows:

An elaborate and cumbersome indoctrination and control machinery permeates the Soviet military establishment. Technocrats in uniform are forced to spend extensive periods of time studying Marxism-Leninism. Professional officers are kept perennially insecure about their careers, which depend on the good will of political officers, many of whom are military ignoramuses. Military processes are exposed to relentless interference from members of the given unit's Party organization, which cuts across both rank and expertise. Internal operations of the unit, therefore, are constantly disturbed. They are changed or rescinded arbitrarily and in defiance of the normal military chain of authority. They may be interrupted by bureaucrats outside the military. Frequently, "collective decisions" in matters of discipline, morale, and the like supplant the individual decisions of the commander, who nevertheless remains personally responsible for the action taken.

The result of these attempts to graft onto a military establishment certain traits peculiar to communist political organizations is the anomaly of an up-to-date military machine that is forced to wear a horse collar of ideological and political controls. The Party has been aware of this incongruity and has tried to deal with it. But the changes have been palliatives rather than solutions; they have been directed only at the symptoms, not the causes, of the problem. The indoctrinational lectures of yesterday have been superseded by indoctrinational "seminars," which give the participants a chance to ask questions as well as to listen. Instead of the political officer who used to dominate the institute or higher staff, there now are Party committees, but few are likely to be taken in by this transparent attempt to make a political control organ appear democratic.

As the situation thus remains unsatisfactory, the Party continues to seek for ways of solving its own dilemma. Most desirable from its point of view would be, of course, an officer corps that consisted only of dedicated and unquestionably loyal men, each of whom combined the best traits of the commander with those of the commissar. Whenever an attempt has been made, however, to realize this ideal—most recently after Zhukov's ouster—the results have been disappointing; for it has proved difficult, if not impossible, for the officer to maintain with equal fervor the dual loyalty to his profession and to the Party, notwithstanding the theoretical principle that ideological motivation will govern both loyalties and preclude any possible conflict. In practice, while the officer can take pride in the performance of his military duties and derive personal and professional pleasures from the military's complex lore and traditions, the Party offers him only slogans and the promise of an impersonal role in a vast historical movement.

The adherence of the Soviet military to the traditions and objectives, the values and symbols, that resemble those of other large military establishments reveals the simple truth that professional loyalties in such guild-like organizations are very intense and virtually proof against ideological onslaughts from outside the profession. The Party, therefore, is less likely to achieve its aims by trying to induce dual loyalty than by changing the priorities in the pursuit of its objectives.

In effect, the Party has three options: It can acknowledge that the military must be spared oppressive controls and constant indoctrination if it is to be highly effective; it can reduce those of its political objectives that necessitate the use of the military; it can reorganize and thereby reduce the military establishment to the point where it ceases to be a significant factor in Soviet politics.

E · THE PROSPECT IN THE LIGHT OF THE PAST

In charting the revolution of the proletariat, the Communist Party's assumption of power, and the creation of a communist society, neither Marx nor Lenin came to grips with the problem of what would be the nature and the role of the military forces in such a society. Marx and Engels originally saw the successful revolution in utopian terms of a massive uprising of the lower classes, led by a communist vanguard. After the fiasco of the Paris Commune, they began to realize the need for a well-organized, well-armed, and well-directed military organization, but they never abandoned the view that standing professional armies were alien to a communist state. Lenin, who so meticulously described most other aspects of the communist society-to-be, remained vague on the role of the military in it. And even Trotsky, the creator of the Red Army, who consciously ignored the communist tenets about the dangers of militarism, subordinating ideology to expediency, reverted to impractical, utopian views once the danger of further anti-Soviet military campaigns had passed.

It was Stalin, the mediocre ideologue and ruthless pragmatist, who finally tackled this central problem of the rulers of any communist society, the question of what should be the status of the military in the one-party totalitarian state. He defined the military's role, its organization, its relations with the Party, and its social and political functions. In doing so, Stalin borrowed from Marx, Engels, Lenin, Trotsky, and even from Kerensky, but added ideas of his own. The Red Army emerged from this process as an adjunct of the ruling Party elite; its officers were denied the full authority necessary to the practice of the military profession; they were kept in a perennial state of uncertainty about their careers; and the military community, which tends toward exclusiveness, was forcibly kept open through an elaborate system of control and indoctrination.

It is not difficult to understand Stalin's uneasiness about the military. The main objective of the Party being to retain its hegemony in the state, and given the lack of formal or traditional provisions for the transfer of power in the event of the dictator's death, those in power, as well as those waiting on the sidelines to grasp it, regarded everyone, both within and without the Party, as a potential challenger. The citizenry as a whole thus appeared as an amorphous, untrustworthy mass, to be manipulated by the Party leadership and to be prevented by it from coalescing into groups or institutions that could challenge or oppose the Party's direction. This distrust found formal expression in the Soviet Union's network of police and control organs and in the fostering of mutual suspicion among the citizenry. In this way it became possible to respond ruthlessly to the slightest sign of real or potential opposition to the dictator's will.

Yet, while the dictator could threaten, imprison, and even kill ordinary citizens and members of most professional and ethnic groups without much danger to the well-being of Party or state, the military presented a special problem which demanded special methods. Notwithstanding its avowals of faith in the invincibility of the community ideology, the Party leadership realized early that the survival of the new state rested largely on the effectiveness of its armed forces. Stalin, therefore, embarked on a massive program intended to provide the Soviet army with modern weapons, equipment, and logistics. But he remained wary of the military's tendency toward elitism and exclusiveness, a propensity that grew with its professional renascence. So overwhelming did his distrust become that, at a time of acute danger of war in Europe, Stalin struck at the military in the massive purges of 1937.

Throughout his reign, Stalin, it appears, looked upon the military as a giant on the Party's leash. Hemmed in on all sides by secret police, political organs, and Party and Komsomol organizations, the military's freedom of action was severely circumscribed. Whenever there was an acute external threat, or when the Party was internally divided, the Party would slacken the leash and toss scraps to the military in the form of concessions and freedom to articulate grievances. When the crisis had passed, the leash was tightened again, and many of these recently won privileges were rescinded.

As long as Stalin's terror machine was in operation, the military was not able to develop an active elite and spokesmen for its interests, nor was it afforded an opportunity for articulating institutional views, objectives, and ideals. However, with Stalin's death and the division in the Party leadership that followed, the control mechanisms were weakened, and the military's own interests and values emerged into the open. In the person of Marshal Zhukov, broad sectors of the military had found their spokesman. Zhukov was able to rid the establishment of the political organs' pervasive controls; he introduced strict discipline and the separation of ranks; he demanded the rehabilitation of purged military leaders and the punishment of their tormentors; he called for better pensions and higher living standards for the military; and he moved the military out of its social and political limbo and into the limelight. Above all, he dared to express in public opinions on major military issues that often deviated from the prevailing Party line.

Seen in retrospect, Zhukov's attempts were doomed to failure, because a large number of ranking military leaders who were his personal and political enemies lent their support to Khrushchev and sought ultimately to replace Zhukov and his followers in the officer corps. These members of the Stalingrad Group, at the time a strongly pro-Khrushchev faction, did indeed achieve their objectives, as we have seen, but only at the price of renewed Party controls and the sacrifice of some of the military's gains in professional autonomy and institutional independence.

In recent years, however, despite the setback suffered with the ouster of Zhukov, the military has been advancing toward greater professional and institutional freedom. Although it remains subject to control, various developments within and outside the Soviet Union have contributed to its growing role. (1) The officer corps is gradually being transformed from a body of interchangeable commanders with minimal skills into a group of more sophisticated, self-assured young specialists. (2) Individually and collectively, these technocrats are becoming indispensable to the effective maintenance of increasingly complex military weapons and equipment. (3) The Soviet Union's extensive political-military commitments, both to countries of the bloc and *vis-à-vis* the West, would be severely compromised by any serious crisis in the relations between the Party and the military, making mutual accommodation imperative. (4) A perceptible moderation in the Party's methods of ruling and a general easing in the social life of the Soviet Union has permitted the ascent of the professional managers and scientists, among others, as well as of the officer corps, which is the professional group *par excellence.* (5) A growing antimilitarist, pacifist trend in Soviet society has prompted the Party to try to enhance the military profession by paying greater tribute to officers and granting them concessions. (6) The movement toward emancipation among the satellites and the split between the Soviet Union and Red China contain a strongly nationalistic element. As Moscow's ideological and economic hold over these dissenters weakens, it may yet fall to the military to halt or even to roll back the divisive trends in the communist bloc. (7) A corollary of the increasingly nationalistic orientation of the bloc countries is that the Soviet military may gain in stature as the major patriotic entity and symbol of the power of communist nations.

Until now, Stalin's terror machine and Khrushchev's tactics through the Stalingrad Group have successfully prevented the Soviet military establishment from developing and playing its great potential role in Soviet politics. However, the last of the Bolsheviks in the Party are on their way out, and their followers in the military are aging and ready to retire. These men are likely to be succeeded by a new kind of elite, more pragmatic and politically less firmly committed, and such a development can only enhance the chances of the military's acquiring a more active role in Soviet politics. As Kremlin leaders continue to be faced with the serious problems of dealing with recurrent challenges from Peking, with unrest in the satellites, with the domestic pressures that accompany rising expectations in Soviet society, and with the perennial conflict with the West, they will almost certainly follow the example of their predecessors in leaning on the military for support in times of stress. Indeed, they may feel freer to do so than earlier leaders, in the knowledge that, contrary to the Party's fears and predictions, the military in the past has shown neither disloyalty nor any appreciable tendency toward Bonapartism.

It is ironical that communist parties, which in principle condemn standing professional armies as an evil force of suppression, cannot do without such large standing forces once they themselves have achieved political control, and indeed depend on the professional military to maintain them in power. This is not to say that the Communists' condemnation of standing armies is merely a tactical device. Their fear of the men who carry the guns, fly the planes, man the missiles, and command the obedience of millions of soldiers is real enough. However, they are today more dependent on this powerful element than in the past.

In dealing with an institution that it regards as alien and inherently hostile, the Party apparatus has, in the past, adopted a policy of "containment," that is to say, it has imposed multiple controls and other inhibiting shackles on most of the military community, while coopting select military personages into the high Party councils. For a time, this cooptation of top military leaders into positions of power and prestige had the desired effect of preventing the larger military establishment from developing a focus, direction, and institutional identity of its own. More recently, however, there has been a change, as the attack on the personality cult, the lessening charisma of individual Party leaders, and the doubts cast on some previously sacrosanct ideological tenets, combined with the evident importance of the military factor in the foreign policy of the Soviet Union, have favored the professionalization and heightened the institutional loyalty of the officer corps in a manner that reaches into the upper layers of the military hierarchy. Thus, men like Malinovskii, Zakharov, and Krylov have shown a remarkably steadfast adherence to their own professional standards and their view of the national interest in the face of the dire consequences that have been known to attend any such opposition to the Party's policies.

In the final analysis, the military's role and influence in Soviet politics must depend on the extent to which the officer corps is aware of itself as an elite with specific institutional objectives, interests, and values. The conditions for the development of such an awareness were inauspicious during the oppressive Stalinist era. Yet, even then, the Soviet officer corps exhibited institutional characteristics and elitist tendencies similar to those of officer communities in noncommunist societies. Since the death of Stalin, the military's desire to develop and indulge these propensities more fully has become manifest. It has caused deep concern to the political leadership, and has resulted in the ambitious socio-political reforms of the military community by which the Party has sought (a) to minimize the conditions that breed elitism by forcing egalitarian, collectivist procedures and values on the military community, (b) to "open up" the military community to the impartial, and not necessarily sympathetic, scrutiny of civilian Party organs, (c) to deprive the officers of their automatic authority as commanders and force them to reclaim it in each instance from the collective authority of the Party organizations in their units, and (d) to undermine the officers' security by exposing them to the ritual of criticism/self-criticism, including the ignominy of criticism from the professionally and militarily lower-ranking Komsomols.

These reforms have been far from successful from the Party's point of view, having merely added to the friction between commanders and Party functionaries, and thus revealed the need for a more radical solution of the problem. As for the direction that such a solution is likely to take, the progressive ideological disillusionment of Soviet society, the stress on functional and professional excellence, the emergence of a mild form of pluralism, and the absence of the terror machine provide fertile soil for the military's conscious growth as a powerful institution. The Soviet military already is potentially able, and aware of its ability, to play an active role in Soviet politics. To transform this potentiality into a reality it must be led by men whose focus is clear and whose primary loyalty is to the military, not to the

Party. The prospects for the emergence of such leadership are very good.

The Soviet political scene has changed in several significant respects since the last months of Khrushchev's rule. To be sure, the change is more in the nature of a shift of official and publicly expressed attitudes than in any major revision of policies. Soviet policy-making is essentially still the private affair of a small number of men, and few others are privy to its secrets. Major shifts in the public attitude on important issues become significant, therefore, not necessarily as signs of impending changes in national policy, but as indicators of a need for adjustment, the reason for which may be either internal or external. At the time of writing, in the spring of 1966, the official stance of the Party leadership seems harder, less committed to détente, than it appeared a year ago. This shift may well be due in large measure to external events: to the growing military firmness of the United States and the American involvement in Southeast Asia; to continuing vituperations from Peking regarding Soviet "appeasement" in the face of the allegedly growing Western militancy; to rising concern about the problem of Germany; and to the waning of however slender a hope there may once have been of finding a way to prevent the proliferation of nuclear weapons.

External developments alone, however, do not fully explain the change in the official Soviet line. There are strong indications that the tensions and frictions between institutions, temporarily forgotten in the common effort to remove Khrushchev, are active factors once more. The military, for one, seems to be dissatisfied with those détente-motivated foreign policies and consumer-oriented domestic policies that threaten its basic institutional interests. At the Twenty-third Party Congress, numerous Party and managerial leaders emphasized the priorities of the civilian sectors of the economy while skirting the issue of war and defense requirements, yet they failed to persuade the military, who in recent months have shown their dissatisfaction with the proceedings of the Congress. Chief of the General Staff Marshal Zakharov, in a "Report to the Armed Forces Concerning the Twenty-third Party Congress,"[27] barely acknowledged the Party's program for raising the living standards of the people. Instead, he drew the attention of his audience to historical lessons of the prewar years, in the 1930's, when the statistics on Soviet steel production "sounded to us like the best kind of poetry" and when "we saw quite clearly how our class enemies, who were preparing

[27] *Tekhnika i vooruzhenie* (Moscow), No. 4, 1966, pp. 1-9.

war against us, counted seriously on weakness in the Soviet economy." Exhorting the Party "not to forget for a minute the possible coming trials which may once again face the Soviet people," Zakharov reiterated the traditional military view that victory in that war was achieved mainly because of "the economic preparedness of the country, including specifically the production of metal."

The military's criticism of important Party policies comes at a time when the Soviet leadership is presented with difficult choices, as well as with opportunities, that have resulted from the Vietnamese crisis, the growing dissent in the communist camp, and some profound changes in the Eastern and Western alliance systems. These and other developments have led the military to demand a more powerful indigenous defense establishment. Its attitude is expressed in this sentence from an editorial in the military's chief professional journal: "One of the most important tasks of military science is to improve existing weapons for waging war and to create new ones."[28]

The voice of the military is again being heard, and the Party leaders are submitting to the need to satisfy the military's pride and some of its demands. Though they may well believe the policy of détente to be the most desirable course for the Soviet Union, they may be forced by internal pressures to take a firmer line. In the internal politics of the Soviet Union, especially under a collective leadership, the military is a formidable institution, whose needs and demands must be considered.

[28] *Voenno-istoricheskii zhurnal,* No. 4, April 1966, p. 6.

Appendices

APPENDIX A

The Stalingrad Group

Appendix A-I

PATTERNS OF POLITICAL ASSOCIATIONS IN THE SOVIET HIGH COMMAND

	STALIN	KHRUSHCHEV
Prominent members of the military	Voroshilov, Budennyi, Timoshenko, Tukhachevskii, Frunze, Bubnov, Gusev, Ordzhonikidze, Shvernik	Konev, Malinovskii, Moskalenko, Chuikov, Biriuzov, Grechko, Eremenko, Zakharov, Epishev, Golikov, Krylov
Origin of the association	In battles of the civil war, mostly on the Southern Ukrainian front and at Tsaritsyn (later Stalingrad, now Volgograd).	During World War II battles on the southern front, especially the battle of Stalingrad.
Added reasons for the community of interests between political leader and his allies in the military	Opposition of field commanders to centralization of Party and military authority, as personified in Trotsky and the *Revvoensovet Respubliki.* Reasons for opposition: (1) personality conflicts between the authoritarian Trotsky and Stalin; (2) reduced authority of field commanders; (3) preferential treatment accorded to Trotsky's appointees as compared with the poor treatment of field commanders.	Opposition of field commanders to the central Party-military authority of the *Stavka* as personified by Zhukov. Reasons for opposition: (1) personality conflicts between authoritarians, such as Zhukov, and the field commanders; (2) the reduced authority of field commanders; (3) the central authorities' preferential treatment of the *Stavka* people and their slighting of field commanders.
Cases of mutual assistance between the leader and his military followers	(1) Stalin, with the aid of Bubnov, Gusev, Frunze, Voroshilov, and Budennyi, replaced Trotsky appointees (Vatsetis, Smilga); (2) he caused dismissal of Trotsky from *Revvoensovet Respubliki*; (3) he placed his own men (Frunze, Voroshilov, etc.) in command.	(1) Khrushchev (in 1955-1956) had his men promoted to the highest ranks and to the CC; (2) assisted by his men and Zhukov, he removed his intra-Party opponents (Malenkov and "anti-Party group"); (3) assisted by his military followers, Khrushchev removed Zhukov from Ministry of Defense; and (4) he promoted his followers to highest positions in the armed forces.
Tensions between the leader and his military following	Issues involving unity of command, collectivization, and purges eventually split the intramilitary elite: Tukhachevskii and his followers were purged; the head of the political organs and his followers also were purged; Voroshilov, Budennyi, and Timoshenko were retained.	Issues involving strategic-doctrinal and economic policy differences caused schism in the Stalingrad Group: Biriuzov, Chuikov, and Eremenko remained very loyal to Khrushchev, while Malinovskii, Zakharov, and Krylov disputed his policies. Khrushchev also replaced the head of the political control organs, Golikov, with the more loyal Epishev.

Appendix A-II

CAREER PATTERNS OF MEMBERS OF THE STALINGRAD GROUP: ASSIGNMENTS TO MAJOR COMMANDS BETWEEN 1945 AND 1965

Key Military Districts

Moscow		*Leningrad*		*Kiev*	
Moskalenko	1949-1953*	Zakharov	1953-1957	Grechko	1945-1953
Moskalenko	1953-1960	Krylov	1957-1960	Chuikov	1953-1960
Krylov	1960-1962	Kazakov	since 1960	Koshevoi	1960-1965
Beloborodov	since 1963			Iakubovskii	since 1965

Force Group Commands

Warsaw Pact Forces		*Soviet Forces in E. Germany*		*Southern Force Group*	
Konev	1957-1960	Chuikov	1949-1953	Kazakov	1955-1960
Grechko	since 1960	Grechko	1953-1957	Batov	1960-1962
		Zakharov	1957-1960		
		Iakubovskii	1960-1961		
		Konev	1961-1962		
		Iakubovskii	1962-1965		
		Koshevoi	since 1965		

Major Force Commands

Ground Forces		*Strategic Missile Forces*		*PVO-Strany*		*General Staff*	
Konev	1946-1950	Moskalenko	1960-1962	Biriuzov	1954-1955*	Zakharov	1960-1963
Malinovskii	1956-1957	Biriuzov	1962-1963	Biriuzov	1955-1962	Biriuzov	1963-1964
Grechko	1957-1960	Krylov	since 1963	Sudets	since 1962	Zakharov	since 1964
Chuikov	since 1960						

* Served as Deputy Commander

Appendix A-III

COOPTATION OF STALINGRAD GROUP MEMBERS TO HIGH PARTY POSITIONS

	XIXth Party Congress (1952)	*XXth Party Congress (1956)*	*XXIInd Party Congress (1961)*	
Full membership in the Central Committee	Konev	Konev Malinovskii Moskalenko	Konev Malinovskii Moskalenko Grechko Chuikov Biriuzov	Krylov Iakubovskii Golikov Vershinin Bagramian Zakharov
Candidate membership in the Central Committee	Bagramian Grechko Chuikov	Bagramian Biriuzov Grechko Chuikov Eremenko Gorshkov (Admiral) Epishev	Eremenko Sudets Savitskii Pliev Pen'kovskii	Kazakov Getman Varentsov Batitskii

Appendix A-IV

PROMOTIONS IN RANK AND STATUS

	After Malenkov's Ouster (1955)	*After Zhukov's Ouster (1957)*	*After XXIInd Party Congress (1961)*
To Marshal of the Soviet Union	Bagramian Biriuzov Chuikov Eremenko Grechko Moskalenko	Zakharov (1959)	Krylov
To Marshal of an Arm	Sudets Kazakov, V. I. Varentsov Rudenko		
To General of the Army	Krylov Popov Zakharov Kazakov, M. I. Fediuninskii		Iakubovskii Pliev Beloborodov
To Hero of the Soviet Union		Malinovskii (1958) Grechko (1958)	

Appendix A-V

CHRONOLOGY OF THE STALINGRAD GROUP'S SURGE TO POWER

Key to abbreviations: A = Army; AF = Air Force; C/S = Chief of Staff; C/GS = Chief of General Staff; CIC = Commander-in-Chief; DOSAAF = Voluntary Society for Assistance to the Army, Air Force, and Navy; F = Forces; FE = Far East; FG = Force Group; PVO-S = Antiaircraft Defense of the Country; SFG = Soviet Force Group

	Wartime Commands at Stalingrad	*1945-1953*	*1953-1957 (Period of Transition)*	*After 1957 (Under Khrushchev)*
Malinovskii	66A, 2nd Guards	FE Command	CIC Ground F	Min of Def
Chuikov	62A	SFG in Germany	Kiev MD	CIC Ground F
Grechko	18A, 56A[1]	Kiev MD	SFG in Germany	CIC Ground F; CIC Warsaw Pact F
Moskalenko	1st Guards, 38A	C/S Moscow MD	Moscow MD	Strat Miss F
Biriuzov	C/S 2nd Guards	Central FG	PVO-S	Strat Miss F; C/GS
Zakharov	C/S Stalingrad Front	Dep Comm FE Cmd[2]	Leningrad MD	SFG in Germany; C/GS
Konev	Steppe Front[3]	CIC Ground F	Carpathian MD	CIC Warsaw Pact F
Krylov	62A	C/S & Dep Comm FE Cmd[4]	Ural MD	Leningrad MD; Moscow MD; CIC Strat Miss F
Bagramian	C/S SW Front[5]	Baltic MD	Voroshilov Acad	Comm of the Rear
Epishev	Member Mil Council	Party & MGB Work		Head MPA
Eremenko	Comm Stalingrad Front	West Siberian MD	N Caucasus MD	Dep Min of Def
Golikov	Comm SE Front	Head of Bd of Cadres		Head MPA

Secondary Level[6]

Iakubovskii	Comm Brigade[7]		Dep Comm SFG in Germany; Comm SFG in Germany
Getman	Comm Army[8]	Unspecified MD	Carpathian MD
Koshevoi		Siberian MD	Kiev MD; SFG in Germany
Babadzhanian	Comm Brigade		Odessa MD
Kazakov, M. I.			SFG in Hungary; Leningrad MD
Fediuninskii		Transcaucasian MD	Turkestan MD
Pen'kovskii		FE Command	Belorussian MD
Leliushenko		Transbaikal MD	Ural MD; DOSAAF
Rybalko	1st Ukrainian Front		Dep Comm Strat Miss F
Gusakovskii	Voronezh Front		Baltic MD
Liudnikov	Stalingrad Front	Crimea MD	Crimea MD[9]
Rotmistrov	7th Tank Corps[10]	CIC Armor	CIC Armor
Skripko	Strat Aviation; Stalingrad Front	Comm Mil Transp Aviation	Dep CIC AF
Rudenko	8th Air Army		Dep CIC AF
Sudets			Dep CIC AF; PVO-S

[1] On southern flank of the Stalingrad Front.
[2] Served under Malinovskii; later became Deputy Chief of Staff.
[3] In the battle of Kursk; later served with Khrushchev at the 1st Ukrainian Front.
[4] Served under Malinovskii; later commanded the Far Eastern MD.
[5] The SW Front became the Stalingrad Front in August 1942.
[6] All served with Khrushchev at the Stalingrad Front and in the battle of Kursk.
[7] The brigade was part of Getman's army at Kursk.
[8] This army was under Khrushchev's political supervision.
[9] This MD was eventually abolished.
[10] The 7th Tank Corps was part of Malinovskii's 2nd Guards Army at Stalingrad.

Appendix A-VI

CAREER PATTERNS OF POLITICAL FUNCTIONARIES IN THE MILITARY ASSOCIATED WITH KHRUSHCHEV

The Main Political Administration of the Soviet Army and Navy (MPA) is the Party's central control organ in the military establishment. Organizationally, it operates as a section of the Central Committee, to which it is directly responsible for its activities. It also has a horizontal link to the Ministry of Defense. During Zhukov's tenure as Minister of Defense, the MPA's functions and role were severely curtailed; since his ouster, the MPA has again become an authoritative and influential force within the military.

The MPA heads a complex control network consisting of political departments attached to major commands of political sections at intermediate levels, of Party Commissions and Party Committees at various levels, Primary Party Organizations at lower levels, and all levels of Komsomol organizations. Functionaries of political organs have wide authority in dealing with political and military matters and with questions of morale and personnel within the units. They are also responsible for maintaining cooperation between the units and the local civilian Party organizations.

There have been five heads of the MPA since 1945: (1) Colonel General Shikin, who is generally associated with Zhdanov, introduced very severe controls over the military during the early postwar period. (2) Colonel General F. F. Kuznetsov replaced Shikin in May 1949. Little is known about his administration of the MPA, except that it presumably was less severe than that of his predecessor. He also had to share some of his duties with a co-equal, Admiral Zakharov, the head of political organs for the Navy. (3) In the spring of 1953, Colonel General Zheltov took over as head of the MPA, and his administration was marked by a lessening of his organization's role and influence, due mostly to the Party's reluctance to alienate the military by maintaining strict political controls, and to Zhukov's well-known dislike of political officers in the military. Zheltov remained in the relatively low rank of colonel general and was not coopted to the Central Committee. (4) In January 1958, soon after Zhukov's dismissal, F. Golikov took over the MPA. He was eventually promoted to Marshal of the Soviet Union and given full membership on the Central Committee. During most of his tenure, the MPA enjoyed wide authority and influence, but these seem not to have been able to counter the growing opposition in military circles to certain military policies of Khrushchev, and Golikov ultimately was dismissed. (5) In May 1962, General of the Army A. A. Epishev replaced Golikov as head of the MPA. Almost from the beginning his regime was marked by a sharpening of the MPA's relations with the military professionals. In distinction to Golikov, who had been a professional officer with broad commanding experience during World War II, Epishev was a Party *apparatchik* and a former secret police functionary.

Following is a brief overview of Khrushchev's successive efforts to place trusted associates in the political control organs within the military, as illustrated by the careers of Epishev, Mironov, and Golikov.

The 1945-1953 Period

A. A. Epishev served first with Khrushchev at the Stalingrad Front, and later with Moskalenko's 38th Army. In 1946 he returned to the Ukrainian Party apparatus, Khrushchev's domain, until 1951, when he followed Khrushchev to Moscow and became Deputy Minister of Security (MGB).

N. R. Mironov also came from the Ukrainian Party apparatus. Having served with Khrushchev during the war, he returned to the Ukraine after the war, where he held positions in the Ukrainian Party. In 1951 he followed Epishev to Moscow and entered the central security organs.

F. F. Golikov served with Khrushchev at the Stalingrad Front. Later he returned to Moscow to assume the vital position of head of the Cadre Board within the Ministry of Defense, a post he retained until almost the end of the Stalin era.

The Zhukov Period—1953-1957

Epishev left the security organs after Stalin's death, and returned again to the Ukrainian Party apparatus, where he became first secretary of the Odessa *Obkom* Party Committee. After the ouster of Malenkov he was appointed Ambassador to Rumania; in 1961 he became Ambassador to Yugoslavia.

Mironov, in 1956, was promoted within the security organs to the position of head of KGB organs for the Leningrad *oblast.*

Golikov was acting within the central organs of the Ministry of Defense during this period.

Consolidation of Power—1957-1962

In January 1958, Golikov replaced Zheltov, the ineffectual political general, as head of the MPA. This move had two effects: the military was conciliated by the appointment of a professional officer, while Khrushchev gained a tighter hold over the MPA by placing it more closely under his control, establishing a direct relationship between the MPA and the Central Committee, and having his loyal associate Golikov in charge.

Mironov, in 1959, moved up into the vital position of head of the Section on Administrative Organs of the Central Committee, where he dealt with security, judicial, and police matters and with some military affairs.

Tightening the Hold on the Military—1962-1963

In 1960 Khrushchev announced a series of measures which created widespread disaffection among the military. He then took several steps to contain the growing opposition, including the tightening of political controls in the military.

In May 1962, Epishev replaced Golikov and instituted a policy of more severe supervision and indoctrination of officers. Mironov became actively involved in military affairs, and predominantly in those touching on coercive functions.

The practical effect of these measures was a much tighter control network in the military, which was now manned by people who were personally responsible and extremely loyal to Khrushchev. The symbolic effect of these changes was also significant, as the political control network in the military had been entrusted to Party *apparatchiks* who, in addition to their close relationship to Khrushchev, had a long history of antimilitarism and of careers in the security organs.

Appendix A-VII

THE FRONTS IN THE FALL AND WINTER OF 1942-1943

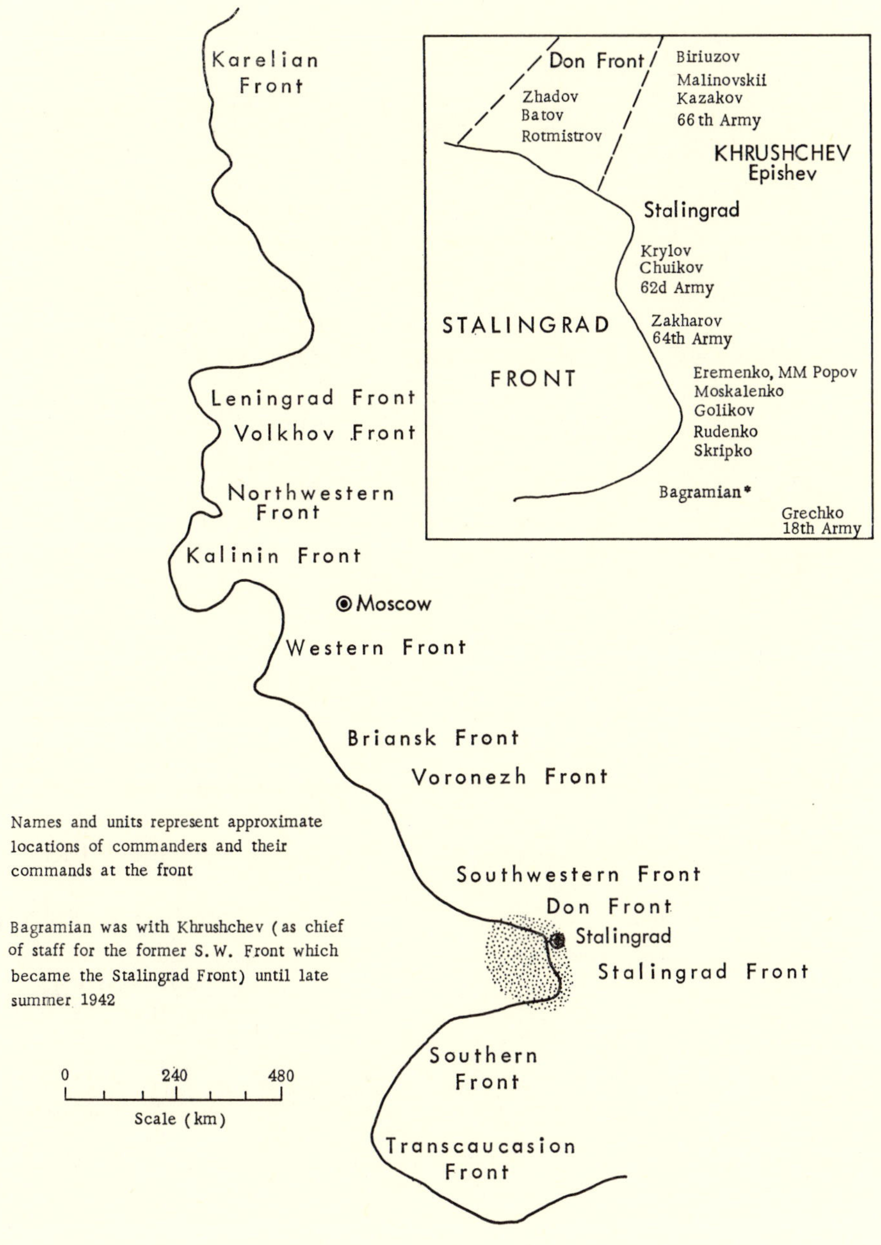

Appendix A-VIII

BIOGRAPHICAL INDEX OF RANKING MEMBERS OF THE STALINGRAD GROUP*

Key to abbreviations: cand = candidate member; CC = Central Committee [of the CPSU]; chmn = chairman; C/S = Chief of Staff; CIC = Commander-in-Chief; comm F = commander of a Front; CP = Communist Party of the Soviet Union; dep = deputy; F = Front; Fr = Frunze Military Academy; GS = General Staff; GS Acad = Academy of the General Staff; HSU = Hero of the Soviet Union; MSU = Marshal of the Soviet Union; MD = military district; memb = member; mil ed = military education; mil car = military career; pol stndg = political standing; PVO-S = Protivovozdushnaia oborona strany (Antiaircraft Defense of the Country); SA = Soviet Army; VVS = Voenno-vozdushnye sily (Air Forces)

BAGRAMIAN, Ivan Khristoforovich—1897, Armenian, worker
- mil ed : Fr 1934; GS 1938
- mil car : Army 1915; SA 1920; comm of SW & W Fs 1941-43; comm of Baltic F 1943-45; comm of Baltic MD 1945-54; chief inspector Min of Def 1954-55; dep Min of Def 1955-56 & since 1958; MSU 1955
- pol stndg: memb CP 1941; cand CC 1952 & 1956; memb CC 1961

BATITSKII, Pavel Fedorovich—1910, Ukrainian, worker
- mil ed : Fr 1938; GS 1948
- mil car : SA 1924; WWII C/S div to comm inf corps; C/S PVO *raion* 1948-50; Transcaucasian MD: C/GS of VVS of SA, 1950-53; dep comm MD 1953-54; Moscow district PVO since 1954; Army General
- pol stndg: memb CP 1938; Moscow City Party Cmte 1958 & 1960; cand CC 1961

* Sources: *Istoriia Velikoi Otechestvennoi voiny Sovetskogo Soiuza, 1941-1945* (The History of the Great Patriotic War of the Soviet Union, 1941-1945), Voenizdat, Moscow, 1961; *Deputaty Verkhovnogo Soveta SSSR, shestoi sozyv* (The Deputies of the Supreme Soviet of the USSR, Sixth Convocation), Moscow, 1962; *Ezhegodnik Bol'shoi Sovetskoi entsiklopedii, 1962* (Yearbook of the Large Soviet Encyclopedia, 1962), "Sovetskaia entsiklopediia," Moscow, 1962; Institute for the Study of the USSR, Munich, *Who's Who in the USSR*, eds. Dr. Heinrich E. Schulz and Dr. Stephen S. Taylor, Intercontinental Book & Publishing Co., Ltd., Montreal, 1962; Hans Koch (ed.), *5000 Sowjetköpfe* (5000 Soviet Leaders), Deutsche Industrieverlags-GmbH, Cologne, 1959. See also the Soviet military memoirs listed in the Bibliography.

BATOV, Pavel Ivanovich—1897, Russian, peasant

mil ed : Fr 1928

mil car : Red Army 1918; comm div in Sov-Finn war 1939-40; comm army (Stalingrad) 1941-45; comm army (Germany) 1945-49; comm forces Kaliningrad dist 1949-50; comm Ciscarpathian MD 1955-58; comm Baltic MD 1959-60; 1st dep C/GS USSR since 1962; C/S Warsaw Pact Armed Forces 1962-11/65; Army General; HSU 1943 & 1944

pol stndg: memb CP 1929; CC Ukraine 1956

BIRIUZOV, Sergei Semenovich—1904, Russian [died 10/19/64]

mil ed : Fr 1937

mil car : SA 1922; WWII C/S of 3rd & 4th Ukr Fs (until 10/44); acting chmn Allied Control Commission in Bulgaria 1944-47; dep comm Ground Forces 1946-47; comm Kiev MD 1947-53; comm Central Forces Group 1953-54; 1st dep comm PVO-S 1954-55; comm PVO-S, dep Min of Def 1955-62; comm Missile Forces 1962; C/GS 1963-10/64; MSU 1955

pol stndg: memb CP 1926; cand CC 1956; memb CC 1961

CHUIKOV, Vasilii Ivanovich—1900, Russian, peasant

mil ed : Fr 1925

mil car : SA 1918; comm brigade to army 1936-40; WWII comm army; dep supr comm Ground Forces 1946-49; CIC Soviet Forces in Germany, chmn Allied Control Commission Germany 1949-53; comm Kiev MD 1953-60; comm Ground Forces, dep Min of Def since 1960; HSU 1944 & 1945; MSU 1955

pol stndg: memb CP 1919; cand CC 1952 & 1956; memb CC 1961

EPISHEV, Aleksei Alekseevich—1908, Russian, worker

mil ed : Technical Acad 1938

mil car : SA 1930-38; Mil Council of Stalingrad F 1940-43; SA political work 1943-46; head, Main Polit Admin SA since 1962; Army General 1962

pol stndg: memb CP 1929; CP work since 1938; 1st sec Kharkov *obkom, gorkom* CP Ukr, in apparatus of CC CPSU 1940-43; sec of CC CP Ukr 1946-51; dep Min of State Security 1951-53; 1st sec Odessa *obkom* CP Ukr 1953-55; amb to Rumania 1955-61; amb to Yugoslavia 1961-62; cand CC 1961; memb CC 11/1964

EREMENKO, Andrei Ivanovich—1892, Ukrainian, peasant
mil ed : Fr 1935
mil car : SA 1918; WWII comm W, Briansk, SE, Stalingrad, S, Kalinin, 2nd Baltic, & 4th Ukr Fs; comm various MDs 1945-58; gen inspector in Min of Def since 1958; HSU 1944; MSU 1955
pol stndg: memb CP 1918; cand CC 1956 & 1961

FEDIUNINSKII, Ivan Ivanovich—1900, Russian
mil ed : Fr 1930
mil car : SA 1919; comm infantry corps 1939-41; WWII comm 54th Army, 2nd Army; post-WWII Col-Gen; comm Arkhangelsk MD 1946-51; dep chmn Sov Control Comm Germany 1952-54; dep comm & comm Transcaucasian MD 1954-57; comm Turkestan MD since 1958; Army General 1955; HSU
pol stndg: memb CP 1930; Presidium CC Georgia 1956-57; Presidium CC Uzbek 1960

GALITSKII, Kuzma Nikitovich—1897
mil ed : Technical Acad mid-30's
mil car : comm 2nd Guards Army 1945; comm troops, East Prussia 1945-46; comm Ciscarpathian MD 1946-54; comm Odessa MD 1954-55; head, Kuibyshev Mil Acad in Moscow 1955-57; comm Transcaucasian MD 1957-61
pol stndg: memb CP 1918; memb CC Ukr 1949, 1952, 1954; memb Presidium CC Georgia 1958-61

GETMAN, Andrei Lavrent'evich—1903, Ukrainian
mil ed : Mil Acad Armored Troops 1937
mil car : SA 1924; WWII comm tank division, dep comm tank army; comm armored troops of various MDs 1945-48; C/S MDs 1948-54; dep chief armored troops 1954-56; comm Carpathian MD since 1958; Col-Gen armored troops 1953
pol stndg: memb CP 1927; memb CC CP Ukr 1960; cand CC 1961

GOLIKOV, Filipp Ivanovich—1900, Russian, peasant
mil ed : Fr 1933
mil car : SA 1918; comm corps 1931-WWII; WWII comm Briansk & Voronezh Fs; dep comm Stalingrad F; dep Min of Def & head, Main Division of Cadres 1943-50;

head, Main Polit Admin SA 1958-62; with Min of Def since 1962; MSU 1961
pol stndg: memb CP 1918; memb CC 1961

GRECHKO, Andrei Antonovich—1903, Ukrainian
mil ed : Fr 1936; GS 1941
mil car : SA 1919; comm regiment, C/S division before WWII; WWII comm div-army, dep comm 1st Ukr F; comm Kiev MD 1945-53; comm Sov Forces Germany 1953-57; CIC Ground Forces 1957-60; 1st dep Min of Def 1958-60; CIC Warsaw Pact Forces since 1960; MSU 1955; HSU 1958
pol stndg: memb CP 1928; memb CC CP Ukr 1952-53; cand CC 1952 & 1956; memb CC 1961

IAKUBOVSKII, Ivan Ignat'evich—1912, Belorussian, peasant
mil ed : GS 1948
mil car : SA 1932; WWII comm tank regiment; dep comm tank corps 1944-46; comm tank div 1948-52; comm armored forces Carpathian MD 1952-53; dep comm Sov Forces Germany 1957-60; comm Sov Forces Germany 1960-61; dep comm Sov Forces Germany 1961-62; Army General 1962; CIC Sov Forces Germany 1962-10/65; comm Kiev MD since 10/65; HSU Jan & Sept 1944
pol stndg: memb CP 1937; memb CC 1961

KAZAKOV, Mikhail Il'ich—1901, Russian
mil ed : Fr 1931; GS 1937
mil car : SA 1920; Party-political work until 1925; command work 1925; dep & C/S Central Asia MD 1937-41; WWII C/S of F, comm army, dep comm F; post-WWII C/S, dep comm & comm of MDs (including Ural); Army General 1955; dep supr comm Ground Forces 1955; comm Southern group in Hungary 1955-60; comm Leningrad MD 1960-11/65; C/S Warsaw Pact Armed Forces since Nov 1965
pol stndg: memb CP 1919; cand CC 1961

KHETAGUROV, Georgii Ivanovich—1903, Ossetin
mil ed : no mil acad cited
mil car : SA 1920; comm div to comm corps 1931-WWII; WWII C/S artillery corps to comm army; comm troops, Northern group & Poland since 1956; Col-Gen; HSU
pol stndg: memb CP 1924

KONEV, Ivan Stepanovich—1897, Russian, peasant
mil ed : Fr 1934
mil car : SA 1918; WWII comm of Kalinin, Steppe, 1st & 2nd Ukr, and other Fs; comm Ground Forces, dep Min of War 1946-11/50; chief inspector SA 1950-51; comm Carpathian MD 1951-55; 1st dep Min of Def, CIC Warsaw Pact Forces 1955-60; CIC Sov Forces Germany 1961-62; gen inspector in Min of Def since 1962; MSU 1944; HSU (2)
pol stndg: memb CP 1918; cand CC 1939-52; memb CC 1952-61

KOSHEVOI, Petr Kirillovich—1904, Ukrainian, worker
mil ed : Fr 1939; GS 1948
mil car : SA 1920; WWII comm div, corps, army; Col-Gen 1954; dep comm Sov Forces Germany 1955-57; comm Siberian MD 1957-60; comm Kiev MD 1960-10/65; CIC Sov Forces Germany since 10/65; HSU (2)
pol stndg: memb CP 1925; cand CC 1961; cand Presidium CC CP Ukr 1961

KRYLOV, Nikolai Ivanovich—1903, Russian
mil ed : secondary
mil car : SA 1919; WWII C/S army, comm army (Stalingrad, Odessa, Sevastopol); comm Far East, Ural, Leningrad MDs 1946-60; Moscow MD 1960; CIC Strategic Missile Forces since 1963; MSU 1962; HSU (2)
pol stndg: memb CP 1927; memb CC 1961

LELIUSHENKO, Dmitrii Danilovich—1901, Ukrainian, peasant
mil ed : Fr late 1920's; GS (no date available)
mil car : SA 1919; WWII comm 4th tank army (Ukr 1943-45, Saxony 1945-47); memb Mil Council in MDs, staff Min of Def 1947-56; comm Transbaikal MD 1956-58; comm Ural MD 1958-60; chmn of CC/USSR/DOSAAF since 1960; Army General; HSU 1940 & 1945
pol stndg: memb CP 1924; cand CC CP Ukr 1954

LIUDNIKOV, I. I.
mil ed : not available
mil car : WWII comm army; dep comm Sov Forces Germany 1951-53; comm Crimean MD since 1954; Col-Gen
pol stndg: memb CC Moldav; cand CC CP Ukr 1956

MALINOVSKII, Rodion Iakovlevich—1898, Ukrainian
mil ed : Fr 1930
mil car : SA 1918; WWII comm Guards Army at Stalingrad; comm South, SW, 3rd & 2nd Ukr Fs; Transbaikal F 1945; post-WWII Mil Dist, FE Forces; 1st dep Min of Def, comm Ground Forces 1956 (March); Min of Def since 1957; MSU 1944; HSU 1944 & 1958
pol stndg: memb CP 1926; cand CC 1952 & 1956; memb CC 1956 & 1961

MIRONOV, Nikolai Romanovich—1913, Russian [died 10/19/64]
mil ed : Dnepropetrovsk State Univ
mil car : WWII polit worker in armed forces; Major General
pol stndg: memb CP 1940; 1st sec Oktiabr' *raikom* (Dnepropetrovsk) CP Ukr 1947-49; 1st sec Kirovograd *obkom* CP Ukr 1949-51; state security organs since 1951; head, KGB of Leningrad *oblast* 1956-59; head, Dept of Admin Organs CC CPSU 1959-64; memb Central Audit Comm CC 1961

MOSKALENKO, Kirill Semenovich—1902, Ukrainian, peasant
mil ed : Artillery Academy Dzerzhinskii 1939
mil car : SA 1920; Sov-Finn war 1939-40; WWII comm corps; comm of SW, Stalingrad, Voronezh, 1st & 4th Ukr Fs since 1941; comm Moscow dist PVO 1948-53; comm Moscow MD 1953-60; comm Missile Forces & dep Min of Def 1960-62; chief inspector in Min of Def & dep Min of Def since 1962 (April); MSU 1955; HSU 1943
pol stndg: memb CP 1926; memb CC 1956

PAVLOVSKII, Ivan Grigor'evich—1909, Ukrainian, peasant
mil ed : GS (no date available)
mil car : SA 1931; WWII "leading mil work," comm div to comm army; 1st dep comm Transcaucasian MD 1958-61; comm Volga MD since 1961; Col-Gen
pol stndg: memb CP 1939

PEN'KOVSKII, Valentin Antonovich—1904, White Russian
mil ed : GS 1947
mil car : SA 1920; WWII comm div, C/S of army, C/S of SW F; comm Far East MD 1956-61; comm Belorussian MD since 1961; Army General
pol stndg: memb CP 1926; memb CC Belorus 1961; cand CC 1961

PLIEV, Issa Aleksandrovich—1902, Ossetin, peasant
mil ed : Fr 1933; GS 1941 & 1949
mil car : SA 1922; WWII comm Cossack cavalry div, corps; comm cavalry army: Ukraine (Right Bank), Bobriusk, Minsk, 2nd Ukr F in Hungary 1944 (spring); comm Mongolian Popular Revolutionary Army 1945; post-WWII comm Baku MD; dep comm North Caucasus MD 1946-56; comm North Caucasus MD since 1956; Army General 1962; HSU (2)
pol stndg: memb CP 1926; memb CC Azerbaidjan 1954; cand CC 1961

POPOV, Markian Mikhailovich—1902, Russian
mil ed : Fr 1920
mil car : SA 1920; C/S, comm MD 1936; WWII comm army, C/S F, comm F; comm Tauric MD 1946-55; C/S, Gen Staff of Ground Forces 1956-63; leading work in Min of Def since 1963; Army General
pol stndg: memb CP 1921

RUDENKO, Sergei Ignat'evich—1904, Ukrainian, handicraftsman
mil ed : Zhukovskii A 1936
mil car : Sov Aviation 1923; WWII comm Air Army; C/GS VVS 1949-58; 1st dep comm VVS since 1958; Marshal of Aviation 1955; HSU 1944
pol stndg: memb CP 1928; cand CC 1961

SKRIPKO, Nikolai Semenovich—1902, Russian, worker
mil ed : GS 1950
mil car : SA 1919; WWII command posts in VVS, dep comm Strategic Air Forces; Gen Staff VVS since 1950 (1st dep comm Strategic Air Forces to asst comm Airborne Troops); comm Mil Transp Aviation of VVS since 1955; Marshal of Aviation 1944
pol stndg: memb CP 1927; memb Central Audit Comm CC 1961

STUCHENKO, Andrei Trofimovich—1904, Ukrainian
mil ed : Fr 1938
mil car : SA 1920; WWII comm forces on W, 2nd Baltic, and Leningrad Fs; comm rifle corps 1947-51 & 1953-54; comm Northern MD 1956-59; comm Volga MD 1959-61; comm Transcaucasian MD since 1961 (May); Col-Gen

pol stndg: memb CP 1929; memb CC Lithuania 1954; memb Presidium CC Karelia 1956; cand CC 1961; memb CC Georgia

SUDETS, Vladimir Aleksandrovich—1904, Ukrainian
mil ed : GS 1950
mil car : SA 1925; WWII command posts in Sov Air Force; C/S VVS & dep comm VVS 1946-49; comm Air Army 1951-55; dep comm VVS & comm Strategic Air Forces 1955-58; comm Strategic Air Forces 1958-62; comm PVO-S, dep Min of Def since 1962; Marshal of Aviation 1955; HSU 1945
pol stndg: memb CP 1924; cand CC 1961

ZAKHAROV, Matvei Vasil'evich—1909, Russian
mil ed : Fr 1928; GS 1937
mil car : SA 1917 & 1918; WWII C/S Kalinin F 1941; Leningrad F 1943; 2nd Ukr F 1944; Transbaikal F 1945; dep comm Sov Far East Forces after WWII; head, GS Acad 1945-49; dep chief, Army Gen Staff 1949-52; chief inspector, SA 1952-53; comm Leningrad MD 1953-57; comm Sov Forces in Germany 1957 (Nov)-1960 (Apr); C/GS & 1st dep Min of Def 1960-63; C/GS since 11/1964; MSU 1959; HSU
pol stndg: memb CP 1917; memb CC 1961

APPENDIX B

Cycles in Party-Military Relations, 1918-1963

The relationship between Party and military in the Soviet Union is marked by conflicts of a peculiarly cyclical and repetitive nature. The graph on the next page is an attempt to trace these cycles on a time-conflict axis, on the basis of the following factors:

1. The relative position, authority, and prominence of the Party-political control organs in the military. (Rises in authority are reflected in a rising curve, and weakening authority in a dropping of the curve.)
2. The relative position, freedom of action, scope of authority, and prominence of the military professionals. (Here, rising authority is reflected in the lowering of the curve, and decline in authority shows up in the rising curve.)
3. Direct coercion of the military; discrediting of military historical achievements.

The curve on the graph must be read in the light of the following historical events and developments:

1921–1925	Trotsky and other proponents of the nonprofessional, mass army struggle against Frunze, Voroshilov, Tukhachevskii, and Stalin, champions of the professional, cadre army.
1929	Silent purges in the military.
1932–1936	The Red Army is modernized and enlarged.
1937	The military purges.
1940	Removal of military commissars from the units.
1941	Reintroduction of the military commissars.
1942–1945	The period in World War II in which the military gained many concessions from the Party.
1946–1949	The Zhdanov (postwar) period characterized by anti-military measures. (Zhukov and other professionals in obscurity, political generals in control, political organs given broad authority under Shikin.)
1949–1952	Military professionals are returned to public life; security organs and Zhdanovites in disfavor.
1953–1957	The Zhukov era: the military's role ascending; political controls in the military at a minimum.
1957	The ouster of Zhukov.

1957–1960	Khrushchev's new strategic policies, which discriminate against the conventional forces and cause discontent in the military.
1962	The military's dissatisfaction becomes more intense, and finds acute expression during the Cuban missile crisis of October 1962.
1963	Party-military tensions abate, but the conflict is not fully resolved.

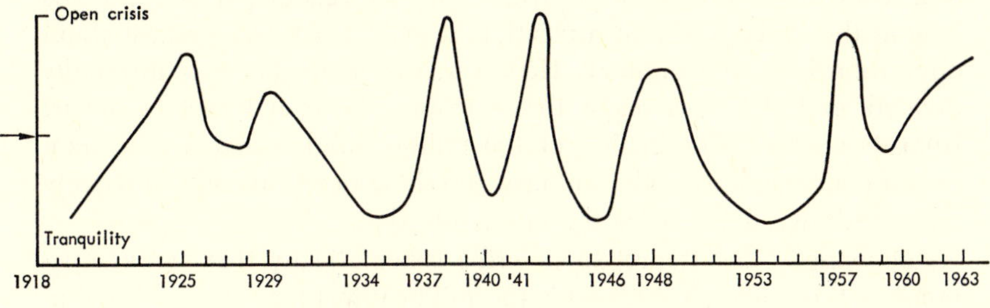

A tension scale of Party-military relations

APPENDIX C

Patterns of the Party's Treatment of the Military Under Given Conditions

The relations between the Party's ruling elite and the military are in the nature of an armed truce, which on occasion erupts into conflict, usually as a result of the Party's attempt to keep the military under tight control while demanding from it high levels of performance. As long as the Party is in a firm position, it need not worry greatly about opposition from the military. However, when the Party is internally divided, or is facing a major threat from outside, it is apt to depart from its absolute domination of the military and follow a more empirical course, granting the military certain concessions, which usually are withdrawn again after the crisis subsides.

Following is an attempt to describe schematically this *modus operandi* of the Party elite *vis-à-vis* the military in four types of circumstance: during periods of rising Party-military tensions; during a war or in the face of a threat of war; during periods of internal Party crisis; and during periods of political and military tranquillity and firm Party authority. From the historical evidence, the Party's behavior in these situations would seem to resemble a predictable reflex action.

1. *Actual or Alleged Military Opposition to the Party*
   (a) Political controls are intensified and the authority of the commanders is curtailed.
   (b) The military is subjected to overt or covert purges.
   (c) Younger, "untainted" officers are promoted in large numbers.
   (d) The role and authority of the Komsomol are enhanced.
   (e) The closure-prone military community is forcibly "opened up" through a massive enlistment of local civilian Party organs in military activities.
   (f) As the crisis ebbs and the Party regains a firm hold, political controls are relaxed, and some concessions are made to the military, usually involving greater status and more socio-economic privileges, to maintain its sense of commitment and to show the Party's good will.

2. *During War or at the Threat of War*
   (a) The first "reflex action" is a tightening of political controls paralleled by severe curtailment of commanders' authority.

(b) This initial panic reaction is followed by the Party's relaxation of political controls and granting of greater commanding authority and status to the military.

(c) Having thus relinquished its firm political controls, the Party builds up its organizational network through massive recruitment of military personnel into the CPSU.

(d) As the crisis subsides, controls are intensified once again and many of the recently granted privileges are rescinded.

3. *During Internal Party Crises*

(a) The military is greatly favored with concessions and privileges.

(b) Ranking military leaders are included in the Party's political affairs.

(c) Political controls are relaxed.

(d) With the passing of the crisis, political controls are restored, some of the recent privileges are rescinded, and ranking military leaders (e.g., Tukhachevskii and Zhukov) may be purged and some of them killed.

4. *Firm Party Unity and Political Tranquillity*

(a) Undesirable elements in the military are weeded out as a routine measure.

(b) The subordination of the military to Party leadership and controls is unquestioned.

(c) By a methodical process the military community is immunized and indoctrinated to ensure its unfailing loyalty to the regime.

APPENDIX D

The Party's Control Network in the Soviet Military

In the accompanying diagram, the solid line represents the regular chain of command within the individual organizations; a broken line shows channels of control (indicating authority over, or access to, a given level in the military hierarchy); and a two-directional arrow points to mutual, balanced controls.

The Military Council is mainly responsible to the Central Committee, answering to the Ministry of Defense only in operational matters. It includes representatives from (a) the military (the Commander of the District), (b) the MPA (the head of the Political Administration of the District), (c) the Party *apparat* (the secretary of the Republican or *krai* Party Committee), and (d) the security organs ("the regular cadre member from the political workers").

The MPA is mainly responsible to the Central Committee, of which it is a section; it coordinates its activities with the Ministry of Defense in an operational sense.

Members of the local Party organs frequently participate in the activities and meetings of the Political Administrations and Sections as well as in the proceedings of the Party Committees. Their main function is to serve as an additional information and control link between the Central Committee apparatus and the military.

The security organs and the *prokuratura* are responsible to their own superior levels of authority and to the Central Committee Section on Administrative Organs. They usually collaborate with the political organs in the units and with the commanders.

The accompanying chart clearly indicates the various channels of control and information that keep the military under close surveillance. By interrupting the military chain of command at a crucial level (i.e., the Military Council at the district level), by placing civilian Party *apparatchiks* at the middle and top of the MPA structure, and by introducing functionaries from the political organs in the military into the appropriate civilian Party organs, the Central Committee apparatus seeks to achieve a balanced power structure in the military districts and in the military organization.*

* Our understanding of the Party's control of the military establishment may be aided by this overview of the functional subdivisions of the Central Committee apparatus.

The central agents of control and information in the military are the political control organs, of which one is attached to headquarters at almost every level of the military establishment. One member of these organs is appointed to serve at each step of the military hierarchy (the Ministry, the Military Council, the *zampolit* of the *soedinenie* and *chast'*, and the *partorg* at the company level), and at each level of the Party and Komsomol organization (as secretary of the respective Party *biuro*). Members of the political organs participate in the proceedings of local civilian Party and governmental bodies. They also collaborate with the security organs.

A. *Commissions*:
   1. Commission for Party-Organizational Problems
      a. Section for Party Organs
      b. Section for Administrative Organs
      c. Main Political Administration of the Soviet Army and Navy (which functions as a CC Section)
   2. Commission for Ideological Problems

B. *Committee for Party and State Control*
C. *Administration for External Affairs*
D. *Bureaus for Production Problems*
E. *Regional Bureaus*
F. *Other Sections of the CC Apparat*

(Adapted from Boris Meissner, "Chruschtschowismus ohne Chruschtschow," *Osteuropa*, No. 3, 1965, pp. 159-161.)

PARTY CONTROLS IN THE SOVIET MILITARY ESTABLISHMENT

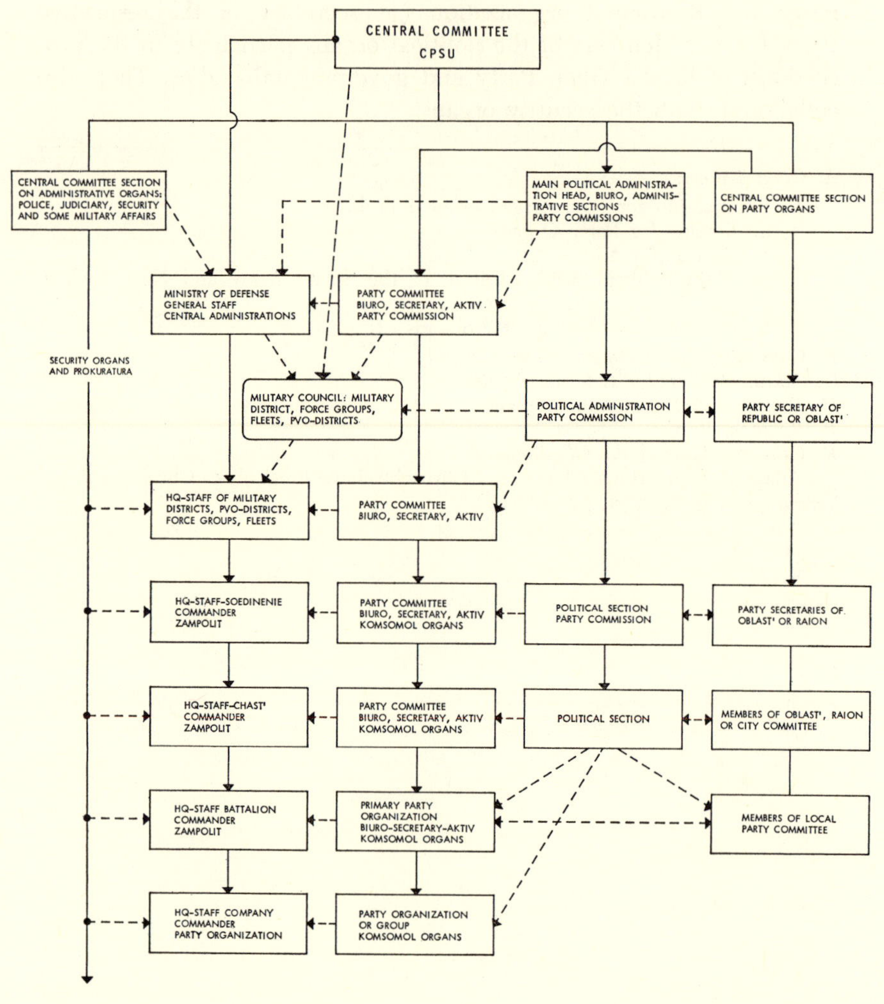

APPENDIX E

Structure and Functions of the Party's Chief Political Organs in the Military

The Political Apparatus of a Chast' and Ship: the Zampolit

The political section of the regiment is headed by the political officer, or *zampolit* (*zamestitel' po politicheskoi chasti*), whose staff includes:

(a) The secretary of the Party *biuro*
(b) The regimental propagandists
(c) The head of the regimental club
(d) The secretary of the regimental Komsomol organization
(e) Part-time agitators, lecturers, and other functionaries

The duties of the *zampolit* as described in Soviet manuals may be summed up as follows:

(a) The *zampolit* participates in all military planning and training as well as in political education.
(b) He organizes and directs all political work in his unit.
(c) He personally conducts educational activities of personnel.
(d) Though immediately subordinate to the regimental commander, he is directly above the personnel.
(e) In matters of Party-political work he is subordinate to the head of the political section of the *soedinenie.*
(f) He is personally responsible for the work of the Party organization. Together with the Party *biuro* he organizes Party work in the regiments and units.
(g) The *zampolit* directs and controls those activities in the unit that come under the heading of "socialist competition." He instructs the officers on them, and participates in setting the unit's goal.

The Primary Party Organization (PPO)

The Primary Party Organization (PPO) is the key element of the Party apparatus in the military. It is normally located at the regimental level as well as in independent smaller units. The PPOs are created by the Political Department of the *soedinenie* (the formation, or larger unit) in regiments and separate units and ships of 1st, 2nd, and 3rd class, and also in all military institutions and institutes that have at least three Party members. Where there are less than three members, a candidate or Komsomol group is created, headed by a *partorg* (Party organizer) who is appointed by the Political Department of the *soedinenie.*

The Party members in the PPO fall into three categories: full-time Party functionaries; part-time Party functionaries; and general membership.

Nominally, the PPO is built on the democratic elective principle, and the majority rules. The internal organization of the PPO is as follows:

(a) Its chief ruling body is the General Meeting of the total membership which convenes once a month.
(b) The General Meeting elects a Party *biuro*, which actually directs and controls the activities of the PPO. The *biuro* consists of not more than eleven members, who are elected by secret vote.
(c) From among its members the *biuro* then elects, by open vote, a secretary and one or two assistants. PPOs with fewer than fifteen members have no *biuro*; instead, the General Meeting elects, by secret vote, a secretary and one assistant.

The functions of the PPO and its *biuro* as they have been described in Soviet manuals for the political organs are:

(a) to educate the personnel in the spirit of Marxism-Leninism;
(b) to inculcate in them a high political awareness, discipline, and loyalty;
(c) to work systematically on bringing into the Party new members who are loyal, active, and conscientious;
(d) to direct the Komsomol;
(e) to strengthen ties with the masses of soldiers, and explain to them the policies and decisions of Party and government;
(f) to perceive the moods and problems of the personnel; to enter into all aspects of their lives; and to assist the *zampolit.*

APPENDIX F

A Political Morality Tale

In December 1960, the central organ of the Main Political Administration of the Soviet Army and Navy, *Kommunist Vooruzhennykh Sil*, carried a "feature story," entitled "Dangerous Sickness," by a Colonel A. Grishchenko. It described at length the recent case of Major General Rogatiuk, whose professional and private conduct had brought him into conflict with the Party and its egalitarian principles, and who had thereupon been subjected to investigation, Party-disciplinary proceedings, and humiliation. Both the timing and the directness of the report are significant. At the time of its appearance, there was growing turbulence in the officer corps, a reaction to the Party's planning to release about a quarter-million officers from active duty and transfer them to reserve or retirement status. The plan had been announced by Khrushchev in January 1960 and had been implemented by a massive campaign of indoctrination, intimidation, and a forced "egalitarianism" intended to weaken the officer corps. The military was deeply shocked by this new policy and the assault on its independence.

This was the background against which to read the very unusual report on the affair of Major General Rogatiuk, published no doubt as a warning to other recalcitrant officers and as a demonstration of the power of the political organs in the military. The substance of the case is quickly told. The general had been called before the Party Commission attached to the Political Section of his staff, to be reprimanded for several acts that were not in the interest of the Party. The charges were (a) that he maintained several dwellings, one on the post, another in the city, and a *dacha*; (b) that he led an immoral personal life, having gone to a picnic with the wife of another officer; and (c) that he had reacted in an "uncommunist" manner to criticism expressed by one of his subordinates at a Party meeting. While such accusations would appear to warrant disciplinary proceedings, evidence of this kind of conduct is very rarely found against a general officer, and even rarer is it to encounter a detailed public account of such a lurid affair. There can be little doubt that the story about General Rogatiuk and his violation of the Party's interests and moral standards was designed to compromise the entire officer corps.

The published story, which makes use of the flash-back technique, follows the classic dramatic pattern of such moral tales in the Soviet

Union: (a) the conflict is staged; (b) the Party, having demonstrated to the transgressor the nature and extent of his wrongdoing, offers him a chance to go straight; (c) the accused, who is "an immature Communist," cannot adhere to the straight and narrow path, as he is weakened by human impulses, and his weakness leads him into anti-Party behavior; (d) he is finally punished, but the Party, though omnipotent, is also kind, and tempers its punishment with mercy: The offender will ultimately find the right path, having been shown the frightening consequences of excommunication.

The following is a greatly abbreviated version of the little drama. For their relevance to the subject of this study those items of dialogue and description have been singled out that illuminate the special relationship between the General and his "assistant for political affairs"; the General's attitude toward the Party functionaries who sit in judgment on his future; the generally tense and volatile relations between officers and political functionaries in the military; and the moralistic attitudes of the Party functionaries, whose language and symbolism recall those of religious institutions.

Act I, "The General and the Apparatchik": The Party insists on faithful practice of the ritual of *kritika/samokritika*, by which every Party member, regardless of position, rank, experience, and age, is urged to confess his own weaknesses and mistakes at regular Party meetings and to point out those of his comrades. The General, having been publicly criticized at such a Party meeting by one of his officers, meets the head of the Political Section attached to his command (and nominally his subordinate) and pleads with him rather obsequiously to discipline the officer, Kuzmenko. *General*: "It would be nice, Ivan Andreevich, if you reprimanded Kuzmenko." *Political officer*: "But wasn't he right?" *General*: "In a way . . . but my authority must not be publicly undermined." *Political officer*: "The authority of a leader is undermined not by those who criticize his mistakes but by those who worsen such mistakes by their self-interest and lack of principles." *General*: "You never listen to my opinion . . . you are supposed to support *edinonachalie* [full military authority]." *Political officer*: "True. I have supported and will support Soviet *edinonachalie* as one of the fundamental principles of the development of our armed forces, but only on the basis of Party interests. . . ."

Act II, "The Growing Conflict": The General begins to feel the pressure from the political organs and their functionaries within his command. The *kritika/samokritika* methods, intensified after October 1957 (when Zhukov was ousted from the Ministry of Defense), are destructive to his sense of authority and military propriety: "I know that I am right. What do they want from me? Why do they constantly point their fingers at me—that's right, that's wrong, don't do this, don't do that?" He finally resorts to addressing an appeal to the Party's Central Committee in Moscow, persuaded and helped by a subordinate who says to him: "Believe me, they [the political functionaries] do it because of jealousy. But don't you give in. True friends will never let you down. Do you want me to write a letter to the CC? Let them know how they persecute a general?" To which the General answers: "Why not? Write! We will take care of ourselves."

Act III, "The General's Temptation": The Central Committee responds to the General's letter with a measure of sympathy and corrects some (unnamed) abuses. At the same time, it finds the General's charges exaggerated and refers the matter back to the local Party authorities, thus leaving the conflict between the General and his political "assistants" unresolved. In the grace period that follows, the General submits to the ultimate human temptations: to the weakness of the flesh (by "going on a picnic" with another officer's wife) and to abusing his authority, a sacred trust of the Party. The dialogue quoted is the reporter's attempt to show the General's abuse of his authority.

Unable to forget that he, a "proud and strong man," has been strongly criticized at a Party meeting, the General threatens the critic, who has come to ask his permission to go to a hospital and sanatorium because of illness. *General*: "I won't give you a pass." *Kuzmenko*: "Is this your answer to my criticism?" *General*: "We are now reducing the Armed Forces. If you don't want to understand that, Comrade Lieutenant Colonel. . . ." *Kuzmenko*: "I understand you, Comrade General, and will therefore have to go to our Supreme Soviet representative—the commander of the Military District." *General*: "So, go."

Act IV, "The General's Canossa": Called before the Party Commission that is attached to the Political Section of his command, the General now must suffer the Party's inquisition and, possibly, the ultimate penalty of excommunication. The account of the meeting strikingly conveys the ritualistic quality of the proceedings, as the General is forced to admit his guilt, then humbles himself by pleading with the assembled functionaries, and the latter piously condescend to his human failings and grant him forgiveness and a final chance to redeem himself.

Commission member: "Yes, Comrade Rogatiuk, you suffer from a dangerous sickness. And you became infected because you don't have an antidote against the corrupting influence of the survivals of the past [a reference to the time before October 1957, when the military, under Zhukov, had asserted itself *vis-à-vis* the Party]. . . . The trouble with you, Rogatiuk, is that you are an immature Communist." *The General*: "Have faith in me, Comrades, I am not completely lost to the Party." *Commission secretary*: "You have given us your oath before." *The reporter*: "Rogatiuk lowered his head. After a while, he quietly asked: 'Trust me for the last time, Comrades. Without the Party there is no life for me.' He said that emotionally, from the soul. And the members of the Party Commission understood his feelings of open-hearted repentance." *Commission secretary*: "You deserve to be excluded from the ranks of the Party. Only after taking into consideration your irreproachable service record and your open-hearted repentance has the Party Commission decided to trust you for the last time. We have decided to transfer you to [Party] candidacy for one year. . . . If your word is good and you show political maturity, you will become a Party member again. If not—then blame yourself." *Reporter*: "Rogatiuk received the severe Party penalty with sorrow, though he knew that he deserved it. . . . From now on it would depend on him; on his being principled, brave, and firm; on his ability to lean on the inexhaustible capabilities of the collective, the indestructible power and spirit of the Soviet people and the Communists. He would become healthy again."

APPENDIX G

The Ascendance of the Military Viewpoint: Comparisons with the Recent Past

How much the official, publicly stated view of the role of the defense establishment in Soviet politics is changing becomes apparent when one compares some of Khrushchev's statements, made as recently as 1964, with official pronouncements and expressions in leading newspapers in 1965. For example,

Of late, a certain relaxation of tension has become apparent in international affairs.
(Khrushchev, 1964)

. . . the current international situation is characterized by a sharpening of tension and increased danger of war.
(*Kommunist*, No. 7, May 1965)

The highest calling of Soviet man, his primary duty, consists of creating, amassing wealth for the country, for a better life. . . .
(Khrushchev, 1964)

. . . CPSU regards readiness to defend socialist achievements from imperialist aggression as the most important function of the Soviet state.
(Editorial, *Kommunist*, No. 7, May 1965)

The tasks of the [defense industry] could be solved more successfully with less expenditure.
(Khrushchev, 1964)

The Communist Party continues to believe that it is its sacred duty to strengthen the defense power of the USSR.
(Editorial, *Kommunist*, No. 7, May 1965)

We are now considering the possibility of a further reduction in the size of our armed forces . . . to reduce military expenditures . . . next year.
(Khrushchev, 1964)

[The Party and the government] are giving their attention . . . to the further strengthening of the country's armed forces and to the development of the defense industry.
(Shelepin, July 1965)

. . . a foundation has been laid for solving controversial international

We have no right to forget the continuous dangers which threat-

problems through negotiations.
(Khrushchev, 1964)

en us in the form of a potential military attack by the imperialist aggressors.
(Shelepin, July 1965)

[Revolutionary] passion is a fine thing, of course, but after the passion we must tackle the economy . . . so that we can eat well, have good housing . . . this is far better than merely revolutionary passion.
(Khrushchev, 1964)

It would be most incorrect to see as the central purpose of Communism mainly the satisfaction of the "needs of the stomach". . . .
(The editor-in-chief of *Kommunist,* as quoted in *Pravda,* May 17, 1965)

. . . the defense of the country is at a suitable level.
(Khrushchev, 1964)

Our dedication to the cause of peace not only does not contradict but, on the contrary, compels the most attentive and concerned attitude toward the defense of our country.
(Brezhnev, July 3, 1965)

A similar juxtaposition might be made to illustrate the change that took place between Malenkov's polemical statements of 1953 and some of the official pronouncements of 1954, the year after Khrushchev had won out over his rival Malenkov in their struggle for power. For then, too, one of the main points at issue between the two men was that of their proposed defense policies, which were bound to affect the military very differently. It will be recalled that it was Khrushchev, at that time, who was courting the military and was espousing policies that would meet its interests, while Malenkov was advocating détente in foreign policy and an internal economy geared to the consumer.

The international situation at present is characterized first and foremost by the great success achieved by the Soviet Union . . . in the struggle to ease international tension, strengthen peace, and prevent war.
(Malenkov, 1953)

So far, no changes have occurred in the international situation that would give us grounds for lessening in any degree our attention to questions of strengthening our defense capability.
(Marshal Bulganin, November 1954)

. . . The easing of international tension should not be overestimated.
(Marshal Timoshenko, November 1954)

Our main task—ensuring the further improvement in the material well-being of . . . all the Soviet people.
(Malenkov, 1953)

That is the main thing: the further development of heavy industry.
(Khrushchev, December 1954)

. . . it is necessary to increase significantly the investment of resources . . . in the program for the production of consumer goods.
(Malenkov, 1953)

Heavy industry is the foundation of foundations of our socialist economy.
(*Voennaia mysl'*, organ of the General Staff, October 1953)

Bibliography

SOVIET SOURCES

Books and Pamphlets

Abramov, V. K., *Chelovek i tekhnika v sovremennoi voine* (Man and Equipment in Modern Warfare), Voenizdat, Moscow, 1960.

Aleksandrov, N. I., *Druz'ia-tovarishchi* (Friends and Comrades), Voenizdat, Moscow, 1963.

Aleksandrov, P. N., *et al.*, *Komandarm Uborevich* (Army Commander Uborevich), Voenizdat, Moscow, 1964.

Al'shits, Z. S., *Osnovy nastupatel'nogo boia* (The Principles of Offensive War), Voenizdat, Moscow, 1964.

Anfilov, V. A., *Nachalo Velikoi Otechestvennoi voiny (22 iiunia—seredina iiulia 1941 goda)* (The Start of the Great Patriotic War [June 22—mid-July 1941]), Voenizdat, Moscow, 1962.

Avtoritet komandira (The Authority of the Commanding Officer), Voenizdat, Moscow, 1963.

Azarov, Vice Admiral I. I., *Osazhdennaia Odessa* (Besieged Odessa), Voenizdat, Moscow, 1962.

Bachurin, A. P., *Frontovye zapiski politrabotnika* (The Front Line Memoirs of a Political Worker), Voenizdat, Moscow, 1962.

Bakaev, N. V., *Partiinoe vliianie* (The Party Influence), Voenizdat, Moscow, 1961.

Barabanshchikov, A. V., *Pedagogicheskie osnovy obucheniia sovetskikh voinov* (The Pedagogic Principles of Training Soviet Soldiers), Voenizdat, Moscow, 1962.

Baranov, Lieutenant Colonel A. O., *Voennaia tekhnika i moral'no-boevye kachestva voina* (Military Technology and the Combat Morale of the Soldier), Voenizdat, Moscow, 1961.

Batov, General of the Army P. I., *V pokhodakh i boiakh* (On Marches and in Battles), Voenizdat, Moscow, 1962.

Bazanov, A. G., *Pedagogika: ocherki po teorii i praktike obucheniia i vospitaniia sovetskikh voinov* (Pedagogy: Essays on the Theory and Practice of Training and Educating Soviet Soldiers), Voenizdat, Moscow, 1964.

Belousov, G. G., *Organizatorskaia rabota partiinogo biuro* (The Organizational Work of the Party Bureau), Voenizdat, Moscow, 1963.

Berkhin, I. B., *Voennaia reforma v SSSR, 1924-1925 gg.* (Military Reform in the USSR, 1924-1925), Voenizdat, Moscow, 1958.

Binevich, A., and Z. Serebrianskii, *Andrei Bubnov*, Politizdat, Moscow, 1964.

Biriuzov, Marshal of the Soviet Union S. S., *Kogda gremeli pushki* (When the Guns Thundered), Voenizdat, Moscow, 1961.

——, *Sovetskii soldat na Balkanakh* (The Soviet Soldier in the Balkans), Voenizdat, Moscow, 1963.

——, *Sviashchennyi dolg* (The Sacred Duty), "Znanie," Moscow, 1964.

Bitva pod Kurskom (The Battle at Kursk), Voenizdat, Moscow, 1963.

Bliukher, Vasilii K., *Stat'i i rechi* (Articles and Speeches), Voenizdat, Moscow, 1963.

Bochkarev, Konstantin S., *et al.*, *Programma KPSS o zashchite sotsialisticheskogo otechestva* (The CPSU Program on the Defense of the Socialist Fatherland), Voenizdat, Moscow, 1963.

Boegotovnost' v zapas ne ukholdit (Preparedness Is Not Going into the Reserve), Voenizdat, Moscow, 1960.

Boevoi put' Sovetskikh Vooruzhennykh Sil (The Battle Path of the Soviet Armed Forces), Voenizdat, Moscow, 1960.

Boevoi put' Sovetskogo Voenno-Morskogo Flota (The Battle Path of the Soviet Navy), Voenizdat, Moscow, 1964.

Boevye podvigi chastei Krasnoi Armii, 1918-1922 (Battle Feats of Red Army Units, 1918-1922), Voenizdat, Moscow, 1957.

Boldin, Colonel General I. V., *Stranitsy zhizni* (Pages from Life), Voenizdat, Moscow, 1961.

Bor'ba partii za zavershenie sotsialisticheskoi rekonstruktsii narodnogo khoziaistva. Pobeda sotsializma v SSSR (1933-1937 gody) (The Struggle of the Party to Complete the Socialist Reconstruction of the National Economy. The Victory of Socialism in the USSR [1933-1937]), "Moskovskii rabochii," Moscow, 1963.

Borzunov, Colonel S. M. (ed.), *Resheniia oktiabr'skogo Plenuma TsK KPSS v deistvii* (Decisions of the CPSU Central Committee October Plenum in Action), Voenizdat, Moscow, 1959.

Brychev, N. F., *O voinskoi sluzhbe* (On Service in the Military), Izdatel'stvo DOSAAF, Moscow, 1960.

Bubnov, A. S., *O Krasnoi Armii* (On the Red Army), Voenizdat, Moscow, 1958.

Budennyi, Marshal of the Soviet Union S. M., *Proidennyi put'* (The Road Traveled), Voenizdat, Moscow, 1958.

Bushmanov, K. A., *Trebovatel'nost' k podchinennym i zabota o nikh* (Exactingness Toward Subordinates and Concern for Them), Voenizdat, Moscow, 1961.

Chuikov, Marshal of the Soviet Union V. I., *Nachalo puti* (Beginning of the Road), Voenizdat, Moscow, 1959.

——, *Vystoiav, my pobedili* (Holding on, We Won), "Sovetskaia Rossiia," Moscow, 1960.

Chuprynin, S., *Ofitser i starshina* (The Officer and the Sergeant-Major), Voenizdat, Moscow, 1962.

Danilevskii, A. F., *V. I. Lenin i voprosy voennogo stroitel'stva na VIII s"ezde RKP(b)* (V. I. Lenin and Questions of Military Development at the Eighth Congress of RKP[b]), Voenizdat, Moscow, 1964.

Demin, Major General N. S., *V nogu s zhizn'iu* (In Step with Life), Voenizdat, Moscow, 1960.

Denisov, E., and Ia. Buchilov, *Sovetskaia Armiia—nadezhnyi oplot mira i bezopasnosti nashei rodiny* (The Soviet Army—The Reliable Bulwark of Peace and Security of Our Motherland), Gospolitizdat, Moscow, 1951.

D'iachenko, Lieutenant Colonel M. I., *Individual'nyi podkhod v vospitanii voinov* (The Individual Approach in the Training of Soldiers), Voenizdat, Moscow, 1962.

Dolgopiatov, G. M., and I. S. Rozanov, *Sovetskoe zakonodatel'stvo o poriadke podachi i razresheniia zhalob v Vooruzhennykh Silakh SSSR*

(Soviet Law on the Order for Submitting and Redressing Complaints in the Armed Forces of the USSR), Voenizdat, Moscow, 1961.

——, *Ustavnoi poriadok podachi i razresheniia zhalob v Vooruzhennykh Silakh Soiuza SSR* (The Statutory Order for Submitting and Redressing Complaints in the Armed Forces of the USSR), Voenizdat, Moscow, 1957.

Dushen'kin, V. V., *Ot soldata do marshala: zhizn' i boevoi put' Marshala Sovetskogo Soiuza V. K. Bliukhera* (From Soldier to Marshal: The Life and Military Career of Marshal of the Soviet Union V. K. Bliukher), 2nd ed., Gospolitizdat, Moscow, 1961; 3rd ed., Politizdat, Moscow, 1964.

XXII (Dvadtsat'-vtoroi) s"ezd Kommunisticheskoi partii Sovetskogo Soiuza: stenograficheskii otchet (The Twenty-second Congress of the CPSU: Stenographic Record), Gospolitizdat, Moscow, 1962.

XX (Dvadtsatyi) s"ezd Kommunisticheskoi partii Sovetskogo Soiuza: stenograficheskii otchet (The Twentieth Congress of the CPSU: Stenographic Record), Gospolitizdat, Moscow, 1956.

Dzhuraev, T., *Uzbekistan v dni velikoi bitvy na Volge* (Uzbekistan During the Great Battle on the Volga), Gosizdat Uzbekskoi SSR, Tashkent, 1963.

Epishev, General of the Army A. A., *Delo ogromnoi vazhnosti* (A Matter of Utmost Importance), "Znanie," Moscow, 1965.

——, *Istoriia uchit* (History Teaches), "Znanie," Moscow, 1965.

Eremenko, Marshal of the Soviet Union A. I., *False Witnesses*, Foreign Languages Publishing House, Moscow, n.d.

——, *Stalingrad*, Voenizdat, Moscow, 1961.

Ermokhin, M. M., *Pooshchreniia i distsiplinarnye vzyskaniia—sredstva vospitaniia sovetskikh voinov* (Encouragements and Disciplinary Penalties—Means for Training Soviet Soldiers), Voenizdat, Moscow, 1961.

Ezhegodnik Bol'shoi Sovetskoi Entsiklopedii. 1962 (Yearbook of the Large Soviet Encyclopedia, 1962), "Sovetskaia Entsiklopediia," Moscow, 1962.

Fediuninskii, General of the Army I. I., *Podniatye po trevoge* (Roused by the Alarm), Voenizdat, Moscow, 1964.

Frunze, M. V., *Izbrannye proizvedeniia* (Selected Works), Partizdat, Moscow, 1934.

Gamburg, I. K., *et al.*, *M. V. Frunze: zhizn' i deiatel'nost'* (M. V. Frunze: Life and Activity), Gospolitizdat, Moscow, 1962.

Geroi grazhdanskoi voiny (Heroes of the Civil War), "Molodaia gvardiia," Moscow, 1963.

Goranskii, M. N., *XXII s"ezd KPSS ob ukreplenii ekonomicheskogo i oboronnogo mogushchestva SSSR* (The Twenty-second Congress of the CPSU Regarding the Strengthening of the Economic and Defensive Might of the USSR), "Zvezda," Minsk, 1962.

Grechko, Marshal of the Soviet Union A. A., *Vysokoe prizvanie* (The High Calling), Voenizdat, Moscow, 1962.

——, (ed.), *Iadernyi vek i voina* (The Nuclear Age and War), Izdatel'stvo "Izvestiia," Moscow, 1964.

Grudinin, I. A., *Voprosy dialektiki v voennom dele* (The Dialectical Problems in Military Affairs), Voenizdat, Moscow, 1960.

Gurov, A. A., *Tekhnicheskii progress i militarizm* (Technical Progress and Militarism), Voenizdat, Moscow, 1963.

Iakovlev, B. N., and I. P. Barbashin, *Vazhneishie daty geroicheskoi istorii Vooruzhennykh Sil SSSR* (The More Important Dates of the Heroic History of the Armed Forces of the USSR), Izdatel'stvo DOSAAF, Moscow, 1958.

Ideologicheskaia rabota KPSS na fronte (1941-1945) (Ideological Work of the CPSU at the Front [1941-1945]), Voenizdat, Moscow, 1960.

Isachenko, Colonel S. M., *Pochemu v armii neobkhodimo edinonachalie* (Why There Must Be *Edinonachalie* in the Army), Voenizdat, Moscow, 1965.

Istoriia Velikoi Otechestvennoi voiny Sovetskogo Soiuza, 1941-1945 (The History of the Great Patriotic War of the Soviet Union, 1941-1945), Voenizdat, Moscow, 1961.

Kalashnik, Lieutenant General M. Kh., (ed.), *Narod i armiia—ediny* (The People and the Army Are United), Voenizdat, Moscow, 1959.

Kalinin, M. I., *O Sovetskoi Armii: sbornik statei i rechei* (On the Soviet Army: Collected Articles and Speeches), Voenizdat, Moscow, 1958.

Kardashov, I. S., *Internatsional'nyi dolg Vooruzhennykh Sil SSSR* (The International Duty of the Armed Forces of the USSR), Voenizdat, Moscow, 1960.

Kashirin, Colonel P., *Rol' moral'nogo faktora v sovremennykh voinakh* (The Role of the Moral Factor in Modern Wars), Voenizdat, Moscow, 1953.

Kazakov, Marshal of Artillery V. I., *Na perelome* (At the Turning Point), Voenizdat, Moscow, 1962.

Khrushchev, N. S., *O vneshnei politike Sovetskogo Soiuza, 1960 g.* (On the Foreign Policy of the Soviet Union in 1960), Gospolitizdat, Moscow, 1961.

Kiriaev, Major General N. M. (ed.), *KPSS i stroitel'stvo Sovetskikh Vooruzhennykh Sil* (The CPSU and the Development of the Soviet Armed Forces), Voenizdat, Moscow, 1965.

Koblikov, A. S., A. G. Mazalov, and V. E. Smol'nikov, *Nauchno-prakticheskii kommentarii k polozheniiu o voennykh tribunalakh* (A Scientific-Practical Commentary on the Military Tribunals Statute), Gosiurizdat, Moscow, 1961.

Kolganov, K. (ed.), *Razvitie taktiki Sovetskoi Armii v gody Velikoi Otechestvennoi voiny (1941-1945 gg.)* (The Development of Tactics by the Soviet Army During the Great Patriotic War [1941-1945]), Voenizdat, Moscow, 1958.

Komandarm Iakir: vospominaniia druzei i soratnikov (Army Commander Yakir: Reminiscences by Friends and Companions-in-Arms), Voenizdat, Moscow, 1963.

Komandir—organizator vospitaniia voinov (The Commanding Officer—The Organizer of Troop Education), Voenizdat, Moscow, 1963.

Komkov, G. D., *Istoki pobedy sovetskogo naroda v Velikoi Otechestvennoi voine* (The Sources of the Soviet People's Victory in the Great Patriotic War), Izdatel'stvo Akademii nauk SSSR, Moscow, 1961.

Kommunisticheskaia moral' i voinskii dolg (Communist Morality and the Soldier's Duty), Voenizdat, Moscow, 1960.

Kommunisticheskaia partiia v period Velikoi Otechestvennoi voiny, iiun' 1941-1945 god (The Communist Party During the Great Patriotic War, June 1941-1945), Gospolitizdat, Moscow, 1961.

Koniukhovskii, V. N., *Territorial'naia sistema voennogo stroitel'stva* (The Territorial System of Military Organization), Voenizdat, Moscow, 1961.

Korobeinikov, Colonel M. P., *Serzhantu o psikhologii* (To the Sergeant Regarding Psychology), Voenizdat, Moscow, 1962.

Kotlar, A. I., and B. V. Kozhevnikov, *Voprosy pensionnogo obespecheniia voennosluzhashchikh i ikh semei* (Problems of Pension Provisions for Military Personnel and Their Families), Voenizdat, Moscow, 1956.

Kozlov, S. N., *et al., O sovetskoi voennoi nauke* (On Soviet Military Science), Voenizdat, Moscow, 1964.

KPSS i stroitel'stvo Vooruzhennykh Sil SSSR, 1918-iiun' 1941 (The CPSU and the Development of the Armed Forces of the USSR, 1918-June 1941), Voenizdat, Moscow, 1959.

KPSS o Vooruzhennykh Silakh Sovetskogo Soiuza: sbornik dokumentov, 1917-1958 (The CPSU on the Armed Forces of the Soviet Union: A Collection of Documents, 1917-1958), Gospolitizdat, Moscow, 1958.

Krasovskii, Marshal S. A., *Zhizn' v aviatsii* (Life in Aviation), Voenizdat, Moscow, 1960.

Krupnov, S. I., *Dialektika i voennaia nauka* (Dialectics and Military Science), ed. S. N. Kozlov, Voenizdat, Moscow, 1963.

Krylov, S. M., *Povyshat' bditel'nost' narodov v otnoshenii voennoi opasnosti* (Raise the Vigilance of Peoples Regarding the Danger of War), "Znanie," Moscow, 1961.

Kuz'min, G. V., *Grazhdanskaia voina i voennaia interventsiia v SSSR* (The Civil War and Armed Intervention in the USSR), Voenizdat, Moscow, 1958.

Kuznetsov, Lieutenant General P. G., *Dni boevye* (The Fighting Days), Voenizdat, Moscow, 1964.

Larkov, A. M., and N. T. Filippov, *Edinonachalie v Sovetskikh Vooruzhennykh Silakh* (*Edinonachalie* in the Soviet Armed Forces), Voenizdat, Moscow, 1960.

Lenin, V. I., *Collected Works*, International Publishers, New York, 1942.

——, *O voine, armii i voennoi nauke* (On War, the Army, and Military Science), Voenizdat, Moscow, 1957.

——, *Selected Works*, International Publishers, New York, 1943.

——, *Selected Works*, Lawrence & Wishart, Ltd., London, 1936.

Levanov, I. N., *et al.* (eds.), *Marksizm-leninizm o voine i armii* (Marxism-Leninism on War and the Army), Voenizdat, Moscow, 1958.

L'goty dlia voennosluzhashchikh, uvol'niaemykh iz armii (Privileges for Military Personnel Discharged from the Army), Gosiurizdat, Moscow, 1960.

L'goty, pensii i posobiia voennosluzhashchim i ikh sem'iam: spravochnik (Privileges, Pensions, and Allowances for Military Personnel and Their Families: A Handbook), Voenizdat, Moscow, 1958.

Loboda, Major General V. F., *Komandnye kadry i zakonodatel'stvo o kadrakh v razvitii Vooruzhennykh Sil SSSR* (The Commanding Cadres and Legislation on Cadres in the Development of the Armed Forces of the USSR), Voenizdat, Moscow, 1960.

Lukov, Colonel G. D., *Vospitanie voli u sovetskikh voinov* (Training the Will of Soviet Soldiers), Voenizdat, Moscow, 1961.

Lupalo, I., *Podvig Generala Karbysheva* (The Victory of General Karbyshev), Gospolitizdat, Moscow, 1962.

Makridin, A. V., and A. A. Shpakovskii, *Komsomol'skaia organizatsiia i dosug voinov* (The Komsomol Organization and the Soldiers' Leisure), Voenizdat, Moscow, 1960.

Malan'in, K. A., *Razgrom fashistskikh voisk v Belorussii* (Defeat of Fascist Forces in Belorussia), Voenizdat, Moscow, 1956.

Malinovskii, R. Ia., *Bditel'no stoiat' na strazhe mira* (Vigilantly Stand Guard over the Peace), Voenizdat, Moscow, 1962.

——, *Velichie pobedy* (The Grandeur of Victory), "Znanie," Moscow, 1965.

Marksistsko-leninskaia ucheba ofitserov (The Marxist-Leninist Training of Officers), Voenizdat, Moscow, 1957.

Marksizm-leninizm o voine, armii i voennoi nauke (Marxism-Leninism on War, the Army, and Military Science), Voenizdat, Moscow, 1955.

Marksizm-leninizm o voine i armii (Marxism-Leninism on War and the Army), Voenizdat, Moscow, 1956.

Maryganov, I. V., *Peredovoi kharakter sovetskoi voennoi nauki* (The Progressive Character of Soviet Military Science), Voenizdat, Moscow, 1953.

Materialy k politicheskim zaniatiiam (V pomoshch' rukovoditeliam grupp) (Materials for Political Studies [To Aid Group Leaders]), Voenizdat, Moscow, 1958.

Medvedev, E. V., and A. S. Milovidov, *Rol' narodnykh mass v sovremennykh voinakh* (The Role of Popular Masses in Modern Wars), Voenizdat, Moscow, 1960.

Metodicheskoe posobie po doprizyvnoi podgotovke (A Methodic Textbook for Pre-Conscription Training), Voenizdat, Moscow, 1959.

Milovidov, A. S., *Moral'nyi kodeks i nravstvennoe vospitanie voinov* (The Moral Code and the Moral Education of Soldiers), Voenizdat, Moscow, 1964.

Molodezhi o Sovetskoi Armii i Voenno-Morskom Flote (To the Youth Regarding the Soviet Army and Navy), Biblioteka im. V. I. Lenina, Moscow, 1960.

Muratov, Kh. I., *Revoliutsionnoe dvizhenie v russkoi armii v 1917 g.* (Revolutionary Movement in the Russian Army in 1917), Voenizdat, Moscow, 1958.

Na obshchestvennykh nachalakh (On a Social Basis), Voenizdat, Moscow, 1963.

Na strazhe rodiny stroiashchei kommunizm (Guarding the Fatherland Which Is Building Communism), Voenizdat, Moscow, 1962.

Narod i armiia—edinaia sem'ia (The People and the Army Are One Family), Lenizdat, Moscow, 1961.

Narodnoe khoziaistvo SSSR v 1956 godu. Statisticheskii sbornik (The National Economy of the USSR in 1956: Collected Statistics), Gosstatizdat, Moscow, 1957.

Nekotorye voprosy partiino-organizatsionnoi raboty v Sovetskikh Vooruzhennykh Silakh (Some Problems of Party-Organizational Work in the Soviet Armed Forces), Voenizdat, Moscow, 1963.

Nekotorye voprosy partiino-organizatsionnoi raboty v Sovetskoi Armii i Flote (Some Problems of Party-Organizational Work in the Soviet Army and Navy), Voenizdat, Moscow, 1959.

Nekrasov, Viktor, *V okopakh Stalingrada* (In the Trenches of Stalingrad), "Sovetskii pisatel'," Moscow, 1947.

Nenakhov, Colonel I. N., *O Sovetskoi voennoi nauke* (On Soviet Military Science), Voenizdat, Moscow, 1954.

Nikol'skii, N., *Osnovnoi vopros sovremennosti* (The Principal Contemporary Question), IMO, Moscow, 1964.

O komissarakh i politrabotnikakh v Krasnoi Armii (About Commissars and Political Workers in the Red Army), Central Committee, 1922.

O samostoiatel'nosti i initsiative ofitserov flota (On Independence and Initiative of Naval Officers), Voenizdat, Moscow, 1959.

Oreshkin, A. K., *Oboronitel'naia operatsiia 9-i armii* (The Defensive Operation of the 9th Army), Voenizdat, Moscow, 1960.

Orlov, I., *Partiinaia gruppa v podrazdelenii* (The Party Group in the Subunit), Voenizdat, Moscow, 1957.

Osipov, Major General Z. S., (ed.), *K novomu pod"emu partiino-politicheskoi raboty v Sovetskoi Armii i Flote* (Toward a New Intensification of Party-Political Work in the Soviet Army and Navy), Voenizdat, Moscow, 1960.

Os'kin, G. I., *Sovetskaia Armiia—detishche sovetskogo naroda* (The Soviet Army—The Offspring of the Soviet People), Izdatel'stvo DOSAAF, Moscow, 1963.

Osnovy sovetskogo voennogo zakonodatel'stva (The Foundations of Soviet Military Legislation), Voenizdat, Moscow, 1961.

Osnovy voennoi pedagogiki i psikhologii (The Fundamentals of Military Pedagogy and Psychology), Voenizdat, Moscow, 1964.

Ovsianko, D. M., *Vospitatel'naia rol' ofitserskikh tovarishcheskikh sudov chesti* (The Educational Role of Officers' Comrades' Courts of Honor), Voenizdat, Moscow, 1962.

Partiia v bor'be za uprochenie i razvitie sotsialisticheskogo obshchestva: usilenie oborony strany (The Party in the Struggle for the Strengthening and Development of the Socialist Society: The Strengthening of the Country's Defense), Moskovskii rabochii, Moscow, 1962.

Partiinaia organizatsiia chasti, korablia (The Party Organization of *Chast'* and Ship), Voenizdat, Moscow, 1960.

Partiino-politicheskaia rabota v Sovetskikh Vooruzhennykh Silakh (Party-Political Work in the Soviet Armed Forces), Voenizdat, Moscow, 1964.

Partiino-politicheskaia rabota v Sovetskikh Vooruzhennykh Silakh v gody Velikoi Otechestvennoi voiny, 1941-1945 (Party-Political Work in the Soviet Armed Forces During the Great Patriotic War, 1941-1945), Voenizdat, Moscow, 1963.

Partiino-politicheskaia rabota v Sovetskoi Armii i Voenno-Morskom Flote (Party-Political Work in the Soviet Army and Navy), Voenizdat, Moscow, 1960.

Partiinyi komitet chasti (korablia) (Party Committee of the *Chast'* [of the Ship]), Voenizdat, Moscow, 1963.

Pered litsom obshchestvennosti (In the Face of Society), Voenizdat, Moscow, 1961.

Perednia, I., and M. Riabchikov, *My—voennye stroiteli* (We—The Military Builders), Voenizdat, Moscow, 1962.

Petrov, Iu. P. *KPSS—rukovoditel' i vospitatel' Krasnoi Armii (1918-1920 gg.)* (The CPSU—The Leader and Educator of the Red Army [1918-1920]), Voenizdat, Moscow, 1961.

——, *Partiinoe stroitel'stvo v Sovetskoi Armii i Flote, 1918-1961* (Party Development in the Soviet Army and Navy, 1918-1961), Voenizdat, Moscow, 1964.

Platonov, Lieutenant General S. P., (ed.), *Vtoraia mirovaia voina* (World War II), Voenizdat, Moscow, 1958.

Pobezhimov, I. F., *Pravovoe regulirovanie stroitel'stva Sovetskoi Armii i Flota* (Legal Regulation of the Development of the Soviet Army and Navy), Gosiurizdat, Moscow, 1960.

Pokrovskii, Major General G. I., *Nauka i tekhnika v sovremennykh voinakh* (Science and Technology in Modern Wars), Voenizdat, Moscow, 1956.

——, *Rol' nauki i tekhniki v sovremennoi voine* (The Role of Science and Technology in Modern Warfare), "Znanie," Moscow, 1957.

Polozhenie o tovarishcheskikh sudakh (The Regulation on Comrades' Courts), Gosiurizdat, Moscow, 1962.

Popel', Lieutenant General N. K., *Tanki povernuli na zapad* (The Tanks Turned West), Voenizdat, Moscow, 1960.

——, *V tiazhkuiu poru* (In Difficult Times), Voenizdat, Moscow, 1959.

Popov, Colonel General V. S., *Vnezapnost' i neozhidannost' v istorii voin* (Surprise and Suddenness in the History of Wars), Voenizdat, Moscow, 1955.

Portiankin, I. A., (ed.), *Sovetskaia voennaia pechat'* (The Soviet Military Press), Voenizdat, Moscow, 1960.

Posobiia, pensii i l'goty voennosluzhashchim i ikh sem'iam (Allowances, Pensions, and Privileges for Military Personnel and Their Families), Voenizdat, Moscow, 1943.

Pozdniakov, E. I., *Iunost' komissara* (A Commissar's Youth), Voenizdat, Moscow, 1962.

Proektor, D. M., *Cherez Duklinskii pereval* (Through the Dukla Pass), Voenizdat, Moscow, 1960.

Rotmistrov, Chief Marshal of Armored Troops P. A., (ed.), *Istoriia voennogo iskusstva* (The History of Military Art), Voenizdat, Moscow, 1963.

Rybkin, E. I., *Voina i politika* (War and Politics), Voenizdat, Moscow, 1959.

Rybkin, P. A., *Vospitanie molodykh kommunistov* (Educating Young Communists), Voenizdat, Moscow, 1961.

Samsonov, A. M., *Stalingradskaia bitva* (The Battle of Stalingrad), Izdatel'stvo Akademii nauk SSSR, Moscow, 1960.

——, *Velikaia bitva na Volge* (The Great Battle on the Volga), "Znanie," Moscow, 1963.

Sandalov, Colonel General L. M., *Perezhitoe* (The Past), Voenizdat, Moscow, 1961.

——, *Pogorelo-Gorodishchenskaia operatsiia* (Pogoreloe Gorodishche Operation), Voenizdat, Moscow, 1960.

Sbornik zakonov SSSR i ukazov Prezidiuma Verkhovnogo Soveta SSSR, 1938-1961 gg. (Collection of USSR Laws and USSR Supreme Soviet Presidium Decrees, 1938-1961), "Izvestiia Sovetov deputatov trud. SSSR," Moscow, 1961.

XVII (Semnadtsatyi) s"ezd Vsesoiuznoi Kommunisticheskoi partii (b): stenograficheskii otchet (The Seventeenth Congress of the All-Union Communist Party [b]: Stenographic Record), Partizdat, Moscow, 1934.

Sharipov, A. A., *General N. V. Krisanov*, Permskoe knizhnoe izd., Perm', 1963.

Shatagin, N. I., *Organizatsiia i stroitel'stvo Sovetskoi Armii v period inostrannoi voennoi interventsii i grazhdanskoi voiny (1918-1920 gg.)* (The Organization and Development of the Soviet Army During the Foreign Military Intervention and Civil War [1918-1920]), Voenizdat, Moscow, 1954.

Shilin, A. P., *Ustavnoi poriadok—osnova organizovannosti i distsipliny* (The Regulation Procedure Is the Foundation of Organization and Discipline), Voenizdat, Moscow, 1957.

Shtabnaia partiinaia organizatsiia (The Staff Party Organization), Voenizdat, Moscow, 1961.

Sibilev, M., *Zavety V. I. Lenina sovetskim voinam* (Lenin's Legacy to Soviet Soldiers), Voenizdat, Moscow, 1964.

Skopin, V. I., *Militarizm: istoricheskie ocherki* (Militarism: Historical Essays), ed. Major General N. V. Pukhovskii, 2nd ed., Voenizdat, Moscow, 1957.

Sokolov, P. V., *Voina i liudskie resursy* (War and Human Resources), Voenizdat, Moscow, 1961.

Sokolovskii, Marshal of the Soviet Union V. D., (ed.), *Voennaia strategiia* (Military Strategy), Voenizdat, Moscow, 1962; rev. ed. 1963.

Somin, N. I., *Vtoraia mirovaia voina (1939-1945 gg.)* (World War II [1939-1945]), Vysshaia partiinaia shkola pri TsK KPSS, Moscow, 1954.

Spravochnik partiinogo rabotnika (The Party Worker's Handbook), No. 5, Politizdat, Moscow, 1964.

Stalin, J. V., *Leninism*, Foreign Languages Publishing House, Vol. 2, Moscow, 1933.

——, *Problems of Leninism*, Foreign Languages Publishing House, Moscow, 1940.

——, *Selected Works*, International Publishers, New York, 1943.

Stuchenko, A. T., *Zavidnaia nasha sud'ba* (Our Fate Is Enviable), Voenizdat, Moscow, 1964.

Sudebnyi protsess po ugolovnomu delu agenta angliiskoi i amerikanskoi razvedok grazhdanina SSSR Pen'kovskogo O. V. i shpiona-sviaznika poddannogo Velikobritanii Vinna G. M. 7-11 maia 1963 goda. (The Court Trial of the Criminal Case of the English and American Intelligence Services' Agent, Citizen of the USSR O. V. Penkovskii and the Spy-Liaison Man, Subject of Great Britain G. M. Wynne on May 7-11, 1963), Politizdat, Moscow, 1963.

Sviridov, V. P., V. P. Iakutovich, and V. E. Vasilenko, *Bitva za Leningrad, 1941-1944* (The Battle for Leningrad, 1941-1944), Lenizdat, Leningrad, 1962.

Tel'pukhovskii, B. S., *Velikaia pobeda Sovetskoi Armii pod Stalingradom* (The Great Victory of the Soviet Army at Stalingrad), Gospolitizdat, Moscow, 1953.

Tiulenev, General of the Army I. V., *Cherez tri voiny* (Through Three Wars), Voenizdat, Moscow, 1960.

Tiushkevich, S. A., *Neobkhodimost' i sluchainost' v voine* (Necessity and Chance in War), Voenizdat, Moscow, 1962.

Todorskii, A. I., *Marshal Tukhachevskii*, Politizdat, Moscow, 1963.

Tolmachev, I., *Ustavy o moral'no-boevykh kachestvakh sovetskikh voinov* (The Statutes on the Morale and Fighting Qualities of Soviet Soldiers), Voenizdat, Moscow, 1961.

Tovarishch komissar (Comrade Commissar), Voenizdat, Moscow, 1963.

Trifonenkov, P. I., *Ob osnovnykh zakonakh khoda i iskhoda sovremennoi voiny* (On the Basic Laws of the Progress and Outcome of Modern War), Voenizdat, Moscow, 1962.

Trotsky, L., *Kak vooruzhalas' revoliutsiia* (How the Revolution Armed), Vysshii voennyi redaktsionnyi sovet, Moscow, 1924.

Tsygankov, V. P., *Geroicheskaia Moskva* (Heroic Moscow), Voenizdat, Moscow, 1960.

USSR Academy of Sciences, Institute of History, *SSSR v Velikoi Otechestvennoi voine, 1941-1945 gg. Kratkaia khronika* (The USSR During the Great Patriotic War, 1941-1945: A Short Chronicle), Voenizdat, Moscow, 1964.

USSR Main Archival Administration, *Iz istorii mezhdunarodnoi proletarskoi solidarnosti* (From the History of International Proletarian Solidarity), Vol. 6 (1938-1945), "Sovetskaia Rossiia," Moscow, 1962.

USSR Ministry of Defense, *Distsiplinarnyi ustav Vooruzhennykh Sil Soiuza SSR* (The Disciplinary Statute of the Armed Forces of the USSR), Voenizdat, Moscow, 1960 and 1964.

USSR Ministry of Defense, *Ustav garnizonnoi i karaul'noi sluzhb Vooruzhennykh Sil SSSR* (The Statute of Garrison and Guard Services of the USSR Armed Forces), Voenizdat, Moscow, 1963.

V pomoshch' ofitseram izuchaiushchim marksistsko-leninskuiu teoriiu (An Aid to Officers Studying Marxist-Leninist Theory), Voenizdat, Moscow, 1959.

Vinokur, L., *Sed'maia gvardeiskaia* (The Seventh Guards [Brigade]), Volgogradskoe knizhnoe izd., Volgograd, 1962.

Vneocherednoi XXI s"ezd Kommunisticheskoi partii Sovetskogo Soiuza: stenograficheskii otchet (Extraordinary Twenty-first Congress of the CPSU: Stenographic Record), Gospolitizdat, Moscow, 1959.

Vodolagin, M. A., *U sten Stalingrada* (By the Walls of Stalingrad), Gospolitizdat, Moscow, 1958.

Voennye voprosy v resheniiakh KPSS: ukazatel' k sborniku "KPSS v rezoliutsiiakh i resheniiakh s"ezdov, konferentsii i plenumov TsK" (Military Problems in the Decisions of the CPSU: An Index to the Compilation *CPSU in Resolutions and Decisions of Congresses, Conferences and Central Committee Plenums*), Biblioteka im. Lenina, Moscow, 1962.

Voennyi inzhener—aktivnyi vospitatel' (The Military Engineer—An Active Educator), Voenizdat, Moscow, 1962.

Voinov, Aleksandr, *Trevozhnaia noch'* (An Alarming Night), Voenizdat, Moscow, 1960.

Volykhin, A., *Ustav vnutrennei sluzhby—zakon zhizni voennosluzhashchikh* (The Intra-Service Statute—The Law of the Servicemen's Life), Voenizdat, Moscow, 1961.

Voprosy istorii KPSS perioda Velikoi Otechestvennoi voiny (Problems of CPSU History During the Great Patriotic War), Izdatel'stvo Kievskogo Universiteta, Kiev, 1961.

Vorob'ev, F., and V. M. Kravtsov, *Velikaia Otechestvennaia voina Sovetskogo Soiuza, 1941-1945* (The Great Patriotic War of the Soviet Union, 1941-1945), Voenizdat, Moscow, 1961.

Voronov, Chief Marshal of Artillery N. N., *Na sluzhbe voennoi* (In the Military Service), Voenizdat, Moscow, 1963.

Vorozheikin, Major General of the Air Force A. V., *Nad Kurskoi dugoi* (Over the Kursk Bend), Voenizdat, Moscow, 1962.

Vyshe kachestvo politicheskikh zaniatii (Political Studies of a Higher Quality), Voenizdat, Moscow, 1960.

Zav'ialov, A. S., and T. E. Kaliadin, *Bitva za Kavkaz, 1942-1943 gg.* (The Battle for the Caucasus, 1942-1943), Voenizdat, Moscow, 1957.

Newspapers and Periodicals

Ambarian, Lieutenant General of the Guards Kh., "Edinonachalie—vazhneishii printsip stroitel'stva Vooruzhennykh Sil" (*Edinonachalie*—The Most Important Principle in Developing the Armed Forces), *Voennyi vestnik*, No. 8, August 1962, pp. 12-15.

Antipenko, Lieutenant General (Reserve) N., "Ot Visly do Odera" (From the Vistula to the Oder), *Voenno-istoricheskii zhurnal*, No. 3, March 1965, pp. 69-79.

Antonov, Colonel General N., "Povyshat' aktivnost' inzhenerov i tekhnikov v politiko-vospitatel'noi rabote" (Increase the Activity of Engineers and Technicians in Political-Educational Work), *Kommunist Vooruzhennykh Sil*, No. 2, January 1961, pp. 30-34.

Azovtsev, Colonel N., "Leninskie printsipy stroitel'stva Sovetskikh Vooruzhennykh Sil" (Leninist Principles of the Development of the USSR Armed Forces), *Kommunist Vooruzhennykh Sil*, No. 7, April 1963, pp. 9-19.

Bagramian, Marshal of the Soviet Union I. Kh., "Nastuplenie voisk 1-go Pribaltiiskogo fronta v Belorusskoi operatsii" (Attack by the Troops of the First Baltic Front During the Belorussian Operation), *Voenno-istoricheskii zhurnal*, No. 4, April 1961, pp. 12-27, and No. 5, May 1961, pp. 15-31.

——, "Slavnyi boevoi put' (K 40-letiiu Sovetskikh Vooruzhennykh Sil)" (The Glorious Fighting Road [on the 40th Anniversary of the Soviet Armed Forces]), *Kommunist*, No. 2, February 1958, pp. 34-48.

——, "Zabota o liudiakh—vazhneishaia cherta leninskogo stilia rukovodstva" (Concern About People—The Most Important Trait of Lenin's Style of Leadership), *Kommunist Vooruzhennykh Sil*, No. 3, February 1961, pp. 24-29.

Baranov, S., and E. Nikitin, "Rukovodstvo KPSS—osnova osnov sovetskogo voennogo stroitel'stva" (The CPSU's Leadership—The Very Basis of Soviet Military Development), *Kommunist Vooruzhennykh Sil,* No. 8, April 1963, pp. 17-25.

Beloborodov, Colonel General A. P., "Rabotu s ofitserskimi kadrami—na uroven' trebovanii XXII s"ezda KPSS" (Work with Officer Cadres—On the Level Defined by the Twenty-second Congress of the CPSU), *Kommunist Vooruzhennykh Sil,* No. 2, January 1962, pp. 19-26.

"Berlinskaia operatsiia v tsifrakh" (Data on the Berlin Operation), *Voenno-istoricheskii zhurnal,* No. 4, April 1965, pp. 79-88.

Binevich, A., and Z. Serebrianskii, "Slavnyi syn Kommunisticheskoi partii" (An Illustrious Son of the Communist Party), *Voenno-istoricheskii zhurnal,* No. 3, March 1963, pp. 35-48.

Biriuzov, Marshal of the Soviet Union S. S., "Velikaia bitva na Volge" (The Great Battle on the Volga), *Politicheskoe samoobrazovanie,* No. 2, 1963, pp. 33-41.

Boltin, E. A., "Pobeda Sovetskikh Vooruzhennykh Sil na zakliuchitel'nom etape Velikoi Otechestvennoi voiny" (The Soviet Armed Forces' Victory in the Closing Stage of the Great Patriotic War), *Voprosy istorii,* No. 5, May 1955, pp. 9-22.

——, "Vazhnaia zadacha sovetskikh istorikov" (An Important Task for Soviet Historians), *Voprosy istorii,* No. 11, November 1957, pp. 219-222.

Boltin, E. A., and A. S. Filippov, "Ser'eznye nedostatki 'Ocherkov istorii Velikoi Otechestvennoi voiny'" (Serious Shortcomings of *Essays on the History of the Great Patriotic War*), *Voprosy istorii,* No. 5, May 1956, pp. 146-156.

Bor-Ramenskii, E. G., Review of *Velikaia pobeda Sovetskoi Armii pod Stalingradom* (The Great Victory of the Soviet Army at Stalingrad), by B. S. Tel'pukhovskii, *Voprosy istorii,* December 1954.

Bukov, Major General A., "Organizatorskuiu rabotu politorganov—na uroven' trebovanii partii" (The Organizational Work of the Political Organs—On the Level of Party Demands), *Kommunist Vooruzhennykh Sil,* No. 10, May 1962, pp. 22-28.

Chuikov, Marshal of the Soviet Union V. I., "Kapituliatsiia gitlerovskoi Germanii" (The Surrender of Hitler Germany), *Novaia i noveishaia istoriia,* No. 2, March-April 1965, pp. 3-25.

——, "Konets tret'ego reikha" (The End of the Third Reich), *Oktiabr',* Nos. 3-5, 1964.

Dozorov, Lieutenant Colonels I., and E. Smotritskii, "Navyki politiko-vospitatel'noi raboty—vsem inzheneram i tekhnikam" (All Engineers and Technicians Should Have Training in Political-Educational Work), *Kommunist Vooruzhennykh Sil,* No. 1, January 1962, pp. 69-72.

"XXII s"ezd KPSS i zadachi voenno-istoricheskoi nauki" (The Twenty-second Congress of the CPSU and the Tasks of Military-Historical Science), *Voenno-istoricheskii zhurnal,* No. 2, February 1962, pp. 3-13.

Efimov, Colonel General P., "Sviazi armii i naroda nerazryvny" (The Ties Between the Army and the People Are Unbreakable), *Partiinaia zhizn',* No. 3, February 1963, pp. 8-14.

Epishev, General of the Army A. A., "Na strazhe mirovogo truda sovetskogo naroda" (Guarding the Peaceful Work of the Soviet People), *Politicheskoe samoobrazovanie*, No. 1, January 1963, pp. 13-24.

——, "O vozrastaiushchei roli KPSS v rukovodstve Vooruzhennymi Silami" (Regarding the Growing Role of the CPSU in Leading the Armed Forces), *Voprosy istorii KPSS*, No. 2, February 1963, pp. 3-14.

——, "Tverdo provodit' v zhizn' politiku partii v Vooruzhennykh Silakh" (Firmly Carry out the Party's Policy in the Armed Forces), *Kommunist Vooruzhennykh Sil*, No. 19, October 1962, pp. 2-15.

——, "Vospitanie voina-grazhdanina" (Education of the Soldier-Citizen), *Kommunist*, No. 5, March 1964, pp. 64-73.

Eremenko, Marshal of the Soviet Union A. I., "Istoricheskaia pobeda pod Stalingradom" (The Historic Victory at Stalingrad), *Kommunist*, No. 1, January 1958, pp. 26-40.

Evstigneev, V., B. Zhilin, and S. Roginskii, "Glubzhe izuchat' istoriiu Velikoi Otechestvennoi voiny" (Study More Profoundly the History of the Great Patriotic War), *Kommunist*, No. 10, July 1956, pp. 59-74.

Fel'dman, O., and V. Cheremnykh, "Ser'eznyi razgovor" (A Serious Conversation), *Voenno-istoricheskii zhurnal*, No. 5, May 1961, pp. 105-110.

Golikov, General of the Army F., "O nekotorykh voprosakh propagandistskoi raboty" (On Some Problems of Propaganda Activities), *Kommunist Vooruzhennykh Sil*, No. 5, December 1960, pp. 16-25.

Golub, P. A., "Kogda zhe byl uchrezhden institut voennykh komissarov Krasnoi Armii?" (When Was the Red Army Institute of Military Commissars Founded?), *Voprosy istorii KPSS*, No. 4, April 1962, pp. 155-160.

Grechko, Marshal of the Soviet Union A. A., "Boevoe sodruzhestvo bratskikh narodov" (The Fighting Solidarity of Fraternal Peoples), *Voenno-istoricheskii zhurnal*, No. 5, May 1965, pp. 16-25.

——, "Novye ustavy Vooruzhennykh Sil SSSR" (The New Statutes of the Armed Forces of the USSR), *Krasnaia zvezda*, September 7, 1960.

Kalashnik, Lieutenant General M., "Krepit' edinstvo ideologicheskoi i organizatorskoi raboty v voiskakh" (Strengthen the Unity of Ideological and Organizational Work Among the Troops), *Kommunist Vooruzhennykh Sil*, No. 22, November 1962, pp. 7-18.

——, "Partiino-politicheskaia rabota v Berlinskoi operatsii" (The Party-Political Work During the Berlin Operation), *Voenno-istoricheskii zhurnal*, No. 5, May 1965, pp. 42-55.

Khrushchev, N. S., "Za tesnuiu sviaz' literatury i iskusstva s zhizn'iu naroda" (For a Close Tie of Literature and Art with the Life of the People), *Kommunist*, No. 12, August 1957, pp. 11-29.

Konev, Marshal of the Soviet Union I. S., "Sila Sovetskoi Armii i Flota—v rukovodstve partii, v nerazryvnoi sviazi s narodom" (The Might of the Soviet Army and Navy Lies in Its Leadership by the Party and in Its Indestructible Tie with the People), *Pravda*, November 3, 1957.

"Kontrol' i proverka ispolneniia—gvozd' vsei nashei raboty" (Control and Verification of Execution Is the Crux of All Our Work), *Kommunist Vooruzhennykh Sil*, No. 1, January 1963, pp. 6-10.

Korotkov, Colonel I., "O razvitii sovetskoi voennoi teorii v poslevoennye gody" (The Development of Soviet Military Theory in Postwar Years), *Voenno-istoricheskii zhurnal*, No. 4, April 1964, pp. 39-50.

Kozlov, Colonel S. N., "O kharaktere voin sovremennoi epokhi" (On the Nature of Present-day Wars), *Kommunist Vooruzhennykh Sil*, No. 2, January 1961, pp. 13-20.

——, "Tvorcheskii kharakter sovetskoi voennoi nauki" (The Creative Character of Soviet Military Science), *Kommunist Vooruzhennykh Sil*, No. 11, June 1961, pp. 48-56.

——, "Voennaia doktrina i voennaia nauka" (Military Doctrine and Military Science), *Kommunist Vooruzhennykh Sil*, No. 5, March 1964, pp. 9-16.

Krasil'nikov, Lieutenant General S., "O kharaktere sovremennoi voiny" (On the Character of Modern War), *Krasnaia zvezda*, November 18, 1960.

Krylov, Marshal S. M., "Vsemerno ukrepliat' edinonachalie" (Strengthen *Edinonachalie* in Every Possible Way), *Krasnaia zvezda*, September 27, 1961.

Kurasov, General of the Army V., "Voprosy sovetskoi voennoi nauki v proizvedeniiakh V. I. Lenina" (Problems of Soviet Military Science in the Works of V. I. Lenin), *Voenno-istoricheskii zhurnal*, No. 3, March 1961, pp. 3-14.

Kurochkin, General of the Army P., "Kniga o velikom perelome" (A Book About the Great Turning Point), *Voenno-istoricheskii zhurnal*, No. 3, March 1962, pp. 85-92.

Loboda, Major General V., "Komandnye kadry v razvitii Vooruzhennykh Sil SSSR" (Commanding Cadres in the Development of the USSR Armed Forces), *Voennyi vestnik*, No. 2, February 1958, pp. 12-21.

Lomov, Colonel General N., "O sovetskoi voennoi doktrine" (On Soviet Military Doctrine), *Kommunist Vooruzhennykh Sil*, No. 10, May 1962, pp. 11-21.

Malinovskii, Marshal of the Soviet Union R. Ia., "Moral'naia i psikhologicheskaia podgotovka voinov v sovremennykh usloviiakh" (The Moral and Psychological Training of Soldiers Under Contemporary Conditions), *Kommunist Vooruzhennykh Sil*, No. 12, June 1965, pp. 3-13.

——, "Nasushchnye voprosy vospitaniia lichnogo sostava Vooruzhennykh Sil SSSR" (Urgent Problems in the Education of USSR Armed Forces Personnel), *Kommunist Vooruzhennykh Sil*, No. 11, June 1962, pp. 3-15.

——, "Programma KPSS i voprosy ukrepleniia Vooruzhennykh Sil SSSR" (The CPSU Program and Problems of Strengthening the USSR Armed Forces), *Kommunist*, No. 7, May 1962, pp. 11-22.

Nenakhov, Colonel I. N., "The Policy of the Communist Party in Strengthening the Active Defense of the Soviet State," *Voennaia mysl'*, No. 10, October 1953, pp. 3-18.

"Neotlozhnye zadachi istorikov KPSS" (Immediate Tasks of Historians of the CPSU), *Voprosy istorii KPSS*, No. 2, 1957, pp. 220-229.

"O rabote partiinogo komiteta i partorganizatsii shtaba i upravleniia tyla Ministerstva oborony SSSR" (About the Work of the Party Committee and Party Organization of the Staff and Administration of the Rear by the USSR Defense Ministry), *Kommunist Vooruzhennykh Sil,* No. 5, March 1962, pp. 55-57.

"O rabote partkoma i partiinykh organizatsii shtaba i upravlenii Sukhoputnykh voisk" (About the Work of the Party Committee and Party Organizations of the Staff and Administrations of the Ground Forces), *Kommunist Vooruzhennykh Sil,* No. 15, August 1962, pp. 38-41.

"O razrabotke istorii Velikoi Otechestvennoi voiny Sovetskogo Soiuza" (On Preparing the History of the Great Patriotic War of the Soviet Union), *Voprosy istorii,* No. 5, May 1955, pp. 3-8.

"Ob 'Ocherkakh istorii Velikoi Otechestvennoi voiny'" (Regarding *Essays on the History of the Great Patriotic War*), letters to the editor by A. Samsonov, E. A. Boltin, and A. S. Filippov, *Voprosy istorii,* No. 1, January 1957, pp. 210-220.

Pavlenko, Major General N., "Letopis' surovykh ispytanii i pervykh pobed sovetskogo naroda v Velikoi Otechestvennoi voine" (Chronicle of Bitter Trials and First Victories of the Soviet People in the Great Patriotic War), *Voenno-istoricheskii zhurnal,* No. 11, November 1961, pp. 93-103.

——, "Novyi trud voennykh istorikov" (A New Work by Military Historians), *Kommunist,* No. 14, September 1965, pp. 117-121.

Pechorkin, V. K., and A. M. Samsonov, "Mezhdunarodnoe znachenie pobedy na Volge" (International Significance of the Victory on the Volga), *Novaia i noveishaia istoriia,* No. 2, February 1963, pp. 65-74.

Petrov, Iu. P., "Deiatel'nost' Kommunisticheskoi partii po provedeniiu edinonachaliia v Vooruzhennykh Silakh, 1925-1931 gody" (The Activity of the Communist Party in Introducing *Edinonachalie* in the Armed Forces, 1925-1931), *Voenno-istoricheskii zhurnal,* No. 5, May 1963, pp. 3-11.

——, "Nekotorye voprosy partiino-politicheskoi raboty v Vooruzhennykh Silakh v predvoennye gody" (Some Problems of Party-Political Work in the Armed Forces in the Prewar Years), *Voprosy istorii KPSS,* No. 11, November 1963, pp. 57-72.

Pigurnov, Lieutenant General A., "Deiatel'nost' voennykh sovetov, politorganov i partiinykh organizatsii po ukrepleniiu edinonachaliia v period Velikoi Otechestvennoi voiny" (Activity of Military Councils, Political Organs, and Party Organizations in Strengthening *Edinonachalie* During the Great Patriotic War), *Voenno-istoricheskii zhurnal,* No. 4, April 1961, pp. 47-56.

Pliev, General of the Army I., "Novaia tekhnika i voprosy ukrepleniia distsipliny" (The New Technology and Problems of Strengthening Discipline), *Kommunist Vooruzhennykh Sil,* No. 19, October 1962, pp. 21-28.

Pozniak, Lieutenant General V., "Zavershaiushchie udary po vragu" (The Final Blows to the Enemy), *Voenno-istoricheskii zhurnal,* No. 5, May 1965, pp. 26-35.

Prochko, Lieutenant General of Artillery I., "Memuarnaia literatura o Velikoi Otechestvennoi voine," (Memoir Literature About the Great Patriotic War), *Voenno-istoricheskii zhurnal,* No. 5, May 1961, pp. 95-104.

——, "'Tanki povernuli na zapad'" ("The Tanks Turned West"), *Voenno-istoricheskii zhurnal,* No. 7, July 1962, pp. 83-89.

Prusanov, I. P., "Povyshenie organizuiushchego i napravliaiushchego vliianiia partii v Vooruzhennykh Silakh, 1956-1964" (The Growth of the Party's

Organizing and Guiding Influence in the Armed Forces, 1956-1964), *Voprosy istorii KPSS*, No. 2, February 1965, pp. 3-14.

Rokossovskii, Marshal of the Soviet Union K., "Severnee Berlina" (To the North of Berlin), *Voenno-istoricheskii zhurnal*, No. 5, May 1965, pp. 36-41.

Rotmistrov, Chief Marshal of Armored Troops P., "Boevoi uchastok ideologicheskoi raboty" (The Fighting Sector of Ideological Work), *Kommunist*, No. 12, August 1964, pp. 123-127.

——, "Istoricheskaia pobeda (K 20-letiiu razgroma gitlerovskikh voisk pod Kurskom)" (Historic Victory [on the 20th Anniversary of Crushing the Hitlerite Forces at Kursk]), *Agitator*, No. 8, April 1963, pp. 19-21.

——, "O roli vnezapnosti v sovremennoi voine" (On the Role of Surprise in Contemporary War), *Voennaia mysl'*, No. 2, February 1955.

——, "O sovetskom voennom iskusstve v bitve na Volge" (Regarding Soviet Military Art in the Battle on the Volga), *Voenno-istoricheskii zhurnal*, No. 12, December 1962, pp. 3-14; and No. 1, January 1963, pp. 8-20.

Rybkin, Lieutenant Colonel E. I., "O sushchnosti mirovoi raketno-iadernoi voiny" (On the Essence of World-wide Missile-Nuclear War), *Kommunist Vooruzhennykh Sil*, No. 17, September 1965, pp. 50-56.

Rytov, Lieutenant General A. G., "Komandir i partiinaia organizatsiia" (The Commander and the Party Organization), *Vestnik vozdushnogo flota*, No. 7, July 1957, pp. 25-34.

Samsonov, A. M., "Volgogradskaia partiinaia organizatsiia v period oborony goroda-geroia" (The Volgograd Party Organization During the Defense of the Heroic City), *Voprosy istorii KPSS*, No. 2, February 1963, pp. 44-54.

——, "Za glubokoe issledovanie istorii Velikoi Otechestvennoi voiny" (For a Thorough Research of the History of the Great Patriotic War), *Voenno-istoricheskii zhurnal*, No. 3, March 1965, pp. 17-24.

Shatagin, N. I., "Kommunisticheskaia partiia—organizator Sovetskoi Armii" (The Communist Party—The Organizer of the Soviet Army), *Voprosy istorii KPSS*, No. 1, 1958, pp. 10-28.

Shtemenko, Colonel General S., "Kak planirovalas' posledniaia kampaniia po razgromu gitlerovskoi Germanii" (How the Last Campaign for the Destruction of Hitler Germany Was Planned), *Voenno-istoricheskii zhurnal*, No. 5, May 1965, pp. 56-72.

Sidorov, Colonel P., "Neustanno krepit' oboronosposobnost' strany" (Strengthen Tirelessly the Defense Capability of the Country, *Kommunist Vooruzhennykh Sil*, No. 12, June 1961, pp. 59-65.

Simonov, K., "Bessmertnyi garnizon" (The Undying Garrison), *Novyi mir*, No. 5, 1955.

"Slavnaia godovshchina" (The Glorious Anniversary), *Voennyi vestnik*, No. 4, April 1956, pp. 2-9.

Sokolovskii, Marshal of the Soviet Union V. D., "O sovetskom voennom iskusstve v bitve pod Moskvoi" (Regarding Soviet Military Art in the Battle Around Moscow), *Voenno-istoricheskii zhurnal*, No. 11, November 1961, pp. 15-28.

"Sovershenstvovat' partiinuiu rabotu v akademiiakh i uchilishchakh" (Improve Party Work in the Academies and Institutes), *Kommunist Vooruzhennykh Sil*, No. 12, June 1962, pp. 40-43.

Sulimov, E., "Nuzhno glubokoe issledovanie temy" (Thorough Research of the Subject Is Necessary), *Voenno-istoricheskii zhurnal*, No. 10, October 1962, pp. 90-95.

Sushko, Colonels N., S. Tiushkevich, and G. Fedorov, "Razvitie marksistsko-leninskogo ucheniia o voine v sovremennykh usloviiakh" (The Development of Marxist-Leninist Teaching Regarding War in Modern Conditions), *Kommunist Vooruzhennykh Sil*, No. 18, September 1961, pp. 19-29.

Talenskii, Major General N. A., "The Late War: Some Reflections," *International Affairs*, No. 5, May 1965, pp. 12-18.

Tarasov, Colonels E., and S. Il'in, "Vsemerno sovershenstvovat' rabotu partiinykh komitetov akademii" (Constantly Improve the Work of the Party Committees in the Academies), *Kommunist Vooruzhennykh Sil*, No. 5, December 1960, pp. 26-32.

Telegin, Lieutenant General (Reserve) K., "Na zakliuchitel'nom etape voiny" (At the Last Stage of the War), *Voenno-istoricheskii zhurnal*, No. 4, April 1965, pp. 54-70.

Tel'pukhovskii, B. S., "Kommunisticheskaia partiia—vdokhnovitel' i organizator pobedy sovetskogo naroda v Velikoi Otechestvennoi voine" (The Communist Party—Inspirer and Organizer of the Victory of the Soviet People in the Great Patriotic War), *Voprosy istorii KPSS*, No. 2, 1958, pp. 34-56.

"V glavnom politicheskom upravlenii Sovetskoi Armii i Voenno-Morskogo Flota" (In the Main Political Administration of the Soviet Army and Navy), *Kommunist Vooruzhennykh Sil*, No. 22, November 1961, pp. 57-60.

Vakhrushev, Major General L., "Vsemerno uluchshat' rabotu s kadrami politsostava" (Improve Work with the Political Cadres in Every Possible Way), *Kommunist Vooruzhennykh Sil*, No. 23, December 1962, pp. 22-28.

"Velikii prodolzhatel' dela Lenina" (The Great Successor to Lenin's Work), *Voprosy istorii*, No. 12, December 1954, pp. 3-10.

Vlasenko, B., "Partiinaia organizatsiia i sem'ia kommunista" (The Party Organization and the Communist's Family), *Kommunist Vooruzhennykh Sil*, No. 22, November 1962, pp. 74-75.

Voronov, Chief Marshal of Artillery N., "Operatsiia 'Kol'tso'" (Operation 'Ring'), *Voenno-istoricheskii zhurnal*, No. 6, June 1962, pp. 67-76.

"Vsemirno-istoricheskaia pobeda sovetskogo naroda" (The Historic Victory of the Soviet People), *Kommunist*, No. 7, May 1965, pp. 3-14.

"Za leninskuiu partiinost' v istoricheskoi nauke" (For a Leninist Party Spirit in Historical Science), *Voprosy istorii*, No. 3, March 1957, pp. 3-19.

Zakharov, Marshal of the Soviet Union M. V., "Uroki istorii (K 20-letiiu s nachala Velikoi Otechestvennoi voiny)" (The Lessons of History [20 Years Since the Start of the Great Patriotic War]), *Voennyi vestnik*, No. 6, June 1961, pp. 3-8.

Zhadov, General of the Army A., "Na strazhe zavoevanii Velikogo Oktiabria" (On Guard over the Achievements of the Great October), *Voennyi vestnik,* No. 10, October 1957, pp. 9-15.

——, "O nasushchnykh zadachakh voenno-istoricheskoi raboty" (The Urgent Tasks in Military-Historical Work), *Krasnaia zvezda,* January 25, 1963.

Zheltov, Colonel General A., "Rukovodstvo KPSS stroitel'stvom Sovetskikh Vooruzhennykh Sil v poslevoennyi period" (The Leadership of the Party in the Construction of the Soviet Armed Forces in the Postwar Period), *Voenno-istoricheskii zhurnal,* No. 2, February 1965, pp. 3-11.

Zhilin, Major General P., "KPSS—organizator pobedy v Velikoi Otechestvennoi voine" (The CPSU—The Organizer of Victory in the Great Patriotic War), *Voenno-istoricheskii zhurnal,* No. 5, May 1965, pp. 3-15.

Zhukov, Marshal of the Soviet Union G. K., "Na berlinskom napravlenii" (On the Berlin Axis), *Voenno-istoricheskii zhurnal,* No. 6, June 1965, pp. 12-22.

Zimin, Colonels Ia., and V. Morozov, "KPSS i stroitel'stvo Sovetskikh Vooruzhennykh Sil" (The CPSU and the Development of the Soviet Armed Forces), *Voenno-istoricheskii zhurnal,* No. 8, August 1965, pp. 74-81.

NON-SOVIET SOURCES

Books and Pamphlets

Abrams, Philip, "Democracy, Technology, and the Retired British Officer," ed. Samuel P. Huntington, *Changing Patterns of Military Politics,* The Free Press of Glencoe, Inc., New York, 1962.

Alexandrov, Victor, *The Tukhachevsky Affair,* trans. John Hewish, Prentice-Hall, Englewood Cliffs, N.J., 1964.

Allen, W. E. D., and Paul Muratoff, *The Russian Campaigns of 1941-1943,* Penguin Books, New York, 1944.

The Anti-Stalin Campaign and International Communism, Columbia University Press, New York, 1956.

Antonov, Colonel G. I., "The March into Poland," *The Red Army,* ed. B. H. Liddell-Hart, Harcourt, Brace and Company, New York, 1956.

Armstrong, John A., *The Soviet Bureaucratic Elite,* Frederick A. Praeger, Inc., New York, 1959.

Atkinson, Littleton B., *Dual Command in the Red Army,* Air University Documentary Research Study, Maxwell Air Force Base, Alabama, 1950.

Bramson, Leon, and George W. Goethals (eds.), *War: Studies from Psychology, Sociology, Anthropology,* Basic Books, New York, 1964.

Bronska-Pampuch, Wanda (ed. and trans.), *Geköpfte Armee. Lew Nikulin: Die Affäre Tuchatschewskij. General Gorbatow: Verlorene Jahre,* Propyläen Verlag, Berlin, 1965.

Brzezinski, Zbigniew (ed.), *Political Controls in the Soviet Army,* Research Program on the USSR, New York, 1954.

Buchheit, Gert, *Soldatentum und Rebellion: Die Tragödie der Deutschen Wehrmacht,* Grote, Rastatt/Baden, 1961.

Chamberlain, W. H., *Russia's Iron Age,* Little, Brown & Co., Boston, 1934.

Coles, Harry (ed.), *Total War and Cold War: Problems in Civilian Control of the Military,* Ohio State University Press, Columbus, 1962.

Conquest, Robert, *Power and Policy in the USSR*, St. Martin's Press, Inc., New York, 1961.

Dinerstein, H. S., *War and the Soviet Union*, Frederick A. Praeger, Inc., New York, 1959.

Dittmar, Lieutenant General Kurt, "The Red Army in the Finnish War," *The Red Army*, ed. B. H. Liddell-Hart, Harcourt, Brace and Company, New York, 1956.

Djilas, Milovan, *Conversations with Stalin*, Harcourt, Brace and Company, New York, 1962.

Duranty, Walter, *The Kremlin and the People*, Reynal & Hitchcock, New York, 1941.

Erickson, John, *The Soviet High Command, 1918-1941*, St. Martin's Press, Inc., New York, 1962.

Fedotoff-White, D., *The Growth of the Red Army*, Princeton University Press, Princeton, N.J., 1944.

Finer, S. E., *The Man on Horseback: The Role of the Military in Politics*, Frederick A. Praeger, Inc., New York, 1962.

Friedrich, Carl J., and Z. K. Brzezinski, *Totalitarian Dictatorship and Autocracy*, Frederick A. Praeger, Inc., New York, 1956.

Gallagher, Matthew P., *The Soviet History of World War II: Myths, Memoirs, and Realities*, Frederick A. Praeger, Inc., New York, 1963.

Garder, Michel, *Histoire de l'Armée Soviétique*, Plon, Paris, 1959.

Garthoff, Raymond L., "The Marshals and the Party: Soviet Civil-Military Relations in the Postwar Period," *Total War and Cold War: Problems in Civilian Control of the Military*, ed. Harry Coles, Ohio State University Press, Columbus, 1962.

——, *Soviet Military Doctrine*, The Free Press, Glencoe, Ill., 1953.

——, *Soviet Strategy in the Nuclear Age*, Frederick A. Praeger, Inc., New York, 1958.

Goerlitz, Walter, *History of the German General Staff, 1657-1945*, Frederick A. Praeger, Inc., New York, 1962.

Gorce, Paul-Marie de la, *The French Army: A Military-Political History*, trans. Kenneth Douglas, George Braziller, New York, 1963.

Hahlweg, Werner (ed.), *Klassiker der Kriegskunst*, Wehr und Wissen Verlagsgesellschaft mbH, Darmstadt, 1960.

Halder, General Franz von, "Diary: Campaign in Russia" (unpublished manuscript), cited in R. L. Garthoff, *Soviet Military Doctrine*, The Free Press, Glencoe, Ill., 1953.

Höhn, Reinhard, *Die Armee als Erziehungsschule der Nation: Das Ende einer Idee*, Verlag für Wissenschaft, Wirtschaft und Technik, Bad Harzburg, 1963.

——, *Sozialismus und Heer*, Verlag Dr. Max Gehlen, Bad Homburg, 2nd ed., 1961.

Horelick, Arnold, and Myron Rush, *Strategic Power and Soviet Foreign Policy*, University of Chicago Press, Chicago, 1966.

Howard, Michael (ed.), *Soldiers and Governments*, Eyre & Spottiswoode, London, 1957.

Huntington, Samuel P., "The New Military Politics," *Changing Patterns of Military Politics*, ed. Samuel P. Huntington, The Free Press of Glencoe, Inc., New York, 1962.

——, *The Soldier and the State*, Harvard University Press, Cambridge, Mass., 1957.

Janowitz, Morris, *The Professional Soldier*, The Free Press of Glencoe, Ill., 1960.

Kellen, Konrad, *Khrushchev: A Political Portrait*, Frederick A. Praeger, Inc., New York, 1961.

Kolkowicz, Roman, *Conflicts in Soviet Party-Military Relations: 1962-1963*, The RAND Corporation, RM-3760-PR, August 1963.

——, *The Impact of Technology on the Soviet Military: A Challenge to Traditional Military Professionalism*, The RAND Corporation, RM-4198-PR, August 1964.

——, *The Use of Soviet Military Labor in the Civilian Economy: A Study of Military "Shefstvo,"* The RAND Corporation, RM-3360-PR, November 1962.

Lasswell, Harold D., "The Garrison-State Hypothesis Today," *Changing Patterns of Military Politics*, ed. Samuel P. Huntington, The Free Press of Glencoe, Inc., New York, 1962.

Lasswell, Harold D., Daniel Lerner, and C. Easton Rothwell, *The Comparative Study of Elites* (Hoover Institute Studies, Series B: Elites, No. 1), Stanford University Press, Stanford, Cal., 1952.

Leites, Nathan, *A Study of Bolshevism*, The RAND Corporation, R-239, 1953.

Liddell-Hart, B. H. (ed.), *The Red Army*, Harcourt, Brace and Company, New York, 1956.

Mackintosh, J. M., "The Red Army, 1920-1936," *The Red Army*, ed. B. H. Liddell-Hart, Harcourt, Brace and Company, New York, 1956.

Mehnert, Klaus, *The Anatomy of Soviet Man*, trans. Maurice Rosenbaum, Weidenfeld and Nicolson, London, 1961.

Meissner, Boris, *Russland unter Chruschtschow*, R. Oldenbourg Verlag, Munich, 1960.

Millis, Walter, Harvey Mansfield, and Harold Stein, *Arms and the State*, The Twentieth Century Fund, New York, 1958.

Nemzer, Louis, "Civil-Military Relations in the USSR," unpublished MS.

Nitschke, August, *Der Feind*, W. Kohlhammer Verlag, Stuttgart, 1964.

Obermann, Emil, *Soldaten, Bürger, Militaristen*, J. G. Cotta'sche Buchhandlung Nachf., Stuttgart, 1958.

Paloczi-Horvath, George, *Khrushchev: The Making of a Dictator*, Little, Brown and Company, Boston, 1960.

Pistrak, Lazar, *The Grand Tactician: Khrushchev's Rise to Power*, Frederick A. Praeger, Inc., New York, 1961.

Pool, Ithiel de Sola, *Satellite Generals* (Hoover Institute Studies, Series B: Elites, No. 5), Stanford University Press, Stanford, Cal., 1955.

Pruck, Erich F., *Der rote Soldat*, Günter Olzog Verlag, Munich, 1961.

Ruge, Friedrich, *Politik, Militär, Bündnis*, Deutsche Verlagsanstalt, Stuttgart, 1963.

Rush, Myron, *The Rise of Khrushchev*, Public Affairs Press, Washington, D.C., 1958.

Schapiro, Leonard, *The Communist Party of the Soviet Union*, Random House, New York, 1960.

——, "The Great Purge," *The Red Army*, ed. B. H. Liddell-Hart, Harcourt, Brace and Company, New York, 1956.

Scharndorff, Werner, *Moskaus permanente Säuberung*, Günter Olzog Verlag, Munich, 1964.

Senger und Etterlin, Frido von, *Krieg in Europa*, Kiepenheuer & Witsch, Berlin, 1960.

Sokolovskii, Marshal V. D. (ed.), *Soviet Military Strategy*, U.S. eds. H. S. Dinerstein, L. Gouré, and T. W. Wolfe, Prentice-Hall, Inc., Englewood Cliffs, N.J., 1963.

U.S. Military Academy, Department of Military Art and Engineering, *The War in Eastern Europe*, West Point, New York, 1949.

Vagts, Alfred, *A History of Militarism*, Meridian Books, Inc., New York, 1959.

Waldman, Eric, *Soldat im Staat*, Harald Boldt Verlag, Boppard am Rhein, 1963.

Wolfe, T. W., *A First Reaction to the New Soviet Book "Military Strategy,"* The RAND Corporation, RM-3495-PR, February 1963.

Newspapers and Periodicals

Adams, Arthur E., "The Hybrid Art of Sovietology," *Survey*, No. 50, January 1964, pp. 154-162.

Boltin, Major General E., "O publikacji 'Historia Wielkiej Wojny Narodowej Zwiazku Radzieckiego'" (On the Publication of *The History of the Great Patriotic War of the Soviet Union*), *Wojskowy Przeglad Historyczny* (Military Historical Review), No. 4, 1964, pp. 206-219.

Brzezinski, Zbigniew, "From the Other Shore," *Encounter*, No. 3, 1963.

Bulletin of the Institute for the Study of the History and Culture of the USSR, Supplement, Vol. 2, No. 5, May 1955.

Bulletin of the Institute for the Study of the USSR, Vol. 9, No. 1, January 1962.

Charles, David A., "The Dismissal of Marshal P'eng Teh-huai," *The China Quarterly*, No. 18, 1964, pp. 63-74.

Conquest, Robert, "In Defense of Kremlinology," *Survey*, No. 50, January 1964, pp. 163-173.

"The Coup and After," *Problems of Communism*, January-February and May-June 1965. A symposium including articles by Merle Fainsod, Richard Lowenthal, Robert Conquest, Adam Ulam, and others.

"Das Echo auf Chruschtschows Sturz," *Osteuropa*, Nos. 3 and 4, 1965, pp. 166-176 and 228-240, respectively. A symposium of articles.

"The Fall of Khrushchev," *Bulletin of the Institute for the Study of the USSR*, Vol. 11, No. 12, December 1964. A symposium including articles by P. Kruzhin, A. Avtorkhanov, S. Stolte, and A. Kashin.

Frank, Victor S., "The Unsolved Crisis," *Bulletin of the Institute for the Study of the History and Culture of the USSR*, Vol. 2, No. 2, February 1955, pp. 3-9.

Galay, Nikolai, "The Significance of Golikov's Removal," *Bulletin of the Institute for the Study of the USSR*, Vol. 9, No. 8, August 1962, pp. 34-40.

——, "The Significance of the Reestablishment of the Supreme Command of the Soviet Armed Forces," *Bulletin of the Institute for the Study of the USSR*, Vol. 11, No. 7, July 1964.

Hackett, General Sir John Winthrop, "The Profession of Arms, Part II: Today and Tomorrow," *Military Review*, Vol. 43, No. 11, November 1963.

Horelick, Arnold L., "The Cuban Missile Crisis: An Analysis of Soviet Calculations and Behavior," *World Politics*, Vol. 16, No. 3, April 1964, pp. 363-389.

Joffe, Ellis, "The Conflict Between Old and New in the Chinese Army," *The China Quarterly*, No. 18, 1964, pp. 118-140.

Kolkowicz, Roman, "The Role of Disarmament in Soviet Policy: A Means or an End?" The RAND Corporation, P-2952, August 1964.

——, "Soviet Strategic Debates: An Important Recent Addendum," The RAND Corporation, P-2936, July 1964.

Lowenthal, R., David Burg, and Herman Achminov, "Nach Chruschtschow," *Osteuropa*, No. 11, 1964.

Lyons, Gene M., "The New Civil-Military Relations," *American Political Science Review*, No. 55, March 1961, pp. 53-63.

Martens, M., "Providing for the Soviet Officer," *Bulletin of the Institute for the Study of the USSR*, Vol. 3, No. 2, February 1956, pp. 26-32.

Meissner, Boris, "Chruschtschowismus ohne Chruschtschow," *Osteuropa*, Nos. 1, 2, 3, 4, 1965.

——, "Party and Government Reforms," *Survey*, No. 56, July 1965.

Miksche, Ferdinand O., "The Soldier and Technical Warfare," *Military Review*, Vol. 42, No. 8, August 1962, pp. 71-78. Orig. publ. in the *Revue de Défense Nationale* (France).

Millis, Walter, "Puzzle of the 'Military Mind,'" *The New York Times Magazine*, November 18, 1962.

Nove, Alec, "The Uses and Abuses of Kremlinology," *Survey*, No. 50, January 1964, pp. 174-182.

Reddaway, P. B., "The Fall of Khrushchev," *Survey*, No. 56, July 1965.

Rigby, T. H., "Crypto-Politics," *Survey*, No. 50, January 1964, pp. 183-184.

Scharndorff, Werner, "Die Stabilität der heutigen Sowjetführung," *Politische Studien*, No. 161, May-June 1965.

Wiatr, Jerzy J., "Militaryzm: pojecie i problematyka socjologiczna" (Militarism: Conceptualization and Sociological Approaches), *Studia Socjologiczno-Polityczne*, No. 6, 1960, pp. 33-61.

——, "Niektore problemy socjologiczne armii socjalistycznej" (Some Sociological Problems of the Socialist Army), *Studia Socjologiczno-Polityczne*, No. 14, 1963, pp. 23-56.

THE NEWSPAPER AND PERIODICAL LITERATURE: A SELECTED, ANNOTATED LIST

Soviet

Agitator	Semimonthly journal of the CPSU Central Committee
Aviatsiia i kosmonavtika (Aviation and Cosmonautics)	Monthly journal of the Soviet Air Force
Biuleten' Verkhovnogo suda SSSR (Bulletin of the USSR Supreme Court)	Monthly bulletin of the USSR Supreme Court
Izvestiia	Daily organ of the Soviet government
Kommunist	Semimonthly theoretical and political journal of the CPSU Central Committee
Kommunist Vooruzhennykh Sil (Communist of the Armed Forces)	Semimonthly central organ of the Main Political Administration of the Army and Navy
Komsomol'skaia pravda (Komsomol Truth)	Main organ of the Komsomol, published six times a week
Krasnaia zvezda (Red Star)	Daily publication of the Ministry of Defense
Kryl'ia rodiny (Wings of the Fatherland)	Monthly organ of the DOSAAF USSR
Literaturnaia gazeta (Literary Gazette)	Main organ of the Union of Soviet Writers, published three times a week
Mezhdunarodnaia zhizn' (International Affairs)	Monthly, dealing mainly with international political problems
Morskoi sbornik (Naval Review)	Monthly theoretical journal of the Soviet Navy
Novaia i noveishaia istoriia (Modern and Recent History)	Published by the Institute of History, USSR Academy of Sciences, biweekly
Novoe vremia (New Times)	Weekly, dealing with international affairs
Novyi mir (New World)	A monthly publication of the Union of Writers, dealing with sociopolitical and literary problems
Partiinaia zhizn' (Party Life)	Semimonthly organ of the CPSU Central Committee
Politicheskoe samoobrazovanie (Political Self-Education)	Monthly organ of the CPSU Central Committee
Pravda	Main organ of the CPSU, published daily
Sovetskaia aviatsiia (Soviet Aviation)	Published daily by the Soviet Air Force until 1960, when it was merged with *Krasnaia zvezda*

Sovetskii flot (Soviet Navy)	Issued daily by the Ministry of Defense until 1960, then merged with *Krasnaia zvezda*
Sovetskii patriot (The Soviet Patriot)	Daily organ of the Central Committee of the DOSAAF USSR
Sovetskii voin (The Soviet Soldier)	Monthly, issued by the MPA
Sovetskoe gosudarstvo i pravo (Soviet Government and Law)	Organ of the Academy of Sciences, dealing with legal and economic problems
Tyl i snabzhenie (Rear and Supply)	Monthly, issued by the Ministry of Defense, dealing mainly with logistics and technical problems
Voennaia mysl' (Military Thought)	Professional military journal, published monthly
Voenno-istoricheskii zhurnal (Military-Historical Journal)	Monthly, issued by the Ministry of Defense
Voennye znaniia (Military Knowledge)	Monthly, issued by DOSAAF
Voennyi vestnik (Military Herald)	Monthly, issued by the Ministry of Defense
Voprosy istorii (Problems of History)	Monthly organ of the Academy of Sciences
Voprosy istorii KPSS (Problems of CPSU History)	Bimonthly publication of the Central Committee's Institute of Marxism-Leninism
Zaria vostoka (Eastern Dawn)	Daily, published by the Central Committee of the Georgian Communist Party and the City Committee in Tbilisi

Polish

Nowe Drogi (New Ways)	Monthly publication of the Central Committee of the Polish Communist Party, dealing with theoretical and political problems
Polityka (Politics)	Weekly, dealing with political and social problems
Studia Socjologiczno-Polityczne (Sociological-Political Studies)	Quarterly, published in Warsaw
Trybuna Ludu (People's Forum)	Daily, published by the Central Committee of the Polish Communist Party
Wojsko Ludowe (People's Army)	Theoretical-political journal, published monthly by the Main Political Administration
Wojskowy Przeglad Historyczny (Military-Historical Review)	Quarterly publication, dealing with problems of military theory and history

Zolnierz Polski (Polish Soldier)	Weekly publication of the Main Political Administration
Zolnierz Wolnosci (Freedom's Soldier)	Military daily
Zycie Warsazawy (Warsaw Life)	Daily

East German

Einheit	Theoretical journal, published monthly by the Central Committee of the Socialist Unity Party (SED)
Volksarmee	Military weekly

West German

Bulletin of the Institute for the Study of the USSR	Monthly, published in Munich
Osteuropa	Monthly, concerned with East European and communist problems
Ost-Probleme	Biweekly, on international communist affairs
Wehrkunde	Monthly military journal
Wehrwissenschaftliche Rundschau	Monthly, dealing with questions of European security
Die Zeit	Weekly, dealing with political-social and cultural problems

Other European

Neue Zürcher Zeitung	A Swiss daily
Survey	A British journal of Soviet and East European studies, published quarterly

United States

East Europe	Published monthly by the Free Europe Committee
Military Affairs	Quarterly publication of the American Military Institute
Problems of Communism	Bimonthly, on Soviet bloc affairs, published by the USIA

Index

Index

OTHER RAND BOOKS IN THE SOCIAL SCIENCES

Brodie, Bernard. STRATEGY IN THE MISSILE AGE. Princeton University Press, Princeton, New Jersey. September 1959.*

Davison, W. Phillips. THE BERLIN BLOCKADE: A STUDY IN COLD WAR POLITICS. Princeton University Press, Princeton, New Jersey. April 1958.

Dinerstein, H. S., and Leon Gouré. TWO STUDIES IN SOVIET CONTROLS: COMMUNISM AND THE RUSSIAN PEASANT; MOSCOW IN CRISIS. The Free Press, Glencoe, Illinois. February 1955.

Dinerstein, H. S. WAR AND THE SOVIET UNION: NUCLEAR WEAPONS AND THE REVOLUTION IN SOVIET MILITARY AND POLITICAL THINKING. Frederick A. Praeger, Inc., New York. April 1959.*

Fainsod, Merle. SMOLENSK UNDER SOVIET RULE. Harvard University Press, Cambridge, Massachusetts. September 1958.

Garthoff, Raymond L. SOVIET MILITARY DOCTRINE. The Free Press, Glencoe, Illinois. May 1953.

George, Alexander L. PROPAGANDA ANALYSIS: A STUDY OF INFERENCES MADE FROM NAZI PROPAGANDA IN WORLD WAR II. Row, Peterson and Company, Evanston, Illinois. February 1959.

Goldhamer, Herbert, and Andrew W. Marshall. PSYCHOSIS AND CIVILIZATION. The Free Press, Glencoe, Illinois. June 1953.

Gouré, Leon. CIVIL DEFENSE IN THE SOVIET UNION. University of California Press, Los Angeles, California. January 1962.*

Gouré, Leon. THE SIEGE OF LENINGRAD. Stanford University Press, Stanford, California. June 1962.*

Halpern, Manfred. THE POLITICS OF SOCIAL CHANGE IN THE MIDDLE EAST AND NORTH AFRICA. Princeton University Press, Princeton, New Jersey. October 1963.

Horelick, Arnold L., and Myron Rush. STRATEGIC POWER AND SOVIET FOREIGN POLICY. University of Chicago Press, Chicago, Illinois. April 1966.

Hsieh, Alice Langley. COMMUNIST CHINA'S STRATEGY IN THE NUCLEAR ERA. Prentice-Hall, Inc., Englewood Cliffs, New Jersey. March 1962.*

Janis, Irving L. AIR WAR AND EMOTIONAL STRESS: PSYCHOLOGICAL STUDIES OF BOMBING AND CIVILIAN DEFENSE. McGraw-Hill Book Company, Inc., New York. June 1951.

Johnson, John J., (ed.). THE ROLE OF THE MILITARY IN UNDERDEVELOPED COUNTRIES. Princeton University Press, Princeton, New Jersey. May 1962.

Johnstone, William C. BURMA'S FOREIGN POLICY: A STUDY IN NEUTRALISM. Harvard University Press, Cambridge, Massachusetts. March 1963.

Kecskemeti, Paul. STRATEGIC SURRENDER: THE POLITICS OF VICTORY AND DEFEAT. Stanford University Press, Stanford, California. April 1958.*

* Also available in paperback.

Kecskemeti, Paul. THE UNEXPECTED REVOLUTION. Stanford University Press, Stanford, California. October 1961.

Leites, Nathan. THE OPERATIONAL CODE OF THE POLITBURO. McGraw-Hill Book Company, Inc., New York. February 1951.

Leites, Nathan. A STUDY OF BOLSHEVISM. The Free Press, Glencoe, Illinois. December 1953.

Leites, Nathan, and Elsa Bernaut. RITUAL OF LIQUIDATION: THE CASE OF THE MOSCOW TRIALS. The Free Press, Glencoe, Illinois. October 1954.

Leites, Nathan. ON THE GAME OF POLITICS IN FRANCE. Stanford University Press, Stanford, California. April 1959.

Mead, Margaret. SOVIET ATTITUDES TOWARD AUTHORITY: AN INTERDISCIPLINARY APPROACH TO PROBLEMS OF SOVIET CHARACTER. McGraw-Hill Book Company, Inc., New York. October 1951.

Melnik, Constantin, and Nathan Leites. THE HOUSE WITHOUT WINDOWS: FRANCE SELECTS A PRESIDENT. Row, Peterson and Company, Evanston, Illinois. June 1958.

Rush, Myron. THE RISE OF KHRUSHCHEV. Public Affairs Press, Washington, D.C. January 1958.

Rush, Myron. POLITICAL SUCCESSION IN THE USSR. Columbia University Press, New York. February 1965.

Scalapino, Robert A. THE JAPANESE COMMUNIST MOVEMENT: 1920-1965. University of California Press, Berkeley, California. February 1967.

Selznick, Philip. THE ORGANIZATIONAL WEAPON: A STUDY OF BOLSHEVIK STRATEGY AND TACTICS. McGraw-Hill Book Company, Inc., New York. February 1952.

Smith, Bruce Lannes, and Chitra M. Smith. INTERNATIONAL COMMUNICATION AND POLITICAL OPINION: A GUIDE TO THE LITERATURE. Princeton University Press, Princeton, New Jersey. December 1956.

Sokolovskii, V. C., (ed.). SOVIET MILITARY STRATEGY. Prentice-Hall, Inc., Englewood Cliffs, New Jersey. April 1963.

Speier, Hans. GERMAN REARMAMENT AND ATOMIC WAR: THE VIEWS OF GERMAN MILITARY AND POLITICAL LEADERS. Row, Peterson and Company, Evanston, Illinois. July 1957.

Speier, Hans, and W. Phillips Davison (eds.). WEST GERMAN LEADERSHIP AND FOREIGN POLICY. Row, Peterson and Company, Evanston, Illinois. October 1957.

Speier, Hans. DIVIDED BERLIN: THE ANATOMY OF SOVIET POLITICAL BLACKMAIL. Frederick A. Praeger, Inc., New York. October 1961.

Tanham, G. K. COMMUNIST REVOLUTIONARY WARFARE: THE VIETMINH IN INDOCHINA. Frederick A. Praeger, Inc., New York. November 1961.

Trager, Frank N., (ed.). MARXISM IN SOUTHEAST ASIA: A STUDY OF FOUR COUNTRIES. Stanford University Press, Stanford, California. December 1959.

Whiting, Allen S. CHINA CROSSES THE YALU: THE DECISION TO ENTER THE KOREAN WAR. The Macmillan Company, New York. November 1960.

Wolfe, Thomas W. SOVIET STRATEGY AT THE CROSSROADS. Harvard University Press, Cambridge, Massachusetts. November 1964.